THE CAMPAIGN
FOR
GUADALCANAL
A Battle That Made History

WRITTEN AND ILLUSTRATED BY

JACK COGGINS

DOUBLEDAY & COMPANY, INC. | *Garden City, New York* | 1972

ISBN: 0-385-04354-6

Library of Congress Catalog Card Number 75-140063
Copyright © 1972 by Jack Coggins
All Rights Reserved
Printed in the United States of America

CONTENTS

CONTENTS

INTRODUCTION

The military historian, in choosing a topic, usually looks for a battle or campaign which either had a decisive effect on—or marked a turning point in—the outcome of a war. The struggle for control of Guadalcanal was such a campaign. Further, from the writer's angle it had everything—bloody battles on land, vicious fighting in the air, and a series of the most deadly naval actions of modern times.

The campaign was fought on and around an island few had ever heard of—certainly not one which either the Japanese or American High Commands would have picked for a battle-ground. Yet upward of 26,000 men left their bones there, and the many rusting hulls, each with its grim complement of skeletons, gave the once-peaceful waters off the landing beaches a new name—Ironbottom Sound.

For the men who fought there it was sheer hell; an almost constant battle waged on or around a stifling, sodden, disease-ridden, insect-infested nightmare of an island, surrounded by treacherous uncharted waters teeming with man-eating sharks. It is not fashionable these days to glorify war in any way. Yet there must be many who will still feel a glow of pride in the deeds of the men who waged the six-month struggle for the prize of Guadalcanal.

It is impossible, in a single volume, to do justice, or even to mention, all the units and personalities involved in such a long-drawn-out series of actions, spread over so vast an area. So to the readers who served in that campaign this book may be a disappointment. But if, by means of a simple text and many maps and drawings, I have made this most crucial of campaigns a little more understandable to the average reader, I shall have accomplished my purpose. And that is a salute to the thousands, Allied and Japanese, who fought and died in the bitter battles for the island of Guadalcanal.

SYMBOLS

UNIT SYMBOLS

Infantry

PARA Parachute

• Field Artillery

E Engineers

P Pioneers

RDR Raider

Tank

LVT Amphibian Tractor

• DB Defense Batalion

(+) + = reinforced
− = less one or
more units

Command Post

I Company

II Battalion

III Regiment

XX Division

Bn./Rgt. (2/5 = 2nd Bn,
5th Marines)

EXAMPLES

2 2nd Marine Regiment

C 1 DB C Co. 1st Defense Battalion

1RDR 1st Raider Battalion

11 11th Marine Regiment

Command Post, 1st Marine Div.

ABBREVIATIONS

AA — Antiaircraft
AAF — Army Air Force
ABDACOM — American, British, Dutch, Australian Command
AKA — Attack Cargo Ship
Amtrack — Amphibian Tractor
ANZAC — Australian, New Zealand Army Corps
AP — Navy Transport
APC — Small Coastal Transport
APD — Destroyer Transport
ATO — Ocean Tug — Old
BAR — Browning Automatic Rifle
BB — Battleship
Bn — Battalion
Btry — Battery
CA — Heavy Cruiser
CAP — Combat Air Patrol
Cal — Caliber
CAM — Combined Army & Marine
Cardiv — Carrier Division
CL — Light Cruiser
CNO — Chief of Naval Operations
CO — Commanding Officer
Co — Company
COMSOPAC — Commander South Pacific Area
COMAIRSOPAC — Commander, Air, So Pac
CP — Command Post
CV — Aircraft Carrier
CVE — Aircraft Carrier, Escort
CVL — Aircraft Carrier, Light
DD — Destroyer
Desdiv — Destroyer Division
Desron — Destroyer Squadron
DMS — High Speed Mine Sweeper
F4F-3 — "Wildcat" fighter plane
FO — Forward Observer
G-2 — Intelligence office (r) Division or above
GHQ — General Headquarters
HIJMS — His Imperial Japanese Majesty's Ship
HMAS — His Majesty's Australian Ship

HMNZS — His Majesty's New Zealand Ship
IFF — Identification, friend or foe (radio device)
LCM — Landing Craft, Mechanized
LCP — Landing Craft, Personnel
LCT — Landing Craft, Tank
LCVP — Landing Craft, Vehicle and Personnel
LOA — Length Over All
LVT — Landing Vehicle, Tracked
MG — Machine Gun
MLR — Main Line of Resistance
Mm — Millimeter
OD — Officer of the Deck
OP — Observation Post
OS2U — "Kingfisher" Navy Float Plane
Para — Parachute
PBY — "Catalina" Patrol Bomber
PT — Motor Torpedo Boat
RAAF — Royal Australian Air Force
RAN — Royal Australian Navy
Reinf — Reinforced
RN — Royal Navy
RPM — Rounds per minute or revolutions per minute
SBD-3 — "Dauntless"
SONAR — Echo-ranging Sound Gear
SOPAC — South Pacific
SS — Submarine
SWPA — Southwest Pacific Area
TBF-3 — "Avenger" torpedo-bomber
TBS — Talk Between Ships Short range voice radio
TF — Task Force
TG — Task Group
TT — Torpedo Tubes
USS — United States Ship
VF — Navy Fighter Squadron
VMF — Marine Fighter Squadron
VMSB — Marine Scout-Bomber Squadron
VP — Navy Patrol Squadron
VT — Torpedo Plane or Squadron
YP — Small Patrol Craft

SERVICE TIME

2400 or 0000 — Midnight	0600	1200 — noon	1800 — 6:00 P.M.
0100	0700	1300 — 1:00 P.M.	1900 — 7:00 P.M.
0200	0800	1400 — 2:00 P.M.	2000 — 8:00 P.M.
0300	0900	1500 — 3:00 P.M.	2100 — 9:00 P.M.
0400	1000	1600 — 4:00 P.M.	2200 — 10:00 P.M.
0500	1100	1700 — 5:00 P.M.	2300 — 11:00 P.M.

I

Prelude to Act One

JAPAN SWEEPS THE FAR EAST
EIGHT MONTHS OF WAR
GUADALCANAL

The circumstances which led Japan to risk all in the throw for the hegemony of the East have their roots in the past, perhaps to the day when the island kingdom was first awakened to the ways of the West. Few at that distant date could foresee the phenomenal changes which swept the Japanese abruptly out of a medieval society into the modern industrial world. But, the changeover once made, it was impossible that a people, industrious, war-like, racially homogeneous and bound by a fanatical reverence for their emperor and the spirit of Japan, could be confined to the boundaries of a small group of densely populated islands—lacking in both arable land and natural resources.

As was natural, the initial expansion took place at the expense of Japan's neighbors, Korea and China, both militarily weak and industrially un-developed. And just as inevitably, the westward thrust against the Asiatic mainland brought the emergent nation into head-on collision with the eastward march of the Russian empire. The im-pact of the resulting victory of an Asiatic nation over one of the mightiest of the Western states was felt throughout the East, and besides shaking the established colonial order to its foundation, raised Japan to the rank of a world power.

This is a story of a campaign—not of the genesis of a war. Briefly, the rising influence of ultra-

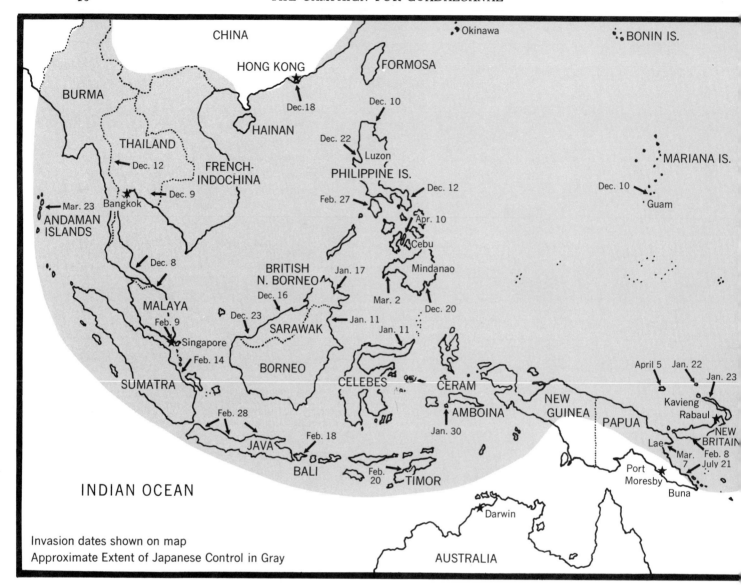

Invasion dates shown on map
Approximate Extent of Japanese Control in Gray

CAPITULATION DATES

Dec. 9 Bangkok, Tarawa and Makin	Jan. 19 British North Borneo	March 23 Andaman Is.	May 3 Tulagi
Dec. 10 Guam	Jan. 23 Rabaul and Kavieng	April 5 Mannu Is.	May 6 Corregidor
Dec. 23 Wake	Feb. 8 Gasmata, New Britain	April 9 Bataan	May 10 Mindanao
Dec. 25 Hong Kong	Feb. 15 Singapore	April 20 Cebu and Panay	May 20 Burma
Jan. 2, 1942 Manila and Cavite	Feb. 23 Amboina Island	April 30 Central Burma	June 9 Philippine Is.
	March 9 Java		July 21 Buna, New Guinea

nationalistic Army elements, the involvement in China (culminating in 1931 in actual hostilities), and the need for the oil and rubber of the East Indies to keep the growing Japanese war machine in operation made a clash between Japan and Britain, the Netherlands and perhaps Soviet Russia a distinct possibility. America, as the other great Pacific power, had long been considered a menace

to Japanese aspirations despite the warnings of many high-ranking Japanese (including the Commander in Chief of the Imperial Japanese Navy, Admiral Isoroku Yamamoto) that a long-drawn-out conflict with the United States could only end in defeat. A struggle for political power, one made deadly by the activities of the fanatical terrorist groups, such as the powerful Black Dragon society,

JAPANESE CONQUESTS
December 8, 1941 to July 21, 1942

Dec. 23
→ WAKE

PACIFIC OCEAN

MARSHALL
IS.

Dec. 9 → GILBERT
IS.
TARAWA
& MAKIN

Jan. 23
Bougainville
May 3
Tulagi
SOLOMON IS.

ELLICE IS.

NEW
HEBRIDES
FIJI IS.

dangerously low, and she must either seize the oil producing areas of the NEI or accede to American demands and withdraw from China and Indochina. This latter course was completely unacceptable to the militarists, and plans for the opening blows of the war, long in preparation, were rushed to completion.

The first paragraph of a Japanese Naval dispatch—from the Chief of Naval General Staff to the CinC Combined Fleet—dated 5 November 1941, read: "In view of the fact that it is feared war has become unavoidable with the United States, Great Britain, and the Netherlands, and for the self-preservation and future existence of the Empire, the various preparations for war operations will be completed by the first part of December."

And three weeks later . . .

25 November 1941.

"FROM: CinC Combined Fleet
To: First Air Fleet
(Pearl Harbor Attack Force)

The task force, keeping its movement strictly secret and maintaining close guard against submarines and aircraft, shall advance into Hawaiian waters, and upon the very opening of hostilities shall attack the main force of the United States Fleet in Hawaii and deal it a mortal blow. The first air raid is planned for the dawn of X-day (exact date to be given by later order).

Upon completion of the air raid, the task force, keeping close coordination and guarding against the enemy's counterattack, shall speedily leave the enemy waters and then return to Japan.

Should the negotiations with the United States prove successful, the task force shall hold itself in readiness forthwith to return and reassemble."

ended with the Army and those in favor of drastic military action in full control of the government.

World War II, with the subsequent defeat of the Netherlands and France, and the involvement of Britain in a life and death struggle in Europe and Africa, opened the way for Japan to play an active role as the leader of a Greater East Asia Co-Prosperity Sphere. The movement of Japanese troops into French Indochina (July 1940) resulted in the freezing of all Japanese assets in the United States, and an embargo on the sale of petroleum to Japan. Britain and the Netherlands followed suit, and war became almost inevitable. Negotiations were futile. Japan's reserves of oil were

The surprise attack on Pearl Harbor was the signal for the beginning of the campaign which was to give Japan control of the whole of Southeast Asia. And as the planes with the red circle insignia on their wings flew triumphantly back to their carriers, the invasion machinery was set smoothly in motion. While Imperial Navy forces in overwhelming strength swept the invasion routes clear and veteran Army and Navy pilots roared overhead, in a series of rapid blows the Japanese Army slashed its way through the Indies and down the Malay Peninsula.

A map and the chronology (*See* also Appendix) show how swift the conquest was.

YAMATO CLASS BATTLESHIP (2 Ships)

Launched July, November 1940
Displacement: 64,170 tons (71,659 tons full load). LOA: 863 Beam: 127¾ Draft: 35½ ft.
4 screws. 150,000 hp=27½ knots. Armor: main belt 16 in., deck 7¾ in., turrets 20–24 in.
Armament 9–18 in. (3✕3), twelve 6.1 in. (4✕3), twelve 5 in. (6✕2),
twenty-four 25-mm. AA (8✕3), four 13-mm. (2✕2), six aircraft Complement: 2500
  (As with many vessels, both Japanese and Allied, changes in armament were made during
the war, usually involving the addition of AA weapons. Sister-ship Musashi was sunk Battle
of Leyte October 24, 1944, Yamato, en route engage U.S. forces off Okinawa April 7, 1945.
Both by U.S. carrier planes.)

Japanese losses for the overrunning of so vast and populous an empire were surprisingly light. Casualties in the land forces were far below those estimated and the Navy's losses in ships had been negligible. Despite overoptimistic claims by both the U. S. Navy and Army Air Force no major units had been sunk. In fact, up to April 22, 1942, at which date Anzac Command terminated, in a period in which the Pacific war had cost the Allies seven battleships, a small carrier, nine cruisers, twenty-two destroyers, a seaplane tender, and some dozen or more submarines, besides many auxiliary craft, the Japanese had lost a mere four destroyers and seven submarines.

As the lines were drawn for the coming struggle in the Pacific, the Japanese fleet was at its peak. The battle fleet had just been strengthened by the addition of the mighty *Yamato*, the world's most powerful battleship, and would soon be joined by her sister ship, *Musashi*. These 64,000 ton giants each mounted nine 18-inch guns, housed in massive turrets protected by armor over 25 inches thick. The fleet's first-line carriers numbered six, with four light carriers, while her pilots, many of them veterans of the war in China, were first-class.

The Japanese seamen were as good as any in the world and their rigorous training, with emphasis on night fighting, ensured their making the best use of their superb forces of cruisers and destroyers. Equipped with the most deadly torpedo in any navy, they were to prove their courage and efficiency in battle after battle.

At the outbreak of war the U. S. Navy had in service seventeen battleships—two of them new (with two more launched and fitting out, and another about to slide down the ways)—seven first-line carriers, a cruiser fleet with a tonnage a quarter again as large as the Japanese cruiser squadrons, a third more destroyers and a submarine force nearly twice as large as her enemy's. But America's was a two-ocean navy, and, facing as she was the threat of a war with the Axis powers in Europe, a considerable proportion of her over-all strength was based in the Atlantic.

The surprise blow at Pearl Harbor was a shattering one. In a few blazing minutes eight battleships of the Pacific Fleet were sunk or badly crippled. Three cruisers, a seaplane tender, a repair ship and a destroyer were damaged, and two more destroyers smashed in drydock. (Fortunately the carriers *Enterprise* and *Lexington* were at sea—the former ferrying Marine fighter planes to Wake Island, the latter, planes for Midway.) USS *Colorado* was the only Allied battleship left in the Pacific—and she was in Bremerton, Washington, for an overhaul. Immediate transfer of ships from the Atlantic to the Pacific was begun; but a war on two oceans was now a fact, and the Axis naval forces in Europe were still strong. Mighty *Bismarck* was down, after sending *Hood*, the pride of the Royal Navy, to the bottom of Denmark Strait; but *Tirpitz*, her sister ship, was still in operation, next to *Yamato* the most powerful dreadnaught afloat. *Scharnhorst* and *Gneisenau* were in Brest, battered by the RAF but still a menace, while the existence of the pocket battleships *Lützow* and *Admiral Scheer* and five cruisers, two heavy and three light, meant that convoys must be guarded against possible surface as well as undersea attack. In the Mediterranean Mussolini's navy—two new super-dreadnaughts and four older vessels along with fifteen fast cruisers and a sizable fleet of destroyers and submarines—tied up ships desperately needed elsewhere.

At the beginning of 1942, the Royal Navy was stretched exceedingly thin. Two capital ships had been sunk since the Pacific war began and *Anson* and *Howe,* sister ships of *Prince of Wales,* were not yet completed. *Nelson* had been damaged by a torpedo in September; in November 1941 the carrier *Ark Royal,* sunk many times already by Axis propaganda, went to the bottom of the Mediterranean, followed a few days later by the battleship *Barham.* Three days after Pearl Harbor *Prince of Wales* and *Repulse* had been sunk off Malaya. And, as a crowning blow, in January limpet lines set by Italian divers sent the battleships *Queen Elizabeth* and *Valiant* to rest on the mud of Alexandria Harbor. Both could be repaired, but the Allies were left perilously weak in heavy ships.

Nevertheless, during the first six months of the war, the new fast battleship *North Carolina* and three older ones of the New Mexico class were sent to bolster the Pacific Fleet, along with the carriers, *Wasp, Hornet, Yorktown,* and the heavy cruisers *Quincy* and *Vincennes.*

By the middle of April the U.S. forces in the Pacific were at least sufficient to act as a deterrent to any Japanese assaults on the Hawaiian Islands or the Antipodes.

In victory the Japanese High Command was now faced with a major decision. With the fall of the East Indies, the Philippines, and Malaya the first phase of the battle for the control of East Asia was over. The problem now was how best to hold the suddenly swollen empire.

The original plan called for consolidation of the areas already won, and the establishment of a strong defense perimeter of naval and air bases. There was not at any time a plan, or even a hope, of physically defeating the United States by direct means—that is, by invasion. The most the Japanese leaders could wish for was that the defenses of their conquered territories could be made so strong that the American people would refuse to pay the necessary price in blood and treasure to retake them. Britain was in no position to launch any immediate counteroffensive, and the streets of Dutch cities and villages rang with the hobnailed boots of the conquering Wehrmacht.

Thus, by a stalemate, the Japanese might be left to develop and exploit the resources of the unwilling members of their Co-Prosperity Sphere at their leisure—trusting that, with the growing strength of the homeland—their conquests, de facto, would become by default, an empire de jure.

But, as has happened to many conquerors before them, success went to the Japanese leaders' heads. The ease with which they had defeated the not-inconsiderable land forces opposed to them, the lack of effective opposition to their air fleets and the smoothness with which they had disposed of the Americans' Pacific Fleet at Pearl Harbor combined to tempt them into further adventures for which they were not sufficiently prepared. For while the Japanese war machine was impressive at first glance it was not backed up by either a sufficiency of trained reserves or an industrial complex capable of turning out military matériel in the vast quantities demanded by modern warfare.

The Japanese soldier, battling with a fanaticism and ferocity which often amazed and shocked his Western opponents, showed throughout the war his willingness to fight and die for his emperor and empire. Too often he merely died, a victim of medieval thinking on the part of leaders who failed to supply him with the ultra-modern equipment needed to combat a great and progressive power fully geared for war. It is no insult to the American fighting man to state that, had the Japanese soldier been as lavishly equipped as he with constantly updated equipment, the war in the East might have taken a far different course.

But in the early spring of 1942, this was all far in the future. Nippon was riding high. Her adversaries on the spot were defeated and her main opponent was in the slow and painful process of changing her economy from peace to war. So perhaps the men who mapped Japanese strategy may be forgiven for overreaching themselves.

There were three main plans proposed, and all were merely extensions of the grand design—to make secure the new empire. One was to attack westward, threatening India and capturing Ceylon, making full use of anti-British elements among the native populations. (In March the Indian Congress Party had rejected the plan, offered by Sir Stafford Cripps, to grant India dominion status after the war was over, and had demanded immediate independence.) This move would forestall, at least for a considerable time, any British counterattack on Burma, Malaya, and the East Indies. Also, at this period Rommel was pressing the British hard in North Africa, while in Russia the Germans were making plans for the massive drive into the Caucasus. There was a chance, therefore, that a Japanese thrust westward might link up with victorious Axis armies driving eastward to the Persian Gulf.

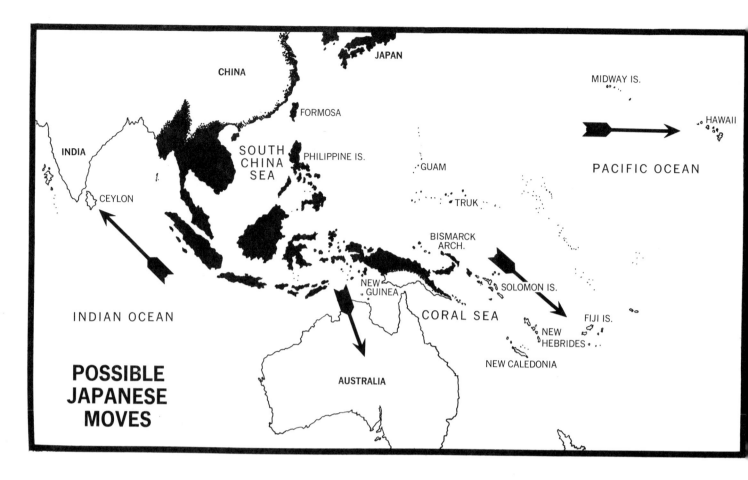

POSSIBLE JAPANESE MOVES

This plan the Army rejected on the grounds that it would call for more troops than could be spared from the operations in China and the defense of the newly conquered territories. War with the old enemy, Russia, was always a possibility; and while the Japanese decision not to attack Russia in 1941 (a decision relayed to Stalin by the master-spy Dr. Richard Sorge, press assistant at the German Embassy in Tokyo) had enabled the Russian ruler to strip his eastern borders of divisions of crack Siberian troops—troops who did much to turn back the Nazis in front of Moscow—there was a good chance that a massive defeat of the Red Army in the Caucasus might bring the Soviet regime down in ruins. The time would then be ripe for a drive into the Far Eastern Areas of the USSR. So the Kwantung Army, stationed in Manchuria, was to be kept at full strength, with sufficient reserves in the home islands as support in the event of a sudden move across the Russian frontiers.

For the same reason another possibility was ruled out, that of an attack on Australia. That vast but thinly populated continent would undoubtedly be used as a jumping-off place for an Allied counter-offensive. An invasion would at the very least forestall such a counteroffensive, and with luck might result in a complete Japanese victory. But the minimum requirements for such a move were estimated at ten divisions (close to a quarter of a million men) and the Army flatly refused to countenance the plan.

As an alternative, the Naval General Staff proposed that Australia be isolated and her vital sea lanes to the United States cut by the capture of the chains of islands lying off her northern and northeastern coasts; the Solomons, the New Hebrides and New Caledonia, and the Fijis.

On the sound principle that the prime consideration of any naval war must be the destruction of the enemy's main fleet, Yamamoto's Chief of Staff, Admiral Matomi Ugaki, was in favor of an attack on Hawaii. This would inevitably draw the American fleet into major battle. With an overwhelming superiority in both carriers and battleships this could only end in a smashing victory—a second Tsushima, the historic site where the Russian Fleet was destroyed by the Japanese Fleet under Admiral Tojo in 1905 during the Russo-Japanese War. Whether or not the Hawaiian Islands were then assaulted and taken, the great American base would be cut off from the mainland, and the U.S. coast laid open to air attack. With the Army firm against an attack on either Ceylon or Australia, this left only the Hawaiian plan open to serious discussion. But while Army and Navy experts were still debating the pros and cons of the Ceylon-Australia-Hawaii question the Japanese CinC had already decided that whatever plan was finally adopted, the British Eastern Fleet should be attacked and, if possible, eliminated. This was a purely naval matter, and accordingly, at the end of March, a powerful force of five large carriers, *Akagi, Hiryu, Soryu, Zuikaku,* and *Shokaku,* accompanied by the battleships *Hiei, Haruna,* and *Kirishima,* six cruisers and twenty destroyers, under Vice-Admiral Chuichi Nagumo, sailed westward across the Indian Ocean.

The British Eastern Fleet was, on paper, a fairly powerful force—five battleships, three carriers, eight cruisers (two of them Dutch), and fifteen destroyers. But the battleships were of World War I vintage, and slow, while one of the carriers was both and small. Admiral Sir James Somerville might have welcomed a night action—night fighting being an art in which His Majesty's Royal Navy was as well versed as the Japanese—but he was well aware that before such an action could be brought about, Nagumo's carriers, veterans of the Pearl Harbor attack, could probably send his ill-assorted fleet to the bottom. Somerville therefore decided that prudence was in this case a virtue, and no clash between the two fleets occurred. A strong carrier raid against an alerted Colombo did comparatively little damage, and several Japanese planes were shot down by the defending fighters and antiaircraft batteries. To offset this, two British heavy cruisers, steaming to rejoin the fleet, were pounced on and sunk. A strike against the naval base at Trincomalee (Ceylon) was picked up by radar, the defenses alerted, and the harbor cleared of shipping. But the small carrier *Hermes,* a destroyer, and a corvette were sunk off the coast.

While Nagumo was operating off Ceylon, a small force consisting of a light carrier and six cruisers, under Rear Admiral Jisaburo Ozawa, was attacking shipping in the Bay of Bengal. In five days this force sank twenty-three merchantmen, totaling over 112,000 tons. But these raids were the extent of Japanese action by surface vessels in the Indian Ocean. Giving up hope of bringing Somerville's fleet to action, Nagumo sailed eastward, passing through Malacca Strait on April 12, followed by Ozawa—nor did any major Japanese warships appear west of Singapore again.

By this time Yamamoto had, in part, accepted the idea of a thrust at Hawaii. But he insisted that first, Midway Island, 1136 miles WNW of Pearl Harbor, must be taken. He also believed that the American carrier fleet must be compelled to fight, and that only by deliberately forcing a major naval engagement and destroying the American carriers could Japan hope to gain the negotiated peace which would save the country from the long-drawn-out war he dreaded.

At the same time Port Moresby in New Guinea was to be seized—as an outlying defense for their recently won stronghold at Rabaul—to safeguard the flanks of the projected advance toward New Caledonia and Fiji, and as a base from which to attack airfields in northern Australia. The place was also an advanced Australian naval base and the northernmost air base from which Allied planes were striking at the Japanese advances in the Bismarcks and Solomons area. New Caledonia and the Fijis might be attacked later, but for the moment Tulagi, in the Solomons, was to be taken and a seaplane base set up there as an adjunct to the invasion of Port Moresby.

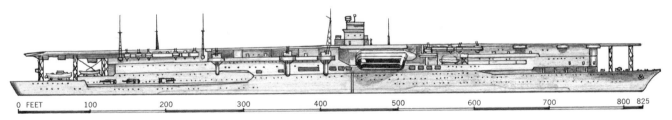

0 FEET   100   200   300   400   500   600   700   800 825

H.I.J.M.S. AKAGI — AIRCRAFT CARRIER

Launched April 22, 1925
Displacement: 36,500 tons LOA: 855½ Beam: 102¾ Draft: 28½ ft. 4 screws.
133,000 hp=31.2 knots Armor: main belt 10 in. Armament: six 8 in. (6×1), twelve 4.7 in.
(6×2), twenty-eight 25-mm. AA ninety-one aircraft Complement: 2000
(Laid down as battlecruiser, completed as carrier. Sunk at Midway, June 5, 1942, by U.S. carrier planes.)

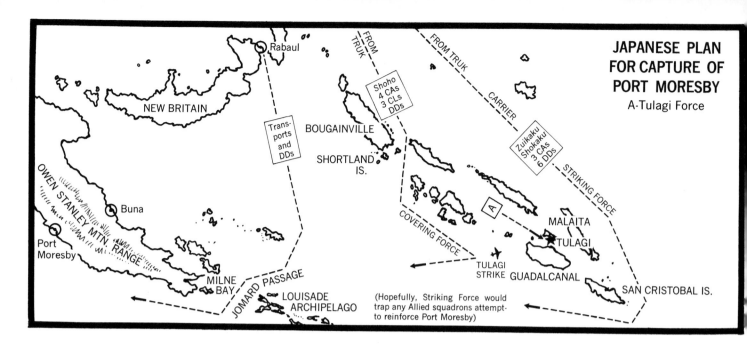

(Hopefully, Striking Force would
trap any Allied squadrons attempt-
to reinforce Port Moresby)

The islands of the Bismarck Archipelago had been included in the original blueprint for conquest, and Rabaul, on New Britain, with the best harbor in the Bismarcks, and with adjacent land suitable for airfields, had been earmarked for capture and development as a major strong point in the defenses of the empire. It was taken on January 23—the 1600-odd Australians of the garrison overwhelmed by a vastly superior landing force after the meager fixed defenses (consisting mainly of a battery of 6-inch guns) had been smashed by a devastating air attack on January 20. Rabaul was swiftly transformed into a major Japanese naval and air base—a vital strong point in the coming struggle for the Solomons.

Kavieng, on the northern tip of New Ireland was taken on January 24 but it was not until March 8 that Japanese forces landed at Lae and Salamaua, on the eastern coast of the southern end of New Guinea. Buka, on the northernmost tip of the Solomons, was occupied on March 13 and a fighter strip commenced. Landings were made on Bougainville, next island in the chain to the south, and air strips were begun at Buin on the south coast of the island and at Kieta on the north. Other landings were made in the Shortlands, just south of Buin.

It is possible that at the same time Port Moresby might then have been taken with little loss, but the Japanese chose to move cautiously—a decision which was to cost them dearly.

Meanwhile an event had occurred which profoundly shocked the Japanese High Command; one which played on the fears of those responsible for guarding the long sea frontier of the empire from attack from the east, and which convinced the many opponents of the Midway operation that it was a necessity instead of an unwarranted risk. At daybreak on April 18, a fishing vessel of the Japanese early warning line, the *Nitto Maru*, sighted an American force, including carriers, steaming toward Japan. The report that U.S. carriers were only 720 miles from Tokyo Bay was flashed to Yamamoto's flagship, and immediately the four battleships of Vice-Admiral Nobutake Kondo's Second Fleet were ordered to sea, while medium bombers took off to try to locate the enemy.

There was no immediate danger. The enemy's reported position meant that the carriers would not be near enough to Japan to launch their strikes before the following dawn. But the American carriers were not closing the coast to launch a conventional carrier strike. Instead, one carrier, *Hornet*, carried sixteen B-25 bombers of Army Air Force under Lieutenant Colonel James A. Doolittle. These were to have been launched 500 miles out, but the unfortunate contact with the *Nitto Maru* meant that the strike must be made immediately. So it was that Kondo's battleships had barely got under way, when the astounding news was flashed to the flagship that Tokyo had been bombed.

Little damage was done, either to the capital, or any of the other target cities, but the shock effect was tremendous. One result was the speed up of the plans for the Midway offensive, which was now expanded to include landing in the Aleutians, and for the capture of Port Moresby.

Japanese intelligence had informed Yamamoto that an Allied force was gathering to contest the Port Moresby landing. He therefore ordered two of Nagumo's carriers, *Zuikaku* and *Shokaku,* on their way back from the Indian Ocean, to proceed to the Fourth Fleet's base at Truk at top speed. Tulagi was to be seized on May 3 and the assault on Port Moresby made the following week.

The Japanese forces, under Vice-Admiral Shige-yoshi Inouye, commander of the Fourth Fleet, were divided into two main groups; the striking force, including the two large carriers (under Rear Admiral Tadaichi Hara), three heavy cruisers and six destroyers, and the occupation force, which included the light carrier *Shoho,* seven cruisers (four heavy and three light), seven destroyers, and fourteen transports.

The Japanese naval code had been broken since Pearl Harbor and U. S. Naval Intelligence was aware of the enemy's intention to attack Port Moresby. (The cracking of the naval code did not mean that every move that the Japanese planned was therefore made known in full to American Intelligence. Tight Japanese security and a minimum of radio transmission saw to that. What it amounted to was that a message, hitherto undecipherable, could be translated to read, "Force A will rendezvous with Force C at position 4X at 0200 on D minus 3." The composition of the forces, the location of 4X and the date of D still had to be determined, or guessed at.) Only two carriers were available, *Yorktown* and *Lexington* (*Saratoga* was still being repaired in Puget Sound after her torpedoing five hundred miles southwest of Oahu in January, while *Enterprise* and *Hornet* were on their way back to Pearl Harbor from the Doolittle raid). Besides the carriers there were eight cruisers—seven heavy and one light (two of them Australian)—and eleven destroyers.

On April 30, 1942, the Japanese occupation force sailed from Truk for the Solomons. This expedition was subdivided into four groups—the main invasion force to come down from Rabaul and round the eastern tip of New Guinea, while the Tulagi group made their landing covered by *Shoho* and her escorts of the covering force. The covering force was then to proceed west to protect the main invasion fleet in its attack on Port Moresby. Meanwhile the striking force, commanded by Vice-Admiral Takeo Takagi was to run down the north side of the Solomons and around the southernmost island, San Cristobal, into the Coral Sea.

Tulagi is a small island just off the southern shore of Florida Island. It affords the best anchorage in the southern Solomons (Earl Jellicoe had once recommended that it be developed as a major fleet base for British empire defense) and was occupied by the Japanese on May 4, 1942. Reports of the landing reached Rear Admiral Frank Jack Fletcher, whose *Yorktown* and *Lexington* groups had rendezvoused in the southeastern Coral Sea on May 1. Leaving the *Lexington* force to finish refueling, Fletcher took *Yorktown* north and on May 4 launched several strikes on the Tulagi area. Important targets were few and the results were disappointing. A destroyer, *Kikutsuki,* and several landing barges were sunk, another destroyer and the 4500-ton minelayer *Okinoshima* were damaged and several planes from a seaplane tender were destroyed.

Fletcher turned back and on the morning of May 5 rejoined *Lexington.* The *Yorktown* group then refueled and the combined squadron, now designated Task Force 17, proceeded on a course a little north of west.

A few hours after *Yorktown* rejoined *Lexington* the Japanese striking force rounded the southern end of San Cristobal into the Coral Sea and also turned on a northwesterly course. Neither Takagi nor Fletcher were aware that enemy carrier forces were definitely in the area—although a sharp turn to the south on the morning of May 6 brought the Japanese carriers within 70 miles of the American Task Force. But by chance the search planes from the American carriers failed to make contact, while a sighting report from a Japanese plane was relayed to Takagi through Rabaul and reached him hours too late.

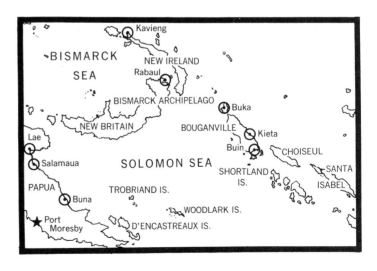

Two-seat Scout Bomber (VSB)
Span: 41′6″ Length: 32′ Height: 13′
Weight empty: 7400 lbs. Max. speed: 260 Cruising: 210
Range at 210: c. 1000 miles Power: one 950-hp Cyclone radial
Armament: two fixed forward-firing .30-cal. MGs., two flexible
.50-cal. in rear cockpit—up to 1000 lb. of bombs

DOUGLAS SBD-3 "Dauntless"

U.S. CARRIER PLANES

GRUMMAN TBF-1 "Avenger"

Three-seat Torpedo Bomber (VTB)
Span: 54′2″ Length: 40′ Height: 16′5″ Weight empty: 12,000 lbs.
Max. speed 278 Range c. 1000 miles
Power: one 1700-hp 14-cylinder Wright Cyclone radial
Armament: three .50-cal., one .30-cal. MGs., one 21 in. torpedo

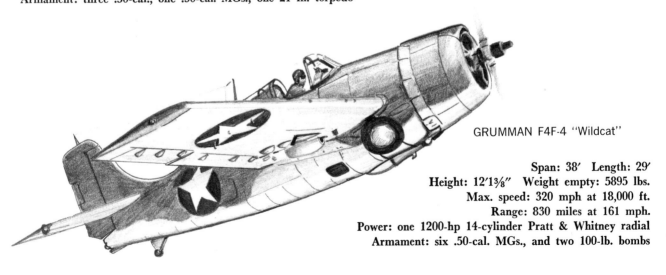

GRUMMAN F4F-4 "Wildcat"

Span: 38′ Length: 29′
Height: 12′1⅜″ Weight empty: 5895 lbs.
Max. speed: 320 mph at 18,000 ft.
Range: 830 miles at 161 mph.
Power: one 1200-hp 14-cylinder Pratt & Whitney radial
Armament: six .50-cal. MGs., and two 100-lb. bombs

Span: 47'2" Length: 33'5" Height: 12'7"
Power: 1070 hp Kinsei Radial
Armament: two fixed forward-firing 7.7-mm. MGs;
one flexible 7.7-mm. in rear cockpit;
one 551-lb. bomb under fuselage;
one 132-lb. bomb under each wing
Wt. empty: 5309 lbs.
Crew: two

AICHI D3A1 NAVY TYPE 99 CARRIER BOMBER
MODEL 11 "Val"

JAPANESE CARRIER PLANES

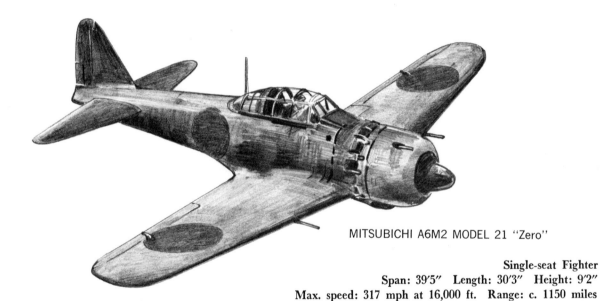

MITSUBICHI A6M2 MODEL 21 "Zero"

Single-seat Fighter
Span: 39'5" Length: 30'3" Height: 9'2"
Max. speed: 317 mph at 16,000 ft. Range: c. 1150 miles
Power: 925-hp 14-cylinder radial
Armament: two 7.7-mm. MGs.; two 20-mm. cannon

Torpedo Bomber
Span: 52' Length: 34' Speed: about 225 mph at 8000 ft.
Range: 500 miles at 190 mph
Armament: two-forward firing 7.7-mm. MGs., one flexible 7.7-mm. in rear cockpit
One torpedo
Crew: two when used as torpedo bomber, three as bomber

NAKAJIMA B5N1 "Kate"

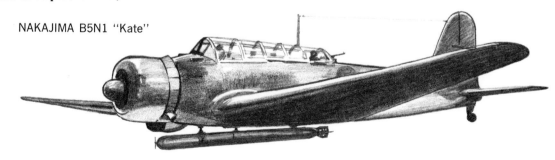

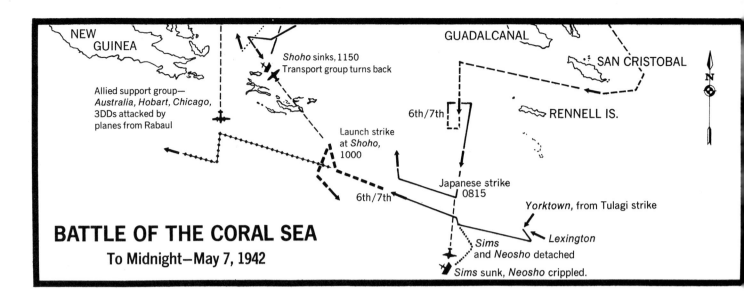

Planes of General Douglas MacArthur's Southwest Pacific command had sighted the Port Moresby invasion force heading for the Jomard Passage through the Louisades, off the eastern end of New Guinea. High level bombing attacks followed, but caused no damage. In the early morning of May 7, Fletcher detached three cruisers and three destroyers under Rear Admiral John G. Crace, RN, in *Australia* to close the Jomard Passage and check the advance of the Japanese invasion force toward Port Moresby. This move was made so that, in the event of disaster overtaking the carriers, there would be at least a surface squadron to defend the approach to the New Guinea base. Fletcher's decision has been criticized, as it robbed his carrier screen of the antiaircraft fire of six ships. On the other hand, Crace's squadron was the object of intensive Japanese air strikes (which fortunately did no damage) which might otherwise have been directed at the American Task Force. (Crace also survived an attack by U.S. B-26s from Australia, whose aim was no better than the Japs.)

Fueling completed, Fletcher had detached the fleet oiler *Neosho* and the destroyer *Sims* to a rendezvous to the south. Here they were sighted by scout planes from the Japanese striking force. Aviators on both sides were prone to make mistakes in identification, and unfortunately for the oiler and her escort, the Japanese scouts reported them as a carrier and a cruiser. A heavy attack by planes from the striking force followed (May 7). Three 500-pound bombs sent *Sims* to the bottom, and *Neosho* became a gutted wreck, floating until May 11, when destroyer *Henley* took off her survivors and sank her.

In the meantime another error in a sighting report sent American planes swarming off *Lexington* and *Yorktown* decks. The report received—TWO CARRIERS AND FOUR HEAVY CRUISERS—was wrongly coded, and should have read, TWO CRUISERS AND TWO DESTROYERS. Thinking, correctly, that near the position indicated—not far north of Misima Island—there should be some sign of the Port Moresby invasion force, Fletcher let the strike proceed and was rewarded when his planes sighted *Shoho* about 1100. Thirteen bomb hits and seven torpedoes sent her down in short order, flaming from bow to stern. It was the American pilots first attack on an enemy carrier, and the exultant shout of a Navy aviator, "Scratch one flattop!" became a warcry.

Takagi by now had a good idea where the American carriers were and his carriers attempted to retrieve the situation by a dusk attack on Fletcher's ships. Twenty-seven of his pilots most experienced in night flying took off but in the foul visibility missed the Task Force, although they came very close.

U.S. radars picked up the strike, and a combat air patrol was vectored out and shot down nine of the attackers. Six of the Japanese aircraft, mistaking *Yorktown* for one of their own carriers, joined the landing circle until recognized and driven off by gunfire, minus one of their number. Eleven others ditched while trying to regain their ships. Japanese pilots reported American carriers within 50 or 60 miles, while *Lexington*'s radar picked up enemy planes circling some 30 miles away. The two forces were too close for comfort and after both commanders had considered ordering their surface forces to attack and had then thought better of it, both ordered withdrawals— Americans southwest and Japanese to the north.

There was little doubt in the mind of either commander that May 8 would be the day of decision. Although they did not know it, both sides were evenly matched. Both had two large carriers —121 planes in Hara's, 122 on Fletcher's. The American carriers had radar; Hara's men were more experienced and had worked together as a team. Also the Jap carriers were now under the overcast, while Fletcher's were under sunny skies.

At 0600 the first Jap search mission took off and the Americans followed suit a few minutes later. Both sides made contact a little after 0800 and strikes were made almost simultaneously (about 1100). *Zuikaku* ran into a squall and the American attack (from *Yorktown*) fell exclusively on *Shokaku*. The torpedoes were all avoided or malfunctioned but dive bombers made two hits. *Lexington's* dive bombers failed to find their target at all, while the torpedo bombers scored no hits. But one scout bomber put another hole in *Shokaku's* flight deck, preventing her from recovering planes.

The Japanese strike, seventy attack planes and twenty fighters, was picked up by radar at a range of 70 miles, but only three of the American CAP (Combat Air Patrol) were able to intercept (later in the war, these things would be managed better).

The smaller and more maneuverable *Yorktown* received only one bomb hit, but *Lexington,* attacked on both bows simultaneously, took two torpedo hits and two bombs. She could still make 24 knots and her ability to fly her planes was unimpaired. A 7-degree list was corrected by shifting fuel.

Yorktown was still operational, and, with *Shokaku* out of action it looked like an American victory. But even as *Lexington's* damage control parties were finishing their job, gasoline vapor from ruptured lines was seeping along between decks— seeping toward a generator carelessly left running. One spark was enough—and at 1247 a tremendous explosion shook the ship. Soon fires were raging out of control, and other explosions followed. At 1707 orders were given to abandon ship and a little later torpedoes from the destroyer *Phelps* sent the "Lady Lex" to the bottom.

Tactically the battle was now to the Japanese— a light carrier, and a destroyer and some small vessels sunk (at Tulagi) against *Lexington, Neosho,* and *Sims.* But strategically it was an Allied victory, for although Japanese pilots optimistically reported both U.S. carriers sunk, Japanese losses in planes had been sufficient for Admiral Inouye to order the postponement of the invasion plan. The invasion fleet turned back to Rabaul. Port Moresby was saved, and while later attacked by land, it was never again threatened by invasion from the sea.

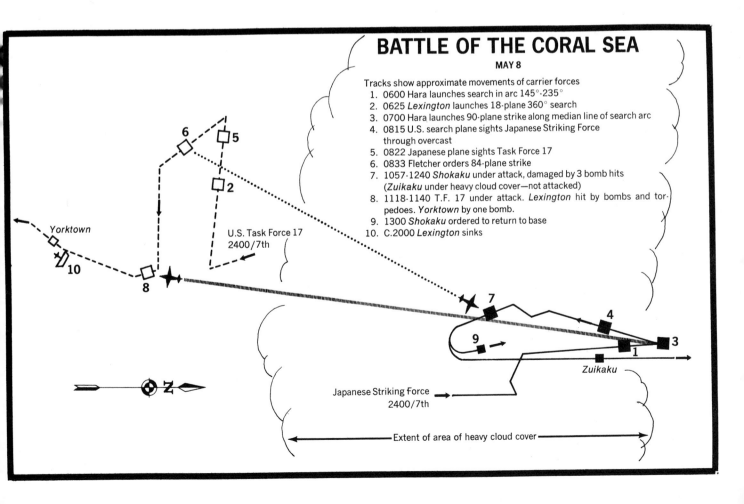

BATTLE OF THE CORAL SEA
MAY 8

Tracks show approximate movements of carrier forces
1. 0600 Hara launches search in arc 145°-235°
2. 0625 *Lexington* launches 18-plane 360° search
3. 0700 Hara launches 90-plane strike along median line of search arc
4. 0815 U.S. search plane sights Japanese Striking Force through overcast
5. 0822 Japanese plane sights Task Force 17
6. 0833 Fletcher orders 84-plane strike
7. 1057-1240 *Shokaku* under attack, damaged by 3 bomb hits (*Zuikaku* under heavy cloud cover—not attacked)
8. 1118-1140 T.F. 17 under attack. *Lexington* hit by bombs and torpedoes. *Yorktown* by one bomb.
9. 1300 *Shokaku* ordered to return to base
10. C.2000 *Lexington* sinks

Yorktown

U.S. Task Force 17
2400/7th

Japanese Striking Force
2400/7th

Zuikaku

N

Extent of area of heavy cloud cover

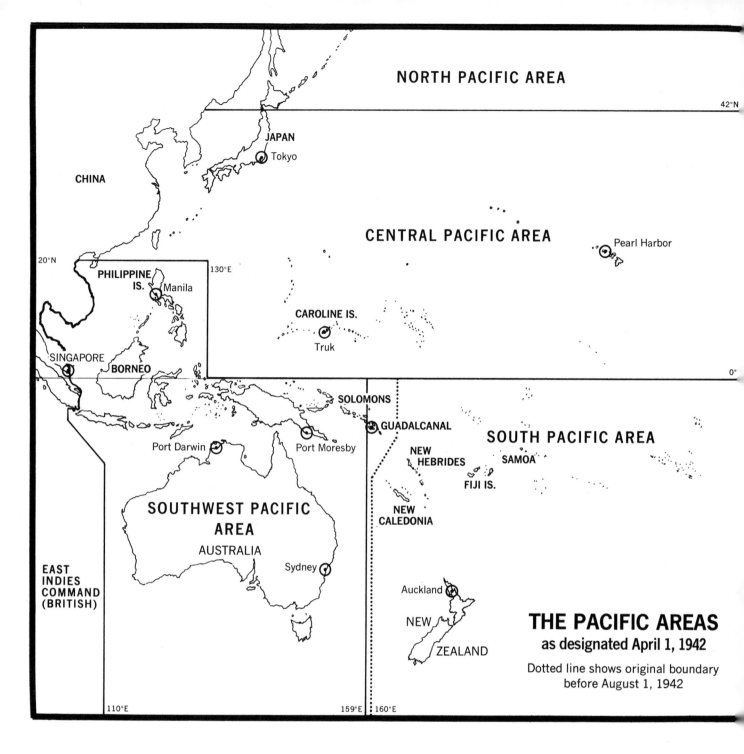

NORTH PACIFIC AREA

42°N

JAPAN
Tokyo

CHINA

CENTRAL PACIFIC AREA

Pearl Harbor

20°N

PHILIPPINE IS.
Manila

130°E

CAROLINE IS.

Truk

SINGAPORE

BORNEO

0°

SOLOMONS

GUADALCANAL

SOUTH PACIFIC AREA

Port Darwin

Port Moresby

NEW HEBRIDES

SAMOA

FIJI IS.

SOUTHWEST PACIFIC AREA

AUSTRALIA

NEW CALEDONIA

Sydney

EAST INDIES COMMAND (BRITISH)

Auckland

NEW

ZEALAND

THE PACIFIC AREAS
as designated April 1, 1942

Dotted line shows original boundary
before August 1, 1942

110°E

159°E

160°E

The Battle of the Coral Sea had saved Port Moresby but the seizure of Tulagi, 300 miles south of Bougainville, and the establishment of a base there seemed to show that the Japanese had every intention of continuing their advance down the Solomons' archipelago.

Tulagi (healthier than the mainland) was the seat of the British Solomon Islands government. When, after frequent air raids, it became obvious that a Japanese landing was imminent, the few people remaining—government officials, civilians, and a handful of Australian riflemen and RAAF personnel—were evacuated. The Japanese, detachments from the 3rd Kure Special Navy Landing Force and some laborers, landed from the minelayer *Okinoshima* unopposed. Work was begun on the seaplane base and defensive positions were organized. Strangely, no steps were taken at that time toward developing a landing field on the large island laying some 20 miles south, called

Guadalcanal. Although warning stations were set up there, it was not until June that surveying parties crossed Sealark Channel from Tulagi to Lunga Point on Guadalcanal. The survey was completed in late June, and work began the first part of July. Then, as if realizing that they were racing against time, the Japanese construction crews outdid themselves. By August 7 they had built wharves, light bridges, machine shops, two radio stations, two power plants, camp buildings, an air-compressing plant, hangars and a nearly completed 3600-feet runway. The fact that Japanese parties were surveying the island's grassy coastal strip was noted and reported by coastwatchers on Guadalcanal, followed by word of the commencement of work on an airfield.

For the Allied reaction to this news we shall have to go back several months to the time when it became apparent that Japan had plans for further expansion to the southeast beyond the area initially conquered.

The Allies were well aware that Japanese takeover of the island chains off Australia's northeastern coast constituted a grave danger to that continent, as well as to any future plans for a counterthrust toward the Philippines and ultimately, the Japanese home islands.

With the fall of the East Indies and Malaya one phase of the Japanese battle for control of east Asia had been completed. The first combined Allied command, established on December 31, 1941, by Roosevelt and Churchill, ABDACOM (American, British, Dutch, Australian Command) had passed out of existence when its commander, General Sir Archibald Wavell, was ordered to India. ANZAC (Australia-New Zealand Army Corps) Area was established by the Joint British and American Chiefs of Staff on January 29 under the command of Vice-Admiral Herbert F. Leary, USN. The area included Eastern New Guinea, the Bismarck Archipelago, Fiji and New Caledonia, the New Hebrides, the Solomons, New Zealand and the seas around eastern Australia. But with the realization that the brunt of the Pacific War was going to be borne by U.S. forces the need for a reorganization of the command structure throughout the whole Pacific Area became apparent.

ANZAC command was therefore terminated on April 22. The whole area was divided into two major theaters. One, Southwest Pacific Area (SWPA) under General Douglas MacArthur, took in almost all the Netherlands East Indies, the Philippines,

the Solomons, and Australia. To Admiral Chester W. Nimitz, USN Commander of the Pacific Fleet, went the rest of the Pacific. So huge an area was divided into three zones; North Pacific Area —north of latitude 42°, Central Pacific Area— containing Midway and the Hawaiian Islands and extending to the equator, and the South Pacific Area, which included New Zealand.

As early as February 18, Admiral Ernest J. King, Commander in Chief, U. S. Fleet, wrote to General George C. Marshall, Chief of Staff, U. S. Army, that in his opinion it was necessary to occupy some of the islands in the South and Southwest Pacific. This was not only to protect the lines of communication between the U.S. and Australia, but also to set up bases from which offensives would be launched against the Japanese strong points in the Solomons and the Bismarcks.

On March 12, U. S. Army and Navy forces occupied Nouméa, capital of New Caledonia, and work on a major air base at Tontouta began. On March 29, the 4th Defense Battalion (reinforced) Fleet Marine Force, made a landing at Port Vila on Efate in the New Hebrides.

General MacArthur was also planning an offensive. The Coral Sea battle in May had taken the pressure off Port Moresby, at least temporarily, and the general was thinking of an attack on Rabaul itself. Operations Division of the War Department General Staff in Washington favored such a move under the leadership of MacArthur. There were three trained infantry divisions in the Southwest Pacific Area, the U. S. 32nd and 41st Infantry Division and the Australian 7th Division. These troops could support a landing once a beachhead had been won, but were neither trained nor equipped to make such a landing themselves. The only force capable of this was the 1st Marine Division, then beginning to assemble at Wellington, New Zealand. Besides these Marine troops (under Nimitz's control) MacArthur would need carriers for fighter support (available Allied airfields were too far off for land-based fighters to operate), transports, and other naval surface ships.

The Navy, reluctant to put its precious carriers, and equally precious 1st Marine Division, under Army control, preferred a step-by-step approach to Rabaul, beginning with an attack on Tulagi. King believed (correctly, as it turned out) that little support would be forthcoming from Southwest Pacific and directed Nimitz to begin the preliminary planning for a Navy operation in the Solomons and Santa Cruz Islands.

So at the outset there was controversy between the services—Marshall favoring an attack on Rabaul under MacArthur; while King wanted an assault through the Solomons, under Nimitz.

Meanwhile the decisive victory at Midway—June 5-6—which saw four carriers, the pride of the Japanese Navy, gutted and sunk, had caused the Japanese Imperial General Headquarters to consider cancellation of the plan for the invasion of New Caledonia, the Fijis, and Samoa. At the same time, it redressed to some extent the balance of naval power in the Pacific, and enabled the Allies to move tentatively from the defensive to the offensive.

Following a series of communications and talks (June 29–July 1) agreement was reached between King and Marshall and on July 2, 1942, the Joint Directive for Offensive Operations in the Southwest Pacific Area, agreed on by the United States Chiefs of Staff, was signed. An offensive was to be mounted immediately, with the ultimate goal the retaking of the northern Solomons, the Bismarcks, and New Guinea. The operation was to be in three phases. Task One called for the seizure of Tulagi, the Santa Cruz Islands, and areas adjacent. This assault was to be under a naval officer appointed by Nimitz. Tasks Two and Three, the occupation of the rest of the Solomons chain, the north coast of New Guinea and Rabaul and the New Britain-New Ireland area were to be under MacArthur's command.

The tentative date for Task One was August 1, and to simplify administrative problems, on that date the boundary between the South Pacific Area and MacArthur's Southwest Pacific Area was shifted west to longitude 159° East—thus placing the target—Tulagi and surrounding areas, Florida Guadalcanal, Malaita, and San Cristobal—in the South Pacific zone of command. South Pacific was to be commanded by vice-Admiral Robert L. Ghormley, under Nimitz as CINCPAC (Commander in Chief, Pacific). Ghormley formally took over as Commander of the South Pacific Area and South Pacific Force (COMSOPAC) on June 19, 1942 with his headquarters in Auckland, New Zealand.

Both preparation, time and means seemed inadequate to Ghormley and when he conferred with MacArthur (who agreed with him) they sent a joint dispatch to Marshall and King urging that the operation be postponed until more forces, especially air power, could be built up. To this the Joint Chiefs of Staff said no, the operation must go forward, and promised that some further air support would be furnished. The problem, as Ghormley saw it, was, "the protection of surface ships against land-based aircraft during the approach, the landing, and the unloading."

The basic problem, of course, was the Anglo-American decision, made at the beginning of hostilities, at the highest levels, that the Allies concentrate their main effort on defeating Germany. This meant that men, ships, planes, and other warlike equipment and supplies for the Pacific were doled out with a niggardly hand. And this in turn meant that commanders in the Pacific areas were usually forced to operate on the proverbial shoestring.

So it was with Watchtower (soon to be nicknamed Operation Shoestring). Ghormley was constantly facing appeals for more this and more that—appeals which, when passed on to the Joint Chiefs, were immediately turned down because of the growing U.S. commitment in Europe. One appeal, that for more time, was granted—one week! And that only because the second echelon of the 1st Marine Division was late in arriving in New Zealand.

This division, less the 7th Marines (reinforced) which had been temporarily detached in March and were now part of the 3rd Marine Brigade in Samoa, was moved from the U.S. to Wellington in two echelons. The last of these did not arrive until July 11. Major General Alexander Archer Vandegrift, USMC, commanding the division, had counted on having several months for training purposes. Instead, his force was to be committed less than a month after the last units had arrived in New Zealand. Worse, his vessels were organizationally loaded—that is, they were loaded in the way most economical of hold space, as opposed to combat loaded, where items are placed so that they can be unloaded in the order of their need in an assault landing.

Due to labor difficulties with the local stevedores the task of unloading and reloading fell on the Marines themselves. This was accomplished, in prolonged foul weather, on wharves equally lacking in dockside facilities and shelter. This was particularly rough on the men of the second echelon. These unfortunates, after a long, cramped voyage from the States, were not disembarked (except onto the docks) but worked eight-hour shifts around the clock in cold, pouring rain, unloading and restowing cargo. The highly organized members of the stevedores union were not popular among the men of the 1st Division.

Lack of shipping was to hamper all operations in the Pacific for many months and when the force was finally loaded there were aboard supplies for sixty days, ten units of fire for all weapons (a unit of fire was the average amount of ammunition necessary for one day's combat) the barest minimum of personal baggage, and less than half the authorized divisional transport. (Most of the ¼- and 1-ton trucks were loaded, but some 75 percent of the heavier vehicles were left in Wellington with the rear echelon.)

Wind, weather, and labor unions had not slowed down the reloading and the force sailed on schedule—at 0900, July 22. For many aboard the transports and escorting warships it was their last voyage.

The makeup of Ghormley's force was complicated and can best be shown with a diagram. It

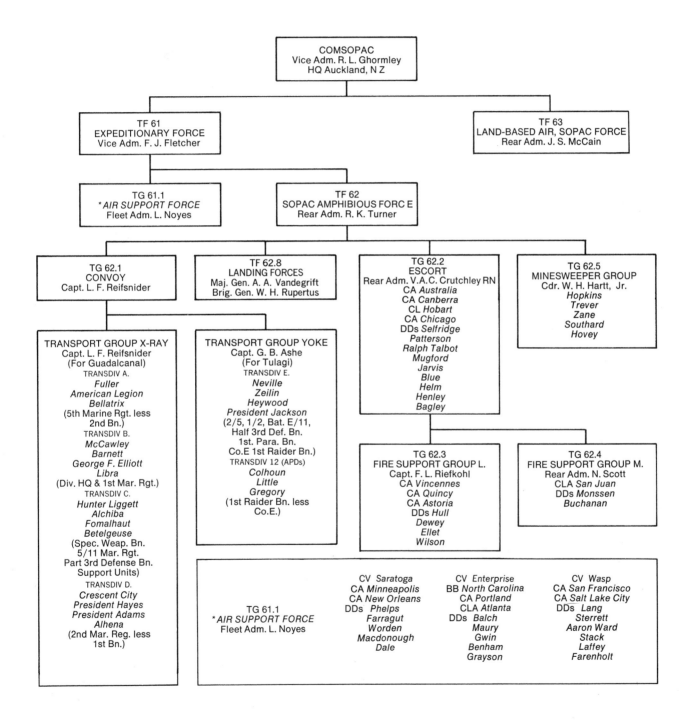

comprised in all eighty-two ships. Ghormley's OTC (Officer in Tactical Command) was Vice-Admiral Fletcher, veteran of Coral Sea and Midway. Loss of *Lexington* at Coral Sea and *Yorktown* at Midway had made Fletcher extremely reluctant to risk the invaluable carriers and this apprehension was to have a damaging effect on the coming operation.

Rendezvous of the invasion fleet was a spot 367 miles south of Fiji. Here on July 2, far from land, a conference of the commanders of the Task Forces —Fletcher, Noyes, McCain, Turner, and Vandegrift, the general in command of the landing force —was held aboard flagship *Saratoga*. Very unfortunately, Ghormley was unable to attend, and he was represented by Rear Admiral Daniel Callaghan.

Right at the beginning of the conference Fletcher exploded a bombshell. He would not, he said, risk his carriers within reach of Japanese land-based air for more than 48 hours after the landing. Turner, commanding the amphibious force, and Vandegrift immediately protested. At least four days would be needed to land the tons of equipment and supplies—without them the whole success of the operation would be jeopardized. From Turner's and Vandegrift's point of view, a complicated invasion by sea was to be turned into a risky hit-and-run raid. But Fletcher would modify his plans only if directly ordered to by Ghormley—and radio silence made such direct control difficult or impossible.

This less than satisfactory conference was followed by equally unsatisfactory landing rehearsals at Kore Island in the Fijis (July 28–30). Some experience in launching landing craft and forming assault waves was gained, but the fragile craft could not be risked on the coral reefs and the operations were, in General Vandegrift's words, "a complete bust." But no more time could be wasted, and on July 31 the fleet sailed; the Carrier Task Force to take up its covering position in the Coral Sea, to the south of Guadalcanal; the Amphibious Force (in two groups) and its screen steaming straight for the target area. Aboard the twenty-three transports were some 19,000 Marines. The first U.S. amphibious invasion since the Spanish-American War was about to begin.

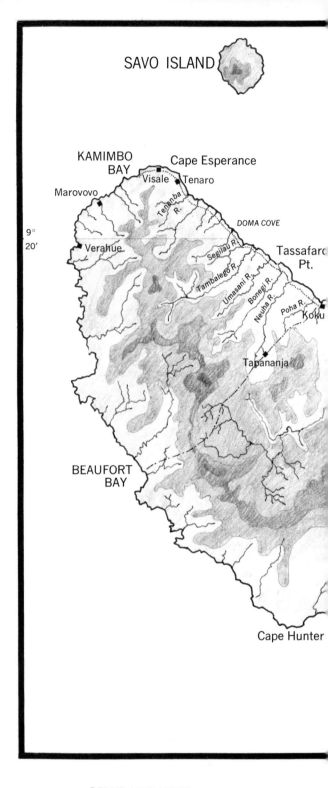

GUADALCANAL

To most dwellers in northern latitudes the words "tropical island" have a romantic connotation—bringing to mind dazzling beaches of shining coral, shaded by stately palms and swept by clean sea breezes. Travelers to such shores are, of course, welcomed by handsome, friendly natives bearing delicious fruits, while dusky belles, wondrous fair

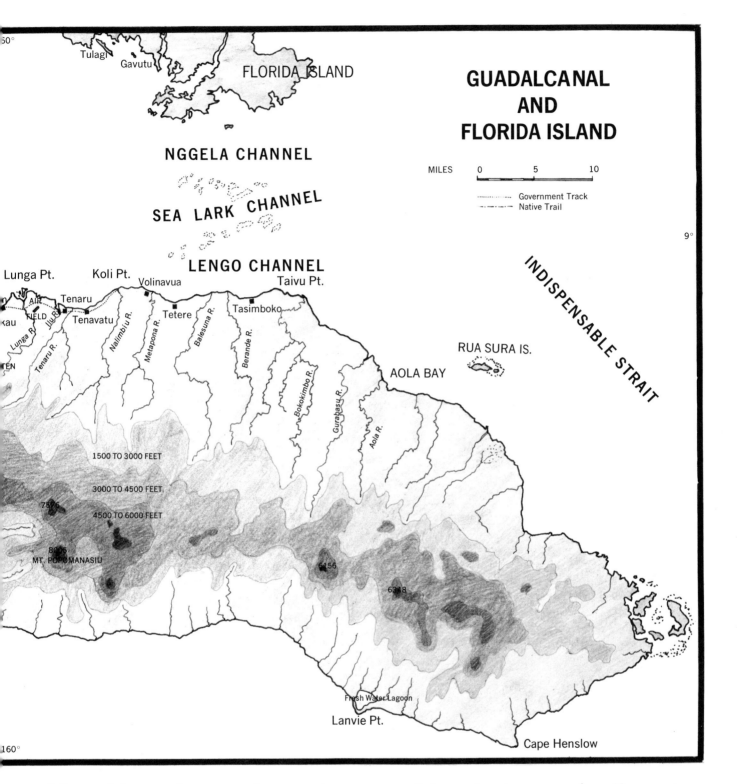

GUADALCANAL
AND
FLORIDA ISLAND

FLORIDA ISLAND

Tulagi
Gavutu

NGGELA CHANNEL

SEA LARK CHANNEL

LENGO CHANNEL

MILES 0 5 10

·············· Government Track
·—·—·— Native Trail

9°

INDISPENSABLE STRAIT

Lunga Pt.   Koli Pt.   Volinavua   Taivu Pt.

Tenaru   Tenaru R.
AIR FIELD
Tenavatu
Lunga R.
Iiu R.
Nalimbiu R.
Metapona R.
Tetere
Balesuna R.
Berande R.
Tasimboko
Bokokimbo R.
Gurabasu R.
Aola R.

RUA SURA IS.

AOLA BAY

1500 TO 3000 FEET

3000 TO 4500 FEET

4500 TO 6000 FEET

7586

8005
MT. POPOMANASIU

6156

6318

Fresh Water Lagoon

Lanvie Pt.

Cape Henslow

of face and form, perform exotic dances to the accompaniment of steel guitars.

Such isles of delight may exist, but Guadalcanal is not one of them. Situated less than ten degrees below the equator, the climate of the island—and of all the Solomons—is wet and hot, averaging in the high 80s. The 90-mile length of the place is liberally drenched with rains (average yearly rainfall at Tulagi, 164 inches) especially during the season of the northwest monsoons—from November to March. Like the other islands of the Solomons chain, Guadalcanal is volcanic. It averages some 25 miles in width with a central spine of jagged peaks, covered with tropical rain forest, rising in places 8000 feet above sea level. On the southwest the mountains slope fairly sharply to the coast. In contrast, on the northeastern side there are some wide plains, cut by numerous rivers, some long, swift, and fordable in spots—others slow and deep with steep mud banks. Since the beginning of the century areas of the plains have been laid out in coconut plantations; the rest is jungle or dense brush, growing in places to the water's edge —interspersed with patches of open ground covered by coarse kunai grass, with stiff seven-foot blades and edges like saws.

The dark humid jungles and evil-smelling swamps swarm with a variety of insects, many of surprising size and ugliness. Less repulsive in appearance than this collection of creeping monsters, but far more deadly, are the mosquitoes. Renowned for their size, numbers, and persistence, they bear malaria, dengue, and other fevers and, despite all the medics could do, they took a large toll of the invaders of their swamps, both American and Japanese. Fungus infections were common. Reptiles abounded and crocodiles haunted the steaming deltas.

The native Melanasians are not noted for their beauty and, at least in the old days, were more likely to greet the traveler with spears and clubs than with fruit. Head-hunting and cannibalism were rife until put down by Government but they are still practiced in the interior of some islands. Theirs is a primitive civilization and, except along the coasts, the white man's culture has made little impression.

Such are the Solomons and such was Guadalcanal. From an island unknown to Americans (except a few readers of Jack London, who wrote of Guadalcanar—the old spelling—in *The Red One*) it became famous—or infamous—a pestilential hell hole hated by soldier, sailor, and Marine.

Not long after the first Marines landed, a blond, bearded young Englishman entered the American lines and offered his services to the American commander. He was Captain Martin Clemens—British District Officer, coastwatcher for the Royal Australian Navy and member of the British Solomon Islands Defense Force. With him were some sixty natives; scouts and members of the Constabulary. The assistance of this veteran of three years in the Solomons and his followers was gladly accepted and the little force proved a valuable addition to Vandegrift's command.

The native population of Guadalcanal had been alarmed by reports of Japanese conquests farther north, by the landing of the yellow men on Tulagi and Guadalcanal and the hasty evacuation of most of the island's whites. Clemens' promise to remain and his assurances (based more on faith than fact)

that some day the little invaders would be driven out and King George's rule restored, helped allay the native headmen's fears. The arrival of a large force of white men, complete with an impressive array of ships and guns, did much to help bolster the loyalty of those whose allegiance wavered. So did the liberal pay scale of the Americans (too liberal, the British thought, and one which resulted in considerable labor unrest and dissatisfaction after the war).

Even more help was the attitude of the Japanese themselves. Forced labor, the wanton looting and destruction of the natives' gardens (painfully hacked out of the jungle and carefully tended), and the arrogance and cold-blooded ferocity of the invaders soon turned every hand against them. The natives, who had once delighted in hunting one another, found it more rewarding (and often less dangerous) to stalk unwary Japanese. How many of the enemy were killed by the inhabitants will never be known but it must have been considerable. Some Japs were believed to have been slaughtered as they fled the area of the American landing that August 7, 1942.

So the loyalty and willingness to help of the natives of the island were seldom in question. The stubborn courage of some of the Constabulary is best exemplified by the case of Sergeant Major Vouza. Vouza, though retired after twenty-five years service, volunteered to help the Marines. On a scouting mission he was captured and "questioned" about Marine strength and positions. He was tied to a tree and, refusing to answer his captors, was stabbed several times with swords and bayonets and left for dead. He recovered consciousness later, slipped his bonds and ultimately found his way to the American lines. His courage was later rewarded with the United States Silver Star and the George Medal, the highest award for bravery that a British civilian can win.

(As a footnote to the "questioning" of prisoners: The Japanese frequently tortured or misused their prisoners, and sometimes executed them. The reason, apart from sheer barbarism, perhaps being that in their eyes a soldier who surrendered was an outcast, a traitor to his flag, who had lost all claim to respect from his enemies. In consequence the Japanese soldier was not instructed in his rights as a prisoner of war: to withhold all information except the usual rank, name, and serial number. Therefore on the rare occasions when a Japanese enlisted man was taken alive, he frequently could be induced to talk, and talk very freely indeed.)

II

"The Marines Have Landed,
and the Situation . . ."

THE AMPHIBIOUS ASSAULT
ON TULAGI AND GUADALCANAL
THE COASTWATCHERS

The course of the U.S. invasion force took it well south of the Solomons, then northward and about 0200 on the morning of August 7, 1942, the convoy was due west of Cape Esperance. The two groups were some six miles apart—speed 12 knots. The hills of Guadalcanal loomed black against the lighter sky to starboard as course was altered to the east and the two groups separated (0240). Transport Group X-ray, steaming in two columns, one of eight and one of seven ships, with a distance of 750 yards between vessels and 1000-yard intervals between columns, heading parallel to the coast, while Yoke proceeded north of Savo Island before turning southeast for Tulagi.

B-17s of 26th Squadron, 11th Bombardment Group, operating under extremely difficult conditions from the partly finished air strips at Efate and Espiritu Santo had bombed Guadalcanal and

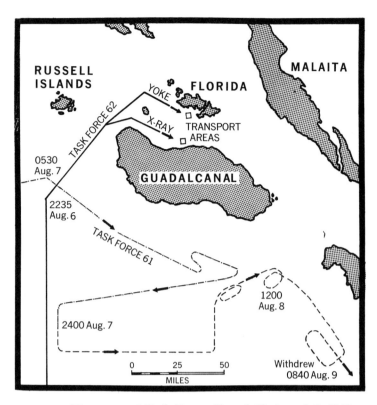

Movement of Task Forces 61 and 62, Aug. 6–9, 1942

after salvo from fourteen 5-inch guns, as did her escorting destroyers *Buchanan* and *Monssen*. At 0800 precisely the 1st Raider Battalion hit the beach (Beach Blue) followed shortly after by 2nd Battalion, 5th Marines. These last, 1085 officers and men, were ashore by 0916.

Tulagi is some 4000 yards long and 1000 yards at its widest. Besides the Residency, there was a prison, hospital, radio station, and other government buildings, as well as some wharves along the northeast beach. The place is hilly, and heavily wooded, and surrounded on three sides with coral reefs. About 3000 yards to the east lie the twin islets of Tanambogo and Gavutu, joined by a causeway 500 yards long. The site chosen for the landing (see map) lay behind one such reef, and the assaulting troops waded ashore, the landing craft being hung up on the coral from 30 to 100 yards off the beach. Fortunately the small Japanese force was concentrated in the southeastern third of the island and no opposition to the landing was encountered.

The Japanese forces in the Tulagi-Guadalcanal area had been greatly overestimated by Navy and Marine Intelligence (7125 and 8400 respectively). Actually there were only some 800 in the Tulagi-Tanambogo-Gavutu area—little more than half the estimated number—and about 2200 troops and laborers on Guadalcanal. Since 0725 the Japanese communication base at Tulagi had been radioing Rabaul that an attack was under way. At 0810 went the final message, "Enemy troop strength is overwhelming. We will defend to the last man." True to their words, the 500-odd defenders of Tulagi proceeded to give the Marines a foretaste of the fanatical bravery and tenacity of which the Japanese fighting man was capable.

The ground at the southeastern end of the island rises to a low hill, and it was in caves, ravines, slit trenches and dugouts in this area that the Japanese defenders were holed up. While the Raider Companies drove across the island and then turned southeast, part of the 2nd Battalion of the 5th Marines turned northwest to clear that end of the island. This was accomplished with no difficulty but by afternoon the Raider Companies were meeting stiffening resistance in the southeastern hill area. Ships' gunfire and dive bombing had had little effect on the defenses—the caves could not be reached, and nothing but direct hits would destroy the dugouts. Grenades and explosive charges placed by hand were used with effect (there were no flamethrowers available at that time) but the

Tulagi for seven days, beginning on July 31. Evidently these raids were not taken as the prelude to an invasion. Incredibly, there were no signs that the approach of the invasion force had been observed. From the invader's standpoint the weather for the last two days had been ideal, low cloud cover and frequent rain squalls, and Japanese patrol planes at Rabaul were grounded on August 5 and 6. Dawn and still no sign of opposition. Then, at 0613, the first salvo from the supporting warships arced into the beach at Guadalcanal. Simultaneously planes from the carriers, then maneuvering some 75 miles to the south, made the first strafing runs over the target area. (Planes from *Saratoga* operated mainly over Beach Red on Guadalcanal—those from *Wasp* attacked Tulagi, while *Enterprise* flew cover for the carriers and patrol missions.)

H-hour at Tulagi was set for 0800, but the first landing (0740) was on Florida Island, near Haleta, to protect the left flank. Here, after a brief bombardment, a reinforced company (B) of the 2nd Marines went ashore unopposed although the enemy had been reported there as late as July 25. The air strikes had started fires on Tulagi, and some eighteen Japanese seaplanes, Kawanishi flying boats and Zero float planes (Rufes), caught like sitting ducks, were destroyed in the harbor. The antiaircraft cruiser *San Juan* poured in salvo

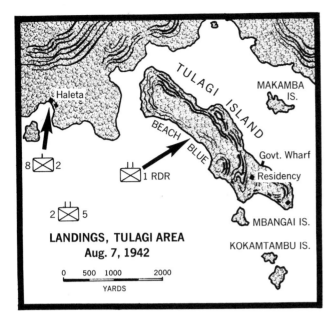

LANDINGS, TULAGI AREA
Aug. 7, 1942

The assault on the twin islets of Tanambogo and Gavutu was set for H plus four hours—1200. (A shortage of landing craft precluded simultaneous attacks on all objectives.) The hill on Gavutu is higher than that of Tanambogo (148 feet to 121 feet) and, in accordance with the old maxim, "Take the high ground," Gavutu was the first target. As a precaution against fire from the Halavo Peninsula (see map) the remainder of 1st Battalion, 2nd Marines landed there at 0845 but met with no opposition.

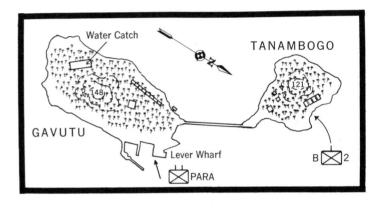

work of clearing the broken ground was slow and it became obvious that Tulagi could not be secured by nightfall. A defensive line was set up, companies of the Raider Battalion, supported by companies of the 2nd Battalion, Fifth Marines, holding a line enclosing the southeastern tip of the island.

During the night the Japanese made numerous attacks, ranging from assaults in strength to attempts at infiltration by small parties or individuals. All were held and in the morning Raiders and 2nd Marines began to close in on the survivors. A heavy concentration of 60- and 81-mm mortar fire prepared the way for the advance and by 1500 Tulagi was in American hands. A few Japanese (estimated at about forty) escaped by swimming to Florida Island. Others holed up and fought on individually for a few days until hunted down. Only three surrendered—the rest died defending their positions. Thirty-six Americans were killed and fifty-four wounded. Two 13-mm antiaircraft guns and a 3-inch gun were among the captured matériel.

The assault on Gavutu was directed against the northeast coast and was made in three waves. After a brief but destructive bombardment by *San Juan* (a 14-gun salvo every twelve seconds for four minutes) and a working over by SBDs from *Wasp*, Company A of the Parachute Battalion made the first landing, getting ashore without casualties. Company B, of the second wave, however, and Company C and miscellaneous detachments of the third wave, were heavily fired upon, both while approaching and landing. Part of this fire came from the northern face of Hill 148, which was protected from the naval gunfire, and part from Tanambogo. Progress was made and by 1430 most of the island was in U.S. hands, but it was obvious that Tanambogo must be taken before the positions in defilade on the northern side of Hill 148 could be reduced.

After a 10-minute strike by planes from *Wasp* and a concentration of fire from *Buchanan* and *Monssen*, at about 1800, Company B, 2nd Marines, who had made the initial landings at Haleta, was ordered to seize the island, believed held only by a few snipers. One of the six LCPs carrying the company hung up on coral, the remaining five

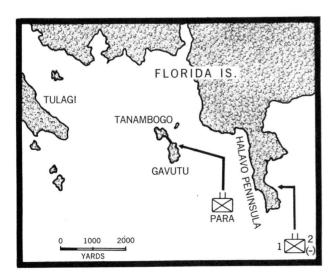

approached the northeastern end of Tanambogo, where there was a small pier. The platoon in the first boat got ashore without drawing fire, but a shell from a support vessel fired a fuel supply and the remaining boats were exposed by the light of the flaming dump. Immediately the defenders opened a heavy fire from rifles and machine guns. There were many casualties, especially among the boats' crews, and it soon became apparent that the company would have to be withdrawn. This was successfully accomplished, although some dozen Marines were forced to work their way to the causeway and so across to Gavutu.

Brigadier General William Rupertus, the division's assistant commander, now requested the release of the rest of Division Reserve (2nd and 3rd Battalions, 2nd Marines, reinforced). This was approved and *President Hayes* and *President Adams* left the transport area off Beach Red and proceeded to the transport area off Tulagi. The 3rd Battalion was ordered to Gavutu to reinforce the troops there (the Japanese, aided by swimmers from Tulagi and Florida, had counterattacked from their cave shelters under cover of darkness, but were nearly all killed) and to seize Tanambogo.

At 1620, August 8, after a ten-minute bombardment by *Buchanan*, Company I preceded by two tanks of 2nd Tank Battalion, landed on Tanambogo. One tank was disabled by an iron bar thrust into the track mechanism and set on fire (forty-two Jap bodies were found piled up around it). Despite close support from the remaining tank, progress was slow.

Enemy concealed in dugouts and caves resisted fiercely, aided by rifle and machine-gun fire from an islet, Gaomi, a few hundred yards away. This was silenced at 1700 by gunfire from *Gridley*, and at the same time a platoon (of Company K) attacked across the causeway from Gavutu. By 2100 most of the island was secure although it was not until late on August 9 that all resistance ended. Five islets close by, including Gaomi, were also secured.

Twenty prisoners were taken, while some thirty are thought to have escaped to Florida Island (to be wiped out later by American patrols or by the natives). Considering the small number, perhaps 350, of the defenders of Gavutu and Tanambogo, American casualties were comparatively heavy, 108 killed or missing, and 140 wounded.

Tulagi was then organized for defense, but although occasionally shelled by Japanese warships, the island was never attacked.

After parting company with the Tulagi forces, X-ray group steered for the designated transport area off Beach Red at 12 knots. At 0613 a salvo of 8-inch guns from *Quincy* signaled the beginning of the preliminary bombardment, the three cruisers and four DDs plastering an area between Kukum and Koli. By 0645 the transports had reached the unloading area, about 9000 yards off the beaches and the traditional order "Land the landing force" roared out over the bullhorns. Zero hour for Guadalcanal was set at 0910 and the first waves hit the beach right on the dot. There had been no reply to the naval bombardment and no ground fire had been reported by the forty-four carrier planes assigned to bomb and strafe the beaches. Now 1st and 3rd Battalions of the 5th Marines (2nd was at Tulagi) landed abreast on a front of some 2000 yards without the slightest sign of opposition. Moving gingerly inland through groves of palm trees and undergrowth shattered by the last furious minutes of fire by the support ships (concentrated in an area 3200 yards long and 200 in depth) patrols of the 5th pressed slowly forward—expecting at any moment a blast of fire from hidden defenders. But the only shots were by trigger-happy Marines. The campaign for an almost unknown island, which before it was over, would bring about the death of thousands, the destruction of hundreds of planes and dozens of warships, had begun with a walkover.

By 0930 the 1st Marines were beginning to come ashore and the assault battalions were establishing a defense perimeter about 600 yards inland.

Three battalions of the 1st were ashore by 1100. Pack howitzers (75-mm) came ashore with the assault troops. The 105s were not ready for action until afternoon. Because of a shortage of ramp-type landing craft their prime movers were not put ashore immediately, and amphibian tractors were pressed into service to haul the weapons into position.

While the artillery, the special weapons and defense battalions, the Pioneers and the 3rd Battalion of the 5th Marines held the beach areas, the 1st Marines pushed inland. There was no opposition, but the heat and the thick steaming jungle slowed the advance of the heavily laden troops—out of condition after weeks crowded into transports—to a crawl. There were not enough salt tablets, and owing to a shortage of canteens, each man was issued only one—and in the extreme heat of the Solomons every man needed two.

By nightfall the weary troops had advanced

ANDING CRAFT, PERSONNEL, RAMP (LCP [R])

Right: LCP. Length: 36′ Beam: 10′8″
Max. draft: 2′6″ Flat bottom
Propeller in tunnel. One 225-hp diesel or gas engine
Speed: 13 knots. Two machine guns in ring mounts
LCP(R) above, is similar in size but has hinged ramp bow

U.S. LANDING CRAFT

LANDING CRAFT, VEHICLES (LCV)

Length: 36′4″
Can carry a light vehicle
or several tons of cargo
or (LCVP) thirty-five or forty men
Same power as LCP above

LANDING CRAFT, MECHANIZED (LCM)

LANDING VEHICLE, TRACKED (LVT) "Alligator"

Unarmored Amphibian Tractor
Powered with 200-hp engine
Armed with one .50-cal.,
one .30-cal. MG
Carried cargo or personnel

some 3500 yards and the three battalions of the 1st dug in astride the Tenaru River. The 1st Battalion of the 5th had reached the mouth of the Ilu River and set up a defense perimeter there.

Troops once landed must be supplied and the amount of paraphernalia a modern division needs to keep it in operation is staggering. First Pioneer Battalion had the job of unloading supplies on Beach Red. With one platoon on Tulagi and one still aboard less than five hundred men were available. In a short time conditions on the beaches were chaotic. Few of the boats had ramp bows and supplies had to be lifted out over the gunwales. The amphibian tractors proved invaluable, but there were too few of them. Sailors from the transports were sent ashore to help the exhausted shore party but the beaches soon became piled with tons of supplies of all descriptions, with not enough manpower and equipment to get it inland. At dusk on August 7 some one hundred landing craft were beached, waiting to be unloaded while fifty more stood off, waiting room to come in. By 2330 the beachmaster reported supplies piling up and at his request unloading ceased until 1000 on August 8.

This foulup on the beach might have been avoided if troops had been assigned to assist the overworked shore party. Complaints were heard that groups of Marines stood idly by, refusing to help on the grounds that their job was to fight, not haul supplies. These complaints were undoubtedly well founded, but Vandegrift and his commanders had expected a stiff fight for their beachhead, and every available unit was earmarked either for the advance or perimeter defense. Most troops seen "idling on the beach" were waiting for their units to move off or were rear elements of some already advancing, and no unit commander was about to let his outfit, expecting soon to be committed to action, be dragooned into pioneer duty!

Lack of proper landing craft, too few amphibians, too few pioneers—Operation Shoestring was living up to its name. Whatever the causes the results, in view of coming events, were to be all but fatal.

Nor was the snafu on the landing beach the only cause of delay. As was to be expected, the news flashed from Tulagi before the Jap radio went off the air brought immediate reaction from Rabaul, headquarters of Vice-Admiral Gunichi Mikawa's Eighth Fleet or Outer South Seas Force. A strike of the Imperial Japanese Navy's 25th Air Flotilla—twenty-seven twin-engined Bettys—escorted by

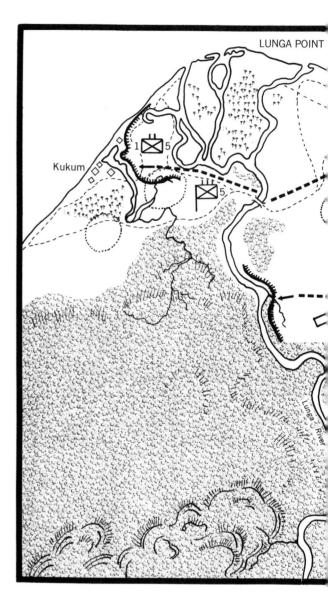

eighteen Zeros, was ordered to attack the invasion force shipping. Rear Admiral Aritomo Goto was summoned from Kavieng with Cruiser Division 6; *Aoba, Kinugasa, Kako,* and *Furutaka.* At the same time, a small force, about 410 men, scraped together from available units and armed only with rifles and machine guns, was ordered aboard transport *Mieyo Maru.*

About 1100 coastwatcher Paul Mason near Buin on Bougainville radioed, "Twenty-four torpedo bombers heading yours." In 25 minutes Admiral Richmond K. Turner had the word, landing craft were ordered off, the ships got under way and a fighting CAP formed over Savo. On H.M.A.S. *Canberra* the bullhorns announced, "The ship will be attacked at noon by twenty-four torpedo bombers. All hands will pipe to dinner at eleven o'clock." At 1320 the strike arrived. The Bettys had been

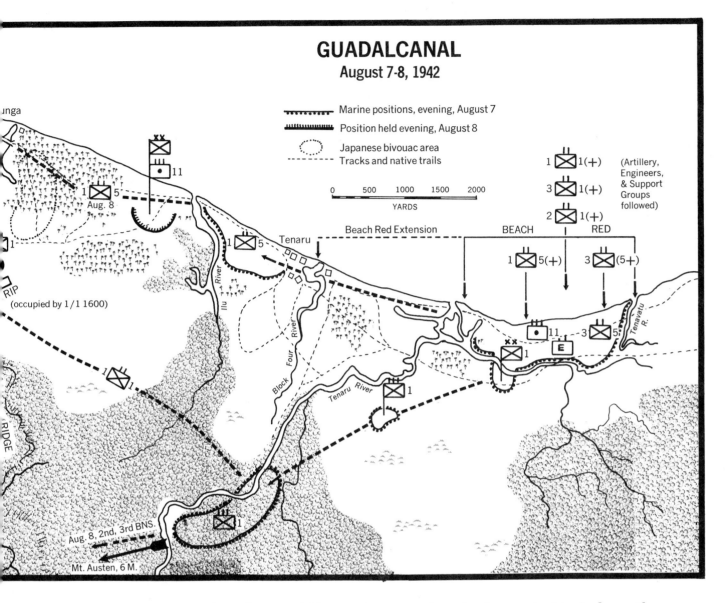

GUADALCANAL
August 7-8, 1942

Marine positions, evening, August 7
Position held evening, August 8
Japanese bivouac area
Tracks and native trails

(Artillery, Engineers, & Support Groups followed)

0   500   1000   1500   2000
YARDS

Beach Red Extension   BEACH   RED

Tenaru

.unga

Aug. 8

RIP
(occupied by 1/1 1600)

Ilu River

Block Four River

Tenaru River

Tenavatu R.

RIDGE

Aug. 8, 2nd, 3rd BNS.

Mt. Austen, 6 M.

loaded for a strike against the airbase at Milne Bay, New Guinea, when the news of the Guadalcanal landings came in and there had not been time to replace bombs with torpedoes. Moving vessels make poor targets, and the Bettys were under attack from Admiral Fletcher's fighters. The bombers failed to score and two were shot down by ships' AA.

The Zero escort, operating at the limit of their endurance, tangled with Wildcats for the first time. Some fourteen bombers and fighters fell to the American airmen. Eleven U.S. fighters and a dive bomber were lost. A later strike of some dozen unescorted Val dive bombers had a little better luck. One hit was made on destroyer *Mugford,* which suffered twenty casualties from a 250-lb. bomb. Three Vals were downed and six more ditched on the way back to Rabaul. Perhaps more

important than the damage to *Mugford* was the three hours' unloading time lost. Fletcher's 48 hours were fast running out!

Mount Austen commands the Lunga Point area and it was Vandegrift's first intention to secure it. However, realizing that it was too formidable an undertaking (as well as being farther inland than the rough maps available had indicated), the 1st Marines were directed on the morning of August 8 to advance toward Lunga and at 1600 their 1st Battalion occupied the airfield and pressed on to the Lunga River. The Japanese, about 450 fighting men and 1700 laborers, had fled, leaving considerable equipment behind. This included some thirty-five serviceable trucks, nine road rollers, two gas locomotives and hopper cars on a narrow-gauge track, hand carts, and tools.

The 1st Battalion, 5th Marines, supported by

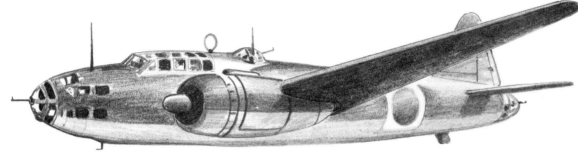

MITSUBISHI G4M1 Type 1 (Betty)

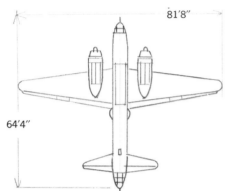

Land Attack Aircraft
Weight empty: 18,500 lbs.
Max. speed: 266 mph at 13,780 ft.
Range: 2260 miles at 196 mph
Power: two 1850-hp 14-cylinder radials
Armament: one 20-mm. in tail, four 7.7-mm. in nose,
dorsal and beam positions;
2200 lbs. of bombs or two 1760-lb. torpedoes
Crew: seven

tanks, crossed Alligator Creek and advanced slowly toward Lunga. Here the first Japanese were encountered and the first shots fired "in anger" (as opposed to many previously fired by mistake). Resistance was light, and a few prisoners, Japanese and Korean laborers, were picked up. Campsites were found abandoned, with every evidence of hasty flight—scattered helmets, rifles, clothing, even half-finished bowls of rice. Obviously no serious resistance was to be expected at the moment so 1st Battalion, 5th Marines, was ordered to cross the Lunga River and advance on Kukum. Some rifle and machine-gun fire was encountered but these positions were soon cleared. Otherwise Kukum was undefended and yielded considerable loot, including two 70-mm and two 75-mm guns, rifles, machine guns, ammunition, oil and gasoline, radio equipment, beer and sake, canned goods and a large supply of rice. The last two were going to be important.

Cessation of unloading on the 7th had allowed some clearing of the beaches, but further delays were caused on the 8th by increased Japanese air activity. Soon after 0900 a warning sent by coastwatcher Jack Read on Bougainville was received, "Forty bombers heading yours." Unloading was stopped once more and the ships got under way in preparation for the attack. Again a fighter CAP was stacked up over Savo, but this time the bombers turned north some 50 miles from that island and when the Bettys, armed with torpedoes this time, swept in low over Florida Island the an-

chorages were without air cover. Probably the Japanese air commander expected an easy slaughter. If so, the accuracy and intensity of the American gunfire must have come as a nasty shock. The heavies used their 8-inch batteries as well as their secondaries and under a hail of fire Betty after Betty disintegrated or went flaming into the sea. One fish went into destroyer *Jarvis*, badly damaging her. A second wave, dive bombers this time, came in a little later and one of these, hit and burning, crashed and exploded on transport *George F. Elliot* off Tulagi setting the ship ablaze. Belatedly the CAP from over Savo tangled with the attackers and their escorting Zeros. Seven American planes were lost. Japanese losses were high and it is probable that many of those damaged failed to make the long trip home. One report has it that only one of the enemy bombers returned to his base, reporting that he had sunk a battleship!

A second alert later in the afternoon—false this time—again sent the invasion armada scurrying about Sealark Channel in defensive tactics. More time wasted, and, although no one knew it, for many in the invasion fleet, time had all but come to an end.

THE COASTWATCHERS

All through the accounts, official or otherwise, of the fighting in the Southwest Pacific run such remarks as, "Enemy planes were reported on their way to Guadalcanal" or "Japanese transports, escorted by warships were sighted steaming south through St. George Channel." Some of these reports came from air reconnaissance and patrolling American submarines but the most numerous, and the most detailed, were sent in by that daring and dedicated group of heroes known as the Coastwatchers.

The organization was originally formed after World War I, with the realization by the authorities that there were large stretches of the long Australian coastline where an enemy's vessels might operate or troops land without even being seen, let alone opposed. So, under Royal Australian Navy sponsorship, a plan was made whereby certain civilians—harbormasters, railroad officials, postmasters, police, and such like—were to pass on information by telegraph to the Navy Office in Melbourne. This still left the north and northwestern coasts almost without coverage; not because there were no inhabitants—although these were few—but from lack of means of communications. With the increasing use of two-way radio by civilians, the system was greatly expanded, and government officials in the chains of islands Americans know as the Southwest Pacific, but which the Australians call the Northeast Area, were made part of the coastwatching organization. By the time World War II began, there were some eight hundred coastwatchers, most of them on the mainland.

But, scattered through the Northeast Area there were district officers, plantation managers and owners, and traders who either had, or had been supplied with, teleradio equipment and who also had received some training in observation and the art of reporting what they had seen with speed and precision. It was these islanders—some of them elderly men, hardly fitted for the guerrilla-type life they were to lead—who faced the full storm of the Japanese invasion. Their equipment, at least the sets issued by the RAN, was bulky—requiring twelve to sixteen porters—but efficient, able to withstand rough transit and the corroding all-pervading jungle damp. Batteries were charged by small gasoline engines, weighing some 70 pounds. Simple ciphers were used, and each teleradio was fitted with a crystal cut to give a certain frequency. Thus loudspeakers at key stations could receive at any hour of the day or night and obviated the use of tight broadcasting schedules.

This odd collection of island officials, planters, miners, missionaries, and naval personnel covered a vast area with an intelligence network which won a high reputation for integrity and efficiency. "The enormous contribution of the Australian Commonwealth to the Allied war effort," wrote General Douglas MacArthur, "contains no brighter segment than this comparatively unknown unit . . ." Operating singly or in pairs, accompanied only by a few trustworthy natives, these men braved months of solitude in some of the most Godforsaken spots on the globe—surrounded by the enemy and often by savage tribesmen, of doubtful loyalty or actively hostile. They faced malaria and all the ills that white men are prone to in tropical jungle country—jungle where even the natives often lived in a state of semi-starvation. At times the jungle country afforded them perfect cover—at others, they lived like fugitives; their hideouts betrayed by treacherous natives and their retreat routes cut by Jap patrols. Forced marches through stinking, crocodile-infested swamps or over thick brush country cut by precipitous ravines wore them down, steaming with tropic heat one day and the next lashed by cold highland downpours. And always there was the knowledge that capture meant first torture and then execution. For large bodies of men to work and fight in such country takes great willpower and endurance. For men to operate in it almost alone takes a special kind of courage. This the coastwatchers had, and the reports they managed to send out materially affected the outcome of the island campaigns.

The coastwatchers' code name was Ferdinand and it was chosen as a reminder that, like Munro Leaf's famous bull, they were to sit quietly under the trees, and to fight only if they were stung. Often an opportunity to strike a direct blow had to be passed—a severe test of discipline to men whose co-workers might have been tied to trees and bayoneted. But a few dead Japanese would not affect the war one way or another, while every effort of Ferdinand was to be focused on one thing only, the gathering and broadcasting of intelligence. This could only be done by drawing as little attention to themselves as possible, and while the Japanese occasionally made concerted drives to find the watchers and destroy their camps and equipment, they seldom succeeded in doing more than running them out of one hideout into one even more inaccessible. Only when the security of their missions was definitely threatened were they to take direct action. When they did it was usually brief, but bloody. More than one small Jap patrol which stumbled on a coastwatcher's hideaway was wiped out to the last man.

Supplies were air dropped (the jungle could support life only for a short time without resort to agriculture and the raising of pigs and fowl) and coastwatchers assigned to new positions or as replacements and reinforcements were often delivered to their destination by submarine. This usually involved making the last stage of their journey by rubber boat, and occasionally parties came to grief in the surf and landed minus much of their equipment and supplies. Coastal travel, where it was possible at all, was usually done in native canoes, while for inter-island travel, launches and small trading boats were pressed into service. Such journeys were mostly made at night, and the craft carried into the jungle or concealed in some inlet during the day.

Much of Ferdinand's success depended on the attitude of the natives. Where Japanese influence and propaganda was strong, the watchers had difficulty purchasing food and hiring carriers, and in many cases, risked betrayal or even attack. Everyone likes to back a winner, and the natives of the Northeastern Area were no exception. On other islands, especially those with energetic district officers, the natives never fell under the spell of Japanese propaganda and held aloof from the invaders, at the same time aiding the watchers, at no small risk to themselves. There were many, often members of the local constabulary units, who staked everything on an Allied victory and gave all out aid to the white men. Not a few gave their lives as well.

By the time the campaign for Guadalcanal got under way, the coastwatching setup in the immediate area was functioning most efficiently. There were coastwatchers on Guadalcanal itself (three parties—one overlooking Lunga Point), on Florida Island, New Georgia, Malaita, Bougainville, Santa Isabel, and later on Choiseul, Vella Lavella, and Kolombangara. Thus the approaches to Guadalcanal from the Japanese bases in the north were well covered and movements of ships and planes duly reported.

The Malaita group, which included a radio expert, became a message center for all coastwatching signals. Here they were recoded in a high-grade cipher and sent to Naval Intelligence at Vila in the New Hebrides. The effects of the coastwatchers' organization was apparent even before the American landings. The observers near Tulagi and Lunga Point reported on the progress of the Japanese installations and the new airfield (native boys were sent in by the coastwatchers to work

on or visit the Japanese installations) while the party on Malaita broadcasted daily weather reports. The report of Japanese ships at Tulagi brought on *Yorktown's* strike of May 4.

The main Japanese air strikes against Guadalcanal came either from Rabaul or Kavieng. If from Rabaul they passed over Buin, if from Kavieng their route lay over Buka Passage. Coastwatchers —Paul Mason, near Buin and Jack Read, overlooking Buka Passage—reported their passing, alerting the Americans at Guadalcanal that a raid was to be expected. Thus, four hours after the Guadalcanal landings began, the watcher at Buin radioed, "From STO" (his code signature) "twenty-four torpedo bombers heading yours." The warning gave time to get the ships under way and the enemy planes were met by blasts of gunfire from the ships and a strong combat patrol of fighters from the carriers, which sent the raiders scurrying back to Rabaul with loss. A message next morning from the watcher overlooking Buka Passage warned, "Forty-five bombers going southeast." And again, ships' guns and the hard-hitting .50-caliber weapons of the fighters splashed a number of Japs and drove off the rest, though not before they had done some damage.

When American fighters were based on Henderson Field, the long-range warnings gave the fliers time to take off and gain altitude—thus giving the Grumman Wildcats an edge over the speedier and more maneuverable Zeros.

Great numbers of ship movements were reported and as Japanese preparations for the counterinvasion of Guadalcanal began to take shape, the area around the Shortlands became crowded with shipping. To aid the watcher there, identification sheets of Japanese vessels were air-dropped. Native scouts, employed by the Japs at their installations, gave the coastwatchers detailed reports—listing numbers of trucks, tractors, etc., and pinpointing such targets as antiaircraft guns, ammunition dumps, radio stations, and fuel stores.

The advantage to the Allies of having each enemy move observed and reported almost as soon as it was made was beyond calculation. Wrote Admiral William F. Halsey: "The intelligence signaled from Bougainville by Read and Mason saved Guadalcanal, and Guadalcanal saved the South Pacific." High praise, but deserved—and equally to be shared by dozens of other men, white and black, who contributed to that remarkable, little-publicized organization named after a well-publicized bull.

III
The Emperor's Admirals
Strike Back

THE BATTLE OF SAVO ISLAND

The air strikes had been Mikawa's immediate answer to the American assault. But even as the remaining planes of the first attack on August 7 were returning to Rabaul, the Japanese admiral was putting to sea. It had not been an easy decision to reach. Obviously the invasion was supported by carriers (even in 1942 this went without saying). Equally obvious, to a fighter like Mikawa, the enemy must be attacked, at the risk of assaults from the air both on the run down the long channel between the islands of the Solomon chain (The

Slot), and on the return journey. A radio message flashed to Tokyo, asking approval of the planned attack. The Chief of the naval General Staff, Admiral Osami Nagano, gave his blessing; reluctantly, because he felt it a rash move, but lacking an alternative. At approximately 1630 on August 7 heavy cruiser *Chokai*, flying Mikawa's flag, led light cruisers *Tenryu, Yubari,* and destroyer *Yunagi* out of Simpson Harbor to rendezvous with Cruiser Division 6. The two forces met about 1800 and course was set for Guadalcanal.

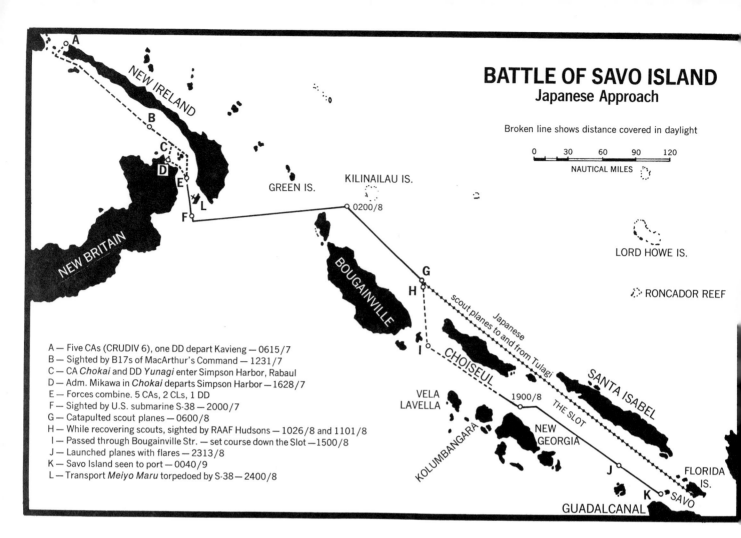

BATTLE OF SAVO ISLAND
Japanese Approach

Broken line shows distance covered in daylight

| 0 | 30 | 60 | 90 | 120 |
NAUTICAL MILES

A — Five CAs (CRUDIV 6), one DD depart Kavieng — 0615/7
B — Sighted by B17s of MacArthur's Command — 1231/7
C — CA *Chokai* and DD *Yunagi* enter Simpson Harbor, Rabaul
D — Adm. Mikawa in *Chokai* departs Simpson Harbor — 1628/7
E — Forces combine. 5 CAs, 2 CLs, 1 DD
F — Sighted by U.S. submarine S-38 — 2000/7
G — Catapulted scout planes — 0600/8
H — While recovering scouts, sighted by RAAF Hudsons — 1026/8 and 1101/8
I — Passed through Bougainville Str. — set course down the Slot — 1500/8
J — Launched planes with flares — 2313/8
K — Savo Island seen to port — 0040/9
L — Transport *Meiyo Maru* torpedoed by S-38 — 2400/8

Also converging on the threatened island were four submarines, one, *I-123* from Truk, *I-121* from Rabaul, and *RD-33* and *RD-54* diverted from New Guinea and the east coast of Australia respectively. Getting ready to sail was transport *Meiyo Maru,* carrying Mikawa's hastily organized relief force, and escorted by a supply ship and a minelayer. Her voyage was a short one. She left Rabaul on the evening of the 8th and about midnight came into the cross hairs of the periscope of the American submarine S-38. Lieutenant Commander H. F. Munson fired two torpedoes. Both smashed into the hull of the 5600-ton vessel and she went down in St. George Channel with fourteen officers and 328 men. Her escorts returned to Rabaul with the survivors. In an hour or two she was to be amply avenged.

The distance from Rabaul to Guadalcanal—steaming north of Buka, to the east of Bougainville and down The Slot—is more than 700 miles. Mikawa could hardly have hoped that his force would travel such a distance undetected. In fact Cruiser Division 6 had been sighted earlier by B-17s of MacArthur's Southwest Pacific Command.

Army pilots were noted for their ignorance of all things nautical (often including the nationality of the shipping they were attacking) and the report merely stated that six unidentified ships were sighted in St. George Channel, course southeast. Had they been identified as warships, traveling at speed, the report might have meant something. As it was they could have been coasters creeping along at 5 knots. However, even a warship sighting, so close to Japanese bases, need not necessarily have been cause for alarm.

The second sighting by the Navy was more illuminating. About 2000 August 7, S-38 sighted the united force steaming south from St. George Channel—so close that she was unable to fire torpedoes. Her contact report: "Two destroyers and three larger ships of unknown type, heading 140 degrees true, at high speed, 8 miles west of Cape St. George . . ." went out immediately. In the darkness Munson overlooked three vessels and confused a destroyer with a small cruiser but at least it was now known that an enemy squadron was heading south, and fast. Even so, the squadron was far away, and barely 60 miles from the Japanese base at Rabaul. The sighting therefore caused no concern.

Sighting number three was different. At 1026 on August 8 a Hudson of the RAAF spotted the Japanese east of Bougainville and some 40 miles northwest of Choiseul. Antiaircraft fire kept the plane at a distance, but the force was reported as: "Three cruisers, three destroyers, two seaplane tenders or gunboats, at Lat. 5° 49′ S., Long 156° 07′ E., course 120°, speed 15." Perhaps noticed is a better word than reported, for the pilot of the Hudson did nothing of the sort. Ignoring instructions to communicate such an important sighting immediately and then to maintain contact, the pilot finished his patrol, landed at his base at Milne Bay on the eastern tip of New Guinea, had his tea and then reported the sighting. About sunset the information reached MacArthur's HQ at Brisbane and from there Canberra sent it out on "Bells" (the Australian broadcast of information and orders to vessels at sea) on which Rear Admiral Victor Crutchley picked it up at 1839. It was also sent by Canberra to Pearl Harbor and broadcast on "Fox" (U. S. Navy counterpart of "Bells") whence Turner received it at 1845, 8 hours and 19 minutes after the sighting. A prompt report might have resulted in a thorough air search in the sector in question, and possible attack by planes of Southwest Command. As it was, the comparatively weak force reported and the identification of "two seaplane tenders, or gunboats" led Admirals Turner and Crutchley to assume (there was to be a lot of assumption that night) that the enemy intended to set up a seaplane base at Rekata Bay on the northeastern coast of Santa Isabel. A logical assumption and one concurred with by MacArthur's HQ (which thought Shortland Island was the probable goal) but unfortunately an incorrect one.

A fourth sighting, by another RAAF Hudson at 1101, reported two heavy cruisers, two light cruisers, and one unidentified vessel. As this information did not reach Turner until the action was in progress, it was completely valueless.

Shortly after the last sighting, Mikawa ordered one float plane up from each of his heavy cruisers. Two of these reconnoitered Tulagi, in spite of antiaircraft fire and fighters, and at noon came back with reports of a battleship, four cruisers, seven destroyers, and fifteen transports off Guadalcanal and two cruisers, twelve destroyers, and three transports off Tulagi. Mikawa, who had slowed his force to wait news from his scout planes, then

raised speed to 24 knots and headed south through Bougainville Strait to the attack.

The area from which enemy attacks on the Guadalcanal landing force might be expected was more or less covered by reconnaissance flights by both B-17s and PBYs of McCain's command and by MacArthur's planes. In places these search sectors overlapped, in places they left gaps.

On August 8, Turner, worried by the incomplete coverage, requested McCain to supplement the reconnaissance with a PBY flight from the tender *Mackinac* (on station off Malaita) to cover a sector including Santa Isabel, Choiseul, and Bougainville. This was covered by B-17s from Espiritu Santo (but only as far as the southern end of Choiseul) and so early in the morning that enemy forces reaching the area later in the day would enter the waters of The Slot after the search planes had left. No reply was received from McCain, so Turner *assumed* that the area had been covered. Actually two B-17s did search part of the area requested but their flights were curtailed by foul weather—and they missed spotting the Japanese by some 60 miles.

Turner had other things to worry him. About the time Mikawa was passing between Choiseul and Vella Lavella the American admiral intercepted a message from Fletcher to Ghormley; "Fighter plane strength reduced from 99 to 78. In view of the large number of enemy torpedo planes and bombers in this area, I recommend the immediate withdrawal of my carriers. Request tankers sent forward immediately as fuel running low." At the same time (the carriers being then some 120 miles from Savo Island) Fletcher, without waiting a reply, ordered his task force to withdraw to the southeast. As the logs of the various ships afterward showed, there was no serious shortage of fuel, most being half full or better. And his fighter force still had one more Wildcat than had the three U.S. carriers at the Battle of Midway.

It was not lack of fuel but fear of air attack (needless, as it happened) that caused Fletcher to retire. Loss of *Lexington* at Coral Sea and *Yorktown* at Midway had made him overcautious. Now three of America's four Pacific carriers were under his command and the responsibility weighed heavily.

No Japanese planes had "snooped" his squadron. No enemy carriers lurked over the horizon. Yet the threat was there and it was too much for Fletcher. And while Mikawa was speeding toward Guadalcanal and action with what he believed to be a vastly superior force, covered by one or more carriers, the "covering force"—a battleship, three carriers, six cruisers, and sixteen destroyers—was speeding in the other direction.

Turner was disgusted. He had not been consulted and, although he knew that Fletcher's ultimatum to retire after forty-eight hours with his carriers expired Sunday morning, he felt that he and his command had been left, as he put it, "bare-arse." Landing of supplies was behind schedule but the loss of his air cover left him little choice but to retire.

At 2032 the harassed admiral sent an urgent message to both Crutchley and Vandergrift to report aboard *McCawley* immediately.

At 2032 the British admiral was on patrol 20 miles away off Savo Island. And Mikawa, his force now in order of battle, was some 125 miles beyond that. The stage was set.

While the Marines on Guadalcanal settled down for a more or less quiet night and the off-loading parties struggled to cope with the great tonnage of supplies and equipment still aboard, the warships of the support groups took up their night stations. They were necessarily divided, one group, the Eastern Force—Rear Admiral Norman Scott with light cruisers H.M.A.S. *Hobart* and the anti-aircraft cruiser *San Juan*, with destroyers *Monssen* and *Buchanan*—patrolled the sector east of a line running north from Lunga Point and the approaches through Sealark Channel. The Western Force, unfortunately, was itself divided into two, North and South, partly because of the location of Savo Island, almost in the center of the western entrance. Also, because Crutchley felt that groups of larger than four heavy ships were too unwieldy to maneuver at night.

Crutchley had immediate command of the Southern Force (three heavy cruisers, two destroyers). Northern Force, also three heavies and two destroyers, was under tactical command of Captain Frederick Riefkohl. Two destroyers, both with SC (Sky Search) radar were assigned to patrol west of Savo to cover both the northern and southern entrances to the Sound.

The Northern Force, in column, cruised at 10 knots in a box pattern about 5 miles on a side, turning 90° to starboard roughly every 30 minutes. *Helm* and *Wilson* were stationed slightly ahead and some 1000 yards to port and starboard of *Vincennes* respectively. Southern Force, also in column, headed by *Australia*, held a course roughly parallel to the coast of Guadalcanal. Cruising at 12 knots some 600 yards apart, they reversed course about every hour. *Patterson* was some 1200 yards broad on *Australia's* port bow (i.e. somewhat ahead and to her left) with *Bagley* in corresponding position to starboard.

Ralph Talbot and *Blue* each cruised a beat some 6 miles long, north and south of Savo respectively along a line roughly northeast-southwest, about 5 miles northwest of the island. Cruising at some 12

SOUTHERN FORCE

		Class	Tonnage	Speed	Armament	Launched
H.M.A.S. *Australia*	(CA)	Kent	10,000	31.5	8 8-in., 4 4-in.	1927
Chicago	(CA)	Northampton	9,300	32.7	9 8-in., 8 5-in.	1930
H.M.A.S. *Canberra*	(CA)	Kent	10,000	31.5	8 8-in., 4 4-in. °	1927
Bagley	(DD)	Craven	1,500	35	4 5-in., 16 21-in. TT	1936
Patterson	(DD)	"	"	"	" "	1937
Blue	(DD)	"	"	"	" "	"

NORTHERN FORCE

		Class	Tonnage	Speed	Armament	Launched
Vincennes	(CA)	Astoria	9,400	32	9 8-in., 8 5-in. °	1936
Quincy	(CA)	Astoria	9,375	"	" " °	1935
Astoria	(CA)	"	9,950	32.7	" " °	1933
Helm	(DD)	Craven	1,500	35	4 5-in., 16 21-in. TT	1937
Wilson	(DD)	McCall	1,500	36.5	" "	1939
Ralph Talbot	(DD)	Craven	1,500	35	" "	1936

° Sunk in the action

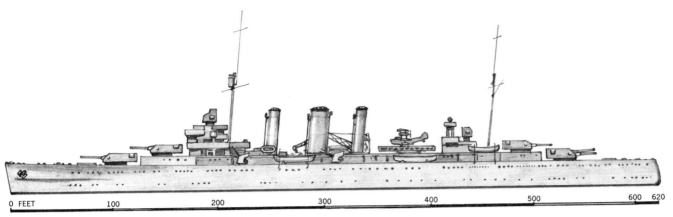

KENT CLASS HEAVY CRUISER (7 Ships. 5 R.N., 2 [Canberra, Australia] R.A.N.)

Launched February 1926–May 1927 Displacement: 10,000 tons LOA: 630 ft.
Beam: 68⅓ ft. Draft: 16¼ ft. 4 screws. 80,000 hp=31.5 knots
Armor: belt 3–5 in.,
deck, 4 in. (waterline), turrets, 2 in.–1½ in.
Armament: eight 8 in. (2×2), four 4 in. (4×1), four 2-pdr. automatic
Aircraft: one Complement: 680

knots, they reversed course about every half hour. When both were at the southernmost end of their beats they were perhaps 15 miles apart.

Ships were at Condition II, that is, half the crews were on watch. The men were tired; the officers doubly so. They had been ordered on full alert the evening of August 6, and between bombardments and air raids, August 7 had been a busy day. August 8 had brought more Jap planes and men looked forward to night and a relaxation of tensions. Tomorrow would presumably bring further air attacks and all those who possibly could tried to get a little much-needed rest. The captains were in their sea cabins, handy to the bridges. There was no indication that that night would be any but a repetition of the preceding one—ships steaming back and forth in orderly columns through the darkness.

On receipt of Turner's request for an immediate conference aboard *McCawley*, Crutchley signaled Captain Howard Bode of *Chicago*; "Take charge of patrol. I am closing CTF 62 [Turner] and may or may not rejoin you later." *Australia* then left her position and headed for the transport area off Lunga Point. Crutchley had been criticized for taking his ship out of line, but it was the logical thing to do under the circumstances. Turner was some 10 miles away and the trip by barge would take considerable time. Turner certainly expected him to come in *Australia* as the latter part of his message indicated; ". . . will send boat as soon as you approach."

Captain Bode held his station astern of *Canberra*. (It was simpler to order a turn together at the end of the next beat, which would have the effect of putting him at the head of the line again than to risk the confusion of a change of position. A further change would then have to be made if and when *Australia* rejoined.) Riefkohl was not informed that the force commander was absent. He was now senior officer in the area but in view of the lack of any definite orders in event of surface action it would probably not have made much difference if he had been.

Crutchley may not have been a great tactician, but he was a fighter of considerable experience. He had won the Victoria Cross, Britain's highest decoration for valor (in a night action, by the way), and assorted other decorations in WW I and in 1940 he was captain of the battleship *Warspite* at the second battle of Narvik. His critics have accused him of not issuing a comprehensive battle plan to his squadron. No doubt experience had convinced him that in the inevitable confusion of a night action the fewer orders the better. In any case he could hardly have foreseen the complete failure of his destroyer screen to alert the squadrons that the Japanese were approaching, nor that the commander of the Southern Force would fail to notify the Northern Force that he was under attack. It is even questionable if *Australia*'s presence with the Southern Force would have tipped the scales in the Allies' favor. Very possibly she would have only presented one more target for the shoals of deadly Japanese torpedoes which laced the black waters of the Sound that night. This is mere speculation, one of wars many "ifs." She was *not* there, and a fighting sailor missed his own squadron's battle.

Mikawa's last daylight reconnaissance, one of *Aoba*'s float planes, failed to return but at 2100 the pilots' reports of the day's raid on the invasion fleet came in from Rabaul—three cruisers, two destroyers, and nine transports sunk, a cruiser and two transports left burning. The odds now appeared to be in favor of Nippon. (The actual damage was one transport left burning and one destroyer holed by a torpedo. Not that it would have made any difference to Mikawa, had he known it. He was already committed, and his battle orders signaled.)

As the sun set (1816) and the brief tropic twilight faded into darkness, officers on the bridges of the speeding Japanese Eighth Fleet heaved a sigh of relief. Incredibly, no American planes had roared in to the attack, in fact, since before noon, no planes had appeared at all. It had all the earmarks of a trap, but a blow must be struck, and Mikawa was the man to strike it. At 2313 the Japanese admiral ordered float planes launched to make a final reconnaissance, lay course markers, and, on signal, to drop flares. At 2342 speed was increased to 26 knots and at midnight, when all hands went to battle stations, was upped to 28 knots. The Japanese order of battle was as follows:

With only thirty-four 8-in. guns as opposed to forty-four on the Allied cruisers and thirty-five lighter guns, 3-in. to 5.5-in., against sixty carried on *Canberra* and the American cruisers and destroyers, Mikawa was at a considerable disadvantage. The disparity in torpedo tubes was also very great, fifty-four Japanese (although forty-four of these carried the deadly 24-in. "long lance" type) against the ninety-six 21-in. tubes of the American destroyers. (American designers did not favor torpedo tubes on cruisers, and *Canberra* had had hers removed before the war.) As a crowning advantage the American vessels had radar, not very

efficient by later standards but still capable of picking up an enemy ship at some 10 miles.

The physical advantages were with his enemies, but Mikawa's edge was of the mental kind. His men were alert and keyed up to fighting pitch and highly trained in night battle tactics—in realistic practice actions which had taken their toll of both ships and men. Of radar they knew next to nothing, but Japanese naval night glasses were superb and all lookouts were picked for their exceptional eyesight, then trained until they could make out a target at more than four miles on a dark night. Now gunners and torpedo men tensed at the controls of their weapons as the great ships, queer and top-heavy looking with their odd stacks and pagoda-like superstructures, swept through the darkness toward Guadalcanal.

A naval action can be as confusing to a reader as to a participant. To clarify the action as much as possible the main events are treated in chronological order. The night is overcast—warm and muggy. A storm is making up over Savo with occasional flashes of lightning. Off Tulagi—*George F. Elliot* is burning. Despite efforts to sink her, she is still blazing, a beacon visible for many miles.

The Allied squadrons are steaming quietly in their formations, sentries *Ralph Talbot* and *Blue* churning up and down on their lonely beat. Then about 2345, a plane is sighted by *Talbot*, quite low and directly overhead, heading toward the Sound. A call goes out on TBS (short range radio telephone, known as Talk Between Ships): "This is Jimmy, Warning, Warning, Plane sighted over Savo Island heading east." (Fateful damaging omission, the aircraft is identified as a float plane—the type carried aboard cruisers and battleships—but no word of this is passed.) The message, repeated several times, is picked up by *Patterson*, who tries to relay it to *McCawley*. Turner never

		Class	Ton.	Speed	Armament	Launched
Chokai	(CA)	*Takao*	9,850	35.5	10 8-in., 4 4.7-in., 8 24-in. TT	1931
Aoba	(CA)	*Aoba*	9,000	34.5	6 8-in., 4 4.7-in., 8 24-in. TT	1926
Kinugasa	(CA)	*Aoba*	9,380	34.5	6 8-in., 4 4.7-in., 8 24-in. TT	1926
Furutaka	(CA)	*Furutaka*	9,150	34.5	6 8-in., 4 4.7-in., 8 24-in. TT	1921
Kako	(CA)	"	"	"	" " " "	1925 *
Tenryu	(CL)	*Tenryu*	3,230	33	4 5.5-in., 1 3-in., 6 21-in. TT	1918
Yubari	(CL)	(1 design)	2,890	35.5	6 5.5-in., 1 3-in., 4 24-in. TT	1923
Yunagi	(DD)	*Kamikaze*	1,270	37.25	3 4.7-in., 4 21-in. TT	1924

* Torpedoed on August 10

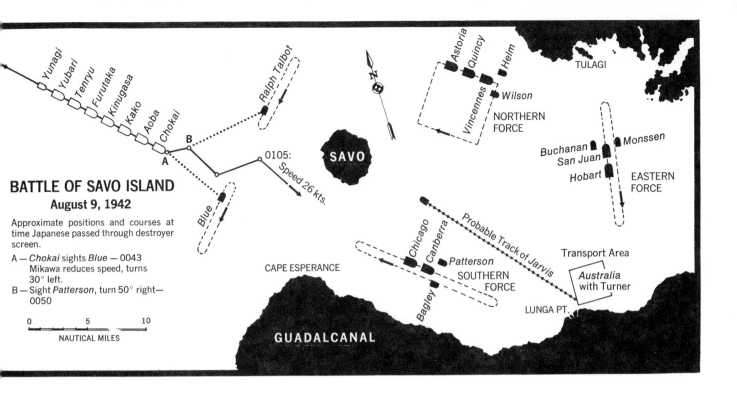

BATTLE OF SAVO ISLAND
August 9, 1942

Approximate positions and courses at time Japanese passed through destroyer screen.

A — *Chokai* sights *Blue* — 0043 Mikawa reduces speed, turns 30° left.

B — Sight *Patterson*, turn 50° right— 0050

0 ____ 5 ____ 10
NAUTICAL MILES

Map labels: Yunagi, Yubari, Tenryu, Furutaka, Kinugasa, Kako, Aoba, Chokai, A, B, Ralph Talbot, Blue, 0105: Speed 26 kts., SAVO, TULAGI, Astoria, Quincy, Helm, Wilson, Vincennes, NORTHERN FORCE, Buchanan, San Juan, Monssen, Hobart, EASTERN FORCE, Chicago, Canberra, Patterson, Bagley, SOUTHERN FORCE, Probable Track of Jarvis, Transport Area, *Australia* with Turner, LUNGA PT., CAPE ESPERANCE, GUADALCANAL

receives it, but *San Juan* hears it, passes it on to *Vincennes* and is overheard by *Astoria*. *Blue* gets the message, and tracks the plane on her radar. Some crewmen claim they see running lights.

Riefkohl, about to turn in, *assumes* the plane is friendly, possibly from Carrier Force. (Not having been told Carrier Force is withdrawing—nor that the plane is of the type carried aboard cruisers.)

Other ships hear planes, even see them. Because they fly low and make no attacks they are *assumed* to be American.

Turner's conference is over. Crutchley is giving Vandegrift a lift back to *Southard*. Midnight and all's well.

0043—Lookouts on *Chokai* sight a destroyer (*Blue*) over 5 miles away, leisurely crossing the Japanese column's line of advance, from starboard to port. As some fifty guns train on the American sentry, Mikawa's orders: "Left rudder. Slow to 22 knots." (The wake of a big ship at high speed piles up astern and is plainly visible.) But no searchlight stabs out from the oncoming vessel, no star shell lob from her 5-in. guns. Unbelievably, she reverses course and steams slowly away to the southeast. A moment later another destroyer is sighted to port. It is *Ralph Talbot* heading peacefully northwest. If her lookouts are watching astern (and lookouts often do not) they see nothing of the enemy sweeping by and the relieved Mikawa orders course changed once more to starboard (0105). And *Blue* plods off on her beat unaware of *Chokai* and her consorts.

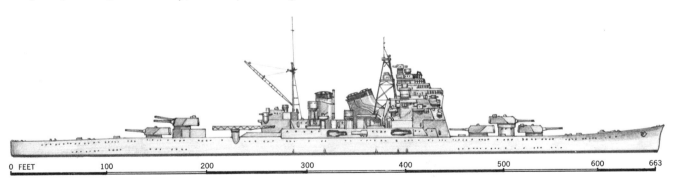

TAKAO CLASS HEAVY CRUISER (4 Ships)

0 FEET   100   200   300   400   500   600   663

Launched May 1930–April 1931
Displacement: 13,160 tons LOA: 670 Beam: 68 Draft: 21⅓ feet
4 screws. 133,100 hp=35.5 knots
Armor: belt, 3–4 in., deck & turrets, 3 in.
Armament: ten 8 in. (5✕2), four 4.7 in. (later eight 5 in.) AA, eight 25-mm., four 13-mm. MGs., sixteen 24 in. torpedo tubes (4✕4) (8 TT [4✕2] in Chokai and Maya)
Aircraft: three Complement: 773

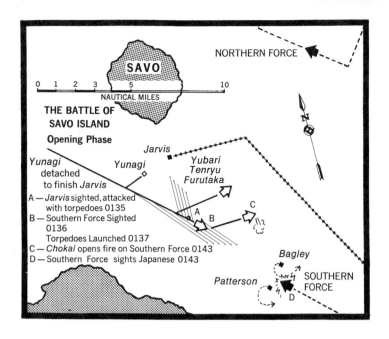

THE BATTLE OF
SAVO ISLAND

Opening Phase

Yunagi
detached
to finish *Jarvis*

A — *Jarvis* sighted, attacked with torpedoes 0135
B — Southern Force Sighted 0136
      Torpedoes Launched 0137
C — *Chokai* opens fire on Southern Force 0143
D — Southern Force sights Japanese 0143

the momentary flare of the launching charges goes unnoticed by any Allied ship and the squadrons speed on, on collision course.

0143—A lookout on *Patterson* shouts, "Ships ahead." General Quarters sounds and out goes the signal, "Warning, Warning, Strange ships entering harbor." At the same instant, flares burst into brilliance over the shipping off Lunga Point, silhouetting the Allied squadron, and *Chokai* opens fire—range 4500 yards.

Canberra (Captain Frank Edmund Getting) had picked up *Blue* on her radar but interference from the land mass of Savo must have prevented her from spotting the advancing Japanese. As *Patterson* flashes out her warning, *Canberra* sights the wakes of the leading enemy vessels. Even as the general alarm sounds—while her guns are still trained inboard and her crew dashing to battle stations—two torpedoes smash into her bow and a hail of shells strike her. A salvo crashes into her bridge, killing or wounding nearly everyone nearby, and a second completes the wrecking of the bridge and smashes into both engine rooms. Blazing and already listing, battered by some two dozen major caliber shells, with eighty-five dead and fifty-five wounded, *Canberra* is out of the fight. Her port 4-in. guns may have got off two rounds apiece. She burned all night, and next morning, about 0800, was sunk by orders of Admiral Turner. The distant flashes of gunfire were seen aboard both *Australia* and *McCawley*. Lacking any information, Crutchley decided to remain with the transports.

Patterson, firing star shell, comes hard left to bring her tubes to bear. The order to fire them goes unheard in the din and, by the time she completes a circle to bring her port tubes on, the Japanese column has disappeared to the northeast.

0125—Mikawa signals; "Three heavy cruisers south of Savo Island," then, "Prepare to fire torpedoes."

0133—Orders, "All ships attack." Speed increased to 30 knots.

0135—Japanese lookouts sight *Jarvis* to the north of them limping slowly westward. Torpedoes are launched (which miss) but no guns are fired.

Yunagi is ordered to drop from the tail of the Japanese column and finish off *Jarvis* (believed by the Japanese to be an Achilles Class light cruiser. The silhouettes were somewhat similar) and engage *Blue*.

0136—Lookouts sight *Patterson* and *Bagley*, then *Canberra* and *Chicago*, range 12,500 yards, and closing at some 1400 yards a minute.

0137—Mikawa orders, "Independent firing" and a ripple of flashes runs down the Japanese line as torpedoes plunge toward their targets. But

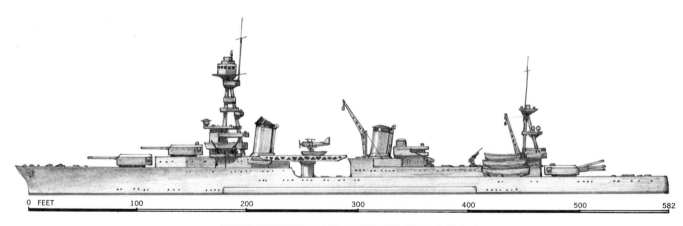

NORTHAMPTON CLASS HEAVY CRUISER (6 Ships)

Launched July 1929–September 1930
Displacement: 9050–9300 tons   LOA: 600¼   Beam: 66¼   Draft: 16½ ft.
4 screws.   107,000 hp=32.7 knots
Armor: belt 3 in.,   deck 3 in.,   turrets 1½ in.
Armament: nine 8 in. (3×3), eight 5 in. (8×1) 1.1 automatics (40-mm. and 20-mm. added later)
Aircraft: four   Complement: 1100

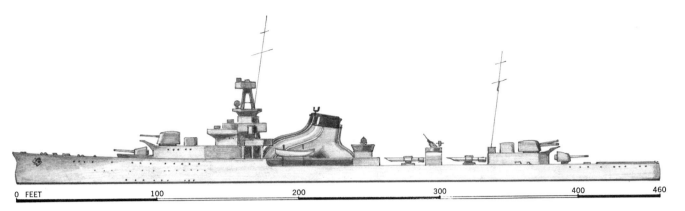

H.I.J.M.S. YUBARI — LIGHT CRUISER

Launched March 1923
Displacement: 2890 tons LOA: 463 Beam: 40 Draft: 11¾ feet
3 screws. 57,900 hp=35½ knots
Armor: belt (amidship) 2 in. Armament: six 5.5 in. (2×2 & 2×1) one 3 in. AA,
two 13-mm. MGs., four 24 in. torpedo tubes, 34 mines
Complement: 328

A couple of Japanese searchlights find and hold her and she sustains a large caliber hit on number 4 gun. She gets off some sixty rounds of regular shell and as far as is known hits nothing. So much for *Patterson*. But not quite. From about 0300 she stood by *Canberra* taking off wounded and helping fight fires. At about 0520 *Patterson's* lookouts reported a strange ship approaching. Her skipper, Commander F. J. Walker, challenged and moved to intercept. As she turned on her searchlight the other vessel opened fire. *Patterson* replied. After three salvos Walker recognized *Chicago*. Both vessels then ceased fire, fortunately with no damage done to either side.

When the firing began, *Bagley* also turned to port to fire torpedoes. Firing primers were not in readiness and, like *Patterson*, by the time she had circled to bring the port tubes to bear she had only fast-disappearing sterns to fire at. She let fly four fish, then went off to eastward. Score for *Bagley*— no hits, nor was she even fired on.

Like *Canberra*, *Chicago* woke up to the crash of gunfire. Her captain, rudely awoken, had just ordered star shells to illuminate two dark shapes ahead when torpedo wakes were reported. Evasive tactics failed and a few seconds later a great column of water smothered her forward as 1200 lbs. of explosive tore off part of her bow. She fired star shells to port and starboard, only six of which ignited. One enemy shell hit, showering the upper decks with splinters. About forty-five common shell were fired from the 5-in. batteries. They made no hits. *Chicago* then wandered off to the westward with two dead and twenty-one wounded. Her part in the battle had been less than spectacular

and she had failed in one vital particular. Captain Bode, in command of the now impotent Southern Force, had neglected to warn his unsuspecting colleagues to the North that his ships had been engaged and that the enemy was approaching.

As the Japanese release their torpedoes and turn north, their column becomes divided. Instead of following *Chokai*, *Furutaka* (perhaps to clear her torpedo batteries) turns more sharply to port. So do *Tenryu* and *Yubari*—so that the Japanese are now in two groups with *Chokai*, *Aoba*, *Kako*, and *Kinugasa* some 4 miles to the east.

0148—*Chokai* fires torpedoes at the cruisers of the Northern Force.

0150—The Japanese cruisers turn searchlights on the Northern Force and open fire.

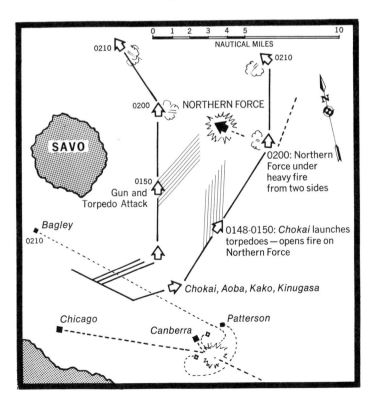

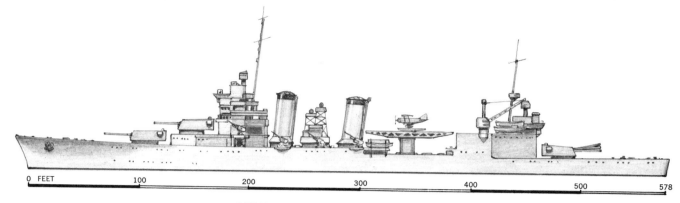

| 0 FEET | 100 | 200 | 300 | 400 | 500 | 578 |

ASTORIA CLASS HEAVY CRUISER (7 Ships)

Launched March 1933–May 1936
Displacement: 9375–9975 tons LOA: 588 Beam: 61¾ Draft: 19½ feet
4 screws. 107,000 hp=32.7 knots
Armor: side, 1½ in. belt (amidships) 5 in. decks, 3 in. and 2 in. turrets, 6 in.–3 in.
Armament: nine 8 in. (3×3), eight 5 in. (8×1), AA Automatics. (more AA
automatic weapons added during war)
Aircraft: four Complement: 1050

Astoria, the last in line, was hit first. Alerted by sight of flares over toward Guadalcanal the gunnery officer, Lieutenant Commander Truesdell, ordered General Quarters. Then came searchlights and a salvo of shells off the port bow. A request to the bridge for permission to open fire went unanswered and Truesdell, his spotter now reporting, "Cruisers of Nachi class," fired two salvos.

Captain William G. Greenman, aroused by the uproar, demanded to know who had sounded the alarm and who had ordered the "Commence firing." Thinking that *Astoria* was firing on her own ships he gave the command, "Cease firing." An urgent appeal from Truesdell at gunnery control and the sight of tall columns of water springing up ahead changed the captain's opinion and he ordered, "Commence firing." But precious time had been lost. The first four salvos, probably from *Chokai,* had missed, but the fifth hit amidships, setting the scout planes and hangars afire and virtually cutting the ship in two with a wall of flame. Once on target the Japanese poured in salvo after salvo. Number 1 turret was knocked out, the bridge hit, the gun deck wrecked. Despite smashed controls and severed communications *Astoria* managed to get off twelve ragged salvos from her 8-inchers, just over fifty rounds in all. The last from number 3 turret hit a forward turret on *Chokai.* The American cruiser's 5-inchers put out some sixty rounds before smashed mounts, exploding ammunition and slaughtered crews put an end to active resistance.

The steady hail of Japanese shells had also raised havoc in *Astoria's* engine spaces. Smoke, flame, and splinters found their way below. A blast destroyed number 1 fire room, others had to be abandoned. In a matter of minutes, the vessel had been reduced to a blazing wreck, nearly all power gone, an increasing list, 216 of her crew dead and 186 wounded. At 0215 shelling stopped, but *Astoria* had ceased to exist as a fighting unit long before that. Heroic efforts were made by a specialist party of her crew and by several destroyers, one of which, destroyer minesweeper *Hopkins,* took her in tow in an attempt to beach her. For hours they fought the flames while others shored up bulkheads and plugged the smaller shell holes. But internal explosions still raked the vessel and the list slowly increased. At last the order was given to abandon ship, and at 1215 she rolled over on her port side and sank.

Quincy, next ahead of *Astoria,* picked up *Patterson's* "Warning" signal. At the same time flares were seen and the general alarm sounded by the senior officer on watch. Unfortunately, the word was not passed to gunnery control, and when *Aoba's* searchlights caught and held her, her guns were still trained in and the Japanese could see men running along her decks.

As the turrets trained to port, the first shells crashed aboard. Two 9-gun salvos flashed out before a shell burst in the well deck starting the inevitable fire. *Quincy* had five planes (SOC-3 biplanes, fabric-covered and each with 135 gallons of gas) one on each catapult, one on deck and two in the hangar, and the well deck blazed like a torch. She was already alight from a hit aft, and now shells came in from both Japanese columns. One shell mortally wounded Captain Samuel Moore and killed almost all bridge house person-

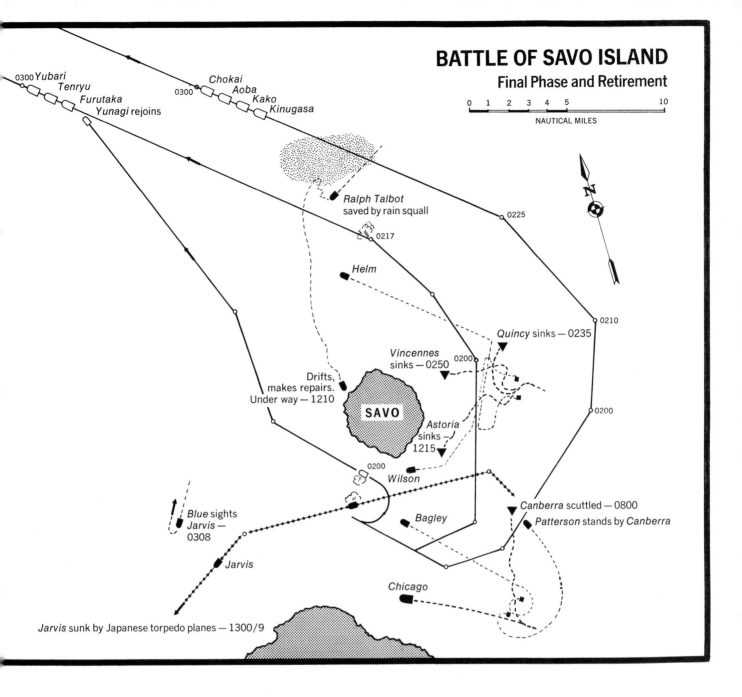

BATTLE OF SAVO ISLAND
Final Phase and Retirement

0 1 2 3 4 5 10
NAUTICAL MILES

0300 *Yubari*
Tenryu
Furutaka
Yunagi rejoins

Chokai
Aoba
0300 *Kako*
Kinugasa

Ralph Talbot
saved by rain squall

0225

0217

Helm

0210

Quincy sinks — 0235

Vincennes
sinks — 0250

0200

0200

Drifts,
makes repairs.
Under way — 1210

SAVO

Astoria
sinks —
1215

0200

Wilson

Blue sights
Jarvis —
0308

Bagley

Canberra scuttled — 0800
Patterson stands by *Canberra*

Jarvis

Chicago

Jarvis sunk by Japanese torpedo planes — 1300/9

nel. Number 3 turret was hit and jammed. Number 1 turret received a direct hit, powder flared and the turret was silent. Number 2 turret also burned and exploded. The 5-in. battery was a tangled wreck of smashed mounts and mangled bodies. The decks were ablaze, while scalding water from a ruptured whistle pipe sprayed down over dead and wounded.

A torpedo exploded into number 4 fire room and the doomed ship took a dangerous list to port. Battered and burning furiously, and all guns silenced, *Quincy* was finished. Her heavy guns had fired twenty-one rounds, one of which wrecked

Chokai's operations room, killing thirty-four men and wounding forty-eight others. At 0235 *Quincy*'s fires were quenched as she went down in 500 fathoms, the first of many vessels to litter the depths of what was to become known as Ironbottom Sound.

Vincennes plowed gently along, leading the column, on the eastward leg of the prescribed square. Captain Riefkohl had just turned in, when the OD heard gunfire and saw star shells and flashes off to the south toward Guadalcanal. The captain was called and the general alarm sounded. Riefkohl assuming (reasonably enough) that if it

CRAVEN CLASS DESTROYER (22 Ships)

Launched September 1936–April 1939
Displacement: 1500 tons LOA: 341½ Beam: 36 Draft: 10 ft.
Twin screw. 49,000 hp=35 knots
Armament: four 5 in., four 1.1 AA, sixteen 21 in. torpedo tubes (4 quadruple)
Complement: 250
(In some vessels two torpedo mounts removed and 40-mm. and 20-mm. AAs added.)

were something serious he would have been informed, put the disturbance down to the Southern Force firing on a Japanese destroyer attempting to sneak in through the southern entrance to the sound. That a larger force could have passed the destroyer guard unseen never entered his mind. Thus, when searchlights stabbed out from the port quarter and illuminated his cruisers Riefkohl *assumed* that they were from vessels of the Southern Force and ordered over voice radio—"Turn those searchlights off us, we are friendly."

As a precaution, the gunnery officer trained his turrets on the right-hand searchlight—radar range some 8000 yards. That the searchlights were not from friendly vessels was immediately made evident. Six tall spouts of water rose majestically some 500 yards off the port quarter. *Kako's* gunnery officer ordered the necessary adjustments and her next salvo smashed aboard *Vincennes* with devastating effect. Shells hit the bridge, the hangar, the carpenter's shop, knocked out gun control and severed all communication lines. Despite loss of power on the turrets, searchlights, and battle phones, *Vincennes* got off a full 9-gun salvo, then another, which hit *Kinugasa*. Screaming shells were now crashing aboard with dreadful regularity and at 0155 Captain Riefkohl ordered, "Hard right." As *Vincennes* turned, two, or perhaps three, torpedoes from *Chokai* hit abreast number 4 fire room on the port side. Despite heavy damage *Vincennes* got off two 6-gun salvos, then 1 and 2 turrets received direct hits. By now the 5-inch battery was a shambles and at about 0203 a torpedo from *Yubari* ripped into number 1 fire room—killing everyone in it.

Searchlights now spotlighted the ship from the east, the unengaged side, and Riefkohl, assuming they must be friendly, ordered a large American ensign raised at the fore. The Japanese gunners, believing they had a flagship in their sights, redoubled their efforts and salvos from both groups poured into the dying ship.

At last, at 0215, the shelling ceased, leaving *Vincennes* dead in the water, battered by some sixty hits and with her vitals ripped by at least three torpedoes. Over three hundred of her men were dead, nearly as many wounded. By 0230 the list was so pronounced that life rafts were ordered overside and the order "Abandon ship" given. About 0250 she rolled on her beam ends, capsized, and sank.

Destroyer *Wilson* sighted three Japanese cruisers attacking the *Vincennes* column (about 0150) and opened fire, firing over her own cruisers, at about 10,000 yards. She continued to fire whenever she saw a target, expending over two hundred rounds.

Helm took no active part in the engagement. She maintained course ahead of the column, and turned south when the cruisers were hit. At 0200 she moved in on a vessel sighted some four miles away but it was identified as friendly (probably *Ralph Talbot*).

Ralph Talbot, the picket destroyer, sighted cruising northwestward by the Japanese when they were approaching Savo, was at first just a spectator of the confusing action taking place far to the south. The battle soon came to her in the shape of *Yubari*, *Tenryu*, and *Furutaka*, moving westward on their way out of action. At about 0215 *Talbot* was caught in the glare of a searchlight and was immediately surrounded by shell splashes. One missile struck one of her torpedo mounts, another the chart house; the after 5-in. was hit and her wardroom wrecked. Her own guns were blazing away and she got off four torpedoes, but she was listing 20° and burning, and probably only the protective curtain of a rain squall saved her from the fate of the cruisers.

The lone Japanese destroyer, *Yunagi*, exchanged shots with what she believed to be a light cruiser (this was *Chicago*) and later she attacked a second alleged light cruiser, which must have been *Jarvis* (*Yunagi*'s report of this encounter doomed the American destroyer and every man aboard). She then tailed on behind the *Furutaka* group as they sped eastward.

The action had lasted some 35 minutes. For an expenditure of 1020 rounds of 8-in. and 885 of smaller caliber shell, plus sixty-one torpedoes, and at a cost of thirty-five dead and fifty-one wounded, with minor damage to two cruisers, Mikawa had sunk four heavy cruisers, sent a fifth limping back to base minus her bow, and beaten up two destroyers. Allied losses totaled 1024 killed and 709 wounded.

There was some doubt in Mikawa's mind as to whether he should regroup west of Savo, return and attempt to destroy the transports. Besides *Australia* and the two light cruisers and two destroyers of the Eastern Force there were six fleet destroyers and five destroyer minesweepers with the transports.

The Japanese admiral's estimation of the completeness of his victory (five cruisers and four destroyers sunk) was only slightly optimistic and

there is no question that had he known that the American carrier force was at that moment out of range and withdrawing out of the area altogether he would have moved to complete his victory. As it was, he calculated that it would take 2½ hours to regroup and reach the anchorage. It would thus be 0500, an hour before sunrise before he could recommence the action, and at first light he could logically expect a swarm of vengeful carrier planes about his ears. With the Midway disaster fresh in his memory Mikawa decided not to risk it. His decision tempered the joy with which news of his victory was received at Combined Fleet HQ and he later came in for some criticism. However, this was after it was known that Fletcher and his carriers were far away and could have done nothing. With little or no air coverage available to Mikawa it is conceivable that had Fletcher attacked the retiring Japanese squadron it might have suffered heavy losses, losses which Japan could ill afford—and then the critics would have sung a different tune.

Understandably, there were repercussions on the American side. The public, of course, was told nothing until a much later date, but feeling in the Navy ran high. Everyone wanted to know exactly what had happened—and no one really knew. Perhaps after long years of peace (the last major American surface fleet action had been off Santiago de Cuba during the Spanish-American War in 1898) Americans were not yet warwise, too complacent, too prone to hesitate—too quick to assume strange objects to be friendly. Lack of battle-mindedness is another way of putting it.

After the war, when the inevitable rehashing of

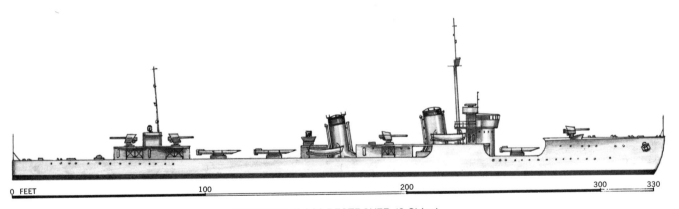

KAMIKAZE CLASS DESTROYER (9 Ships)

Launched December 1922–November 1924
Displacement: 1270 tons LOA: 336 Beam: 32 Draft: 10 feet
Twin screw. 38,500 hp=37¼ knots
Armament: four 4.7 in., two 7.7-mm. MGs., six 21 in. torpedo tubes (3×2)
Complement: 148
   (Note: In 1941–42 one 4.7 and one torpedo mount was removed and 6–10 25-mm. AA added. This AA increased later in war.)

battles and campaigns had begun, some anglo-phobes tried to put the whole blame for the Savo disaster on Crutchley. His dispositions may have been faulty but they had the approval of Turner, and, through no fault of his, Crutchley was not even present at the battle. It is easy to be wise after the event, but both Crutchley and Turner had some justification for their decisions. The transport areas had to be guarded, against even a sneak attack by a single destroyer or submarine. From Cape Esperance to Savo is 7 miles and from the north side of Savo to Buena Vista on the north-western end of the Nggela Group (of which Florida Island is the largest) is 13 miles—a total, plus Savo itself of some 24 miles. It has been suggested that Crutchley should have kept his western squadron together to the west of Savo. His battle line might then have covered about 7000 yards. At the limit of his beat, then, there would have been a gap at the other end of about 15 miles. When one considers that the whole Jap squadron slipped by *Blue* at comparatively close range it is highly likely that on a dark squally night the fox might have got in among the hens while the watch dog was too far away to stop it.

One unsolved mystery is why no cruiser float planes were launched. There were many available and, scouting in relays, they could have kept the approaches under surveillance over a considerable area. As it was, all they did was burn on their catapults, a grave hazard to the ships and a welcome illumination for the Japanese gunners.

There were two post-battle victims. *Jarvis*, on her way to Australia for repairs, was involved briefly in the Savo action. Whether she was hit or inflicted any damage we shall never know. She was intercepted and identified by *Blue* at 0308 and was sighted by a scout plane from *Saratoga*

just after dawn, some 40 miles west by south of Guadalcanal. Thereafter she vanished. Not until after the war was her fate revealed. On receiving *Yunagi's* report of a "damaged Achilles-Class cruiser" sixteen torpedo bombers and fifteen Zeros left Rabaul to finish her off. At 1300 on the 9th the planes found her and in a few minutes it was all over. There were no survivors.

Mikawa ordered Cruiser Division 6 to separate south of Bougainville. *Chokai* and three smaller vessels headed for Rabaul while the other four heavies proceeded to Kavieng. Lack of destroyers proved disastrous. Just before 0800 the column of cruisers was sighted by S-44—Captain John Moore. At 700 yards, Moore fired a salvo of four torpedoes. One or more struck *Kako* and she went down in a few minutes with the loss of thirty-four dead and forty-eight wounded.

Both Admirals King and Nimitz put the defeat down to surprise, and the lack of organization to the hasty way in which Operation Shoestring had been put together.

There was no official witch hunt. Captains Getting and Moore were dead. Captain Riefkohl, who was in line for promotion to rear admiral at the end of his cruise on *Vincennes*, was quietly passed over and Captain Greenman was transferred to Service Forces. Captain Bode, who had been shifted to command of the naval station at Balboa, Canal Zone, shot himself in a fit of depression. Admiral Scott, in charge of the Eastern Force, was also dead, killed at the battle of Guadalcanal.

Admiral Ghormley's subsequent replacement by Halsey was for other reasons than Savo but it may be noted that Fletcher did not command any of the great carrier task forces which were forming for the later Pacific offensive. So one of America's most humiliating naval defeats passed into history.

IV

"...a Boy to Do a Man's Job"

COLONEL ICHIKI AND THE BATTLE OF THE TENARU RIVER

Turner had planned to leave the area just after daybreak. The night's disaster—details of which were just becoming known—made this impossible. *Canberra* and *Astoria* still remained afloat, and rescue operations were continuing in the sound where small groups of survivors floated amid the oil and debris. Efforts were being made to put as much vital equipment ashore as possible, but when the pull-out order was finally made—about 1600 for the Guadalcanal group—much still remained aboard. At about 1800 the final exodus began, led by *San Juan*. While Marines ashore watched in disbelief, the invasion armada sailed away, taking with it food, ammunition, tools, barbed wire, and a hundred other indispensable items. Away went *Fomalhaut* with 85 percent of the earth-moving equipment (only one bulldozer was landed). Away

went *Alchiba*, three-quarters full of supplies, and others followed still half-unloaded. And away went 1390 Marines of various detachments, who had never been put ashore.

If Turner had been left with a bare behind, Vandegrift was practically naked. Left with no sea or air cover, with but four units of fire and food for thirty-seven days, the 10,000 plus Marines on Guadalcanal with their 6000-odd buddies on Tulagi were strictly on their own.

None of the 5-in. coast defense guns of 3rd Defense Battalion had come ashore, nor had any fire control or long-range warning radars. The Marines could have used some of the Navy reconnaissance planes—but they were at the bottom of Ironbottom Sound and many of their pilots with them. Vandegrift and his men would have little

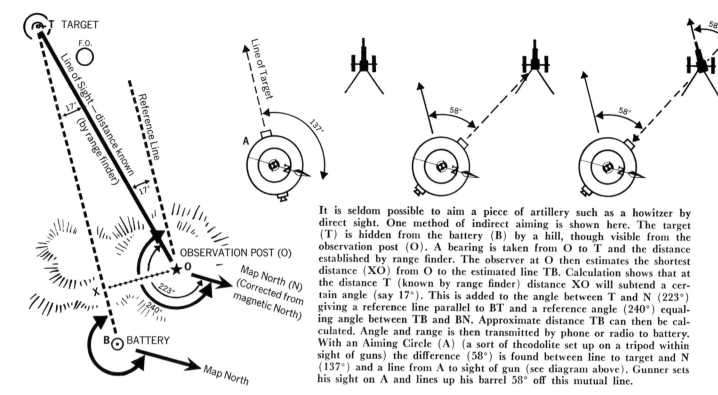

It is seldom possible to aim a piece of artillery such as a howitzer by direct sight. One method of indirect aiming is shown here. The target (T) is hidden from the battery (B) by a hill, though visible from the observation post (O). A bearing is taken from O to T and the distance established by range finder. The observer at O then estimates the shortest distance (XO) from O to the estimated line TB. Calculation shows that at the distance T (known by range finder) distance XO will subtend a certain angle (say 17°). This is added to the angle between T and N (223°) giving a reference line parallel to BT and a reference angle (240°) equaling the angle between TB and BN. Approximate distance TB can then be calculated. Angle and range is then transmitted by phone or radio to battery. With an Aiming Circle (A) (a sort of theodolite set up on a tripod within sight of guns) the difference (58°) is found between line to target and N (137°) and a line from A to sight of gun (see diagram above). Gunner sets his sight on A and lines up his barrel 58° off this mutual line.

notice of the Japanese attacks which were to follow.

No matter what the Japanese might do, and no matter that supplies and equipment of all kinds were lacking, the first and most important task was to make the landing field ready to receive planes. It was doubted by many in the higher command (but not by the Marines on the island) that Guadalcanal could now be held. Even Ghormley was dubious. But there was no doubt at all that if it was to be held it could only be done by the maintenance on the island of a force of fighters and bombers sufficient to thwart any large-scale landing by the enemy and to interdict the passage of reinforcements and supplies. The vulnerable carriers might not be risked but Guadalcanal would provide an unsinkable flight deck for both Navy and Marine—and later—Army planes. The deck might be battered by land, sea, and air and furious attempts made to recapture it, but it had to be held and kept in repair. As long as it was, Guadalcanal and the lower Solomons were safe.

None realized more the importance of the field that they had so obligingly begun, and so precipitantly abandoned, than the Japanese. Reluctantly, little by little, more and more of their forces, naval and military, were thrown into the hot, stinking, insect-infested pest hole that was Guadalcanal. At first overconfident, finally in desperation they poured men, ships, planes, and mountains of supplies down The Slot—and down the drain. For they never regained their strategic

airfield, and for the lack of it they lost Guadalcanal, the Solomons, and ultimately New Guinea, the Bismarck Archipelago and their bases to the north. Probably never in history have a few acres of cleared ground cost so much in ships, men, and treasure as the airstrip which the Marines were to name Henderson Field.

Work on the airstrip was begun on August 9 by the 1st Engineer Battalion. Lacking their own equipment (on its way out with Turner) they did the best they could with the gear the Japanese had abandoned. At the same time combat troops began work on defenses around the field. Rice bags were used (the sandbags were still aboard) and some wire salvaged from the plantations. Hasty positions were in readiness before nightfall of the 9th.

The likelihood of amphibious landings made the beaches the danger spot, and a 9600-yard defense line from Kukum to the mouth of the Ilu River was prepared. The left of the line (Kukum) bent back over flat terrain from the beach to the first hills. On the right the line ran 600 yards along the west bank of the Ilu. Caliber .50 and .30 machine guns and 37-mm guns, plus some riflemen, covered the shoreline. On the land side the line ran through jungle-covered hills and ravines. Lack of troops made it necessary to defend this by a series of unconnected strong points. Troops not otherwise engaged helped move supplies off the beaches.

In support were 60-mm and 81-mm mortars. The 75-mm pack howitzers of the 2nd and 3rd Battalions, 11th Marines, and the 105-mms of the 5th were emplaced where they could bring fire support to all sectors. Besides the howitzers, there were half-tracked 75-mm "tank destroyers" and some light tanks, each mounting a 37-mm gun and machine guns. Against air attack there were a few 90-mm guns, some automatic weapons and searchlights. The Japanese building on the field, nicknamed the "pagoda" was used as a warning station, complete with a captured Japanese siren.

Patrol activity on the 9th brought on a minor clash. A twelve-man patrol reconnoitering the Matanikau River, some 3000 yards west of Kukum, was fired on and suffered casualties. A patrol crossed the next day but was driven back. Unopposed patrolling to the east and inland indicated that the enemy had retreated to the west.

The seas about Guadalcanal were now Japanese property, and submarines, destroyers, and an occasional cruiser made their appearance and lobbed a few shells onto Tulagi or in the direction of the airstrip. There were numerous air raids, although the fire of the few 90-mms, in positions near the field, discouraged bombing below 25,000 feet. Despite these nuisances, work on the field progressed. Captured Japanese trucks, running on Japanese gasoline, carried fill to be rolled by Japanese rollers or tamped by tampers run by air from Japanese air compressors. One stretch, 2600 feet long and 160 feet wide, was finished on August

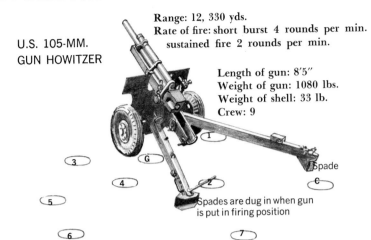

U.S. 105-MM. GUN HOWITZER

Range: 12, 330 yds.
Rate of fire: short burst 4 rounds per min.
sustained fire 2 rounds per min.

Length of gun: 8'5"
Weight of gun: 1080 lbs.
Weight of shell: 33 lb.
Crew: 9

Spade

Spades are dug in when gun is put in firing position

G: Gunner lays for direction
1: Set elevation and fires
2: Loads
3 & 4: Operate fuse setter
5: Prepares charges
6 & 7: Ammunition handlers
C: Chief of Section

Right: Charge in case can be varied. For instance, for lobbing a shell in a high arc for a short distance the shell is removed from case and some of the small powder bags (increments) are removed.

The 105 was the work-horse of the artillery. Its range of elevation, −10° to +65° enabled it to be used as a gun (with a reasonably flat trajectory) or, as a howitzer, lob shells in a high arc into hidden enemy positions. It is usually towed by a 2½-ton 6-wheel truck.

12, while an additional 1178 feet was completed on the 18th. On August 12 the first plane to land on Guadalcanal arrived on the airstrip. This was a Catalina, piloted by Rear Admiral McCain's aide.

U.S. HALFTRACK

with 75 mm. pack howitzer and a .50 caliber machine gun. Used as a tank destroyer.

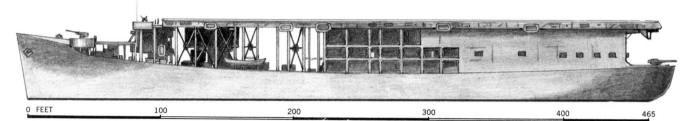

U.S.S. LONG ISLAND — ESCORT CARRIER

Ex-MORMACMAIL Launched January 11, 1940. Converted March–June 30, 1941
Displacement: 11,300 tons LOA: 492 Beam: 69½ Draft: 25¾ feet
Single screw. Diesel motors. 8500 hp=18 knots
Armament: one 5 in. (at stern), two 3 in. AA (2×1)
Aircraft: twenty-one Complement: 950

Although the field lacked taxi ways, revetments, and drainage, he pronounced it ready for fighters. And the planes were coming. U.S.S. *Long Island*, ex-motorship *Mormacmail*, the Navy's first escort carrier, was even then leaving Suva, carrying a load of thirty-five fighters and dive bombers. As a reminder that hard times lay ahead, on the same date meals were cut to two a day—this despite captured stocks of rice and canned goods.

Also on August 12 a Japanese seaman was captured, who told interrogating officers that there were many Japanese and Koreans of the labor force hiding—and starving—in the jungle who might be glad to surrender. A patrol had seen a white flag (probably a Japanese flag so viewed that the red center did not show) west of the Matanikau. Lieutenant Colonel Frank Goettge, Vandegrift's G-2, thought the matter worth investigation and personally led out a 25-man patrol, which included a surgeon and most of the intelligence section of 5th Marines.

The original plan called for a boat landing by daylight about 1200 yards west of the Matanikau but due to delays the party did not get ashore until about 2200. In the dark the proper landing place was missed and the party went ashore from a Higgins boat just west of the Matanikau. They were met by heavy small arms and machine-gun fire and all but three men (sent back to report) were killed, including the prisoner.

On the night of August 15 there arrived the first American vessels to return to Guadalcanal since the hurried exodus of the 9th. The four APDs (high speed transports) of Transdiv 12 brought in Major Charles Hayes, with five officers and 118 enlisted men of a Navy construction base unit from Espiritu Santo. Also aboard were four hundred drums of aviation gasoline, thirty-two drums of lubricant, 282 bombs, ranging from 100 to 500 lbs., ammunition, tools, and spares. Men and supplies were safely unloaded and the APDs retired without incident.

CONSOLIDATED PBY5A (Catalina)

Long-distance Maritime Reconnaissance Amphibian Flying Boat
Span: 104′ Length: 63′10½″ Height: 20′2″ Weight empty: 20,910 lbs.
Max. speed 179 mph at 7000 feet. Range: 2545 miles at 117 mph
Power: two 1200-hp Pratt & Whitney 14-cylinder radials
Armament: two 0.3 in. MGs. in bow, one 0.3 in. MG. in ventral tunnel, one 0.5 MG. in each beam blister, four 1000-lb. bombs (max.) or two torpedoes. Crew: 7–9

SENDAI CLASS LIGHT CRUISER (3 Ships)

Launched October 1923–March 1925
Displacement: 5195 tons LOA: 534 Beam: 46½ Draft: 16 feet
4 screws. 90,000 hp=35¼ knots
Armor: belt (amidships) 2 in., deck (W.L.) 2.5 in.
Armament: seven 5.5 in. (7×1), two 3 in. AA, eight 24 in. torpedo tubes (4×2)
Aircraft: one Complement: 450

To keep events in sequence we must switch briefly from Guadalcanal to Rabaul—and meet one of the leading characters in the Guadalcanal story—Rear Admiral Raizo Tanaka, who became famous as chief engineer of the so-called Tokyo Express. Tanaka had commanded Destroyer Squadron 2—flagship light cruiser *Jintsu* and ten Fubuki-class destroyers—at Midway, escorting the transport group of the invasion force.

On July 14, 1942 the Eighth Fleet under Vice-Admiral Mikawa had been organized, with headquarters at Rabaul. Eighth Fleet had originally been planned for the defense of the Fiji-Samoa-New Caledonia islands after their capture. The defeat at Midway caused the cancellation of the operations against this area and attention switched to the invasion of New Guinea, although work was being done on airstrips on Guadalcanal and Buka and a seaplane base on Tulagi. The newly activated Eighth Fleet was now to defend the area south of the equator and east of 141° East. The Army in the area was represented by Seventeenth Army (Lieutenant General Haruyoshi Hyakutake) with HQ at Rabaul. The air force was Navy—the 25th Air Flotilla, under Eleventh Air Fleet. All energies were being directed to the speedy capture of Port Moresby when news of the Tulagi-Guadalcanal landings exploded like a bomb at Rabaul.

Even then, Seventeenth Army was not particularly interested. Both they and the Navy consistently underestimated the strength and fighting ability of the American invasion forces. Mikawa's dispatch of the ill-fated handful embarked on *Meiyo Maru* was only the beginning of a haphazard method of reinforcing the island by dribs and drabs, putting ashore units never strong enough or well enough supplied to do the job assigned. This

had been put down by a Japanese naval writer to "victory disease"—a combination (born of a series of almost uninterrupted victories) of blind arrogance, supreme confidence, and utter contempt for the enemy. This may be a splendid thing in the individual fighting man but at the tactical and strategic level it can prove a serious handicap. In Japan's case it was fatal.

On August 13 the High Command in Tokyo, alarmed at the presence of an American force in the Solomons, ordered Seventeenth Army to direct ground operations on Guadalcanal. Hyakutake was short of men (he had the New Guinea campaign on his hands, too) and shorter still of transports. But an attempt to oust the invaders was decided on, to have the support of Combined Fleet. So Operation KA was born (in Japanese the first syllable of Guadalcanal is Ka). The unit chosen to drive the Americans off the island was the Ichiki Force, a combat team composed of part of the crack 28th Infantry, artillery and engineers, commanded by Colonel Kiyono Ichiki. This force had originally been picked to spearhead the invasion of Midway. It was finally on its way back to Japan from Guam when it was ordered to Truk, then Rabaul. It was attached to 35th Brigade (usually referred to as Kawaguchi Force, after its commander, Major General Kiyotake Kawaguchi).

In mid-August Tanaka was ordered to join Eighth Fleet as commander of the Guadalcanal Reinforcement Force. His first task was to send an advance force of nine hundred of Ichiki's men in six destroyers to Taivu Point, some 22 miles east of Lunga. The balance were to follow in transports later. This latter reinforcement, under Tanaka's personal command, was to be supportd by a powerful portion of Combined Fleet, under Vice-Admiral Nobutake Kondo. Besides the six destroyers carrying

Ichiki's advance detachment, Tanaka's force consisted of light cruiser *Jintsu,* flagship, escorted by two patrol boats (converted destroyers, similar to the American Navy's APDs) with eight hundred men of the Special Naval Landing Forces, and seven hundred men, mostly service troops, of Ichiki Detachment in two slow transports and two more patrol boats. This force was later reinforced with three more destroyers. The colonel and his nine hundred were landed without interruption on the night of August 18. About the same time some 250 men of the Special Landing Forces were put ashore near Tassafaronga.

U. S. Navy historian Samuel Eliot Morison says the six destroyers made a brief bombardment of American positions before returning, were caught in daylight by some B-17s from Espiritu and one, *Hagikaze,* was damaged by a bomb hit. Tanaka says the three ships of Desdiv 17 returned immediately after the landing, that the other three stayed to guard the beachhead and that at dawn *Hagikaze* was hit, that she and a sister ship left for Truk and that the third remained. In any event the period when Japanese surface ships could safely venture near Guadalcanal during daylight was drawing to a close.

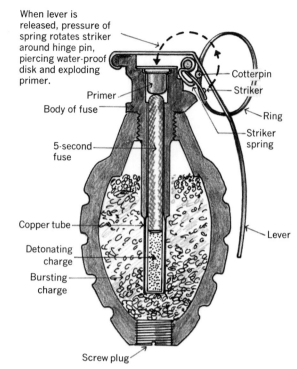

When lever is released, pressure of spring rotates striker around hinge pin, piercing water-proof disk and exploding primer.

Cotterpin
Striker
Ring
Striker spring
Lever

Primer
Body of fuse
5-second fuse
Copper tube
Detonating charge
Bursting charge
Screw plug

U.S. FRAGMENTATION HAND GRENADE

**Weight: 1¼ lbs. Bursting charge: .74 oz.
Case breaks into some 40 pieces
Lethal radius: about 30 yards
Average soldier can throw about 35 yards**

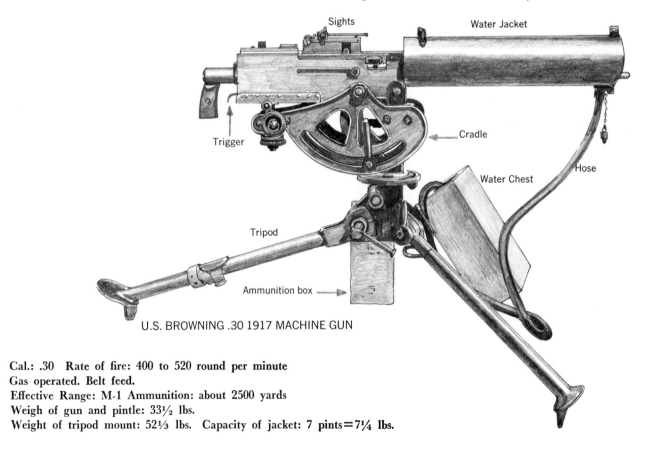

Sights
Water Jacket
Cradle
Hose
Trigger
Water Chest
Tripod
Ammunition box

U.S. BROWNING .30 1917 MACHINE GUN

**Cal.: .30 Rate of fire: 400 to 520 round per minute
Gas operated. Belt feed.
Effective Range: M-1 Ammunition: about 2500 yards
Weigh of gun and pintle: 33½ lbs.
Weight of tripod mount: 52⅓ lbs. Capacity of jacket: 7 pints = 7¼ lbs.**

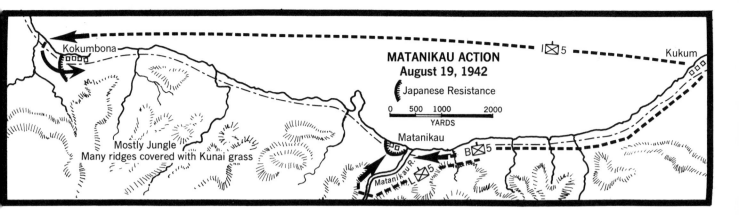

MATANIKAU ACTION
August 19, 1942

Japanese Resistance

0   500   1000   2000
YARDS

Kokumbona

Kukum

Mostly Jungle
Many ridges covered with Kunai grass

Matanikau

On August 19, rumors of a Japanese landing somewhere to the east of the Marine's perimeter caused strong patrols to be sent out. One of these sighted four officers and thirty men on the beach near Koli Point. A neat little ambush killed all but two or three who escaped. A glance at the bodies showed the Marine leader, Captain Charles Brush, that these were no poorly equipped, unkempt remnants of the original garrison. Uniforms and equipment were in good order, and the helmets bore the star of the Japanese Army, not the chrysanthemum and anchor of the Naval Landing Forces. Examination of map cases and pockets revealed not only that a considerable force was ashore and preparing to attack, but also that the Japanese were well informed as to American dispositions around the airfield.

On the same day a small but carefully planned attack was carried out to the west. Two companies of 5th Marines attacked Matanikau from the east and south while another went by landing craft from Kukum to Kokumbona, where it landed and worked east. On the way this force was shelled at long range by a couple of Japanese destroyers but no craft were hit. The eastern attack across the river mouth was checked by heavy fire, but the attack from inland, after crossing the river some distance upstream (made with the assistance of the artillery), took the village. Upward of sixty-five Japanese were killed. Marine casualties were four killed and eleven wounded. The companies then retired within the defense perimeter.

On August 20, *Long Island* arrived at a position 200 miles southeast of Guadalcanal and at 1330 commenced to launch her planes. By 1700 nineteen Wildcats (F4F-4s) of Marine Fighter Squadron (VMF) 223, and twelve Douglas dive bombers of Marine Scout Bombing Squadron (VMSB) 232 had arrived safely at Henderson Field. Twelve hours later they were in action.

August 20 also saw the return of three APDs of Transdiv 12. *Colhoun, Gregory,* and *Little* brought in 120 tons of rations—enough for about three and a half days. They departed safely, after ferrying 2nd Battalion, 5th Marines across from Tulagi.

Vandegrift lost no time in preparing to meet a Japanese thrust from the east. The 2nd Battalion, 1st Marines were dug in along the west bank of the Ilu (Tenaru) River. The 3rd held the beach front along to the Lunga River with the 1st in battalion reserve, on the right rear of 2nd Battalion. Some of the precious wire was laid across the 45-yard-wide sandpit at the river mouth and this was also covered by a 37-mm gun, rifles and machine guns. Supporting artillery was registered on the east bank.

In the evening of August 20, Marine listening posts reported hearing movement and at 0310 a sudden and furious charge was made across the sandbar by some two hundred Japanese. They were met by a hail of rifle and machine-gun fire and blasts of canister from the 37-mm. Despite this a few crossed the bar over the bodies of the dead and dying and overran some of the emplacements, but after savage hand-to-hand fighting a counterattack drove the survivors back to the east bank.

The Japanese now directed a heavy fire from light artillery, mortars, and machine guns on the Marine positions. This was followed by a second assault, made by a considerable body who waded out beyond the breakers and came ashore on 2nd Battalion's flank. This attack was also smashed at the water's edge by canister, rifles, and machine guns.

Fire from the supporting batteries was now called in on the east bank in the area near the river mouth where the enemy seemed to be concentrated. At daybreak it was apparent that the enemy was held. Then 1st Battalion moved upstream, crossed,

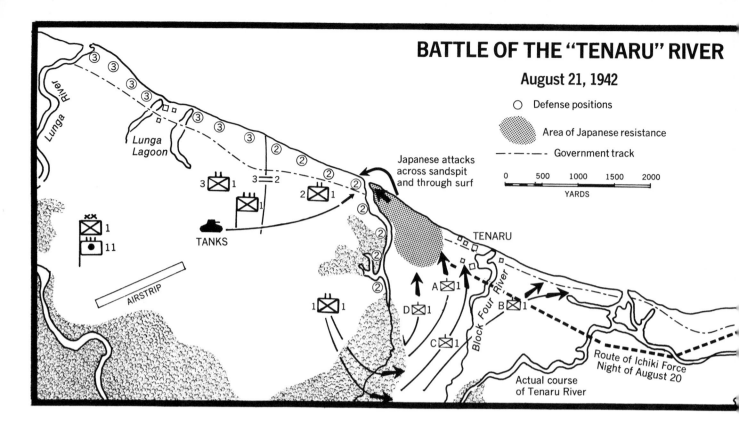

BATTLE OF THE "TENARU" RIVER

August 21, 1942

○   Defense positions

     Area of Japanese resistance

– · – · –   Government track

Japanese attacks
across sandspit
and through surf

0   500   1000   1500   2000
YARDS

Lunga River

Lunga Lagoon

TANKS

AIRSTRIP

TENARU

Block Four River

Route of Ichiki Force
Night of August 20

Actual course
of Tenaru River

and fanned out and advanced on the enemy-held position. Attempts to break out were checked and the remaining Japanese, caught between the Marines, the river, and the sea, were compressed into an ever-decreasing space. Blasted by mortar and artillery fire and strafed by the newly arrived fighter planes (by Admiral McCain's orders the few precious SBDs were to be used only against enemy ships of cruiser size or better) the trapped Japanese died by dozens. Finally Marine tanks clanked across the bar, spitting tracer and canister. A few Japs survived by crawling off into the underbrush. The others died right there. Wrote Vandegrift: "The rear of the tanks looked like meat grinders." The battle was over. Some eight hundred of Japan's finest shock troops had been killed. Fifteen wounded were captured. Many of the others died in the jungle. Colonel Ichiki made his way to Taivu with the regimental color bearer. The colonel then tore the colors to pieces, burned them, and committed hara-kiri. Marine casualties were thirty-four killed, seventy-five wounded. Captured material included thirty machine guns, three 70-mm light field guns, twelve flame throwers (not used in the action) some seven hundred

rifles and assorted sabers, pistols, and grenade launchers.

On August 22, five P-400s of Army's 67th Fighter Squadron arrived at Henderson. On the same day transports Alhena and Fomalhaut landed supplies and some men of the 2nd Marines at Tulagi. The transports had been escorted by destroyers Blue, Helm, and Henley, arriving on August 21. Early on the morning of August 22, Blue and Henley steamed into Ironbottom Sound on the lookout for a possible troop landing from Japanese destroyers. A few minutes before 0400 Blue made radar contact on a high speed vessel some 5000 yards away. She continued on course with guns and torpedo tubes trained on the stranger. The range was down to 3200 yards when at 0359 a Japanese warhead blasted off part of Blue's stern. Eyes on an enemy destroyer (Kagero, which had just landed some reinforcements) had once more been keener than Blue's radar. At daybreak Henley took the crippled Blue in tow toward Tulagi but progress was slow and she was still outside the harbor on August 23. Enemy naval forces were known to be on the way, so she was scuttled.

V

Duel of the Flattops

THE BATTLE OF THE EASTERN SOLOMONS

Operation KA was now under way. News of the destruction of Colonel Ichiki and his nine hundred, while disconcerting, did not alter plans to land the men aboard Tanaka's transports and the naval headquarters set their respective forces in motion with the disputed island as the focal point.

After his retirement from the Guadalcanal area on August 8th Fletcher had kept his force well to the southeast, covering the sea routes to the Solomons.

Dawn of August 23 found Task Force 61 (divided into three smaller groups each with a fleet carrier as its nucleus) about 150 miles east of Henderson Field. It also disclosed the Combined Fleet steaming southeastward from its base at Truk. The Japanese were in five groups: the two fleet carriers *Zuikaku* and *Shokaku* under Naguma; an advance force, Vice-Admiral Kondo (over-all tactical commander of the supporting forces); a vanguard

group, Rear Admiral Hiroaki Abe, with two battleships; a diversionary group, Rear Admiral Hara with light carrier *Ryujo;* and Rear Admiral Tanaka with the transports. With Kondo in the advance force was a seaplane carrier, *Chitose*. With the transports, armed merchant cruiser *Kinryu Maru* and the four patrol boats (destroyer transports), the whole force amounted to fifty-one surface vessels. Far ahead went six fleet submarines in line abreast, while three more took station to the west of the New Hebrides.

Two of the submarine screen were sighted by planes of *Enterprise* on dawn patrol. Then at 0950 one of *Mackinac*'s PBYs from Ndeni sighted Tanaka's transport group. Tanaka reported this to Eighth Fleet at Rabaul and at about 1030 was ordered to turn about. At 1430 he received an order from Eleventh Air Fleet to turn again and carry out the landings as planned—night of August 24—

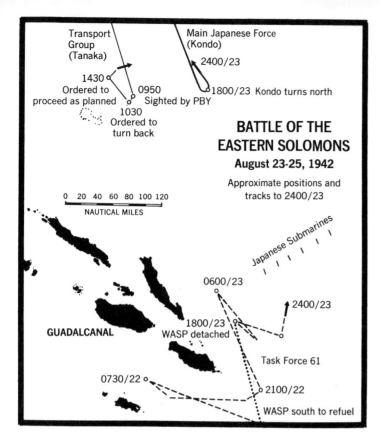

BATTLE OF THE EASTERN SOLOMONS
August 23-25, 1942

Approximate positions and tracks to 2400/23

clearly impossible under the circumstances. At 1800 Kondo himself ordered a reversal of course and the remainder of the Japanese armada duly turned northwest.

On receipt of the PBYs sighting report, search planes took off from Guadalcanal and the carriers, but the weather was bad, and they found nothing. At 1445 *Saratoga* sent off thirty-one SBDs and six TBFs, followed at 1615 by twenty-three planes from Guadalcanal. As before they found nothing (although an *Enterprise* search group did sight and attack another submarine) and at dusk the *Saratoga* planes, low on fuel, landed on Henderson Field.

At the end of the day's excursions, Fletcher was no wiser as to the location, size, or destination of the enemy fleet. It was possible (Pacific Fleet Intelligence thought so) that the main Japanese fleet was still somewhere north of Truk. Fletcher was always concerned about fuel and at 1800 he detached the *Wasp* group (Task Force 18) south to refuel. An unfortunate move, as it turned out, for *Wasp* and her stingers might have turned a drawn battle into a serious Japanese defeat.

Before daylight of the 24th, Kondo again altered course—the diversionary group to the southward—and by 0600 the whole Japanese force was once more steering roughly SSE. At 0800 a radio report from Guadalcanal (Henderson Field was under

Japanese observation from Mount Austen) warned that thirty-six bombers were taking off, and Tanaka, who thought his position had been reported, expected an attack. Actually it was the thirty-seven *Saratoga* planes returning to their carrier, on which they landed about 1100. Their stay on Guadalcanal had been livened by destroyer *Kagero*, which bombarded the Marine positions during the night.

About 0910 a Catalina from Ndeni sighted the *Ryujo* group some 220 miles north of Malaita and 280 miles northwest of Fletcher. At 1028 *Chitose* reported being tracked by another of the ubiquitous PBYs. American "snoopers" were not the only ones in the air and about 1030 Wildcats from *Saratoga* shot down a four-engined flying boat of the "Emily" type some 20 miles from the carrier. An hour later another PBY sighted the *Ryujo* group still on course.

At 1229 *Enterprise* flew off twenty-three search planes while *Saratoga* organized for a strike. And at 1345 the first of thirty SBDs and eight TBFs roared off "Sara's" deck headed for *Ryujo*. Reports of sightings were now coming thick and fast, but Fletcher, with some sixty-five bombers and torpedo planes aloft on various missions, had only fourteen SBDs and twelve TBFs on board his two carriers. At 1430 an *Enterprise* plane spotted *Zuikaku* and *Shokaku* about 230 miles away.

Meanwhile, at 1300 six bombers, escorted by fifteen Zeros, had flown off *Ryujo* to attack Henderson Field.

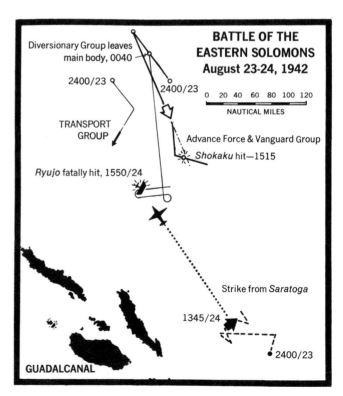

BATTLE OF THE EASTERN SOLOMONS
August 23-24, 1942

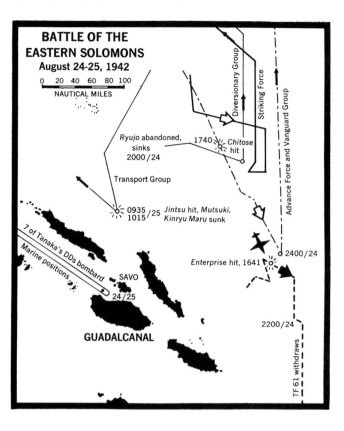

Field. Ten bombers and six Zeros were shot down for the loss of four Marine planes and three pilots. Damage to the field was slight.

At 1507 Nagumo launched his first strike. A few minutes later two search planes from *Enterprise* spotted *Shokaku*. Braving antiaircraft fire and Zeros they dove on the carrier and released their bombs. A hit, or more probably a near-miss did minor damage. Other *Enterprise* planes made scattered contacts on other groups and delivered bomb and torpedo attacks, but without success. But if *Enterprise*'s planes did not accomplish much, the *Saratoga* strike made up for it.

Ryujo was just turning into the wind to launch fighters when the first *Saratoga* SBDs began their dive. Despite heavy fire the dive bombers planted their bombs with great accuracy. At least four and possibly ten 1000-lb. bombs smashed their way into the light carrier's flight deck. Spouting sheets of flame and clouds of smoke the stricken vessel careened in circles, while the TBFs tore in to drop their missiles. At least one torpedo hit her. Listing heavily and with flames pouring through the holes in her shattered flight deck, she lay dead in the water. Rescue operations were interrupted (about 1700) when two B-17s, part of a small group from Espiritu Santo, made an abortive attack. Surviving crew members were taken aboard the destroyers and shortly afterward *Ryujo* turned over and sank. Not long after she had disappeared her planes returned from their raid on Henderson Field. Seven were missing. According to Captain Tameichi Hara, whose *Amatsukaze* took off many of *Ryujo*'s survivors, one of the missing seven was the only radio-equipped one of the lot. So not knowing of the order to land at Buka, they ditched, the pilots being picked up by the two destroyers and the heavy cruiser, *Tone*. Tanaka on the other hand, says that, after circling over his group, they flew off to Buka.

Fletcher, with the two enemy fleet carriers located, tried to divert *Saratoga*'s strike to the bigger quarry. But communications were poor and radio discipline worse—the narrow frequency often jammed with traffic. He could now expect attack himself. Two other Japanese "snoopers" had been splashed by his fighters and he could reasonably assume that some sighting reports had got through to the Japanese admiral. (They had.) More combat patrols were sent aloft and other fighters readied —fifty-four fighters up or set to go. At 1400 *Enterprise* readied her remaining planes, eleven SBDs, seven TBFs, and seven Wildcats.

By that time *Ryujo*'s strike was approaching Guadalcanal, where it was joined by land based twin-engine bombers from Rabaul. At about 1420 they were attacked by fighters from Henderson

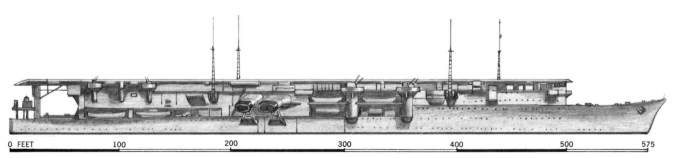

H.I.J.M.S. RYUJO — AIRCRAFT CARRIER

Launched April 1931
Displacement: 10,600 tons LOA: 590⅓ Beam: 68¼ feet Draft: 23½ feet
Twin screw. 66,269 hp=29 knots
Armament: eight 5 in. AA (4×2), four 25-mm., twenty-four 13-mm. AA
Aircraft: forty-eight Complement: 900

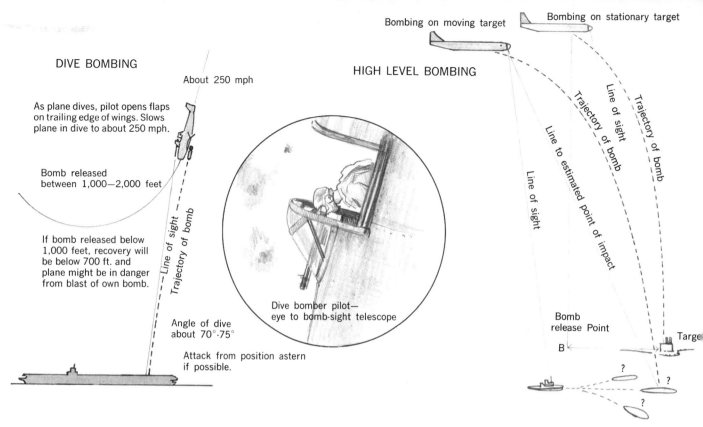

DIVE BOMBING

About 250 mph

As plane dives, pilot opens flaps on trailing edge of wings. Slows plane in dive to about 250 mph.

Bomb released between 1,000—2,000 feet

If bomb released below 1,000 feet, recovery will be below 700 ft. and plane might be in danger from blast of own bomb.

Line of sight

Trajectory of bomb

Angle of dive about 70°-75°

Attack from position astern if possible.

Dive bomber pilot— eye to bomb-sight telescope

HIGH LEVEL BOMBING

Bombing on moving target

Bombing on stationary target

Line of sight

Trajectory of bomb

Trajectory of bomb

Line to estimated point of impact

Line of sight

Bomb release Point

B

Target

?   ?   ?

High-level bombing (right) calls for great accuracy—even on a stationary target. To use bombsight, plane must be held on level course prior to release, and height, speed, course, and wind direction allowed for. Trajectory of missile takes bomb far forward of point where it was actually released. Line B-T might be two miles or more. Even with best bombsights, bombs often missed. Bombing a moving target, such as a ship, was far more dif-

ficult. All factors already mentioned were present plus fact that by time bomb arrived, ship might have moved ¼ mile or more and swung right or left. Even hits by salvos of bombs dropped from bombers in formation were rare. Far more accurate (and more dangerous) was dive bombing (left). Here whole plane was aimed and bomb was released much closer to target. From 1000 feet up bomb would reach target in less than three seconds.

TORPEDO PLANE ATTACK

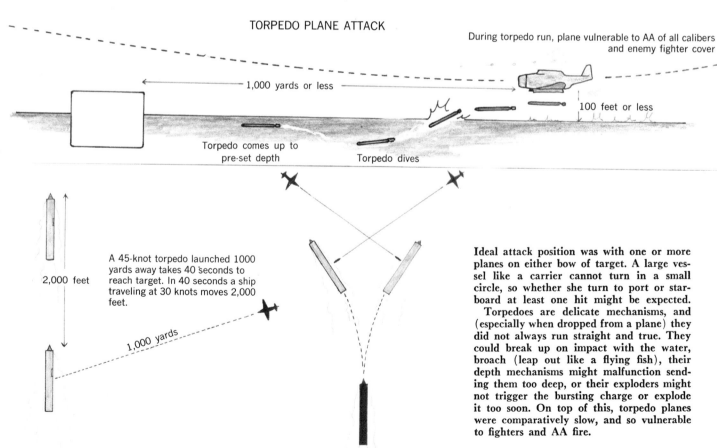

During torpedo run, plane vulnerable to AA of all calibers and enemy fighter cover

1,000 yards or less

100 feet or less

Torpedo comes up to pre-set depth

Torpedo dives

A 45-knot torpedo launched 1000 yards away takes 40 seconds to reach target. In 40 seconds a ship traveling at 30 knots moves 2,000 feet.

2,000 feet

1,000 yards

Ideal attack position was with one or more planes on either bow of target. A large vessel like a carrier cannot turn in a small circle, so whether she turn to port or starboard at least one hit might be expected.

Torpedoes are delicate mechanisms, and (especially when dropped from a plane) they did not always run straight and true. They could break up on impact with the water, broach (leap out like a flying fish), their depth mechanisms might malfunction sending them too deep, or their exploders might not trigger the bursting charge or explode it too soon. On top of this, torpedo planes were comparatively slow, and so vulnerable to fighters and AA fire.

20-knot wind →

Wind along deck—50 knots →

Speed—30 knots ←

The take-off length on a carrier's deck was short. To help aircraft become airborne in shortest possible time, in launching planes, a carrier was headed into the wind and speed increased. This also helped pilot to maintain straight run during takeoff without danger from cross winds. Same applied to landing. Plane's designed landing speed was necessarily slow. This, and wind plus ship's speed enabled planes to land in short space.

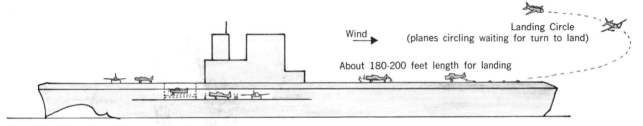

DIVE BOMBERS   TORPEDO

FIGHTERS   SCOUT BOMBERS   PLANES

Speed in launching was essential. As one plane cleared the bow the next was starting to move. Others closely packed behind, were moved or taxied into position on signal from the launching officer. Because they might have been needed to protect the ship, and because they had the more powerful engines in ratio to their size and weight, the fighter planes were stowed farthest forward, then the scout and dive bombers, with the heavier torpedo planes at the stern.

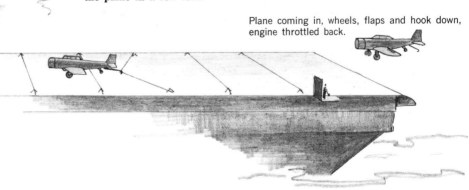

Wind →

Landing Circle
(planes circling waiting for turn to land)

About 180-200 feet length for landing

As planes landed they were moved forward immediately. Planes in need of servicing and repair were taken down to the hangar deck on huge elevators. When planes were all landed they were moved aft to be ready for takeoff.

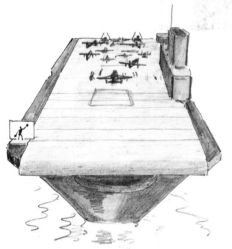

Landing on a small area of flight deck (often heaving and dipping 30 feet or more) is a tricky business. To the pilot coming in for a landing, the most important man aboard was the Landing Signals Officer. Standing on a platform aft, and silhouetted against a white canvas backdrop, the L.S.O. watched the approach carefully. If the plane was coming in at correct height, speed and angle he waved it in with his paddles. If not, he signaled "Too high," "Too Fast," "Right a little," etc. If the approach was too bad, both paddles crossed over head signaled a wave-off, "No good —try again." A paddle tapped on the deck meant: Your landing hook is not down.

To stop quickly, carrier planes have retractable hooks (this is why they have to be built more strongly than land-based planes). These hooks are caught by arrestor wires stretched across the deck (laid flat when not in use). These wires run out under tension when the hook is caught, stopping the plane in a few feet.

Plane coming in, wheels, flaps and hook down, engine throttled back.

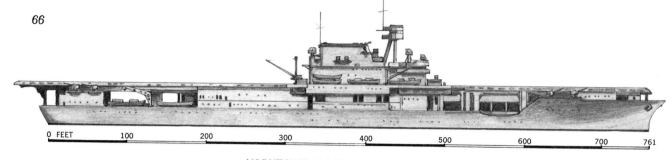

YORKTOWN CLASS AIRCRAFT CARRIER

Launched April 1936–December 1940 Displacement: 19,900–20,000 tons LOA: 809½
Beam: 83¼ Draft: 21¾ feet 4 screws. 120,000 hp=34 knots
Armament: eight 5 in. (8✕1). (Later removed in Enterprise and forty 40-mm. installed.)
Aircraft: 100 Complement: 2200

At 1602 the rotating "bedsprings" atop the masts of Fletcher's command picked up "many bogies": range 88 miles. More Wildcats roared off the decks; there were now fifty-three aloft. *Enterprise* cleared her decks, putting up eleven SBDs and seven TBFs and *Saratoga* launched two SBDs and five TBFs with orders to join the *Enterprise* group and attack the Jap CVs. The American carriers were each roughly in the center of a ring of protective warships—a circle with a radius of some 2000 yards—and about 10 miles apart. Their fighter CAPs were stacked overhead, waiting the word to strike. There were still communication problems, however, and the electronic IFF (Identification, Friend or Foe) system was not then perfected. Consequently, with unidentified sightings all around (the main sighting had temporarily disappeared from the screens), the carriers' fighter-director officers warned all returning search planes away.

At 1625 came a visual sighting report from a Wildcat and the fighter-directors tried desperately to vector their interceptors to hit the strike before it broke up. Unfortunately, the circuit was full of sightings, exhortations, warnings, and other chit-chat so that no coherent directions could get through. At 1629 the commander of the Japanese strike sighted *Enterprise* and split his force into

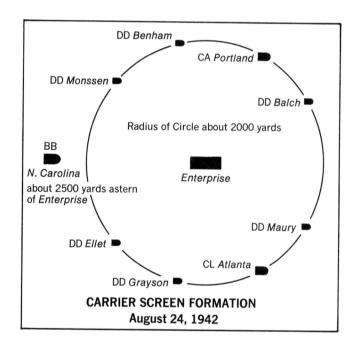

CARRIER SCREEN FORMATION
August 24, 1942

several small attack groups. It was up to the fighters now, and as the Wildcats sought to claw the attacking dive bombers and torpedo planes down before they could reach their objective, so the escorting Zeros fought just as stubbornly to protect their charges. Returning Dauntless and Avenger pilots also joined the fray and they and their rear-gunners took their toll of Japanese planes.

So far, although every eye topside on *Enterprise*

ATTACK ON Enterprise
1641—August 24

NAUTICAL MILES

Although Radar was invaluable, the area to be covered by the CAP was very great. The 24-mile radius circle below covers over 1800 square miles.

88 miles

on Radar—88 m.

Visual Sighting 35 miles

Jap Carriers to *Enterprise*— some 200 miles

Japanese sight *Enterprise* 24 miles out, and split their force

"E"

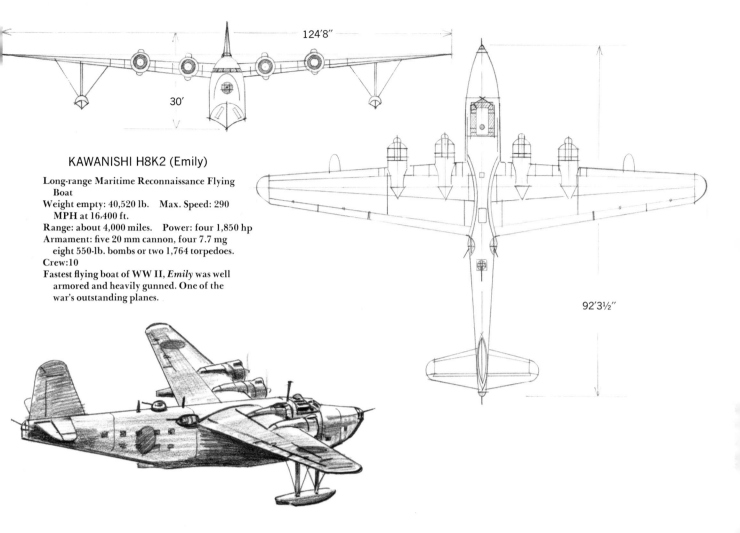

KAWANISHI H8K2 (Emily)

Long-range Maritime Reconnaissance Flying
  Boat
Weight empty: 40,520 lb.   Max. Speed: 290
  MPH at 16,400 ft.
Range: about 4,000 miles.   Power: four 1,850 hp
Armament: five 20 mm cannon, four 7.7 mg
  eight 550-lb. bombs or two 1,764 torpedoes.
Crew:10
Fastest flying boat of WW II, *Emily* was well
  armored and heavily gunned. One of the
  war's outstanding planes.

124'8"

30'

92'3½"

and her screen was raised skyward, there had
been no sight of the enemy—only the audible signs
of a desperate battle coming in over the radio
wave. Then, at 1641, sharp eyes caught a brief
gleam overhead as the sunlight caught a plane
beginning its dive. Down they came spaced a
few seconds apart, like a string of deadly beads.
The ships blasted away at them and the fighters
followed them down into the black burst of antiaircraft fire. At least three Jap planes took direct
hits from 5-in. shells and disintegrated. Water from
near misses deluged the ship as she twisted and
turned in her efforts to spoil the bombers' aim.
But her 800-foot bulk made too good a target.
A bomb struck the corner of the after flight deck
elevator, penetrating to the third deck before exploding. Thirty seconds later she was struck
again, almost in the same place. A third, fortunately
defective, struck the flight deck aft of the island.
Burning, with a list and with part of her 5-in.
battery wrecked, *Enterprise* was in a bad way.
Seventy-four of her crew had been killed and
ninety-five wounded but the remainder set to to

fight fires, repair the flight deck, collect the
wounded and ready the ship to meet further attacks. But none came. No Japanese torpedo plane
put in an appearance. It is probable that they were
all shot down while making their approaches and
Nagumo's second strike missed the carrier by some
50 miles. Low on gas, it was forced to return, its
mission unaccomplished.

Enterprise's own last strike also missed contact.
The Avengers ran low on fuel, jettisoned their
torpedoes and headed back to their carrier. The
Dauntless pilots dumped their loads and landed on
Henderson, guided in by the light of extemporized
gasoline flares. *Saratoga*'s contingent had a little
better luck. The five TBFs at least found a target
—Kondo's forces—and made an unsuccessful attack.
The two SBDs spotted what they took to be a
battleship and bracketed the vessel with two near-
misses. The victim was *Chitose* and the near-hits
caused bad leaks and started fires. Like *Enterprise*,
her damage control crews did a good job and she
was able to reach Truk under her own steam.

Frantic efforts by *Enterprise* repair parties managed to get her flight deck in good enough shape to receive planes, the Avengers from the last strike landing about 2000. *Saratoga's* planes were aboard by this time and Fletcher headed southward. The *Wasp* group had been steaming at full speed toward the action but the American admiral quite rightly did not wish to encounter a superior enemy surface force in a night battle. Kondo, on the other hand, would have liked nothing better and since 1630 his ships, along with those of Abe's vanguard group, had been racing in line abreast toward the American's last known position. But Task Force 61 was well on its way south and just before midnight Kondo turned his forces north.

The main event was over, but the cause of all the bother, Tanaka's transport group, was still plowing along toward its objective. That night seven of his destroyers brazenly paraded up and down off the beachhead, plastering the Marine defenses with 5-inchers while cruiser float planes dropped "daisy cutters" (small anti-personnel bombs). In the morning of August 25 the Marine fliers and their Navy friends on Guadalcanal managed to repay Tanaka for a restless night. At 0935 they stumbled on the Transport Group—put one bomb beween *Jintsu's* two forward guns, which sprayed the bridge with splinters (and knocked Tanaka unconscious) and set *Kinryu Maru* ablaze with

another. The shaken Japanese admiral shifted his flag to *Kagero* and ordered *Jintsu* back to Truk. Other destroyers closed the sinking *Kinryu Maru* and began rescue operations. While *Mutsuki* was alongside the transport, eight B-17s appeared and their bombs sent the destroyer to the bottom while a near-miss damaged *Uzuki*. With his largest transport and a destroyer sunk, his flagship damaged, and his APDs crammed with survivors the disgusted Tanaka ordered a withdrawal. The reinforcement attempt had been a failure. Despite the fact that there had been a massive support group in the vicinity (probably never in history have 1500 men had such an escort) the Japanese High Command had failed to push through to the island. The attempt had cost them a light carrier, a destroyer and a transport sunk, a seaplane carrier, a light cruiser and a destroyer damaged—and the loss of some ninety planes, many of them with their crews. To offset that they had damaged *Enterprise*.

Both Kondo and Fletcher had shown a notable lack of aggressiveness. The victors of this inconclusive affair were the American airmen who had braved antiaircraft fire and the much vaunted Zeros to inflict considerable damage on the enemy fleet and to destroy many hard-to-replace planes and pilots.

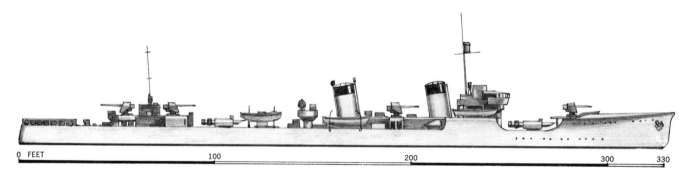

0 FEET   100   200   300   330

MUTSUKI CLASS DESTROYER (12 Ships)

Launched March 1925–April 1927
Displacement: 1313 tons   LOA: 336   Beam: 30   Draft: 9¾ feet
Twin screw.   38,500 hp=37 knots
Armament: four 4.7 in. (4×1), two 7.7-mm. MGs., six 24 in. torpedo tubes (2×3)
Complement: 150

VI
"Maline, You Die!"

THE BATTLE OF BLOODY RIDGE

Since the slaughter of Ichiki's men on August 21 there had been no striking developments on land. Work on the airstrip continued, while a trickle of reinforcements and supplies for both sides filtered into the island, Americans by day and Japanese by night.

On August 27, a reconnaissance in force was made, west of the Matanikau. The plan called for 1st Battalion, 5th Marines, Lieutenant Colonel William Maxwell, to land near Kokumbona, work their way back eastward to the Matanikau, re-embark, and resume their position in the defense perimeter by dark. The Marines went ashore at 0730 without opposition but about 1100 machine-gun and mortar fire from troops dug in in very difficult ground brought the advance to a halt. Poor communication (no walkie-talkies) between companies, dense jungle and intense heat did as much to slow the operation as did the enemy. Constricted by almost impossible terrain inland and with determined resistance along the beach area; and in view of his orders to return to the perimeter by nightfall, Maxwell requested boats sent for a withdrawal and retired a part of his force to the beach. Colonel Leroy P. Hunt, the Commandant of the 5th Marines, had other ideas. He ordered the withdrawal canceled, relieved Maxwell of his command, and later arrived on the scene himself. The battalion was kept in position overnight and in the morning the advance was resumed. The enemy withdrew during the night and the battalion proceeded along the coast road to Matanikau and embarked for the perimeter without further incident.

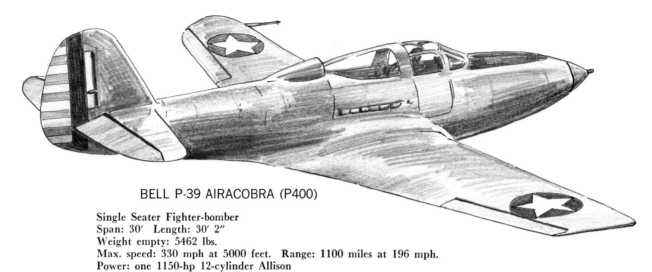

BELL P-39 AIRACOBRA (P400)

Single Seater Fighter-bomber
Span: 30'   Length: 30' 2"
Weight empty: 5462 lbs.
Max. speed: 330 mph at 5000 feet.   Range: 1100 miles at 196 mph.
Power: one 1150-hp 12-cylinder Allison
Armament: one 37-mm. cannon firing through propeller shaft; four 0.3 MGs. in wings, two
0.5's in fuselage.

August 27 also saw the arrival of nine more P-400s of 67th Fighter Squadron at Henderson.

The Japanese had, in the meantime, made preparations for a powerful stroke to shatter the American invaders and recapture the field. Or rather, it might have been judged a powerful stroke if Japanese estimates of Marine strength and capabilities had been correct. The reinforcements this time were to consist of the force under Major General Kawaguchi, plus the remains of the troops of the late lamented Colonel Ichiki. The actual makeup of Kawaguchi's force was the rear echelon of the 2nd Battalion, 28th Infantry (Ichiki); the 124th Infantry under Colonel Akinosuka Oka and the 2nd Battalion of 4th Infantry. To these were attached units of artillery, engineers, signals and antitank gunners—some 6000 men in all.

A first echelon of the force was ordered down to Guadalcanal on destroyers to land on the night of August 27. Not for the first time, Tanaka received conflicting orders and after leaving Shortlands the vessels were ordered to return and the operation was put off until the following night. Tanaka's plan for a safe night landing was frustrated by headquarters and the "Express" arrived too early. With American planes on Guadalcanal this was dangerous, as the little admiral very well knew. As if in answer to his forebodings, at 1800 on August 28, SBDs from Henderson gave the all-too-visible "Midnight Special" a thorough going over. A well-placed 500-lb. bomb struck *Asagiri* which blew up and sank; *Shirakumo* was badly damaged and had to be towed home, while

Yugiri also suffered considerable damage to her upperworks. Needless to say, no troops went ashore that night.

But Tanaka was nothing if not persistent and on August 29, destroyers landed some one thousand men near Taivu Point. After the landing, Captain Yonusuke Murakami, with Destroyer Squadron 24 (*Fubuki, Shirayuki, Kawakaze, Umikaze*) was to have attacked U.S. shipping reported off Lunga Point (probably seven destroyers and APDs which brought supplies to Guadalcanal and Tulagi on the 29th). However, to Tanaka's disgust, Murakami left the shipping untouched, claiming that the moon was too bright and the Henderson fliers active. His lack of enterprise cost him his command.

Tanaka had other troubles besides the reluctant captain. General Kawaguchi disliked the idea of transporting his brigade by destroyers. He was a firm believer in landing barges, as was Colonel Oka, had had great success with them in Borneo, and was not about to change. It was only after much delay (during which time Tanaka sent two patrol boats and the destroyer *Yudachi* with the last of the original Ichiki Force to Guadalcanal, where they landed on the night of August 30) that Seventeenth Army finally ordered Kawaguchi to give in. Colonel Oka remained unconvinced and while the bulk of the Kawaguchi Force went by destroyer, he and about a thousand officers and men transferred to their barges at Gizo Harbor.

The Cactus Air Force (Cactus was the code name for Guadalcanal) also received reinforcements on the 30th. Nineteen Wildcats of VMF-224 and twelve SBD-3s of VMSB-231 landed on

HIGH SPEED TRANSPORT (APD) CONVERTED "FLUSH DECK" DESTROYERS

Launched 1917–1920 Converted 1942–1943
Displacement: 1020 tons LOA: 314½ Beam: 31¾ Draft: 8¾ feet
Twin screw. 13,000 hp=25 knots
Armament: three 3 in., two 40-mm. AA.; 20 mm. Complement: 200

Henderson. But though the island's fliers took their toll of the Japanese bombers, who raided the field whenever weather permitted, they could not stop them. Even while the new planes were landing, a salvo of bombs from a flight of twin-engine bombers struck on and around *Colhoun*, which with *Little* had been escorting the small auxiliary ship *Kopara*. The veteran APD went down in less than two minutes, taking fifty-one of her crew with her.

By the end of the month Cactus Air Force had some sixty-four planes in operation. But the rate of atrition was high. While comparatively few had been lost in actual combat, losses due to operational mishaps and enemy bombing and shelling were serious. As an example, five days after landing from *Long Island* one-third of the original planes were damaged or destroyed and only three of the fourteen P-400s were still operable by September 1. The overworked ground crews did their best —cannibalizing badly damaged planes to keep others in the air—but there was always a shortage of aircraft. The equally hard-working engineers somehow managed to keep the field in shape despite bombing, and shelling from the sea. Dump trucks were kept loaded, and with these and pneumatic tampers repair crews could fill the hole made by a 500-kilogram bomb in half an hour.

By the end of August daily fighter patrols were being flown—0545 to 0830 and 1400 to 1830.

Scout bombers often went up at night to patrol to the east and occasional night attacks were made on the Tokyo Express. But the SBDs only had a radius of some 200 miles, and as the nights close to the equator are twelve hours long, with short dawns and twilights, the enemy was at a great advantage. Within an hour of darkness the fast Japanese destroyers could start their high-speed approach, disembark their cargoes of troops and supplies and be 175 miles up The Slot on their way home before daylight.

Air communication was also a problem. Army planes could not receive on the Navy band and it was necessary to rig up a twin broadcast system. Planes could not usually pick up the field at any range over 20 miles while the field could receive from as much as a hundred. Until October, when radios were available with air forward observers, air-ground communication depended on colored panels, often impossible to see due to the heavy foliage. But despite such handicaps and a chronic shortage of gasoline, the Cactus Air Force remained the deciding factor. During the day, the waters around the island were reasonably safe for U.S. shipping and equally dangerous to the enemy. It was only with the coming of darkness that the picture changed. Then any ships remaining in the area scuttled off to the shelter of Tulagi in anticipation of the almost nightly arrival of the Japanese. These vessels, destroyers, destroyer-

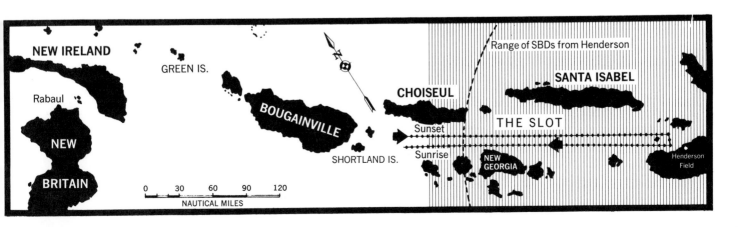

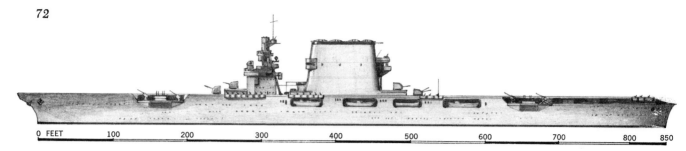

U.S.S. SARATOGA — AIRCRAFT CARRIER

Launched April 1925
Displacement: 33,000 tons LOA: 888 Beam: 105½ Draft: 24¼ feet
4 screws. 180,000 hp=34 knots. Armor: belt 6 in., deck 3 in.
Armament: sixteen 5 in. (8 original 8 in. removed in 1942), four 40-mm. quads, forty plus 20-mm. AA
Aircraft: ninety Complement: 3300

transports, and an occasional cruiser, usually completed their missions (troop and supply landings and/or bombardment of the Marine positions or airfield) shortly after midnight and retired toward the Shortlands at high speed before the Cactus fliers could locate and work them over. This pattern was to be occasionally interrupted by a vicious night surface action as American naval forces sought to intercept a particular Japanese bombardment or reinforcement group. Then the black waters around Savo would be lit with gun flashes and the glare of burning ships and slashed by the wakes of torpedoes. And daylight would find the sound streaked once more with long patches of oil and dotted with wreckage and groups of survivors.

Besides an occasional bombing and shelling, Tulagi was quiet and seemed securely enough held to enable Vandegrift to order his 1st Raider Battalion and 1st Paratroop Battalion across to Guadalcanal. This was on August 31, and both battalions were ferried over without mishap and bivouacked west of Lunga and behind Kukum.

But while the Marines on Guadalcanal were strengthened, the Navy was seriously weakened by the damaging of another carrier. After the Eastern Solomons battle Fletcher's carriers—Saratoga, with Wasp and Hornet—were patrolling in an area (some 9000 square miles in extent) about 260 miles southeast of Guadalcanal. With orders from Ghormley not to proceed north of Latitude 10° S. unless in pursuit of an enemy, the task force steamed slowly back and forth, ready at any moment to move to a position from which its planes could intercept any large-scale Japanese thrust into the lower Solomons.

A submarine had been sighted and driven under by scout planes on August 27 and a suspicious radar "blip" had been investigated in the early morning hours of August 31. At 0655 a change of base course brought Saratoga and her escorting vessels—a battle ship, three cruisers, and seven destroyers—zigzagging back toward the general area of the contact. At about 0745 a "zig" brought the carrier into the periscope cross hairs of submarine I-26. From outside the destroyer screen the submarine fired a spread of six torpedoes. Almost immediately destroyer MacDonough got a strong sonar contact and a few moments later a glimpse of a periscope just ahead. The warning went out and as MacDonough scraped over the submerging submarine, Saratoga began to turn. But she could not swing fast enough. A column of water rose alongside the carrier's superstructure and the reverberations of the explosion told the Japanese skipper that at least one of his fish had gone home. He and his crew felt numerous other—and much closer—explosions as MacDonough, Phelps, and later Monssen, tried to finish him off. But the hunters had no luck and I-26 got away. Saratoga was not badly holed, and the slight list was soon corrected but she was out of the war for almost three months, at a time when she would be badly needed. If she was out of the fight, her planes were not and both bombers and fighters were flown nearly 350 miles to Espiritu Santo and from there many ultimately reached Henderson Field.

On the night of the 31st, 1200 men of the Kawaguchi Brigade, including the general himself, landed to the east of the Marine lines, ferried there by eight destroyers.

Daylight saw the Japanese ships gone and the

waters of the sound once more ready to receive American surface vessels. Transport *Betelgeuse* landed a pair of 5-inch guns on Tulagi. These relatively powerful weapons (coastal defense had heretofore consisted of fire from 105s or 75-mm pack howitzers) were manhandled up the steep coral cliffs of the southern tip of the island and emplaced there. Their wooden firing platforms were floated in. More important than this ordnance for Tulagi was the landing on Guadalcanal of five officers and 387 men of the 6th Naval Construction Battalion (Seabees) with two bulldozers.

On September 2, during a particularly heavy air raid, a SBD was hit by a bomb and exploded, showering hot fragments and flaming gasoline around and causing several destructive fires. It was just another of the series of incidents which beset those responsible for the buildup of Cactus Air Force—one of the daily ups-and-downs—in which some stroke of bad luck seemed almost inevitably to cancel the painfully won gains of the day before. As some consolation, three Bettys and four Zeros were shot down for no American losses.

In the Tasimboko area Kawaguchi's engineers had begun the appalling task of cutting a trail from the coast inland and south of Henderson Field. The Japanese general had planned a textbook-type operation, involving simultaneous assaults from west, south, and southeast by forces separated by both distance and rough terrain. This form of attack is a tricky business—although much admired by tacticians—and often fails because of the vast gap between theory and practice. It was to be so in Kawaguchi's case, and his ultimate defeat was due in part to the steamy jungle, steep ravines, and wandering watercourses of the island.

The unexpected resistance of the Americans had already made its effects felt as far away as New Guinea. On August 31, Japanese General Headquarters had finally admitted the importance of the lower Solomons operation and had given top priority to the immediate recapture of Guadalcanal. This meant a temporary slowdown in the drive to take Port Moresby—a decision which was to have a decisive effect on that campaign. And from the northern end of Santa Isabel the stubborn Colonel Oka was setting out with his thousand men safely stowed in forty-eight landing barges.

JAPANESE LANDING BARGE—TYPE A (ARMY)

Length: 47 ft. Beam: 11½ ft. Draft: 2 ft. 6 in. Twin keel, steel hull, wooden ramp. Steel shield for helmsman. 60-hp diesel Speed: 7½ knots

Although the Japanese were the first to design a vessel specifically for amphibious operations (8000 ton Shinsu Maru—built in 1934 for the army to launch landing barges down a ramp at her stern) they never developed the varied types produced by the U.S. and Britain. There were several variations of the 47-foot barge above and others varying from 33 to 56 feet. All were comparatively crude affairs and there was nothing as sophisticated as the U.S. LCT or LCI. Large vessels capable of landing vehicles on a beach from a bow ramp were not built until 1943 and 1944. They were half the size of the 1600-ton U.S. LSTs and were few in number.

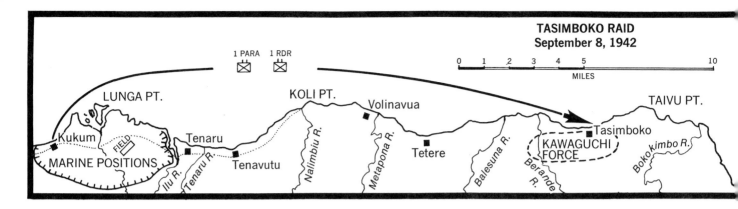

On September 3 the command echelon of 1st Marine Air Wing arrived, in the person of Brigadier General Roy Geiger, with his Chief of Staff and Intelligence Officer. The same day *Fomalhaut* and three APDs landed more supplies. The next day APDs *Gregory* and *Little* ferried two companies of the Raider Battalion to Savo, where Japs had been reported. No enemy was discovered and the Raiders were ferried back again, disembarking at dusk. Instead of anchoring as usual in Tulagi Harbor, the two APDs remained on patrol off Lunga Point. Here at about 0100 on September 5 they made radar contact with a force of three Japanese destroyers, which with some destroyer transports had made a routine troop and supply landing. The destroyers, *Yudachi*, *Hatsuyuki*, and *Murakumo* had begun the usual bombardment of the Marine positions prior to retiring up The Slot. *Gregory* and *Little* had the choice of leaving or, aided by their radar, making a surprise attack with the hope of bluffing the vastly superior enemy into retreating. Unfortunately for them, at the moment of decision a Catalina on patrol saw the flashes from the bombardment and dropped a string of flares. Instead of illuminating the enemy for the shore guns, the flares disclosed the two old APDs to the Japanese. Switching targets, they quickly found the range and salvo after salvo smashed into the two Americans. First commissioned in 1918—now with most of their original armament removed—they were no match for three modern destroyers. The two put up a gallant but brief resistance, but within a few minutes both were reduced to sinking, burning wrecks. Some survivors, struggling to swim clear, were killed as the Japanese steamed in close and blasted the hulks at close range. The rest were picked up next morning by landing boats, directed by planes from Henderson Field.

Other planes from Henderson were also busy with landing craft that morning. Colonel Oka's barge force had left the southern end of Santa Isabel the previous night, under escort of light cruiser *Sendai* and three destroyers for the 50-mile run to Cape Esperance. They were scheduled to land at dawn. Their escort left them some 20 miles from their destination but heavy seas slowed them down and daylight (and patrol planes from Henderson) found them still at sea. For several hours Marine pilots bombed and strafed the helpless barges. Finally some three hundred men, including Colonel Oka (who presumably by now wished he had come via destroyer) got ashore near Cape Esperance, while about the same number sought safety on Savo, whence they reached the mainland next night. The remainder, some four hundred officers and men, were lost at sea.

By September 6 the Japanese forces amounted, according to some accounts, to some three thousand men east of the defense perimeter, including the main body of the 124th Infantry, the second echelon of the Ichiki Force and a few survivors of the first. To the west were parts of the 124th, men of the Special Naval Landing Forces and some of the original garrison, mostly pioneers—perhaps 2200 men.

The almost nightly runs of the Tokyo Express gave ample notice that a Japanese buildup was in progress. To disrupt the mounting of an attack in force, 1st Raiders' Colonel Merritt A. Edson proposed an amphibious raid to the east, in the Tasimboko area. Accordingly, at 1800 on September 7, 1st Raider Battalion embarked at Kukum on APDs *Manley* and *McKean* and two "Yippies" (YPs, in this case, converted California tuna boats). The 1st Paratroop Battalion, also destined for the operation, moved down to Lunga Point and bivouaced in readiness to proceed in support. Together the two battalions numbered some seven hundred men.

At about 0520 (still pitch dark in those latitudes) on September 8 the first of Edson's Raiders went ashore east of Tasimboko village. At daylight the advance toward the village began, supported by a couple of SBDs and four P-400s whose mission was to bomb and strafe the target area. The area was also shelled by *Manley* and *McKean*.

At the time the Raiders were landing, transports *Fuller* and *Bellatrix*, escorted by destroyers, came into view en route to unload supplies at Lunga. It is possible that the sight of the transports, coming on top of the shelling and strafing, convinced the Japanese that a landing in force was imminent. At any rate, the advance was unopposed for some time and it was not until after 0800 that contact was made with enemy forces, who retired toward the village. At 1045 Edson reported further progress and suggested that more troops be landed west of Tasimboko. This suggestion was turned down by Division and a countersuggestion made that Edson re-embark and return to the perimeter. This, in turn, was refused and Edson pressed on against mounting opposition, including point-blank fire from artillery—several pieces of which were taken.

By now (1100) the 1st Parachute Battalion had also been landed and made contact with Edson, who ordered an enveloping attack made on the village. The village was taken but the majority of the defenders succeeded in escaping, leaving behind twenty-seven bodies. Marine casualties were very light, two killed and six wounded. To the surprise of the Marine commanders the attack had done more than scatter a comparatively small force of Japanese. Large quantities of supplies and ammunition, including several 47-mm antitank guns were found and it was estimated that some four thousand men had been in the area

shortly before the raid. Actually the force attacked was the rear echelon of Kawaguchi's expedition, now busily hacking their way into the jungle toward an area to the south of Henderson Field.

There was neither time nor space enough to transport the captured booty to the perimeter, so with the exception of a few machine guns the rest of the matériel was systematically destroyed. Holes were jabbed in tins of food, rice dumped in the sea, shells defused, and breechblocks thrown into the surf. A radio was found and destroyed but not before a report of the "landing" had been sent to Rabaul, where the news caused concern. There were fears that Kawaguchi was "sandwiched" between the landing forces and the Americans at Lunga. More Special Landing Forces men were ordered to Guadalcanal via the Express and a regiment, the 41st Infantry, then on the faraway trail from Buna to Port Moresby, was ordered to prepare for transshipment to Guadalcanal.

Considering the devastation of Kawaguchi's supply base and the "flap" caused at Japanese HQ the raid had been a success. It was also successful from the personal point of view of the raiders—most of whom managed to "save" a load of tinned crab or sliced beef, not to mention a small amount of sake and beer.

A minor but more immediate reaction was the dispatch of planes from Rabaul to bomb the transports, an effort which caused *Fuller* and *Bellatrix* to leave the area before fully unloaded. At the same time Mikawa sent down *Sendai* and eight destroyers to attack the same targets that night. Balked of their prey, the *Sendai* force bombarded Tulagi Harbor, hitting a YP and wounding three men.

JAPANESE MODEL 1 (1941) 47-mm. ANTI-TANK GUN

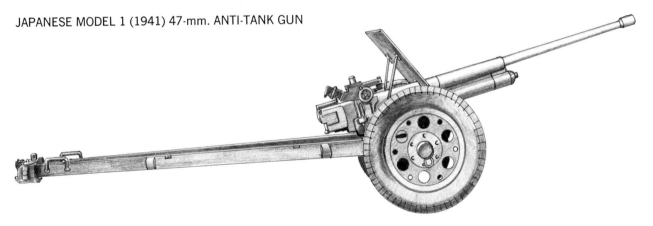

Velocity: 2700 feet per second
Weight of projectile: 3 lbs., 6.4 oz.   Weight of gun: 1660 lbs.

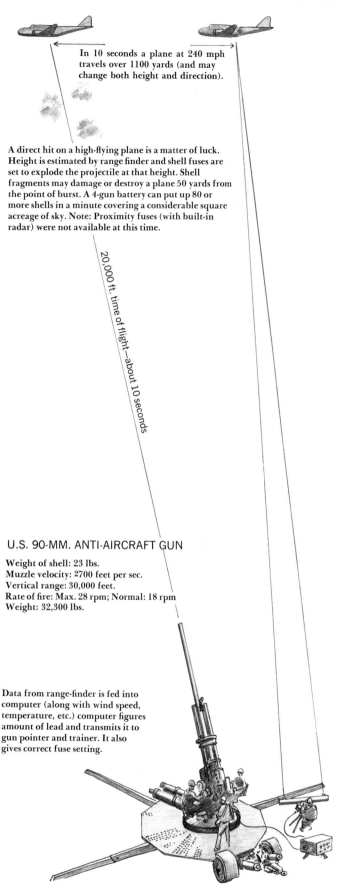

In 10 seconds a plane at 240 mph travels over 1100 yards (and may change both height and direction).

A direct hit on a high-flying plane is a matter of luck. Height is estimated by range finder and shell fuses are set to explode the projectile at that height. Shell fragments may damage or destroy a plane 50 yards from the point of burst. A 4-gun battery can put up 80 or more shells in a minute covering a considerable square acreage of sky. Note: Proximity fuses (with built-in radar) were not available at this time.

20,000 ft. time of flight—about 10 seconds

U.S. 90-MM. ANTI-AIRCRAFT GUN

Weight of shell: 23 lbs.
Muzzle velocity: 2700 feet per sec.
Vertical range: 30,000 feet.
Rate of fire: Max. 28 rpm; Normal: 18 rpm
Weight: 32,300 lbs.

Data from range-finder is fed into computer (along with wind speed, temperature, etc.) computer figures amount of lead and transmits it to gun pointer and trainer. It also gives correct fuse setting.

By September 10, reports from Clemens' natives indicated that the Japanese were less than 5 miles east of the perimeter and working their way painfully to the south of it. An attack was obviously in the making, but while the Marines were making what preparations they could in anticipation, the far-distant Ghormley was requested by the Joint Chiefs (who should have known better) to turn over to MacArthur a reinforced regiment of "experienced amphibious troops" together with their necessary transports and supply ships! ComSoPac referred this request to Turner, who, understandably alarmed, told Ghormley in no uncertain terms that the only experienced troops were deeply committed on Guadalcanal, and that, far from reducing their strength, they were in urgent need of reinforcement.

Under Secretary of the Navy James V. Forrestal had already recommended that the Army Air Force provide interceptors capable of meeting the Japanese at high altitude. The only plane available to meet this requirement was the new P-38 Lightning, which partly due to the commitments of the North African invasion, was in short supply. In answer to an appeal to Southwest Pacific for a few of these planes by ComSoPac, MacArthur replied that he had only six himself.

There were, however, Navy fighters available in the area, but under Fletcher's command (Fletcher, it will be remembered, was operating in ComSoPac's area but under orders from Nimitz). These planes were part of *Saratoga's* Air Group, and, although the carrier would not be serviceable for some time, Fletcher had no wish to see his highly trained carrier group broken up. On September 10, Nimitz finally transferred as many carrier aircraft as could be spared to Ghormley, who on September 11, ordered twenty-four Wildcats flown from Espiritu Santo to Guadalcanal.

This reinforcement, arriving at 1620, was particularly welcome. Japanese raids were frequent and enemy action and accidents, due to hazardous conditions (eight planes cracked up on takeoff on September 8, for instance) kept Cactus Air Force in constant need of planes. The new arrivals were in action the next day. With some of the "old inhabitants" they shot down twelve bombers and three fighters of a forty-two-plane raid which struck at 1100.

In the middle of the air alert Kelly Turner arrived. He brought bad news. Strong enemy naval forces were massing at Truk and Rabaul, transports were loading, and the enemy air forces were being steadily reinforced. Ghormley, short of just about everything, had come to the conclusion that the Guadalcanal operation could no longer be supported. Turner, not so pessimistic as ComSoPac and perhaps more convinced of the seriousness of the situation on the island by a night partly spent in listening to incoming Japanese naval shells, promised to urge Ghormley to send Vandegrift the 7th Marines, then at Samoa. The shells which disturbed Turner's rest came from destroyers bringing in the 3rd Battalion, 4th Infantry which landed near Cape Esperance about midnight.

Vandegrift had by this time improved the defenses of the perimeter. The 1st Marines held a line from the western side of the mouth of the Ilu River some 4000 yards inland, almost due south. On the west, 5th Marines with its 2nd Battalion in reserve held a line inland for about 2000 yards. To the south, and west of the Lunga River were positions of the 1st Amphibian Tractor Battalion and Pioneer Battalion while the line inland was held in a series of strong points and outposts by the bulk of the Pioneers, the Engineers, units of the 1st, and Edson's composite battalion of Raiders and Paratroopers. These last were dug in on the southern end of a long low ridge running roughly northeast and southwest, parallel to the Lunga River and less than a mile south of Henderson Field, which it overlooked and to which it was connected by a narrow road. The ridge, like others in the area, was covered with kunai grass and

appeared as a narrow strip of open ground some one thousand yards long surrounded on all sides by jungle-covered ravines. The ridge presented a likely approach to the field from the south, and, appreciating this, on September 12 Colonel Edson and his staff examined the ridge prior to locating its defenses. They were met with small arms fire from the thick woods to the south, and although the ridge thrust out further than the supporting positions of the Engineers on the east and Pioneers to the west, Edson ordered his men to dig in on its southernmost end.

As if to prove that the Japanese were well aware of the importance of the ridge, and that it was being fortified, a raid by twin-engine bombers plastered the ridge with 500-pounders and "daisy cutters." The "Cactus" fliers went up and out of a forty-two plane strike, twelve bombers and three Zeros were destroyed. One U.S. plane was lost in landing.

The night of the 12th was hardly a restful one. About 2100 a cruiser and three destroyers shelled the ridge, while several small probing attacks were made by the enemy. One of these penetrated the Marine positions but was driven out and the line partially re-established. Early morning attempts by Edson to counterattack met with strong resistance and were called off. This actually was to have been Kawaguchi's big attack, but as he afterward wrote ". . . because of the devilish jungle, the brigade was scattered all over."

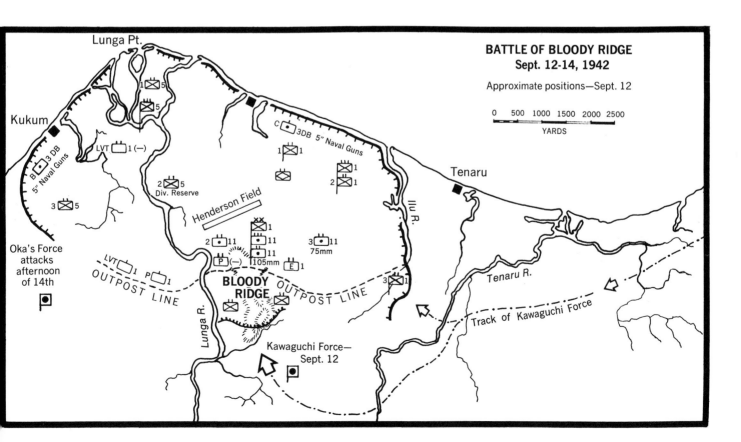

BATTLE OF BLOODY RIDGE
Sept. 12-14, 1942

Approximate positions—Sept. 12

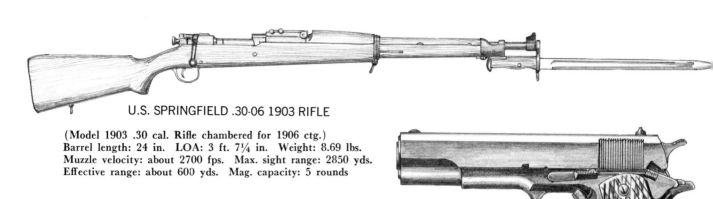

U.S. SPRINGFIELD .30-06 1903 RIFLE

(Model 1903 .30 cal. Rifle chambered for 1906 ctg.)
Barrel length: 24 in.   LOA: 3 ft. 7¼ in.   Weight: 8.69 lbs.
Muzzle velocity: about 2700 fps.   Max. sight range: 2850 yds.
Effective range: about 600 yds.   Mag. capacity: 5 rounds

U.S. .45 1911A1 AUTOMATIC

Barrel length: 5 in.   LOA: 8½ in.   Weight: 39 oz.
Muzzle velocity: 810 fps.
Accurate range: about 75 yds.   Mag. capacity: 7 rounds
Sights: fixed

But Edson was convinced that the main assault was still to come and he decided to both consolidate and contract his lines and provide a clearer field of fire by pulling back somewhat. This was accomplished during the day, and by night the Marines were as ready as they ever would be, with their automatic weapons and mortars in position and fields of fire laid out for the supporting artillery.

Kawaguchi, lurking in the jungle which lapped the Marines' position, was not happy about his arrangements. His assault, which he had planned for the 13th, had been delivered a day earlier on orders from the Seventeenth Army's commander, General Hyakutake—who was concerned about reports of the arrival of a large American convoy in the Fijis. Delivered with what units could be brought into line, the attack had failed and his scheduled take-over of the field postponed. (He had even brought a white dress uniform for the surrender ceremony. Unfortunately, it had been among the baggage taken by Edson's men at Taivu Point.) Further, he may have had misgivings about the overwhelming effect of the "spiritual" ascendancy of Japanese swords and bayonets on this stubborn enemy—an enemy which appeared to be both stronger in numbers and morale than he had been led to believe. However, the banzai charge of veteran troops had traditionally carried everything before it, and although communications between units were almost non-existent and Colonel Oka was still not in position, the general was confident that the concerted rush of two reinforced battalions, nearly two thousand men, would clear the way to the vital field.

After Edson's attack on Kawaguchi's rear echelon at Tasimboko and the destruction of his signals detachment's equipment, Rabaul had not been in contact with the general. At first it was assumed that the airfield had been taken on the 12th as scheduled, but the report of four scout planes sent down to investigate by Eleventh Air Fleet indicated (they came home exhibiting bullet-holes) that the airstrip was not in friendly hands. But planes were ready to fly down to the field, including transport aircraft with maintenance crews and spare parts.

The raids on the field were therefore kept up but it was not considered advisable to bomb the ridge area where the main assault was to come. The area around Tasimboko where the American landing force had gone ashore on September 8 seemed a worthwhile target however, and about noon on the 13th, twenty-six bombers, escorted by twelve Zeros, bombed and strafed the remainder of Kawaguchi's rear echelon!

The 13th brought new arrivals at Henderson. With the Japanese infantry a couple of thousand yards away and with Japanese planes overhead (there were many alerts that day), eighteen F4Fs from *Hornet* and *Wasp* flew in, followed in the afternoon by twelve SBDs and six TBFs (Henderson's first torpedo planes) from *Saratoga's* group.

The Marines on and near the ridge spent the day strengthening their positions and settled down to an uneasy wait for darkness and the attack which all felt was coming.

As the night wore on, the drone of an airplane engine heralded the arrival of one of the almost

JAPANESE MODEL 38 (1905) Arisaka 6.5-mm. RIFLE

Barrel length: 30.3 in. LOA: 50.2 in.
Weight: 8 lb. 12 oz.
Muzzle velocity: about 2400 fps. Sight range: 2400 meters (2623 yds.)
Effective range: about 500 yds. Mag. capacity: 5 rounds

JAPANESE NAMBU 8-mm. 1914 AUTOMATIC

Barrel length: 4½ in. LOA: 9 in. Weight: 31 oz.
Muzzle velocity: about 900 fps. Accurate range: about 75 yds.
Mag. capacity: 7 rounds Sights: adjustable rear (to 500 meters)
no windage adjustment
Note: A wooden shoulder-stock holster can be attached to butt.

nightly intruders. Known as Washing Machine Charley or Louie the Louse these nuisances, twin-engine bombers from Rabaul or float planes from some cruiser, were in the habit of stooging about, dropping an occasional bomb just to keep everyone from having too sound a sleep, or marking the field with a flare or two for the benefit of whatever Japanese vessels happened to be shelling the area that particular night.

At about 2100 the visitor dropped a flare over the field, at which signal seven destroyers (which had been sighted earlier coming down The Slot and which were now cruising in Sealark Channel) opened up with their 5-inch guns.

In answer a flare rose in the jungle at the foot of the ridge and without further warning, Kawaguchi sent in a two-battalion attack against the center and right of Edson's defenses. The forward observers of Colonel Pedro del Valle's artillery called down fire immediately, and the enemy infantrymen

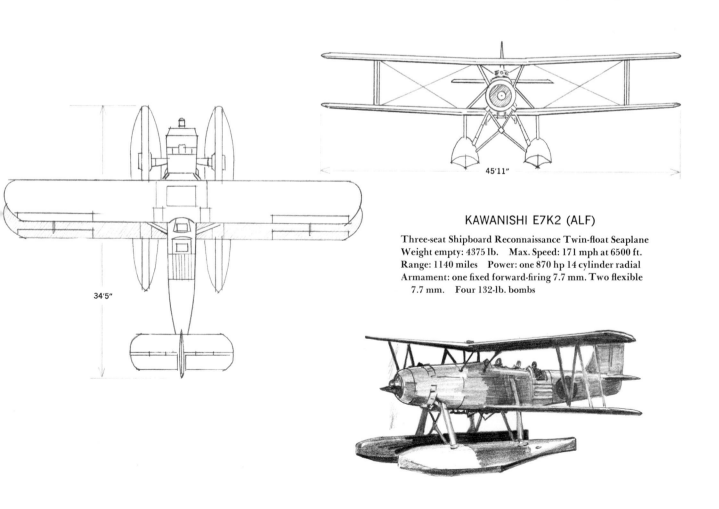

KAWANISHI E7K2 (ALF)

Three-seat Shipboard Reconnaissance Twin-float Seaplane
Weight empty: 4375 lb.   Max. Speed: 171 mph at 6500 ft.
Range: 1140 miles   Power: one 870 hp 14 cylinder radial
Armament: one fixed forward-firing 7.7 mm. Two flexible
7.7 mm.   Four 132-lb. bombs

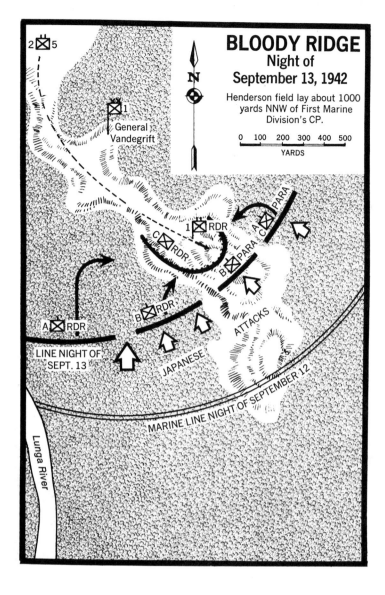

BLOODY RIDGE
Night of
September 13, 1942

Henderson field lay about 1000
yards NNW of First Marine
Division's CP.

0 100 200 300 400 500
YARDS

General Vandegrift

LINE NIGHT OF SEPT. 13

JAPANESE ATTACKS

MARINE LINE NIGHT OF SEPTEMBER 12

Lunga River

and the dark fringe of jungle spewed platoon after platoon of shouting Japanese. The direction of the attack was now more to the east of the ridge. Through clouds of smoke, lit by lurid orange flashes and the ghastly greenish light of the flares, squat figures rushed the slopes. "Gas attack" they yelled —but it was the weight of the charge, not the fear of gas, which drove the thin line of paratroops from their positions. As the Japanese pressed their attacks home, the artillery fire was called in even closer to the forward positions—shells screaming low over the heads of the defenders to burst less than 200 yards ahead. The 105-mm gunners were to fire close to two thousand rounds that night— pouring out shells as fast as they could slam them into the smoking breeches. Then the lines from the forward observers went dead—cut by infiltrators or severed by the pounding mortars. But the gunners still fired, redoubling their efforts when the signal flares which marked each fresh attack shot up out of the jungle.

The ridge—Bloody Ridge in Marine Corps history—was in turmoil. Tracers arced and ricocheted, grenades sprayed their deadly fragments and rifles spat as the fight surged northward. The forward company was exposed on both flanks now, and Edson passed the word for a withdrawal. Scrambling back, the defenders took position for a last-ditch stand on higher ground. The new line was shorter—but there were far fewer to defend it. But defend it they did. In some twelve desperate assaults, Kawaguchi's infantrymen swarmed up and along the bullet-swept ridge. Fighting was often hand to hand as the frantic Japanese hurled themselves at the Marines' last defenses. But even the best of soldiers can only take so much—and many of their best lay sprawled in death or writhing in agony in the scorched stubble and shredded scrub on and around the ridge. As the night wore on, the attacks slackened and it became evident that Edson's men would hold. Other units were moving up in support as Vandegrift committed his scanty reserves and by daylight the fighting on Edson's front had died down to occasional sniping.

Kawaguchi's plans for a coordinated three-prong attack never materialized. While the fight for the ridge was raging, a small force—perhaps two companies—attacked 3rd Battalion, 1st Marines in their position inland of the Ilu. Their lines lay along the edge of the jungle, facing an open plain some 700 yards deep. The tall grass had been burned or cut and wire strung, and the Japanese never had a chance. At the wire they were blasted by auto-

were met, not only with small arms fire, mortar bombs, and grenades, but with a curtain of exploding shells. Yelling "Banzai" and "Maline, you die!" the Japanese swarmed out of the thick cover and up the slopes.

Thrown back in front, despite heavy losses they made a gap in the defenses to the west of the ridge, infiltrating deep into the position. The Marines on that side were forced to swing back and up the ridge. Fighting desperately, the Marines ripped the attackers with streams of automatic fire, and amid the flash of bursting grenades and the glare of the artillery barrage, the Japanese were beaten back. Sullenly, they filtered back into the black cover of the jungle, leaving the slopes littered with dead and dying. But not for long. Shortly before midnight the ridge erupted in flame as the Japanese hurled a torrent of mortar bombs on the Marine positions. Again the flares went up

U.S. M3 LIGHT TANK
(General Stuart)

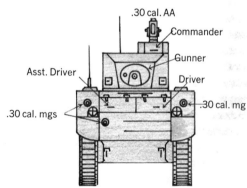

.30 cal. AA
Commander
Gunner
Asst. Driver
Driver
.30 cal. mgs
.30 cal. mg

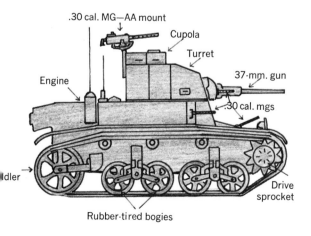

.30 cal. MG—AA mount
Cupola
Turret
Engine
37-mm. gun
.30 cal. mgs
Idler
Drive sprocket
Rubber-tired bogies

Length: 14 ft. 10 in.   Height: 7 ft. 4 in.   Width: 7 ft. 6 in. Weight: 12.9 tons Engine: one 250-hp radial Max. speed: (road) 36 mph Range: 60 miles Armament: one 37-mm. gun with a coaxially mounted .30 cal. MG.; three .30 cal. MGs. mounted in hull; one .30 cal. MG. on AA mount on cupola. Armor: turret face and lower front—2 inches; driver's front, rest of turret—1½ inches. Rest: 1 inch to ⅜ inches.   Crew: 4

matic weapons and 75-mm pack howitzers and the attack petered out into a fire fight which lasted until dawn. An attempt to clear the Japanese out of their position with six light tanks ended in failure. The tanks made the mistake of advancing several times over the same route. They were finally met with antitank fire and three were knocked out. Another rolled down a bank—and the attack was written off.

On the western side of the perimeter, Colonel Oka's attack was not made until the afternoon of the 14th. His men struck suddenly at positions held by part of the 3rd Battalion of the 5th Marines. The Japanese were met by heavy fire and driven back into the jungle by infantry counterattacks and artillery.

The rest was just mopping up. At dawn troops

flushed out infiltrators and snipers, while P-400s strafed the jungle around the southern end of the ridge. The battle for the ridge was over and a saddened Kawaguchi could only collect the shattered remnants of his command and make arrangements for a retreat.

He had a choice of retracing his steps to Tasimboko or carrying on westward to join the forces under Oka. He chose the latter and, putting his badly wounded in litters, began the weary march to Kokumbona. The nightmare journey took over a week. Rations gave out, many wounded died and the weakened survivors abandoned all their heavy equipment in their struggle to hack their way westward. Some four hundred of the original Ichiki Force and part of 2nd Battalion, 4th Infantry went back the way they had come and eventually arrived at Taivu Point, where they joined the hungry remnants of Kawaguchi's rear echelon. There is no accurate count of Japanese losses. More than six hundred bodies were counted on or adjacent to the ridge itself and many more must have fallen in the jungle. To this must be added the two hundred or so who were killed attacking the 1st Marines and an unknown number of Oka's command who died attacking the 3rd Battalion, 5th Marines. The Japanese admit to over five hundred wounded and many of these never lived to reach Kokumbona.

It appears from General Kawaguchi's postwar *Memoir* that one battalion, which should have supported the attack on the ridge, did not engage. (The colonel commanding was scarcely able to walk, due to his strenuous march from Taivu Point, but it would seem strange that his battalion could not be committed without him.) The heavy casualties, then, fell largely on two battalions, which must have been written off as fighting units. Marine casualties on the ridge were thirty-one killed, nine missing (presumed dead), and 103 wounded.

VII
Alarms and Excursions

FIGHTING ALONG THE MATANIKAU—AND *WASP* GOES TO THE BOTTOM

The 7th Marines and part of 5th Defense Battalion with their equipment and vehicles had left Samoa on September 2 under escort and had arrived at Espiritu Santo on September 12. The next day Ghormley ordered the 7th to Guadalcanal.

The 7th Marines, reinforced, including the 1st Battalion of the 11th Marines (75-mm howitzers), were loaded in six transports. They left Espiritu Santo at dawn on September 14, escorted by three cruisers, plus destroyers and minesweepers. Turner's force, designated Task Force 65, was supported by a task force formed around *Hornet* and *Wasp*, the only two fleet carriers then operational. Flagship *Wasp*, Rear Admiral Leigh Noyes, was attended by four cruisers and six destroyers. *Hornet*,

some six miles away had as escort new battleship *North Carolina*, three cruisers and seven destroyers. It was to be an expensive voyage.

At 1420 on September 15, *Wasp*, whose planes that day were flying CAP and antisubmarine patrols, turned to windward to launch and recover planes. As she came back to base course she was struck (1445) by three torpedoes from *I-19*. The effect was catastrophic. Planes on decks were hurled into the air and smashed, fires immediately broke out and spread to planes already tanked and bombed up, and fire mains were ruptured. The ship took a heavy list, which was soon partially corrected by shifting oil. The engine rooms were undamaged but there was no controlling the

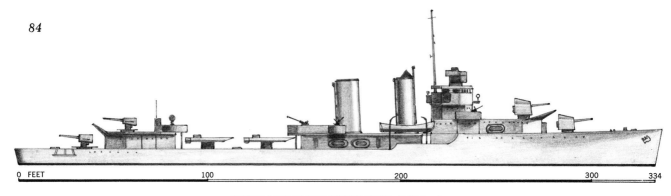

FARRAGUT CLASS DESTROYER (8 Ships)

Launched January 1934–January 1935
Displacement: 1345–1395 tons LOA: 341½ Beam: 34¼ Draft: 9 feet. Twin screw.
42,800=36.5 knots Armament: four 5 in., twin 40-mm. (replaced old No. 3 5 in.)
six/seven 20-mm. AA, eight 21 in. torpedo tubes (2×4). Complement: 250

gasoline-fed fires and *Wasp* blazed like a torch. About fifteen minutes after the torpedoes hit, a terrific explosion took place which killed many men and whirled others about like fallen leaves. Admiral Noyes, his clothes on fire, was blown onto the signal bridge and the blast and flames caused the evacuation of the bridge area. Despite heroic efforts by fire fighters and damage control crews, *Wasp* was doomed and at 1520 the order was given to abandon ship. At 2100 she was sunk by torpedoes from *Lansdowne*.

All but one of the twenty-five planes she had just launched landed aboard *Hornet* but 193 of her 2247 man complement were killed and 366 wounded. *I-19*, whose attack had been made without her being picked up on the screen's sound gear, escaped.

Cruising in company with *I-19* was *I-15*. The column of flame-shot smoke pouring from the stricken *Wasp* encouraged the second submarine's commander to try for a double. He missed *Hornet* but one of his fish caught *North Carolina* and tore

a hole 32 feet long and 18 high. Another struck destroyer *O'Brien* and opened up her bow. The battleship never lost her place in formation and her list was compensated for in a few minutes. She had to be sent back for repairs, however, first to Tongatabu, then to Pearl Harbor. *O'Brien* was patched up sufficiently for a trip to the West Coast, or so it was thought. But her keel and supporting members had been strained and when off Samoa she broke in two and went down. Three ships out of the lineup, two permanently and nothing to show for it. It had been a great day for the Japanese submarine service.

Kelly Turner, although he knew that strong Japanese forces were massed to the north, decided to push on. He had promised Vandegrift to deliver the 7th Marines and although he and the Marine general had disagreed over their use (Turner, who had a reputation for liking to "play soldier" had wanted to extend the area by landing them at Taivu Point, some 20 miles east of the perimeter) deliver them he would. On the 16th,

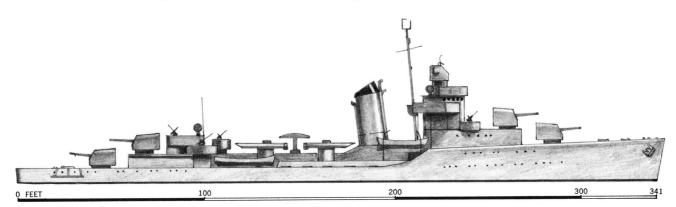

SIMS CLASS DESTROYER (12 Ships)

Displacement: 1570 tons LOA: 348 Beam: 36 Draft: 10 feet
Twin screw. 49,000 hp=38 knots
Armament: four 5 in., six 20-mm., eight 21 in. torpedo tubes (2×4).
Complement: 250
 (Originally had 5–5 in., in some ships 12 (3×4) TTs. One 5 in. removed 1941.)

after a short withdrawal due to reports of Japanese warships off the Shortlands, he made plans for a landing at dawn on September 18.

At 0550 the 7th began going ashore at Kukum. Despite heavy weather (which incidentally assured a raid-free operation by grounding the enemy bombers at Rabaul) the troops—over four thousand of them—and their equipment, guns, ammunition, vehicles, fuel, food, and other supplies went ashore in a steady stream. While they were disembarking, destroyers *Monssen* and *MacDonough* shelled enemy positions, a bombardment which depressed the Japs as much as it elated the Marines.

By 1800 it was time to go. Most of the unloading had been completed and Turner sailed at once for Nouméa and Espiritu Santo, taking with him the remnants of the 1st Paratroop Battalion.

It was the first reinforcements of combat troops the Marines on the island had had since they landed forty-three days before. For a good part of that time they had been fed two meals a day, part of this captured rice. While malaria had not yet become a problem, casualties from dysentery, fungus infections, exhaustion, and malnutrition far exceeded those caused by enemy action. All units were far below strength and the debilitating effect of the tropical climate was beginning to make itself felt on those still fit for duty.

The 1st Division was at last complete and Vandegrift now had on the island nine battalions of infantry, a weak Raider Battalion, four battalions of artillery, two companies of light tanks and a special weapons battalion, plus auxiliary forces —engineers, pioneers, amphibian tractor men, etc. —19,251 on Guadalcanal and 3260 on Tulagi (3rd Battalion, 2nd Marines had been ferried from Tulagi to Guadalcanal on the 14th).

Also on September 18, cargo ship *Bellatrix* with two APDs landed a shipment of aviation gasoline. The three left with Turner. That night enemy naval forces entered Sealark Channel but made no attempt at pursuit.

Patrols in force had been made on the 14th, following the Ridge battle, and again on the 17th. On that date a three-company patrol of 1st Battalion, 1st Marines made contact with the Japanese southwest of the perimeter. A fire fight followed before the patrol withdrew, which cost the Marines eighteen dead and three wounded. But General Vandegrift now felt that more "active defense" was in order. The first such effort to expand and strengthen the perimeter, by clearing the Matanikau River area, ended in failure. The plan was for

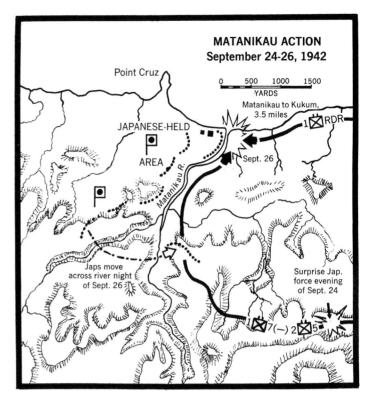

MATANIKAU ACTION
September 24-26, 1942

1st Battalion, 7th Marines, Lieutenant Colonel Lewis B. ("Chesty") Puller, to skirt the foot of the high ground known as Mount Austen, cross the Matanikau and push into the area between the river and Kokumbona. He was to start on September 23, and on the 26th, by which time it was expected he would have reached his objective, 1st Raider Battalion was to advance along the coast to Kokumbona.

On September 24, Puller's men ran into a Jap force at the foot of Mount Austen and routed them, but at the cost of several killed and wounded. The 2nd Battalion, 5th Marines were sent in support and A and B Companies of 7th went back with the stretcher cases (difficult to move in hilly jungle country, and needing protection). It became apparent that the original timetable could not be met, so instead of crossing the river, 2nd Battalion, 5th and the remainder of 1st Battalion, 7th Marines moved northward along its eastern bank. On reaching the river mouth on September 26, heavy fire was encountered from the western bank. Attempts to cross were repulsed, although artillery and air were called in. It was decided to renew the attack on the 27th, with the Raiders crossing some 2000 yards upstream while 2nd Battalion, 5th Marines and C Company of the 7th Marines attacked across the river near its mouth.

When the Raiders moved upstream they found that a Japanese force had crossed to the east bank during the night. Their planned march down the west bank was thus checked but a garbled message gave Edson (who had been sent to take

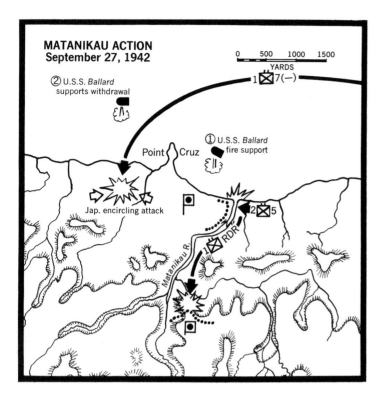

MATANIKAU ACTION
September 27, 1942

0 500 1000 1500
YARDS

② U.S.S. *Ballard*
supports withdrawal

① U.S.S. *Ballard*
fire support

Point Cruz

Jap. encircling attack

Matanikau R.

charge of the operation, with Puller now his executive) to understand that they had succeeded in forcing a passage. He therefore ordered Major Otho Rogers of the 7th Marines to land A and B Companies with parts of D Company on the western side of Point Cruz.

The force landed and moved a few hundred yards inland but was cut off and severely handled. At the same time, attempts by 2nd Battalion, 5th Marines to cross at the river mouth were held by stiff resistance from Japanese dug in on the other bank. Rogers had been killed and 1st Battalion, 7th Marines (its radio had been left behind) could only call for help by spelling the word on a patch of open ground with white T-shirts. Luckily a patrolling SBD spotted this and relayed word of their plight to Edson's HQ. Puller (no man to stay at HQ while his men were fighting) boarded seaplane tender *Ballard* and directed boats which had landed the battalion to take them off. This was finally done—the battalion fighting its way back to the beach, aided by *Ballard's* guns and embarking under heavy fire. The whole operation had been a costly foul-up, some sixty Marines killed and a hundred wounded for no gains.

The last days of September saw increasing air activity which, in most cases, resulted in Japanese losses far outweighing any damage they inflicted. On the 27th, nine Japanese planes out of a fifty-three-plane raid were lost and on the 28th, the Cactus fliers shot down twenty-three bombers and

a fighter. On neither day did the Americans lose any planes in combat. Non-combat losses were always high, however, and the combination of exceedingly variable weather conditions and an often repaired runway (which might be a sea of mud in the morning and choked with fine dust in the afternoon) did much to offset the comparatively light losses in the air. Non-combat losses to the Japanese were also high, and many planes, damaged or low on gas, ditched or made forced landings while attempting to return to their airfields.

It was about this time that the Japanese changed their tactics and began sending a few bombers (perhaps to act as bait) covered by a large number of fighters. The elusive Zero was a more difficult and dangerous target than the bomber and on October 2, the score was only five Japanese planes downed for four Americans.

On the same day that *Wasp* was sunk, first reports of Kawaguchi's defeat reached Rabaul. After conferences between the naval and military staffs, more troops were requested and on the 17th, Imperial GHQ assigned the veteran 38th Division, Lieutenant General Tadayoshi Sano commanding, which had fought at Hong Kong, Java, Timur, and Sumatra, to Seventeenth Army.

The Tokyo Express suffered an occasional "derailment." On October 5, destroyers *Minegumo* and *Murasame* were attacked by SBDs of Cactus Air Force and were badly damaged by near misses. But the Express continued to run and the destroyers, each carrying some 150 soldiers, frequently put as many as nine hundred men ashore in one night's operation.

On October 7, another move was made to clear the enemy from the Matanikau River area. It was in essence a beefed-up version of the attack of September 24–27 with five rifle battalions and another in reserve, a scout-sniper detachment, plus artillery and air support. The 5th Marines (less one battalion) were to advance to the river, while 3rd Battalion, 2nd Marines and the scout-sniper detachment (known as Whaling Group, after its commander) and 7th Marines (less one battalion) crossed the river above the 5th Marines and advanced north toward Matanikau Village and Point Cruz.

Contact with an enemy force of about one company strength was made east of the river by 3rd Battalion, 5th Marines in midmorning. The enemy was located in an area about 75 yards

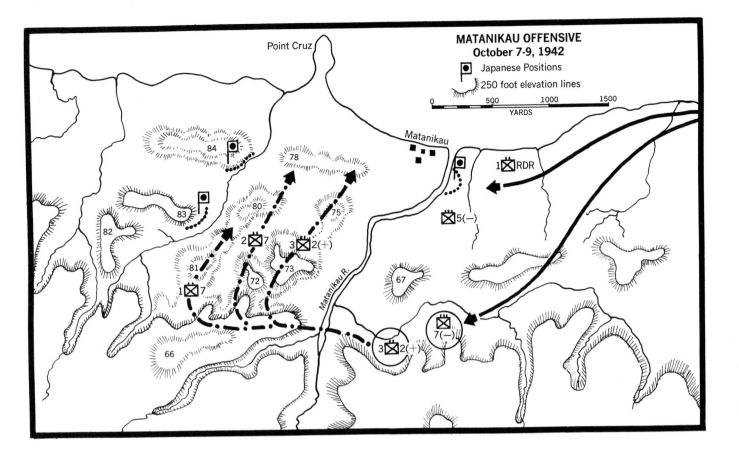

above the river mouth and some 150 yards up-stream. This strong point was defended by about 150 men, and perhaps forty or fifty more had escaped across the river mouth. The 1st Raider Battalion was ordered in as reinforcement in the afternoon. Repeated attempts were made by the enemy to break out of their position during the night. There was little action on October 8 because of the torrential rains, but at 1830 that night the enemy made a final effort to escape. They struck the Raider's position and in heavy hand-to-hand fighting were almost wiped out. Fifty-nine bodies were counted next day. Others escaped across the river mouth or died in the river.

During the 8th, reports from coastwatchers and air observers of troop concentrations and ship movements around Rabaul and the Shortlands indicated that a strong counterattack would soon be launched on the American perimeter.

For this reason General Vandegrift decided that the Matanikau operation must be curtailed. Originally it had been intended that, if the advance across the river upstream had been successful, then the 5th Marines would cross the river mouth and advance west and seize—and if possible, garrison—Kokumbona. This part of the plan was now given up, and after Matanikau had been taken and it

and the enemy in the area destroyed, the force was to return to the perimeter.

The crossing upstream was made successfully next day (October 9) and the force moved north-ward toward the beach in three columns. The Whaling Group pushed downstream on the west-ern bank, parallel to it and some 1000 yards west. The 2nd Battalion, 7th Marines drove against stronger resistance to the base of Point Cruz, while 1st Battalion, 7th attacked along a ridge west of 2nd Battalion, 7th. Puller's 1st Battalion, 7th came upon a sizable enemy force in a deep ravine run-ning roughly north and south and some 1500 yards south (inland) of Point Cruz. Puller called in an artillery concentration into the ravine, at the same time bringing his own mortars into action. The jungle-filled ravine erupted into an inferno of flashes, slashing steel fragments, splintered trees and scrub and upflung earth and bodies. Too de-moralized to rally for counterattacks, the Japanese (of the 4th Infantry Regiment) tried to escape up the steep open slopes. Here they were cut down by grazing fire from automatic weapons or picked off by riflemen. Scrambling down to escape the bullets they were again driven out by shells and mortar bombs. Puller's men kept up the slaughter until they ran out of mortar ammunition, then withdrew to rejoin the other units. By 1400 the combined forces had withdrawn east of the Matanikau. In support of 1st Battalion, 7th, Marine artillery fired over two thousand rounds of 75-mm and more than a thousand rounds of 105-mm ammunition. A captured Japanese diary gave 4th Infantry's losses to 1st Battalion, 7th Marines as 690 officers and men. It was one of the bloodiest and most spectacular encounters of the campaign.

The whole operation, while not carried out to its completion, was a success. Japanese losses were high, while Marine casualties for the three days were sixty-five killed and 125 wounded. It was subsequently learned that a Japanese offensive action had been planned for the 8th. Colonel Nomasu Nakaguma's 4th Infantry were to cross the Matanikau and establish artillery positions within range of the airfield in readiness for the big assault to come later in the month. Needless to say, the shattered 4th Infantry would not launch any attacks for some time.

General Kawaguchi had been back to Rabaul to brief Seventeenth Army HQ on the difficulties of fighting on Guadalcanal and to explain his own defeat. It is doubtful if anyone believed him, so perhaps he felt a little smug when, on stepping ashore that night with General Hyakutake, the latter was informed that a few hours before the 4th Infantry had been slaughtered like sheep.

While disappointed in his plan to establish his forces beyond the Matanikau, Vandegrift had every intention of holding the right, or eastern, bank. Lack of men precluded a continuous line of defense, but enough were available to form a horseshoe, the right arc along the beach and the left some 2000 yards upriver.

Reports of enemy activity on the eastern side of the perimeter led to a landing of three companies of 1st Battalion, 2nd Marines from Tulagi at a point some 25 miles east of the perimeter. These companies attacked two villages, Gurabusu and Koilotumaria, on October 10. About thirty Japanese were killed and a large amount of supplies and radio equipment destroyed. An incident in this operation highlights the invaluable aid given throughout the whole Guadalcanal campaign by Clemens and his native police and scouts. When the American commander landed, he was met by Clemens who gave him a detailed account of the numbers and weapons of the enemy. Questioned by the skeptical commander about the accuracy of this estimate, Clemens informed him that it was an actual count, not an estimate! His natives had offered to help the Japanese unload their supplies and kept an accurate account as they did so. It is interesting to note that the American landing was reported by a Japanese watcher.

In the meantime, air raids kept Henderson's fighter pilots and maintenance crews busy. On October 11, a force of thirty-five bombers escorted by thirty fighters raided the field but did only minor damage. Eight of the bombers and four Zeros were destroyed. But, despite their losses, the raiders served a useful purpose. They kept the Cactus fliers from bothering the Japanese transports then on their way toward Guadalcanal.

VIII

"Bakayaro!"

THE BATTLE OF CAPE ESPERANCE

True to form, the engagement known as the Battle of Cape Esperance was brought on by the necessity for both Americans and Japanese to reinforce their troops on Guadalcanal. Both sides sent in covering forces—and the covering forces met.

The American reinforcement was the 164th Infantry Regiment of the Americal Division. It sailed on October 9 from Nouméa in a convoy consisting of *McCawley* (Kelly Turner's flagship), transport *Zeilin,* with three destroyers, and three DMLs (destroyer mine layers) as escort.

Providing cover were three groups. *Hornet* and her group, Rear Admiral George Murray commanding, was to patrol some 180 miles west of Henderson; *Washington* group, Rear Admiral Willis Lee, to take station about 50 miles east of Malaita; and a cruiser force, TF 64, commanded by Rear Admiral Norman Scott, was to cruise in the area near Rennel about 125 miles south of Guadalcanal.

Scott's orders were to "search for and destroy enemy ships and landing craft" and to carry out these instructions he had under his command two heavy cruisers, two light cruisers, and five destroyers.

At Rabaul plans had been made for transporting the bulk of Maruyama's Sendai Division down The Slot. Mikawa had repeatedly pointed out the difficulty of a major troop movement made under the noses of the American fliers at Henderson. His vessels always made the Express run at considerable peril, and bombings and strafings were all too common. He now asked the Commander of Eleventh Air Fleet, Vice-Admiral Jinichi Kusaka to attempt to neutralize the field. Kusaka agreed, and Mikawa ordered the Tokyo Express loaded and ready for a run which would bring it to the island about 2200 on October 11.

This reinforcement group, under command of

Rear Admiral Takaji Joshima, consisted of sea-plane carriers *Nisshin* and *Chitose*, and destroyers *Akitsukii, Asagumo, Natsugumo, Yamagumo, Mura-kumo,* and *Shirayuki*. Aboard were troops and equipment, a few pieces of artillery including four 150-mm howitzers, four tractors, medical supplies, and a half a dozen landing craft.

Admiral Scott had definite plans for a night action and had just put his command through three weeks' training in night tactics. His plan was a simple one—ships in column, with destroyers ahead and astern. The cruisers were to fire without waiting for orders and their float planes were to drop flares to illuminate the enemy.

For two days, October 9 and 10, Task Force 64 cruised about near Rennel. Scott's presence miles to the south did not interrupt the Japanese reinforcement, however, and on October 9, the Express—light cruiser *Tatsuta* and five destroyers—took in more troops, among them Hyakutake and his headquarter's staff.

Then on October 11, a B-17 of 11th Bombardment Group reported a force of cruisers and destroyers on their way down The Slot some 210 miles from Guadalcanal. Scott was alerted and at 1600 the American admiral ordered speed increased to 29 knots and headed for Guadalcanal. At 1810 another sighting placed the enemy just over a hundred miles from Savo and closing fast.

The approaching Japanese squadron was made up of three heavy cruisers and two destroyers, under the command of Rear Admiral Aritomo Goto, and was to bombard American positions while providing support for the Reinforcement Group. An Air Support Group built around light carriers *Junyo, Hiyo,* and *Zuiho*, under the aggressive Rear Admiral Kakuji Kakuta, had sailed from Truk on October 10 and was cruising well to the north and west of Guadalcanal.

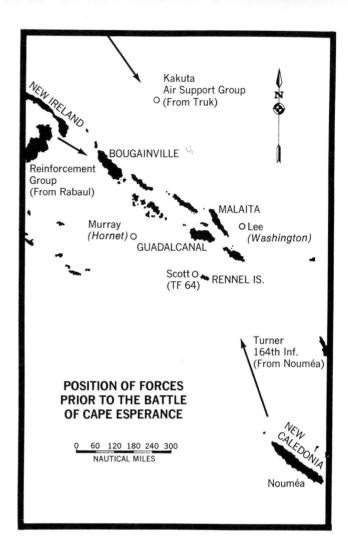

POSITION OF FORCES PRIOR TO THE BATTLE OF CAPE ESPERANCE

At sunset the American crews went to battle stations and Scott set course to take his force around the western end of Guadalcanal. At 2130, speed was reduced and preparations made to launch float planes. At Savo the nests of planes on board the cruisers had provided ready-made bonfires for the Japanese gunners. A lesson had been learned from that sad defeat and the cruisers of Scott's force had already sent their spare planes

JAPANESE FORCES

		Class	Tonnage	Speed	Armament	Launched
Aoba	(CA)	Aoba	9,000	34.5	6 8-in., 4 4.7-in., 8 24-in. TT	1926
Furutaka	(CA)	Furutaka	9,150	34.5	" " "	1925 °
Kinugasa	(CA)	Aoba	9,380	34.5	" " "	1926
Hatsuyuki	(DD)	Fubuki	2,090	34	6 5-in., 9 24-in. TT	1927
Fubuki	(DD)	Fubuki	"	"	" "	1927 °

° Sunk in the action

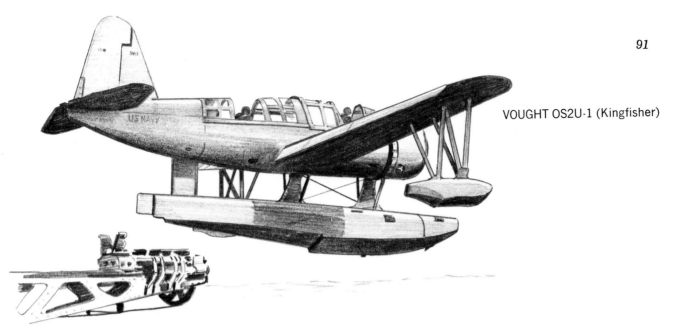

VOUGHT OS2U-1 (Kingfisher)

Two-Seat Observation and Scout Float Seaplane
Span 35'11" Length: 33'10" Height: 15'1½" Weight empty: 4123 lbs.
Max. speed: 164 mph at 5500 ft. Range: 800 miles at 130 mph Power: one 450-hp radial
Armament: one fixed forward-firing 0.3-in., one flexible 0.3-in., two 100-lb. bombs.

to Tulagi. The remaining four Kingfishers were now flying off the catapults. *San Francisco* and *Boise* got theirs off successfully, but *Salt Lake City*'s plane caught fire and crashed on takeoff—lighting the sky for miles—but fortunately not alerting the oncoming Japanese. *Helena* failed to receive the order to launch so jettisoned hers.

At 2228, Cape Esperance bore SE by E, distance 14 miles. Scott headed toward Savo and at 2235 formed his ships in single column, with a distance between cruisers of 600 yards, with 500 yards between the destroyers. *Farenholt*—flagship of Captain R. G. Tobin, ComDesron 12—was in the lead, followed by *Duncan* and *Laffey*. Then came *San Francisco*, Admiral Scott's flag, *Boise*, *Salt Lake City*, and *Helena*. Destroyers *Buchanan* and *McCalla* brought up the rear.

At 2250, *San Francisco*'s scout plane reported, "One large, two small vessels, one six miles from Savo off northern beach, Guadalcanal." These ships were part of Joshima's Reinforcement Group approaching their landing position. But Scott was after bigger game. He determined to attempt to intercept the larger force (now about 30 miles away) and at 2308 changed course to NE so as to pass west of Savo.

U. S. FORCES IN ORDER OF BATTLE

		Class	Tonnage	Speed	Armament	Launched
Farenholt	(DD)	Benson	1,620	37	4 5-in., 10 21-in. TT	1941
Duncan	(DD)	"	"	"	" "	1942 *
Laffey	(DD)	"	"	"	" "	1941
San Francisco	(CA)	Astoria	9,950	32.7	9 8-in., 8 5-in.	1933
Boise	(CL)	Brooklyn	10,000	34	15 6-in., 8 5-in.	1936
Salt Lake City	(CA)	Pensacola	9,100	32.7	10 8-in., 8 5-in.	1929
Helena	(CL)	Brooklyn	10,000	34	15 6-in., 8 5-in.	1938
Buchanan	(DD)	Benson	1,630	37	4 5-in., 10 21-in. TT.	1942
McCalla	(DD)	Benson	"	"	" "	1942

* Sunk in this action

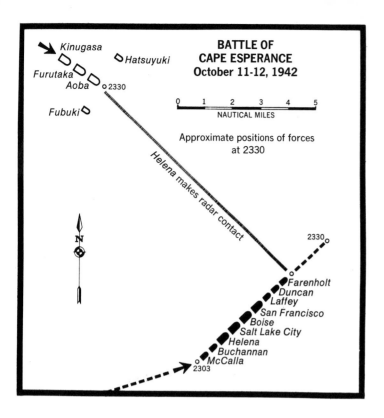

BATTLE OF CAPE ESPERANCE
October 11-12, 1942

Kinugasa
Hatsuyuki
Furutaka
Aoba ○ 2330
Fubuki ○

0 1 2 3 4 5
NAUTICAL MILES

Approximate positions of forces
at 2330

Helena makes radar contact

N

2330 ○
Farenholt
Duncan
Laffey
San Francisco
Boise
Salt Lake City
Helena
Buchannan
McCalla
2303

Helena, last cruiser in line, was equipped with the new and comparatively powerful SG radar, and at 2325 she got a "blip"—distance nearly 14 miles and bearing 315 degrees. *San Francisco* and *Salt Lake City* had the older SC apparatus and as it was known that the Japanese had receivers which could track the SC emissions, Scott had banned their use in his squadron. Unfortunately, perhaps because her captain was unsure of the validity of his sighting, no report of her contact was made by *Helena* to the flagship. *Boise*'s plane had come down with engine trouble and 'Frisco's plane was scouting the enemy force off Guadalcanal. At 2330 this plane reported the same vessels, this time further eastward.

Scott's decision to cover the area between Savo and Cape Esperance necessitated a reversal of course and at 2330 he ordered, "Left to course 230 degrees" over TBS. This called for the cruisers and the following destroyers to reverse course, the ships turning in succession. The lead destroyers would also turn but in a separate movement, then proceed at top speed down the flank of the main column, finally turning in to take their place in the van.

The lead destroyer was only halfway up the cruiser column (on the side from which the enemy could be expected) when *Helena*'s captain finally (2342) made up his mind that his contact was a genuine one, and informed Scott that a target was some 6 miles away, bearing 285°. *Boise* at this moment reported five "Bogies" (Bogies stood for unidentified aircraft, but it was understood that she actually meant ships) bearing 295°. Radar being what it was in those days it was possible that both contacts were Tobin's destroyers and Scott had to make sure. He called Tobin over TBS and was informed that the latter was proceeding up the column's starboard flank.

But only with two destroyers. As *Farenholt* swung wide to make her turn, *Duncan* picked up a contact on her radar screen. Thinking Tobin had seen them too, *Duncan*'s skipper headed for the contact, some 4 miles distant. *Laffey* followed *Farenholt*, closing her from astern.

By now the column was proceeding on its new course with *Farenholt* and *Laffey* some 800 yards to starboard and *Duncan* rapidly closing the enemy on her own. *San Francisco*'s gun control radar had picked up a target 5000 yards away, while *Helena*'s gunnery officer was becoming impatient. Perhaps because being uncertain of the exact whereabouts of Tobin's destroyers, *Helena*'s captain now asked (over TBS), "Interrogatory Roger" (permission to open fire). But in naval signal parlance, "Roger" could also mean "Message received." Some confusion with various "Rogers" ensued, with the end result that *Helena* took an answering "Roger" to mean "Go ahead" and at 2346 she opened fire with both 6-in. and 5-in. guns.

As luck would have it, the Japanese column, flagship *Aoba* in the lead, was approaching the American column at right angles. And the celebrated Japanese lookouts were not up to par that night, for the opening American salvos took them completely by surprise (all the more amazing as the same three cruisers had done the surprising at Savo a month before).

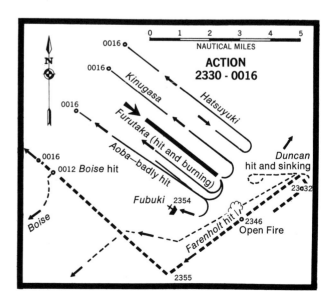

0 1 2 3 4 5
NAUTICAL MILES

ACTION
2330 - 0016

N

0016
0016
Kinugasa
Hatsuyuki
0016
Furutaka
Aoba—badly hit
Duncan
hit and sinking
0016
0012 *Boise* hit
Fubuki 2354
2332
2346
Open Fire
Boise
Farenholt hit
2355

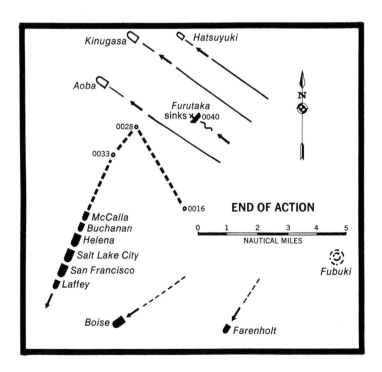

93

FURUTAKA CLASS HEAVY CRUISER (2 Ships)

Launched February, April 1925 Displacement: 9150 tons LOA: 602 feet Beam: 55½
Draft: 18½ feet 4 screws. 103,340 hp=34.5 knots Armor: belt 3 in., deck 2 in.,
turrets 5 in. Armament: six 8 in (3✕2), four 4.7 in. AA (4✕1), eight 25-mm. AA (4✕2),
four 13-mm. MGs., eight 24 in. torpedo tubes (2✕4) Aircraft: 2 Complement: 773

Firing was almost simultaneous. *Salt Lake City* loosed armor piercing shell and star shell a second after *Helena*—and a few seconds later received a hit from a Japanese cruiser in return. *San Francisco* and *Boise* let fly immediately, as did *Farenholt* and *Laffey*, while *Duncan,* only a mile from the enemy, also opened fire and maneuvered to bring her tubes to bear.

The undescribable confusion of a night action now led both commanders into error. Scott (who had never actually ordered "Commence firing" in the first place) was convinced that his ships were firing on his own destroyers, while Goto imagined that *his* cruisers were engaging Joshima's ships. One minute after *Helena* opened fire, Scott ordered, "Cease Firing." And at almost the same moment, Goto, whose flagship *Aoba* was the target for a hail of shells (from Japanese guns, he believed) ordered a 180° turn to the right (which would bring his ships momentarily even closer to the American line). A second later he was mortally wounded. It is said that as he lay dying in the wreckage of his bridge he muttered: *"Bakayaro! Bakayaro!"* ("Stupid bastards! Stupid bastards!")

The gunners on Scott's ships were not as convinced as he that they were firing on friendly vessels and it took repeated orders to bring the firing to a halt. Four precious minutes elapsed before Scott, after finally ordering his destroyers to flash on their recognition lights, gave the command to resume firing. The sudden lull in the shelling gave the startled Japanese a short breathing spell. It came just in time for *Aoba* had been badly hit and was on fire while *Furutaka* was blazing brightly.

As Scott's flagship reopened fire, her gunners made out a shape to the westward about 1500 yards away. A searchlight revealed a Japanese destroyer and in an instant she was blasted by every American vessel in range. It was *Fubuki* and in less than three minutes she went down, ripped by shellfire and torn apart by an explosion.

Up to now the Japanese fire had not been effective. *Duncan* had received severe damage, but her most grievous wounds had probably been inflicted by American shells. *Farenholt* had also been hit (also by both sides) while damage to the cruisers had been negligible. All five destroyers had been in action and at least one of their torpedoes hit *Furutaka*.

At 2355 Scott turned his column northwest, parallel to what was left of the Japanese line. *Furutaka* was a blazing, sinking wreck, *Aoba* badly hit and *Fubuki* on the bottom. *Kinugasa* had saved herself by turning left instead of right, as had *Hatsuyuki*. But there was fight in the Japanese yet.

At 2400 Scott ordered another brief cease-fire to give his ships a chance to regroup. At that moment the cruiser *Kinugasa* opened fire and torpedoes crossed the American line. *Boise* snapped on a searchlight to illuminate a vessel (probably *Aoba*) and was promptly hit by her target and by *Kinugasa*. Powder fires from a direct hit flashed through both forward handling rooms and turrets, and it was only water pouring in through shell holes in the American cruiser's hull that saved her

BROOKLYN CLASS LIGHT CRUISER (9 Ships)

Displacement: 9475–10,000 tons LOA: 608½ Beam: 61¾ Draft: 19½ feet
4 screws. 100,000 hp=34 knots
Armor: belt 1½–4 in., deck 3+2 in., turrets 3–5 in.
Armament: fifteen 6 in. (5×3), eight 5 in. (8×1)
Aircraft: four Complement: 1300

from a magazine explosion. That and the action of her next astern, *Salt Lake City,* whose captain deliberately interposed his ship between the battered light cruiser and the Japanese.

But the action was dying down. Scott's column had become disarranged during the pursuit by ships swinging out to avoid torpedoes and there was danger of the rear cruisers firing at those in the lead. At 0028, Scott changed course to SSW and the battle was over.

Farenholt, by shifting weights, brought her shell holes out of the water and managed to raise speed to 20 knots. *Duncan* was too badly damaged to salvage. Although valiant efforts were made to save her, her spreading fires could not be checked. Before noon the water was level with her main deck and she sank shortly afterward. *Furutaka* managed to stagger some 22 miles northwest before she too went down.

Aoba's hits (she had been struck at least forty times) had not injured her machinery, and she and *Kinugasa* left the area at top speed. A strike from Henderson Field sent in pursuit of the retreating Japanese fleet at 0700 failed to do any damage and both cruisers and *Hatsuyuki* were back at the Shortlands before noon. *Aoba* went home for repairs. The other two were ready for action next day.

While the two cruiser forces were engaged, Joshima's group were busy landing men and supplies near Kokumbona. Among other items were the four 150-mm guns, which were shortly to give the defenders of the airstrip a hard time. All ships were unloaded and on their way out of the sound by 0230. Rear Admiral Joshima could congratulate himself on a job well done, but Mikawa promptly relieved the officer who took over after Goto's death, Captain Kijima. Surprise in such circumstances was inexcusable and the fact that the primary object—the safe passage of the Reinforcement Group—was successfully accomplished did not balance against the loss of two ships and another damaged and out of the war for months.

In the early morning of October 12, destroyers *Shirayuki* and *Murakumo,* which had been attached to the Reinforcement Group, returned to search for survivors. They were attacked at first light by sixteen SBDs with fighter escort north of the Russells and damaged. About 0830, a strike of six SBDs and six TBFs from Henderson found the pair up The Slot 170 miles from the field. A torpedo hit left *Murakumo* dead in the water and later in the afternoon a second mixed strike sank another relief destroyer, *Natsugumo.* Some Japanese survivors of the battle were picked up (forcibly, as the majority preferred drowning to surrender) by *McCalla* on the 12th and more by minesweepers *Trever* and *Hovey* on the 13th.

The Japanese force at Guadalcanal had been reinforced, but at a very high price.

IX

The Sendai Division Is Expendable

THE SECOND MAJOR JAPANESE ASSAULT

American naval reinforcements for the Marines on the island arrived on October 12, with four PT boats towed in behind *Southard* and *Hovey*. Their arrival marked the small beginning of an effort to deny the Japanese undisputed use of the waters off Guadalcanal by night.

A major boost for the fighting strength of the Marines came on October 13. On that day Admiral Turner brought in the 164th Infantry, Colonel Bryant Moore commanding—2852 men with all their equipment. This included forty-four jeeps, twenty ½-ton trucks, seventeen 1½-ton trucks, sixteen British bren gun carriers, twelve 37-mm guns, five units of fire, seventy days' rations, sixty days' supplies, tentage, and a large quantity of supplies for 1st Marine Division. Also landed were 210 ground personnel of 1st Marine Air Wing. Hardly had the first American soldiers to reach

Guadalcanal cleared the beach before they were under fire. Up north, coastwatchers Read and Mason were on the run, and for some reason, Henderson Field's recently installed radar was temporarily out of commission. As a result some two dozen Bettys, escorted by Zeros, hit both Henderson and a new strip some 2000 yards to the east named "Fighter One" without warning. Fighters tried frantically to take off and gain altitude but much damage was done—parked planes destroyed, the runways torn up and 5000 gallons of precious fuel went up in smoke and flame. A second raid later in the day caught many planes refueling and more aircraft were damaged. Only one American scored that day, a newly arrived Marine captain by the name of Joe Foss, who was to pile up an impressive total before the campaign was over.

Worse was to follow. The dust had hardly

JAPANESE MODEL 4 (1915) 150-mm. HOWITZER

Maximum range: 10,464 yards Weight of shell: about 79 lbs., depending on type
Rate of fire: max. 3–4 rpm.; continuous: 30–40 rph
Weight of gun: 9108 lbs. Length over-all: 22 feet Normal crew: 8
(Standard medium artillery piece until 1936. Very light in relation to weight of shell.
Broken into two pieces—tube and cradle—for travel.)

cleared after the second raid before a new sound was heard, the tearing screech of an incoming shell. Hyakutake's 150-mm howitzers had arrived in action. With a range of 12,000 yards these weapons could lob a heavy shell onto Henderson from the other side of the Matanikau, and though the air raids were bad while they lasted, they didn't last very long, but the shelling was an around-the-clock affair. The Marines, who were to become all too familiar with these pieces in the days to come, lumped them together under the nickname Pistol Pete. The Japanese weapons outweighed the Marines' 105s and were almost impossible to locate. They were to provide an added source of annoyance and injury and were both feared and hated.

But larger projectiles were on their way toward Henderson Field. By nightfall, Turner's vessels were safely heading south (taking with them the remnants of 1st Raider Battalion) but coming down from the north was the heaviest armada the Japanese had sent against the island. This was Vice-Admiral Takeo Kurita's Combat Division 3—the old, but powerful, 31,000 ton battleships *Kongo* and *Haruna*, each armed with eight 14-in. guns, light cruiser *Isuzu* and accompanying destroyers. Their mission was to blast Henderson Field and every plane on it. The great guns of the battleships were to fire new bombardment ammunition, Type Zero, which burst with a firecracker-like shrapnel effect. And there were over sixty rounds for each gun.

The Division encountered neither ships nor planes. Just west of Savo speed was reduced and as airplane flares burst greenish-white over Henderson, sixteen 14-in. guns roared as one. Some 17,000 yards away, veteran Marines and newly arrived "doggies" cowered in their foxholes and slit trenches as shell after shell roared in. The field was an inferno of exploding ammunition and fuel dumps. Splintered palms, vehicles, and shattered planes were flung about like playthings as some nine hundred huge projectiles smashed into the area. For 90 minutes the show went on, in Tanaka's words ". . . making the Ryoguko fireworks display seem like mere child's play." Six-inch shells from the battleships' secondary armament, 5.5s from the cruiser and 5-inchers from the destroyers added to the din and destruction. The few coastal defense guns ashore tried valiantly to retaliate, but momentary glares of gunfire on the horizon were their only targets and they scored no hits. As the Japanese withdrew, the four PTs cleared their anchorage at Tulagi and engaged the destroyer screen with torpedoes and automatic weapons. They claimed hits (everyone claims non-existent hits in a night action) but the Jap DDs brushed them aside with closely placed salvos of 5-inchers. Untouched, the Japanese steamed north leaving a lurid glow behind them that could be seen many miles away.

Nor did they have to fear air attacks next day by planes of the Cactus Air Force. In the morning only a half dozen bombers and some thirty-five

KONGO CLASS BATTLESHIP (4 Ships)

| 0 FEET | 100 | 200 | 300 | 400 | 500 | 600 | 700 723 |

Launched May 1912–December 1913 (Extensively remodeled 1930 and 1936)
Displacement: 31,720–31,980 tons LOA: 729½ Beam: 95¼ Draft: 32 feet 4 screws.
136,000 hp=30½ knots Armor: belt 8 in. amidship, ends 3 in., deck 2¾ in.,
turrets 9 in. Armament: eight 14 in. (4×2), sixteen 6 in. (16×1), eight 5 in. AA, twenty
25-mm. AA
Aircraft: three Complement: 1437
(Originally built as battle-cruisers. After remodeling classed as fast battleships.)

fighters could be made operational out of ninety. The field was a shambles. Miraculously only forty-one were dead, although there were many wounded. The runways were cratered, strips of steel runway matting had been hurled hundreds of yards and sixteen Wildcats had been reduced to wreckage.

Henderson was temporarily out of action but "Fighter One" had not been hit as badly and was still usable. Though dazed and shaken, mechanics and repairmen set to work to salvage what they could from the ruins. Harried by two more air raids on the 14th and by interdictory fire from Pistol Pete they managed to get enough planes in the air to make a strike at a big run of the Express —six transports escorted by destroyers, with Zeros flying cover. Four SBDs and seven P-400s armed with bombs made the strike and slightly damaged destroyer *Samidare*, but she kept coming south and so did the others. Close cover for the convoy came along that night in the shape of *Chokai* and *Kinugasa* (none the worse for her last visit 48 hours earlier). Together the two heavies pumped 752 8-in. shells into the Marine positions before turning for home. The six transports, carrying two battalions of the 230th Infantry of the 38th Division and part of Sendai's 16th Infantry and their equipment, stayed to unload, guarded by destroyers. The Guadalcanal battle fleet of four PT boats were unable to attack. One boat had been damaged by running aground, another was out of torpedoes and the other two were on convoy duty between Guadalcanal and Tulagi.

Confident that the pounding of the airfields had drawn the sting of Cactus Air Force, the Japanese did not trouble to leave before dawn. Morning light revealed the embarrassing sight of Japanese

transports calmly unloading off Tassafaronga as if there were no enemy within a hundred miles while destroyers churned the waters of the sound and planes patrolled overhead.

Cactus Air Force made a supreme effort. Supplies of gas were almost exhausted but by rooting out every drum of fuel and even draining the tanks of unserviceable planes, enough was procured to send everything that would fly (and it wasn't much) aloft. It was only a 10-mile hop from the fields to Tassafaronga and Cactus ran a sort of shuttle service—gas up, bomb or strafe the convoy, back to the field and gas up again. The service soon got results. Repeated attacks by SBDs and

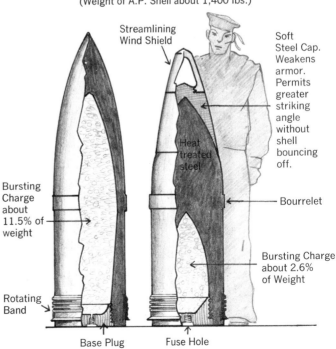

14 in. BOMBARDMENT PROJECTILE (Left) and ARMOR PIERCING PROJECTILE

(Weight of A.P. Shell about 1,400 lbs.)

Streamlining Wind Shield

Soft Steel Cap. Weakens armor. Permits greater striking angle without shell bouncing off.

Heat treated steel

Bursting Charge about 11.5% of weight

Bourrelet

Bursting Charge about 2.6% of Weight

Rotating Band

Base Plug   Fuse Hole

DOUGLAS C-47 PASSENGER AND FREIGHT TRANSPORT

**Span: 95 feet Length: 64 feet, 5½ in. Height: 16 ft. 11 in. Weight empty: 16,976 lbs.
Max. speed: 230 mph at 8800 ft. Range: 1350 miles Power: two 1200 hp
Pratt & Whitney Twin Wasp radials Crew: 4 Armament: None**

strafing and bombing runs by Army P-400s and P-39s set three of the transports alight and they were promptly beached. Most of the troops were already ashore but some equipment was lost. Planes strafing the beach destroyed part of the supplies laboriously landed during the night but not yet carried inland. Ammunition dumps exploded and gasoline stores blazed—a small repayment for The Bombardment (the shelling of October 13–14 was afterward always referred to as The Bombardment). The other transports were damaged but sailed in midafternoon after landing much of their cargo.

It had been a wild day. While Japanese planes bombed the fields and fighters tangled overhead, C-47s from Espiritu Santo roared in with drums of aviation fuel and maintenance crews sweated to unload them, transferring their cargoes to the empty tanks of the returning Cactus fliers. At intervals Pistol Pete added his share of destruction. Over the convoy more fighters milled around while SBDs and B-17s from Espiritu Santo tried to plant their bombs on the juicy targets below. Even a PBY, Geiger's personal plane, *Blue Goose*, piloted by his aide, Major Jack Cram, braved AA fire from several destroyers to attack the transports with a pair of borrowed torpedoes. (Cram managed to hit a beached transport with one of them—collecting some fifty bullet holes in the general's plane, and a Navy Cross.)

It was a noisy night, too, for toward midnight heavy cruisers *Maya* and *Myoko* rained some 1500 8-in. shells down on the field and perimeter defenses. Results—more casualties, more dumps set ablaze, more holes in the runways and fifteen Wildcats demolished.

The buildup of Japanese forces on Guadalcanal had proceeded steadily and by mid-October there were on the island an estimated 20,000 men. These included the 2nd Sendai Division (mustering 9372 men on October 19), two battalions of the 38th Division, one regiment and three batteries of heavy artillery, one battalion and a battery of mountain artillery, a mortar battalion, a tank company (some sixteen vehicles) and three rapid-fire gun battalions. According to Colonel Taguchi, Operations Officer of 2nd Division, since the beginning of the campaign some 176 artillery pieces of all calibers had been landed. (Some of these had been lost or destroyed—i.e. those lost by Kawaguchi.) Also included in the grand total were the survivors of the original garrison, plus the remains

**Maximum range: 3000 yards Effective range: 1500 yards
Weight of Shell (HE): 8.36 lbs. Rate of fire: 10 rpm
Weight of gun: 468 lbs. Length of gun: 87 in.
Crew: five
Normally horse-drawn,
but can be handled
by ten-man section**

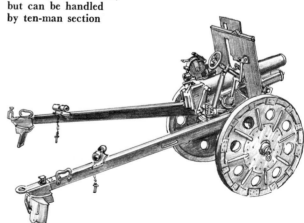

JAPANESE MODEL 92 (1932) 70-mm. HOWITZER

of Ichiki's and Kawaguchi's commands. The climate, exhaustion, and malnutrition had reduced the efficiency of the earlier arrivals (as was also true of General Vandegrift's forces). However, morale was high among the newly arrived units and the troops were in good health and well equipped. The massing of such a force showed that at last GHQ was realizing that the American forces could not be brushed aside as easily as had been anticipated. On the other hand, Hyakutake's decision to leave the bulk of the 38th Division at Rabaul and his refusal to learn from the mistakes of Kawaguchi (that the jungle and the terrain almost certainly doomed any efforts at a concerted attack by units forced to march over great distances and committed to battle too far apart to be of mutual assistance) revealed both the weakness of the Japanese intelligence work and the inflexibility and arrogance of the typical Japanese commander.

October 22 had been set by Maruyama as the date for the capture of the airfield (which the Americans had named Henderson Field in honor of Major Loften Henderson, a Marine flier who had been killed at Midway). A 2nd Division Order, No. 174, gave detailed instructions for the handling of the surrender, and even specified the spot where the defeated American commander should sign the surrender terms. When that had been accomplished—and not until then—the powerful naval forces of Combined Fleet would move in to repulse any American attempt to reinforce the island, remove the remnants of the garrison, or retake the all-important field. The code word to be broadcast when the field was taken was Banzai and its receipt was eagerly, and confidently, awaited in Rabaul.

To accomplish this, two fleets, Second Fleet and Third Fleet, both under the command of Vice-Admiral Kondo, had sortied from Truk on October 11 and were waiting north of the Solomons for news of the successful attack. Admiral Yamamoto still lay at Truk in his mighty flagship *Yamato* but his forces under Kondo numbered four battleships, five carriers, ten cruisers, and twenty-nine destroyers. In the Shortlands was Admiral Mikawa in *Chokai* and Rear Admiral Tamotsu Takama with *Yura* and nine destroyers. There were also at Yamamoto's disposal twelve submarines and four oilers, a destroyer and cruiser and some 220 land based planes of Kusaka's Eleventh Air Fleet.

On October 15, a scout plane from one of Nagumo's carriers reported sighting a cruiser, two

destroyers, and two transports a hundred miles south of Guadalcanal, heading for the island. The vessels sighted were actually a group consisting of transports *Alchiba* and *Bellatrix*, PT tender *Jamestown* and fleet tug *Vireo* escorted by destroyers *Nicholas* and *Meredith*. These had been dispatched to Guadalcanal with gasoline and ammunition—doubly precious since the destruction of bombardment night—and the first four vessels each towed a barge carrying barrels of gas and five hundred 250-lb. bombs.

The sight of an enemy carrier plane overhead gave promise of an early attack, and the two transports and *Jamestown*, escorted by *Nicholas*, were ordered back to Espiritu Santo. *Vireo* took *Bellatrix's* tow and the tug and *Meredith* held course for Guadalcanal. At 1050 they beat off a two-plane attack, but it was then reported that enemy surface vessels were close by and the two vessels headed back. *Vireo*, a converted minesweeper of the Bird Class, vintage of 1919, was too slow to clear the area and *Meredith* ordered her abandoned and prepared to sink her. *Vireo's* crew had hardly reached *Meredith* when a twenty-seven-plane strike from *Zuikaku* roared in and a hail of bombs and torpedoes sent *Meredith* to the bottom. In a matter of a few minutes the swarm from *Zuikaku* were on their way back to the carrier leaving the sea dotted with survivors struggling in a swirl of oil and wreckage. *Vireo* had been untouched and a few survivors managed to scramble aboard as she drifted off. The others, many of them desperately injured, spent a nightmarish three days and nights clinging to rafts before being rescued. As men on the floats died, others in the water took their places. Schools of sharks added to the horror—one monster flinging itself onto a raft to attack a wounded man. One hundred and eighty-five of *Meredith's* men and fifty-one from *Vireo* were lost. *Vireo* and the two barges were salvaged. The enemy spent most of his fury on *Meredith*. A minor attack on the retiring convoy slightly damaged *Bellatrix* and all four ships made Espiritu Santo.

On October 16, seaplane tender *McFarland*, loaded with ammunition and gasoline had just delivered most of her cargo at Guadalcanal and taken aboard some 160 hospital patients, half of them classed as war neurotics. A gasoline barge was still alongside receiving fuel when nine Japanese dive bombers swooped down on her. The barge was cast off and the old ship began to move, her AA guns stuttering into action. As one "Val" splashed into the sea, a bomb hit the barge and 20,000 gal-

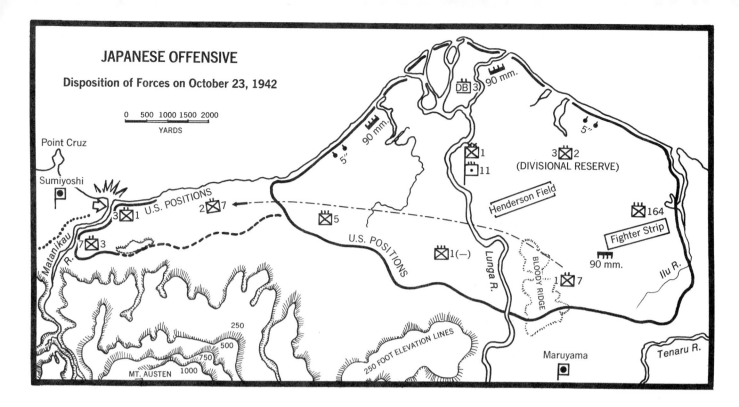

JAPANESE OFFENSIVE

Disposition of Forces on October 23, 1942

lons of high octane gas exploded. A few seconds later another hit *McFarland's* depth charge racks, blowing off part of her stern. To add to the uproar many of the neurotics panicked, hampering the crew's efforts to save their ship. But save her they did. Steering by means of her damaged engines, she made 5 knots to Tulagi and arrived there safely although leaking and minus her rudder, and with twenty-seven men killed and twenty-eight wounded. Her captain, Lieutenant Commander John Alderman, took her into a river mouth on Florida Island, camouflaging her with vines and bushes. By using bits of steel from the former Japanese seaplane base for temporary repairs and rigging a jury rudder from some wooden poles, she was able to sail on November 27 for Espiritu Santo.

On Guadalcanal there was increasing evidence of a major Japanese offensive in the making. At the mouth of the Matanikau, Marines of 3rd Battalion, 1st, noticed considerable enemy activity. On October 20, a Japanese combat patrol headed by two tanks probed the Marine defenses but were driven back into the jungle on the west bank when one tank was knocked out by a 37-mm antitank gun. Sporadic mortar and artillery fire came into the Marine positions during the next 24 hours and at sunset on October 21, nine tanks, supported by infantry, again rolled out of the jungle and headed east for the sandspit. Again one tank was hit and the attack turned back.

The force gathered on the western bank of the Matanikau was led by General Tadashi Sumiyoshi, commander of Seventeenth Army's artillery. It consisted of two battalions of 4th Infantry, a tank company, seven light field guns, three 100-mm guns, and fifteen 150-mm howitzers—some 2900 men. He was to shell the perimeter and then launch a diversionary attack across the river. While Sumiyoshi moved his men and guns into position, Maruyama was leading his troops, eight or nine infantry battalions (about 5600 men), artillery and supporting troops over the narrow and tortuous trail cut by his engineers from near Tassafaronga through the jungle to the assembly area well south of Henderson Field. The jungle did one thing—it concealed the trail from American air observation. But it also slowed Maruyama's march to a crawl and forced him twice to postpone his attack by 24 hours. The Japanese soldier was tough, but the Maruyama Trail was almost too much for him. Troops already weakened on half-rations of rice each had to carry a mortar or artillery shell as well as their heavy loads of combat equipment. It rained hard almost every day and the weary soldiers were forced to manhandle artillery, heavy machine guns and mortars up rugged ridges and into deep valleys, slipping and sliding in the slimy muck on slopes so steep that ropes had to be used.

The narrow trail became hopelessly congested and was soon littered with abandoned equipment, including most of the artillery pieces and mortars. Worse, it was evident that with the attack already delayed, the exhausted troops would have little respite at the end of their ordeal before being committed to battle.

The map shows the general position of the assaulting and defending troops. The attacks had been planned as a coordinated effort but in the event, due to poor communications and almost non-existent intelligence and patrol work, were delivered at widely spaced intervals.

The first attack to go sour was that of Sumiyoshi on the western side of the perimeter. The general was down with malaria (which may have partly accounted for the foul-up) but in retrospect it would appear to be a Japanese version of "someone forgot to pass the word." In any case, though Maruyama had again postponed his attack (from the original date of October 22, to 23, and then to 24) Sumiyoshi made his push on the 23rd, afterward claiming that he had moved ahead of time to divert American defense measures. About 1800 on October 23, the desultory mortar and artillery fire on 3rd Battalion, 1st Marines' position quickened in tempo and at dusk nine 18-ton tanks roared across the sandspit. Armor piercing projectiles from Marine 37-mm guns streaked white hot into their targets and a momentary glow showed where each struck armor. The hardened steel hail

brought eight of the charging vehicles to a halt. One rumbled on across the spit. As it narrowly missed a foxhole, a Marine chucked a grenade into its track. Swerving out of control it churned into the surf and stalled, to be finished off by shells from a half-tracked 75-mm.

A battalion of the 4th Infantry was massed in the area near the spit. As they advanced to the river they were held by rifle and automatic weapon's fire while a heavy barrage was poured into them from Marine mortars and nine batteries of artillery. The range was known by the American gunners, and each battery was assigned a narrow strip of riverfront which it covered by "laddering" (i.e. increasing or decreasing the range). The result of this systematic slaughter, as observed later, showed several hundred bodies and the wreckage of three more tanks. This finished Sumiyoshi's assault (and the 4th Infantry) and apart from a feeble attempt, easily beaten off, to cross the river higher up, the action on the western side was over.

Sumiyoshi's premature attack did have the effect of causing the Marine commander to strengthen that sector. (It must be remembered that no patrols had contacted any enemy to the south or east and it could not be assumed that the main drive was not still to come from the west.) So 2nd Battalion, 1st Marines were pulled out of the southern line and moved to support 3rd

Length: 14 ft. 4 in. Height: 7 ft. Width: 6 ft. 9 in. Weight: 10 tons (laden)
Speed: 28 mph Range: 100 miles
Armament: one 37-mm. gun, one 7.7-mm. MG. rear, one 7.7 MG. in hull
Armor: .47 in. to .24 in. (vulnerable to 75 or 105-mm. H.E. shell)
Crew: three

JAPANESE MODEL 95 (1935) LIGHT TANK

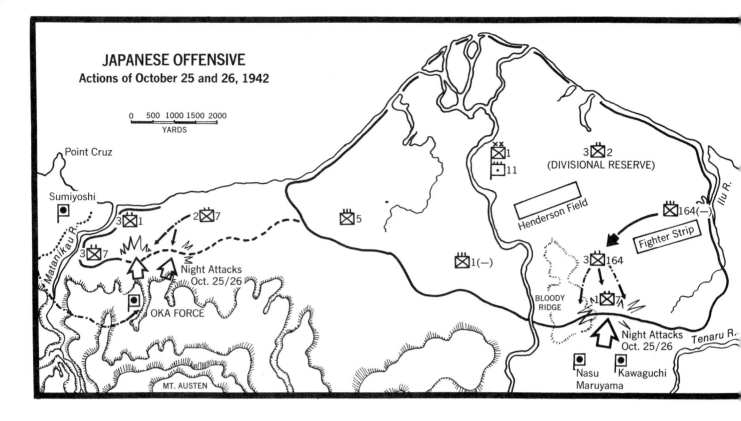

JAPANESE OFFENSIVE
Actions of October 25 and 26, 1942

Battalion, 1st at the mouth of the Matanikau. This left Puller's 1st Battalion, 7th to cover 2500 yards of front. And it was here that Maruyama struck.

In late afternoon of October 24, a Japanese officer was observed south of the perimeter, studying Bloody Ridge through his binoculars. This and the report of a patrol that they had seen the smoke of cook fires in the Lunga Valley a couple of miles south of the ridge was the first indication of a possible Japanese threat from that direction.

The Southern assault, Maruyama's main effort, was to be made in two columns, Major General Yumio Nasu, leading the left or western attack, and Kawaguchi the right. (The right attack was actually commanded by a colonel, Toshinari Shoji. General Kawaguchi had pressed for an attack further to the east of the ill-fated ridge and had been relieved by Maruyama.)

The night of October 24 was pitch black and very wet (a fact which was to hinder both Japanese coordination and physical progress). About 2130 there was a sharp exchange of fire as the Japanese advance engulfed a forty-six-man outpost some distance south of Puller's wire. The advance was reported by the patrol leader of the outpost (he and most of his men finally made their way into the American lines after varying adventures) and

the Marines on the main line of resistance peered through the rain for a glimpse of the enemy. An hour went by, and another—then at 0030, October 25, Nasu's battalions attacked in force on a narrow front, surging out of the jungle and onto the slippery slopes of the ridge. Mortar and artillery fire was called in, and the shouting crowds of Japanese were cut down by rifle and machine-gun fire both from the Leathernecks in the front and from 2nd Battalion, 164th Infantry Regiment on the Marines' left. (The advancing men of the 29th Infantry may have noticed that the rifle fire pouring in from the right of their attack was of unusual intensity. The Army's 164th Infantry were armed with the new 8-shot semiautomatic Garand.) After some 15 minutes the waves of attackers ebbed back into the jungle, only to sweep out again and again. In the darkness and confusion small lodgments were made by fanatical swarms of grenade-throwing Japanese. The positions were always promptly restored but not without some bitter hand-to-hand fighting. Units of 3rd Battalion, 164th Infantry began to move in and were committed as they came up, fed into the Marine line wherever they were needed most.

By early morning the Japanese attacks had begun to slacken through sheer lack of manpower. The 29th Infantry Regiment had suffered heavy casualties (nearly one thousand dead lay in front of Puller's position), and at dawn Maruyama called off the attack to give his units time to regroup. Nasu's men had made the attack without help from the eastern column. Shoji had mistaken his route in the rain and darkness and his command had come up in rear of 29th Infantry instead of on their right flank. It was an unfortunate blunder for the Japanese and robbed the assault of half its punch. The first great attack had been beaten back, leaving the ground in front of the American positions strewn with dead and wounded and accomplishing nothing.

Somehow in the uproar, word was passed to Maruyama that the field had been taken. (A Japanese source has stated that a scout pilot thought he saw the prearranged signal of green-white-green flares. There must have been a good many flares soaring aloft that night so perhaps his mistake is understandable.) In any case, without troubling to confirm the report, Maruyama relayed the good news to Hyakutake's HQ and from there the signal "Banzai! Occupied field at 2300" went out to Rabaul. Signal lamps flashed from Mikawa's flagship and a force of destroyers led by Takama, with light cruiser *Yura* headed for Guadalcanal. The message was also received aboard *Yamato* and aboard the flagships of Combined Fleet. It was not until after daybreak that word was sent by Yamamoto's naval liaison officer on Guadalcanal that the Marines still held the vital field.

October 25 was known afterward as Dugout Sunday, and with some reason. The rains of the preceding days had turned the airfields into a morass and it was not until nearly noon that planes could get off Fighter One. Japanese bombers from Rabaul made two raids and Zeros were overhead often enough to keep the area in an almost continuous Condition Red alert, while Pistol Pete fired at

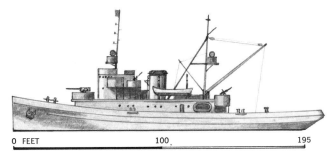

U.S.S. SEMINOLE—Fleet Tug

Displacement: 1235 tons LOA: 205 Beam: 38½
Draft: 15¼ feet Single screw.
Diesel-electric 3000 hp=16 knots
Armament: one 3 in., four 40-mm. AA
Complement: eighty-five

intervals. Early in the morning, three destroyers, *Akatsuki, Ikazuchi,* and *Shiratsuyu* of Takama's squadron steamed into the sound. There they sighted (1000) two destroyer-minesweepers, *Trever* and *Zane* which had arrived earlier at Tulagi, each towing two PT boats, and which had unloaded torpedoes, ammunition, and gasoline. The two destroyer-minesweepers tried to get away through Sealark Channel, but the faster Japanese vessels, making good practice with their batteries of 5-inch guns, would have undoubtedly sent both the old four-stackers to the bottom in short order. In the emergency, *Trever's* Lieutenant Commander Agnew, the senior commander, decided to attempt to escape via the reef-studded passage of Nggela Channel. At the same time, three Wildcats, which had managed to churn their way off water-logged Fighter One started strafing runs on the Japanese destroyers. The attack caused the enemy destroyers to turn back toward Guadalcanal but the minesweepers' reprieve doomed two other American vessels. Tug *Seminole* and YP 284, on a ferry run from Tulagi to Lunga Point, were caught off the beach and sunk, their cargoes of gasoline blazing. The destroyers then proceeded to bombard

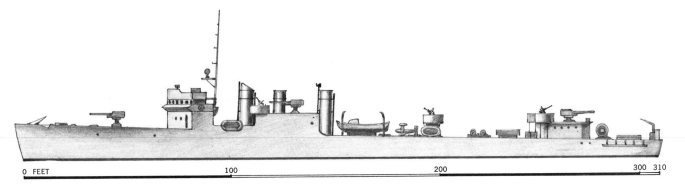

HIGH SPEED MINESWEEPER (DMS)

Converted "Flush Deck" Destroyers
Launched 1918–1921. Converted 1940–1942
Displacement: 1060–1090 tons LOA: 314½ Beam: 31½ Draft: 11½ feet
Twin screw. 26,000 hp=32.5 knots
Armament: four 3 in. plus light AAs Complement: 140

Marine positions ashore; but this was what the 5-inch gun crews of 3rd Defense Battalion were being paid for. They hit *Akatsuki* at least once and the three destroyers then withdrew behind a smoke-screen.

By noon the fields had dried sufficiently for planes to take off and at 1255 a strike was made on *Yura* and the bombardment group. A hit in an engine room slowed the cruiser down and another bomb damaged *Akitsukii*. The force turned north and toward sunset, *Yura*'s captain received permission to beach her on a small island off Santa Isabel's northern coast. A final attack at 1700 by SBDs and B-17s set her afire from stem to stern, and she was ordered sunk by torpedoes from *Harusame* and *Yudachi*.

An offset to this reverse was the loss on the same day of the large U. S. Army transport *President Coolidge* carrying the 172nd Regiment, 43rd Infantry Division, destined for Guadalcanal. Despite frantic warnings from shore stations and patrol boats her merchant marine skipper managed to run her into a protective minefield at Espiritu Santo. Although only two lives were lost she carried to the bottom all the regiment's equipment, weapons, artillery, and vehicles.

Although their takeoffs had been delayed by the condition of the runways, Cactus Air Force fliers more than made up for it. By the end of the day, twenty-two enemy planes had been brought down, four of them by Captain Foss. AA fire had downed five more and only three American planes were lost with all of the pilots safe. So with a score of two destroyers damaged, a cruiser sunk, and twenty-seven Jap planes downed, Cactus Air Force's Dugout Sunday ended a lot better than it had begun.

On the perimeter, Marines spent the day consolidating their positions and preparing for whatever the night might bring. When the expected attacks came they were a repetition of those of the previous night. Once again company after company charged the Marine lines and again they were met with intense artillery and mortar fire and a leaden hail from rifles and machine guns. Where the positions of the 164th Infantry joined those of 7th Marines four 37-mm guns blasted the oncoming Japanese with round after round of canister.

The attacks continued until the early hours of October 26 and succeeded only in adding to the slaughter of the night before. The Sendai Division was wrecked, with half its officers killed or wounded. Major General Nasu was dead, killed leading a charge, as was Colonel Hirayasu (16th Infantry). Over a thousand of the 29th Infantry lay dead or wounded and their Colonel Furumiya with the regimental colors, was missing (he would later be found dead with the shredded colors beneath him).

On October 24, an enemy force had been seen moving eastward across the low hills at the foot of Mount Austen. This was Colonel Oka's detachment, two battalions of his 124th Infantry and one of 4th Infantry. To counter this threat 2nd Battalion, 7th Regiment had been moved into position partially covering the 4000-yard gap between the Matanikau positions and those on the Lunga. These thinly held positions were subjected to artillery fire from the Kokumbona area during daylight hours of the 25th and at 2130 several strong attacks were made in battalion strength. These were at first beaten back with heavy losses but at 0300 some 150 Japanese succeeded in establishing themselves in some Marine foxholes and machine-gun emplacements. Gathering a scratch force of riflemen, runners, signalmen, headquarters and service personnel, messmen and a cook, Major Odell Conoley, executive officer of 2nd Battalion, 7th Regiment successfully counterattacked with grenades, while a heavy mortar barrage cut the enemy off from reinforcements from the jungle below.

With the defeat of Oka's men, the third Japanese effort to drive the Marines off Guadalcanal and retake the airfield had failed. An estimated 3500 dead lay in and around the Marine positions and in the surrounding jungle. The survivors made their weary way back to Tassafaronga or east to Taivu. As before, supplies gave out and starving men ate tree bark, or roots, or chewed their rifle slings.

Each drive had been made in increasing strength —first Ichiki's Battalion—then Kawaguchi's Brigade, then Maruyama's Division. At all levels the Japanese High Command had underestimated their enemy and as each day went by, the toll of Japanese shipping, planes, and men mounted—and the Stars and Stripes still flew over Henderson Field.

X
Too Many Meat Balls

THE BATTLE OF SANTA CRUZ

The carrier battle known as the Battle of Santa Cruz was tied in strategically with the Japanese offensive on Guadalcanal. Hyakutake's attack on the field was spurred on by Yamamoto's threat to withdraw his naval forces under Kondo (which had been cruising impatiently in the waters to the north of the Solomons for two weeks), unless the Army showed some immediate results. The confusion following the premature announcement of the field's capture only added to Kondo's dilemma. For while it was known that an enemy force was operating north of Nouméa, and sightings of a battleship and heavy cruisers indicated that this force most probably included at least one carrier, no sightings of a carrier had been made. And until the enemy flattops had been located, Kondo was reluctant to move southward.

The American team was now under new management. Despite Marine successes on Guadalcanal the over-all situation in the Solomons area remained tense and it was evident that the island could only be held if the most determined efforts were made to reinforce it, even at the risk of a succession of naval engagements. At the outset of the campaign, Ghormley had been thrust into what must have seemed to him an impossible situation—called on to launch an invasion with inadequate forces and to supply and reinforce his beachhead with non-existent troops, ferried in non-existent transports, and covered with a non-existent air force. That much had been accomplished was due in great part to his efforts, but Nimitz felt that now a more determined approach was needed under a more aggressive commander. He therefore, on October 18, relieved Ghormley and appointed Vice-Admiral William F. Halsey in his place.

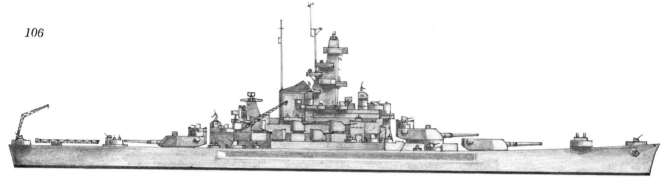

SOUTH DAKOTA CLASS BATTLESHIP

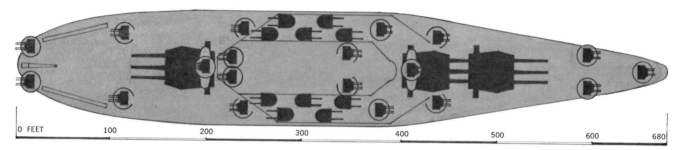

| 0 FEET | 100 | 200 | 300 | 400 | 500 | 600 | 680 |

Above: (4 ships launched between June 1941–February 1942)
Displacement: 35,000 tons LOA: 680 ft. Beam: 108¼ ft.
Draft: 29¼ ft. 130,000 hp=28 knots
Armor: belt 18 in., turrets 18 in. Complement: 2500
Armament South Dakota Class: nine 16-in. guns; twenty

5-in. dual purpose (South Dakota sixteen 5-in. DP); sixty
40-mm. (varied in different ships), numerous 20-mm. The
deck view shows typical arrangement of 40-mm. quad
mounts

The first thing that Halsey did on taking over was to call a conference of his commanders at Nouméa. He was impressed by Vandegrift's steady assurance that his men could hold if given active and adequate support. This Halsey promised, and it was in keeping with this promise that he ordered Rear Admiral Thomas C. Kinkaid, who had led the *Enterprise* group at the Battle of the Eastern Solomons, to take command of a sizable force for operations in the area northeast of Guadalcanal.

On October 24, *Enterprise* rejoined the fleet, the damage received in the action of August 24–25 repaired. With her was battleship *South Dakota*, also returning to the war after an unfortunate encounter with an uncharted chunk of coral near Tongatabu. While at Pearl Harbor the antiaircraft armament of both vessels had been augmented by the addition of numerous Bofors 40-mm. guns. These fine weapons, usually mounted in quadruple mounts, were capable of spitting out explosive shells at the rate of 160 rounds per minute to a maximum distance of 5000 yards. *South Dakota* carried sixty-eight of them, and *Enterprise*, forty. Numerous 20-mm. guns were also mounted in odd corners and these, with their high rate of fire (450 rounds per minute) added greatly to the fleet's antiaircraft capability.

These two ships, with two cruisers and eight

Below: Range: max. about 5000 yds.; effective: about 3000 yds. Rate of fire: 160 rpm (actually governed by speed crew could feed 4-round clips into gun) Crew: single mount 4, twin 7, quad 11 (pointer, trainer, gun captain, and 8 loaders). If mount is under director (remote) control, gunners stand by.

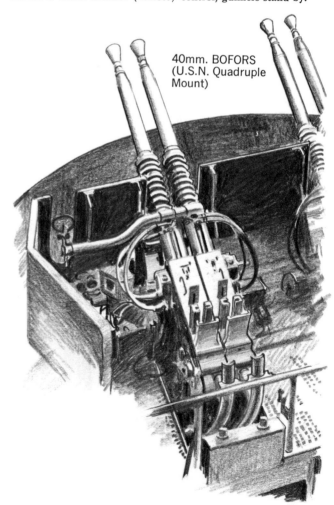

40mm. BOFORS
(U.S.N. Quadruple
Mount)

destroyers, formed the nucleus of Task Force 16 under direct command of Kinkaid. Task Force 17, Rear Admiral George D. Murray, was centered around *Hornet* with four cruisers and six destroyers. A separate Task Force, 64, Rear Admiral Willis A. Lee, was composed of battleship *Washington,* three cruisers, and six destroyers. This force was not engaged in the battle.

The plan was for Kinkaid's two task forces to rendezvous 270 miles NE by E of Espiritu Santo, sweep north of the Santa Cruz islands and to then steam southwestward. By so doing, the combined carrier force would be in a position to intercept any Japanese forces approaching Guadalcanal.

The relative time factors involved in any naval engagement are important and sometimes complex. To avoid confusion and aid continuity the events of the battle are put down chronologically. It must be remembered that, until sightings were made and verified, both commanders were, so to speak, "going it blind" over a battlefield covering many thousands of square miles, and any inkling of the enemy's whereabouts, particularly those of his carriers, was all-important.

U.S. AND JAPANESE FORCES

BATTLE OF SANTA CRUZ OCTOBER 25-26, 1942

TASK FORCE 16

Enterprise (CV)   Rear Adm. Kinkaid
South Dakota (BB)
Portland (CA)
San Juan (CLAA)
Porter (DD)
Mahan (DD)

Shaw (DD)
Preston (DD)
Smith (DD)
Maury (DD)
Conyngham (DD)

TASK FORCE 17

Hornet (CV)   Rear Adm. Murray
Northampton (CA)
Pensacola (CA)
San Diego (CLAA)
Juneau (CLAA)

Morris (DD)
Anderson (DD)
Hughes (DD)
Mustin (DD)
Russell (DD)
Barton (DD)

ADVANCE FORCE   Vice Adm. Kondo

Junyo (CV)
DDs *Kuroshio*   *Hayashio*
Kongo (BB)   *Haruna* (BB)
DDs *Oyashio*   *Kagero*
       Murasame   *Samidare*
       Yudachi   *Murusame*
Atago (CA)   *Takao* (CA)
Myoko (CA)   *Maya* (CA)

Isuzu (CL)

DDs *Naganami*   *Makinami*
       Takanami   *Umikaze*
       Kawakaze   *Suzukaze*

STRIKING FORCE   Vice Adm. Nagumo

Shokaku (CV)   *Zuikaku* (CV)   *Zuiho* (CV)

Kumano (CA)

DDs *Amatsukaze*   *Hatsukaze*
       Tokitsukaze   *Yukikaze*
       Arashi   *Maikaze*
       Teruzuki   *Hamakaze*
Hiei (BB)   *Kirishima* (BB)
Tone (CA)   *Chikuma* (CA)   *Suzuya* (CA)

Nagara (CL)

DDs *Kazagumo*   *Makigumo*
       Yugumo   *Akigumo*
       Tanikaze   *Urakaze*
       Isokaze   12 Submarines

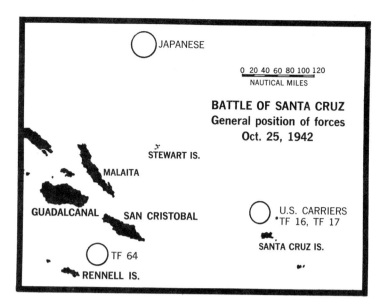

BATTLE OF SANTA CRUZ
General position of forces
Oct. 25, 1942

0 20 40 60 80 100 120
NAUTICAL MILES

JAPANESE

STEWART IS.

MALAITA

GUADALCANAL   SAN CRISTOBAL

U.S. CARRIERS
TF 16, TF 17

SANTA CRUZ IS.

TF 64

RENNELL IS.

OCTOBER 25

1200	A patrolling PBY from Espiritu Santo sighted two Japanese carriers on course SE by S, some 360 miles WNW of Kinkaid's forces. Unfortunately, the area in which the Japanese had been sighted was overcast, with many rain squalls, and the PBY lost contact. Kinkaid decided to launch a search, followed by a strike and at 1330 twelve SBDs left *Enterprise,* followed at
1420	by nineteen SBDs and TBFs, escorted by fighters. The range was long but the fleets were on converging courses, lessening the distance between them by approximately 50 miles per hour. But when *Enterprise's* planes reached the area in which they might have expected to find the Japanese they found nothing but empty ocean. Alarmed by the "snoop" and, as yet, unaware of the American carriers' location, Nagumo had turned north. The planes returned to the carrier after dark. One crashed and six more ditched. Several contacts with battleships and cruisers of the Japanese forces were made during the day by PBYs and B-17s.
2100	The Japanese turned south once more.

OCTOBER 26

0011	A PBY reported the enemy fleet about 300 miles NW of Kinkaid's position. And at
0250	A Catalina narrowly missed *Zuikaku* with a salvo of four bombs—and once more the Japanese turned 180 degrees.

0415	Admiral Abe's battleships and cruisers of the Vanguard catapulted off seven reconnaissance float planes and at
0445	thirteen scout planes were launched by Nagumo's carriers. (Carrier *Junyo* was with the Advance Group. Her sister ship *Hiyo* had developed condenser trouble and on October 22 had been sent back to Truk, escorted by two DDs.)
0500	*Enterprise* launched a search—sixteen SBDs, each with one 500-lb. bomb, to work in pairs. The planes were to comb a 200-mile, 120° sector from north to SW by W. Meanwhile at
0512	a delayed report of a second sighting reached Kinkaid, relayed through Espiritu Santo. This sighting, made about 0300, placed one fleet carrier and six escorting vessels 200 miles away—on course and bearing the same as in the 0011 report —a serious delay in the transmission of an important message. Reading these reports in his HQ at Nouméa, Halsey characteristically broadcast "ATTACK—REPEAT—ATTACK," a stimulating shot in the arm for pilot and boilerman alike.
0630	Two SBDs report sighting the ships of Abe's Vanguard and about the same time a Japanese float plane spotted *Hornet.*
0650	Another pair of SBDs sighted Nagumo's carriers. The two planes began an attack, but were jumped by eight Zeros of the Japanese CAP and forced to seek safety in the clouds—but not until they had shot down three of their attackers. About

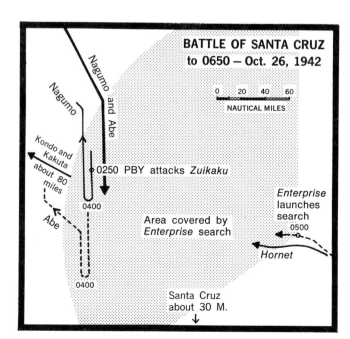

BATTLE OF SANTA CRUZ
to 0650 – Oct. 26, 1942

0 20 40 60
NAUTICAL MILES

Nagumo

Nagumo and Abe

Kondo and Kakuta
about 80 miles

0250 PBY attacks *Zuikaku*

Abe

0400

0400

Enterprise launches search
0500

Hornet

Area covered by *Enterprise* search

Santa Cruz
about 30 M.

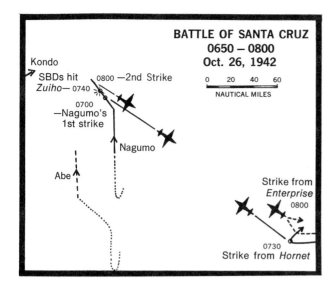

0700	a scout plane from *Shokaku* reported a large enemy unit, including a carrier. Nagumo at once ordered a strike, and the planes, which had been waiting on the carriers' flight decks, took off and climbed into formation. By
0715	the first wave, forty bombers and twenty-seven fighters, was on its way. Nagumo, with a few minutes less warning of his enemy's position, had struck first. Not until
0730	did Kinkaid order his planes up—fifteen SBDs, six TBFs, and eight Wildcats from *Hornet*.

When *Enterprise*'s pair of SBDs had broadcast their sighting of enemy carriers (at 0650) the message had been picked up by two more of her planes, piloted by Lieutenant Stockton Strong and Ensign Charles Irvine. Having drawn a blank in their own section of ocean, Strong and Irvine headed for the position reported. By skillful use of cloud cover, they managed to elude the Japanese CAP and at

0740 roared down through the overcast and planted their two bombs on *Zuiho*'s flight deck aft—opening up a gaping 50-foot hole. As flames burst up through the shattered deck the two SBDs made their getaway, pursued by a swarm of angry Zeros. Not only did they escape, but their rear gunners shot down two of their pursuers. *Zuiho*'s fire was soon under control, but while she could still launch planes she could not retrieve them and later on in the day she was ordered to Truk for repairs. The Japanese deck crews had been working frantically and by

0800	a second wave of planes left *Shokaku* and *Zuikaku* accompanied by *Zuiho*'s sixteen fighters. At the same time, a couple of hundred miles away, *Enterprise* was launching her first strike—three SBDs, eight TBFs, and eight Wildcats (sixteen of her SBDs were on their way back from their early morning search, and six more had been launched to fly an antisubmarine patrol).
0815	*Hornet* flew off a second strike of nine SBDs, nine TBFs, and seven Wildcats. The Japanese first strike was, by now, well on its way toward the American carriers. Some 60 miles out, the *Enterprise* group was attacked by Zeros escorting the Japanese first strike, and in a flurry of action lost four TBFs and four Wildcats. The action warned the American carriers that the expected strike was not far off and at
0857	Radar confirmed an earlier warning and placed the oncoming Japanese 45 miles out. Two minutes later, CAP reported sighting enemy dive bombers at 17,000 feet.

The American carriers were about 10 miles apart, each centered in the middle of a protective ring of ships. Heavy cruisers *Pensacola* and *Northampton* and antiaircraft cruisers *Juneau* and *San Diego* provided heavy support for *Hornet*, along

BATTLE OF SANTA CRUZ
Oct. 25, 1942
0800 — 0857

0   20   40   60
NAUTICAL MILES

Adm. Kakuta

Nagumo

Adm. Kondo

Adm. Abe

Enterprise strike meets Zeros escorting 1st Japanese strike

Enterprise

Hornet's 2nd strike

Hornet

with six destroyers. With *Enterprise* were *South Dakota*, bristling with AA weapons, cruisers *Portland* and *San Juan,* and eight DDs. All fighter direction was controlled from the flagship, a system which had been used by Fletcher. Perhaps it lacked flexibility, or *Enterprise*'s new fighter-director, experience. It was afterward claimed that the CAP was too close—only 10 miles out, and the interception took place too close to the ring of antiaircraft fire. Whatever the cause, when the Japanese arrived, although several were knocked down, too many were able to get through.

About 0900, *Enterprise* disappeared under the protective cover of a rain squall but at

0910 the Japanese signaled "enemy carrier sighted—all planes attacking." The sky over *Hornet* sparkled with flashes, brief winks of light which were instantly replaced with puffs of dirty-brown smoke. Tracer flashed up from dozens of automatic weapons, to arc lazily toward the tiny dots of the enemy bombers. Twisting down through the smoke and flame of their own barrage, bucking with the recoil of their hammering .50s came the Wildcats of the CAP. And down came the Japs—some flaming—some exploding— some trailing smoke and debris. And some undamaged. Too many—a bomb hit *Hornet*'s flight deck aft and a damaged Val plowed into the deck amidship, its bombs bursting in the hangar deck. Two torpedoes exploded in the engine spaces and as the great carrier slid to a halt, spouting flame and smoke, three more bombs struck, one penetrating four decks before exploding. Twenty-five enemy planes had been shot down but as the survivors sped back to their carriers, some ten minutes after the attack began, *Hornet* was burning fore and aft, dead in the water and listing 8 degrees.

Midway through the stricken carrier's ordeal far-distant *Junyo* had launched her strike—twenty-nine planes in three waves.

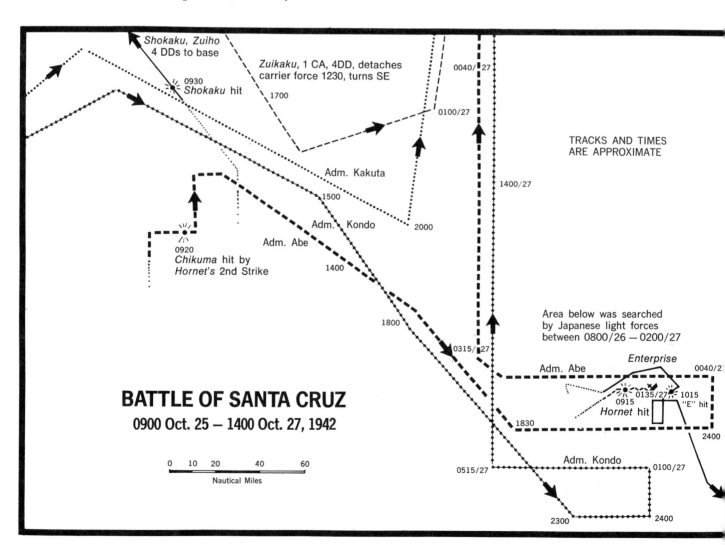

BATTLE OF SANTA CRUZ
0900 Oct. 25 — 1400 Oct. 27, 1942

0   10   20   40   60
Nautical Miles

Shokaku, Zuiho 4 DDs to base

0930
Shokaku hit

Zuikaku, 1 CA, 4DD, detaches carrier force 1230, turns SE

1700

0040/27

0100/27

TRACKS AND TIMES ARE APPROXIMATE

1400/27

Adm. Kakuta

1500

2000

Adm. Kondo

Adm. Abe

0920
Chikuma hit by *Hornet's* 2nd Strike

1400

1800

0315/27

Area below was searched by Japanese light forces between 0800/26 — 0200/27

Adm. Abe

Enterprise

0040/27

0135/27   1015
0915   "E" hit
Hornet hit

1830

2400

0515/27   Adm. Kondo   0100/27

2300   2400

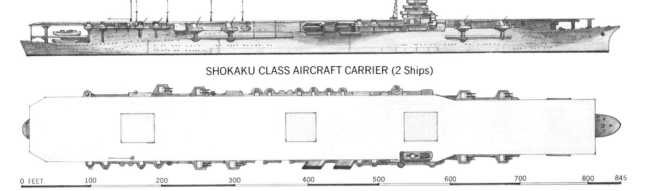

SHOKAKU CLASS AIRCRAFT CARRIER (2 Ships)

Launched June, November 1939 Displacement: 25,675 tons. LOA: 844¾ Beam: 85½
Draft: 29 feet 4 screws.
160,000 hp=34 knots Armament: sixteen 5 in. (8×2),
thirty-six 25-mm. AA (12×3) Aircraft: 84 Complement: 1660

But now it was the American pilots' turn. At

0930 *Hornet's* SBDs found *Shokaku*. While their Wildcat escort fought off a swarm of Zeros, the Dauntlesses attacked. Two were shot down and two were so damaged that they turned back, but the remaining eleven pressed on, their rear gunners blazing away at the Zeros on their tails. Several 1000-pounders plunged into *Shokaku*, bursting open her flight deck and setting her on fire.

Hornet's Avengers, which should have coordinated their attack with the dive bombers', missed sighting the Japanese carrier altogether. Instead, they found Abe's Vanguard Force and for want of a better target launched their fish at heavy cruiser *Suzuya*. All missed. *Hornet's* second strike also failed to find the carrier force, and while several bombs severely damaged *Chikuma*, the strike failed of its purpose. *Enterprise* had no better luck. Her SBDs tried to hit *Kirishima* but missed (the Japanese battleship had nearly three weeks

to live yet) while the TBFs wasted their torpedoes in a vain attack on a heavy cruiser.

Before the last of her attackers were below the horizon, *Hornet's* damage repair crews were hard at work. Chemicals and hoses were brought into play and destroyers *Russell* and *Morris*, lying alongside, pumped in thousands of gallons of water. Three-quarters of an hour after the first bomb hit, the carrier's fires were under control, an attempt was being made to get steam to the after engine room and *Northampton* was getting ready to put a towline aboard.

Yamamoto's far-flung line of submarines now came into action. Destroyer *Porter*, one of the *Enterprise* screen, had stopped to pick up a downed aviator when at

1002 a torpedo from *I-21* exploded in her fire rooms. In normal circumstances she might have been saved but with the enemy in the vicinity it was impossible, and after her crew had been taken off she was sunk by gunfire.

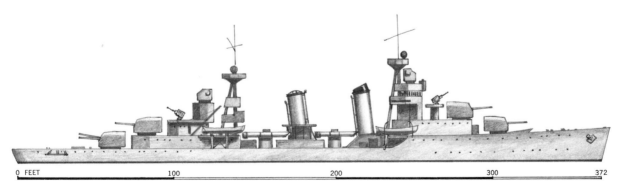

PORTER CLASS DESTROYER (8 Ships)

Launched July 1935–September 1936 Displacement: 1805–1850 tons LOA: 381¼ Beam: 37
Draft: 10½ feet Twin screw 50,000 hp=37 knots Armament: eight 5 in. (4×2),
1.1 AA, eight 21 in. torpedo tubes (4×2) Complement: 290
(Several changes during war; Tripod main mast removed, No. 2 mount replaced by 40-mm.,
No. 3 mount by single gun: 40-mm. quads aft, etc.)

1015   Nagumo's second strike, on its way since just after 0800, now bore down on *Enterprise*. Fortunately for the "*Big E*" the Japanese dive bombers had far outdistanced their torpedo planes. Had the attack been delivered simultaneously, as was the one on *Hornet*, the carrier might not have escaped. The steeply diving Vals were met with devastating fire. *San Juan*'s sixteen 5-inchers erupted so violently that an observer in another ship thought for a moment she was hit and had exploded. Streams of 40-mm projectiles from *South Dakota*, following *Enterprise*'s every maneuver some 1000 yards away, aided the battleship's 5-in. AA in knocking down twenty-six enemy planes, while the carrier and the others of the screen did their part. Again Wildcats of the CAP chased the bombers into the curtain of AA bursts— and again a few got through. One bomb hit *Enterprise* forward, close to the bow, another struck close to the forward elevator, while a near-miss did some damage aft.

While the carrier's crew worked to repair damages, the skies were watched anxiously for the expected attack of the torpedo planes. When the Kates arrived, they were met with furious resistance from the Wildcats of the CAP. One pilot, Lieutenant Stanley ("Swede") Vejtasa, shot down no less than six, other fighters got three or four more and the AA gunners claimed five. That left about nine—and for the next few minutes the huge carrier was the target for their torpedoes. By skillful use of the helm, she evaded all of them, though tracks streaked the water only a hundred feet away. At the same time another Kate made a suicide dive on destroyer *Smith*, hitting her number 1 gun mount and converting the ship from the bridge forward into a flaming torch. Smart handling and quick thinking saved the vessel. By swinging of her bow into *South Dakota*'s wake most of the burning oil and gasoline was washed overboard. Twenty-eight of her crew were dead and twenty-three wounded but, still smoking, she was back in position in the screen and her after guns in action by the time the next attack roared in.

It was not long in coming. At
1101   *South Dakota*'s radar picked up planes to the west (this was *Junyo*'s strike) and at
1121   the planes came down through the overcast. The cloud cover had protected them on the way in but to pick their targets they were forced to make shallow dives and once more the AA gunners made good practice. A near-miss was scored on *Enterprise*, a bomb burst on top of *South Dakota*'s number 1 turret (most of the men inside were unaware they had been hit, but splinters peppered the bridge, wounding Captain Thomas Gatch) and another went right through *San Juan*, exploding underneath the ship. Damage was comparatively light, although she was out of control for a few tense minutes, tearing through the formation with rudder jammed over, siren blowing, breakdown flag flying and her guns still blazing away.

As the attack died away, *Enterprise* began taking in as many of the circling planes as she could. The forward elevator was out of commission and this caused such delay in striking planes below that some were forced to ditch. To help clear the crowded flight deck, thirteen SBDs were flown off to Espiritu Santo. Due to the violent maneuvering during the air attacks the carriers had long since lost sight of each other. After flying off another CAP, *Enterprise* left the area with her attendant ships.

1315   *Junyo* launched another small strike—five of her own planes and ten of *Shokaku*'s and at
1320   *Zuikaku* sent off thirteen more.

While *Enterprise* was under attack, cruiser *Northampton* had tried to take *Hornet* in tow. At
1330   after one parted towline had been replaced, the damaged carrier began to move. A speed of 3 knots was finally attained and it began to look as if *Hornet* might live to fight another day. But at
1515   Japanese planes again attacked. *Northampton* cast off her tow and the escorts filled the air with shell bursts and tracer. But this time there was no fighter cover overhead—and by some misinterpretation of signals, *Juneau* with her massive battery of 5-inchers had gone off to join Kinkaid.

Hornet, now minus much of her protection and unable to maneuver, took another, and fatal, torpedo. The after engine room was flooded and the vessel's list increased to 14 degrees. A little later another group of planes scored one more bomb hit. All wounded and the personnel not actively engaged in fire fighting and damage control had long since been taken aboard destroyers and finally the order to abandon ship was given. A final strike,

1702

by some of *Junyo's* planes which had been hastily rearmed and refueled, hit her again at

and it was obvious that, with a superior Japanese force in the vicinity, she would have to be sent to the bottom. First destroyer *Mustin* fired eight torpedoes, of which only three exploded in their target. She still floated, so *Anderson* fired her salvo. Six of these hit, without any great result, so the two DDs poured over 400

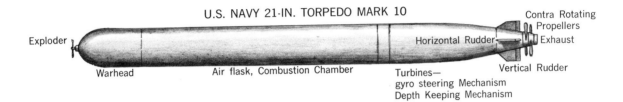

U.S. NAVY 21-IN. TORPEDO MARK 10

Exploder | Warhead | Air flask, Combustion Chamber | Turbines— gyro steering Mechanism Depth Keeping Mechanism | Horizontal Rudder | Contra Rotating Propellers | Exhaust | Vertical Rudder

At the time of Pearl Harbor there were two types of torpedoes in use in the U. S. Navy—the old Mark 10 and the new Mark 14. The Mark 10 was 21 inches in diameter, 21 feet long, weighed 2215 lbs. including a 415 lb. load of TNT in its warhead, and had a range of 3500 yards, at a speed of 36 knots. The Mark 14 was also 21 inches in diameter but was longer, heavier, and could be set to go for 4500 yards at 46 knots or 9000 yards at 31.5 knots. Both were driven by steam, generated by burning alcohol in air carried under high pressure in the air flask. Water was sprayed into the combustion chamber and the resulting mixture of steam and hot gas passed into a turbine which turned two contra-rotating (to counteract torque) propellers. Where they differed was in the exploder. In the Mark 10 this was a simple contact device operating on impact. The Mark 14, unfortunately, was fitted with a new and very secret (so secret that at first not even the torpedomen were informed about it) magnetic exploder. This complicated gadget was designed to go off on contact or when the torpedo passed through the enemy vessel's magnetic field. Thus a torpedo set to run too low or accidentally running too deep would explode under the enemy ship—incidentally

doing (in theory) more damage. There was only one drawback—it didn't work, or at least not often.

Even the old Mark 10 gave trouble—until the Bureau of Ordnance found that the warheads made the missiles run 4 feet deeper than the practice heads used in peacetime. The Mark 14s also ran too low, which accounted for many missed opportunities. When that was straightened out it was found that the exploder was malfunctioning. Bureau of Ordnance suggested modifications in its pet device and finally —but not until March 1944—the magnetic feature of the exploder was ordered deactivated.

The Japanese, on the other hand, had the most powerful torpedo in the world. As far back as 1933 they had developed a torpedo which used oxygen instead of compressed air and which boosted the range and speed to an incredible 21,800 yards at 49 knots while at 32 knots it had a range of over 43,000 yards. This 24-inch monster was 30 feet long and packed a wallop of 1210 lbs. of explosive. More important, its contact-type exploder worked. The Japanese had also paid considerable attention to their reloading arrangements, so that their destroyermen could reload tubes in about ten minutes.

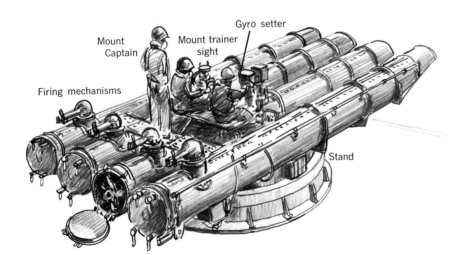

Mount Captain | Mount trainer sight | Gyro setter | Firing mechanisms | Stand

QUADRUPLE TORPEDO MOUNT

Torpedo salvos were usually fired at short intervals, 2–3 seconds, rather than all at once, thus giving a "spread" to the salvo. Torpedoes could also be fired singly. Mount could be trained and torpedoes fired from director-control or manually.

rounds of 5″ into the flaming wreck. But it was time to go. The Japanese vanguard was not far distant and at

2040   the two destroyers followed their companions over the horizon. *Hornet* was now white hot from bow to stern and when the first of Abe's destroyers arrived at the scene a little more than half an hour later, she was obviously beyond all hope of salvage. Four of the Japanese Long Lances finally finished her off and in the early hours of October 27 she went, roaring and hissing, to the bottom.

Kondo now steamed slowly north, planning to renew his pursuit of the retiring American forces at daylight. Next afternoon, evidently not wishing to push his luck, he set course for Truk. His reluctance to pursue may have been prompted in part by a night attack by Black Cats from Espiritu

Santo, one of which damaged destroyer *Teruzuki* while another nearly succeeded in putting a torpedo into *Zuikaku*.

Kinkaid's retirement toward Nouméa was not without incident. While maneuvering to avoid a submarine contact, destroyer *Mahan* collided with *South Dakota*. Both ships were damaged, but not enough to send them out of the war zone.

The battle had cost the Japanese some one hundred planes and the Americans seventy-four. The score card for the ships showed—Japanese; two carriers, a heavy cruiser, and two destroyers damaged, against a carrier and destroyer sunk, a battleship, a carrier, a cruiser, and a destroyer (two if *Mahan* is counted) damaged. There had been happier celebrations of Navy Day (October 27) but on the credit side there had been no triumphal procession of Japanese warships into Sealark Channel—and the Marines still held Henderson Field.

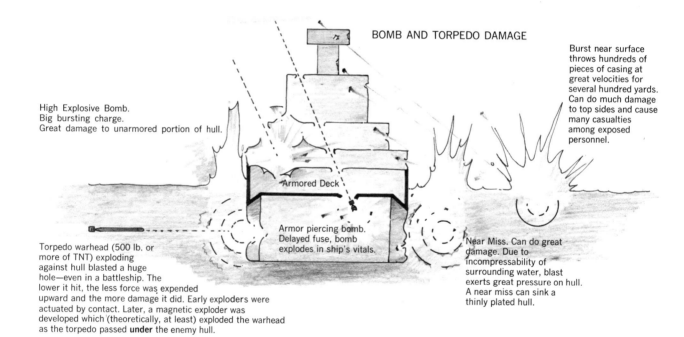

BOMB AND TORPEDO DAMAGE

High Explosive Bomb. Big bursting charge. Great damage to unarmored portion of hull.

Burst near surface throws hundreds of pieces of casing at great velocities for several hundred yards. Can do much damage to top sides and cause many casualties among exposed personnel.

Armored Deck

Armor piercing bomb. Delayed fuse, bomb explodes in ship's vitals.

Torpedo warhead (500 lb. or more of TNT) exploding against hull blasted a huge hole—even in a battleship. The lower it hit, the less force was expended upward and the more damage it did. Early exploders were actuated by contact. Later, a magnetic exploder was developed which (theoretically, at least) exploded the warhead as the torpedo passed **under** the enemy hull.

Near Miss. Can do great damage. Due to incompressability of surrounding water, blast exerts great pressure on hull. A near miss can sink a thinly plated hull.

XI

"A Left! A Right! Then Another Left!"

ACTIONS AT POINT CRUZ AND KOLI POINT

General Vandegrift had no intention of giving the enemy time to recover from his costly defeat of October 25–26. Even while burial details and salvage squads were clearing up the battlefield, plans were under way for an advance west of the Matanikau River to clean the Japanese out of the Kokumbona area. Acquisition of this ground would put the enemy's long-range artillery beyond reach of Henderson Field and also deprive the Japanese of an assembly area close to the western side of the perimeter defenses.

The troops earmarked for this operation were 5th Marines, 2nd Marines (ferried over from Tulagi) less the 3rd Battalion, and a Whaling Group of scout-snipers and 3rd Battalion, 7th Marines. The 11th Marines and U. S. Army artillery and engineers were in support. The Cactus Air Force was ready and the Navy stood by for shore bombardment.

The plan was much the same as that for the earlier advance on October 7. At 0630 on November 1, Edson's 5th Marines, with 2nd Marines in support, were to cross the river (on foot bridges this time, not across the river mouth), and push along the coast, supported by artillery, a bombardment by naval vessels and air attacks from Henderson. The Whaling Group would cross higher up and also sweep west, protecting Edson's flank.

In preparation for this, at midnight on October 31, men of the 1st Engineer Battalion began throwing three foot bridges (planking on empty fuel drums) across the river. A company of 2nd Battalion, 5th Marines crossed the river in rubber boats to cover the crossing. By 0700 the two battalions of the 5th were over and ready to push on; 1st Battalion, 5th on the coast and 2nd Battalion, 5th on higher ground a little farther inland.

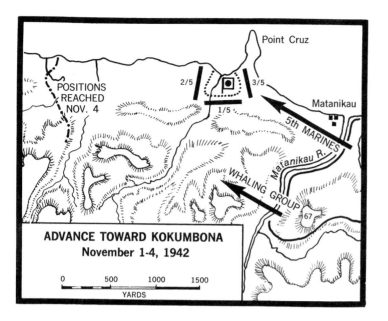

ADVANCE TOWARD KOKUMBONA
November 1-4, 1942

Cruisers *San Francisco* and *Helena* and destroyer *Sterett* pumped shells into the Santa Cruz area, while B-17s from Espiritu Santo and SBDs and P-39s from Henderson bombed and strafed enemy positions around Kokumbona.

Opposition to the advance of 2nd Battalion, 5th was light but the main Japanese force in the area was located close to the foot of Point Cruz and it was here that 1st Battalion, 5th ran into stiff resistance. Edson's reserve, 3rd Battalion, 5th, was brought up and the advance halted for the night. On November 2, 2nd Battalion, 5th swung in to help and the Jap force was boxed in a small area just south of the Point. The enemy was well dug in and the heavy mortar and artillery fire plus a bombardment by DDs *Shaw* and *Conynham* failed to flatten their positions. Progress was very slow and it was not until just after noon on November 3 that all pockets of resistance was finally overrun. Over three hundred enemy dead were counted and booty included a field piece, twelve 37-mm guns and thirty-four machine guns.

The way now seemed clear for a push to Kokumbona, but new dangers threatened to the east. On the night of November 2, the Tokyo Express steamed in once more, this time to land some 1500 men near Koli Point. This was in accordance with a new Japanese plan for yet another troop buildup and another grand attempt to sweep the Americans off the island. This time the bulk of the 38th Division (two battalions were already on Guadalcanal) were to be landed at Koli Point, thus putting pressure on the Marine perimeter from both sides. There were even plans to hack out an airstrip at Koli to counterbalance those at Lunga

Point. A powerful Japanese squadron under Kondo, including carriers and battleships, was ready at Truk; to give air cover to the operation, to pulverize Henderson Field by bombardment and to escort transports carrying the major elements of the 38th Division and all its heavy weapons, artillery transport, and equipment. (It must be noted that while at various times many thousands of men were carried to the island on fast destroyers, these craft could not transport any equipment other than a few light artillery pieces, machine guns, and mortars.)

U. S. Intelligence (by piecing together information from coastwatchers, reconnaissance flights, and decoded radio chatter) was able to alert Vandegrift that a buildup to the east of his perimeter was probable. And so it was that on November 1, while Edson's men were advancing west, 2nd Battalion of the 7th, under Lieutenant Colonel Herman H. Hanneken, moved to the Tenaru River. On the following day they marched across the base of the curve of land forming Koli Point and dug in for the night of November 2 along the coast east of the Metapona River, some 13 miles east of the perimeter.

Unknown to Hanneken, Colonel Shoji had also arrived at the coast with some 2500 veterans (or survivors) of the counteroffensive of late October. The Japanese troops, mostly of the 230th Infantry Regiment, were concentrated in an area about a mile east of Hanneken's force. Just before midnight of November 2, the Marines on the right flank of Hanneken's command found themselves in the frustrating position of being forced to watch the unloading of the Express without being able to do anything to stop it. About 2200, six ships, dimly made out through the dark and rain, put

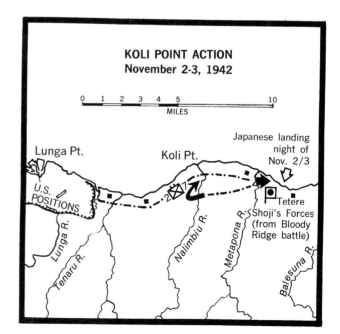

KOLI POINT ACTION
November 2-3, 1942

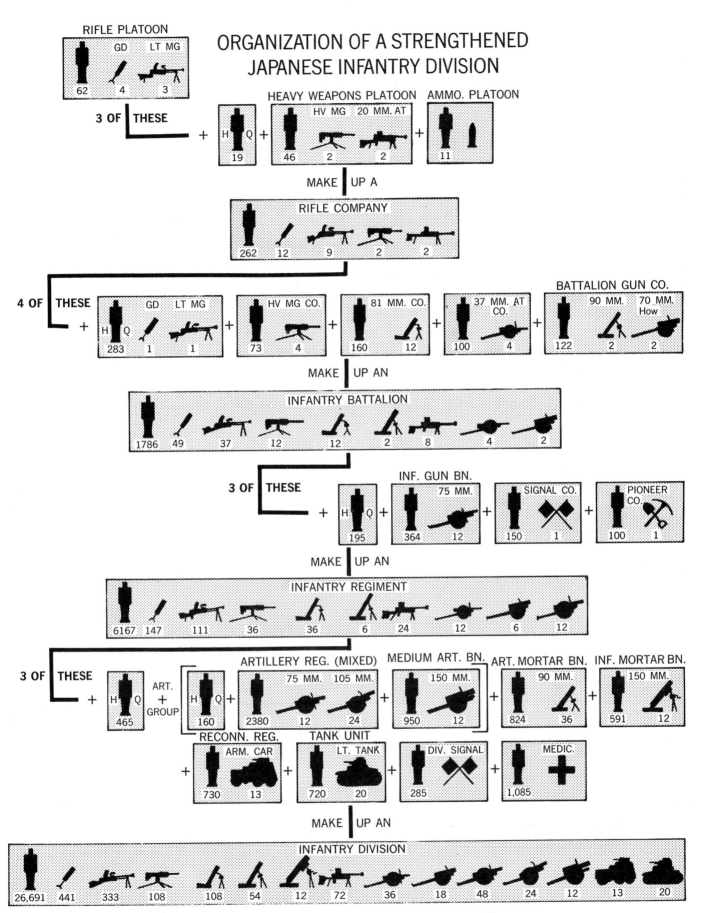

ORGANIZATION OF A STRENGTHENED JAPANESE INFANTRY DIVISION

Note: The Japanese Divisions on Guadalcanal were never at full strength. They arrived piecemeal, minus much equipment (either not shipped or lost en route).

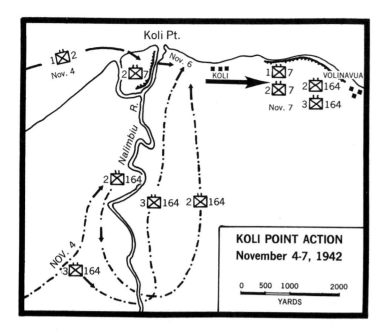

KOLI POINT ACTION
November 4-7, 1942

0   500   1000   2000
YARDS

ashore the 1500 men of the 228th Infantry Regiment. Hanneken's radio was out—the jungle march and tropical rainstorms had proved too much for it—and he was unable to relay information of the landing. By 0200, their mission accomplished, the Japanese vessels had withdrawn unmolested.

An exchange of mortar fire in the morning was followed by an attempt by a large force of Japanese to flank Hanneken's battalion, whereupon 2nd Battalion of the 7th withdrew to positions along the west bank of the Nalimbiu River, about 5000 yards to the west. Hanneken was now in radio contact with division and called for air support (he soon wished he hadn't, as Cactus planes bombed and strafed some of his own troops) and for landing craft to take out his wounded. Vandegrift complied with these requests, and also asked for naval support. *San Francisco, Helena, Lansdowne,* and *Sterett* thereupon shelled the area east of Hanneken's position.

The 2nd Battalion of the 7th was obviously faced with a strong body of troops and it was at this point that it was decided to curtail operations in the Kokumbona area and concentrate on the eastern flank. Two battalions of 164th Infantry were ordered to march to attack the enemy from the south while 1st Battalion of the 7th moved in to aid Hanneken. Batteries of the 1st Battalion of the 10th were in general support. General William Rupertus had come over from Tulagi and newly arrived Brigadier General Edmund B. Sebree was with the 164th Infantry Regiment of the U. S. Army's Americal Division. The commander of the 7th Marines was also present—a large amount of brass for what was to prove a generally disappointing action.

Progress for the next few days was very slow, although the Japanese had already begun a withdrawal to positions east of the Metapona. For the enemy had suddenly changed their plans. The two-prong offensive idea had been given up and instead the main buildup was to be in the west. Shoji was therefore ordered to march back to Kokumbona (no small feat in itself) and it was his rear guard which was involved in the fighting at Koli Point and the Metapona.

Koli Point was cleared of the enemy by November 6 and the next day, 7th Marines and the 164th Infantry moved to a position about one mile west of the mouth of the Metapona where they dug in to await a possible landing. But although the Tokyo Express ran that night, it did not stop east of Lunga Point, nor would it again. On November 8, the Marines and Army troops moved to surround the remaining Japanese located just east of Gavago Creek. Fighting was sharp and it was not until the next day that the final movement to wipe out the pocket began, with 2nd Battalion of the 7th on the east, 1st Battalion of the 7th on the west, and 2nd Battalion of the 164th on the south. Artillery and aircraft pounded the Japanese, but some succeeded in breaking out of the trap.

Two companies of the 164th Regiment's 2nd Battalion failed to make contact across the creek and although the battalion commander was replaced on November 10, the gap remained open and many of the surviving enemy escaped up the swampy river. It was not until November 12 that the pocket was entirely cleared. About 450 Japanese dead were counted. American casualties totaled some forty dead, with 120 wounded, including 1st Battalion of Puller's 7th Marines. Considerable amounts of rice, two howitzers, many mortars and machine guns and fifty collapsible landing boats were part of the booty.

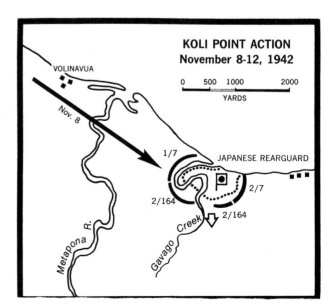

KOLI POINT ACTION
November 8-12, 1942

0   500   1000   2000
YARDS

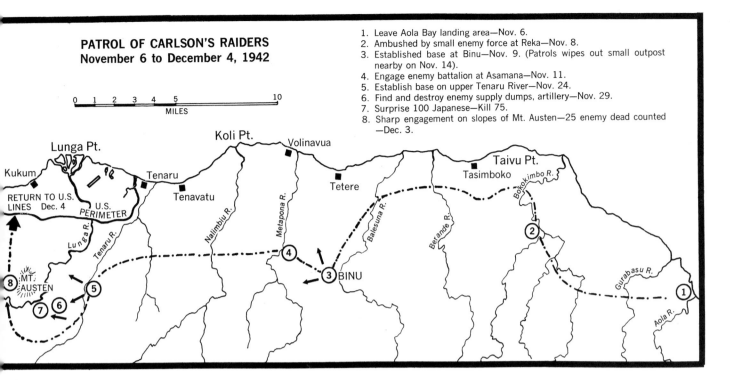

PATROL OF CARLSON'S RAIDERS
November 6 to December 4, 1942

1. Leave Aola Bay landing area—Nov. 6.
2. Ambushed by small enemy force at Reka—Nov. 8.
3. Established base at Binu—Nov. 9. (Patrols wipes out small outpost nearby on Nov. 14).
4. Engage enemy battalion at Asamana—Nov. 11.
5. Establish base on upper Tenaru River—Nov. 24.
6. Find and destroy enemy supply dumps, artillery—Nov. 29.
7. Surprise 100 Japanese—Kill 75.
8. Sharp engagement on slopes of Mt. Austen—25 enemy dead counted—Dec. 3.

Mention has been made of Admiral Turner's weakness for "playing soldier." One of his pet schemes—which he had succeeded in selling to Halsey—was the extension of Vandegrift's hold on the island by a landing at Aola Bay, some 30 miles east of Koli. Here a back-up airfield was to be constructed (although a survey team had long since declared the swampy area unsuitable). On November 4, three transports and two APDs unloaded 1700 men of 1st Battalion, 147th Infantry (originally scheduled for Ndeni, but diverted when that landing and occupation was happily canceled), two companies of Lieutenant Colonel Evans Carlson's 2nd Marine Raider Battalion, artillery units, and five hundred Seabees. By this time it was apparent that it was impractical to try to turn the waterlogged land into a field and Vandegrift (who, with the commanders on the spot, had condemned the move from the outset) finally recommended to Turner that the project be abandoned. Halsey concurred and by December 3 the whole force had been shifted back to Koli Point where more artillery, more Seabees, and 3rd Battalion of the 147th Infantry Regiment were landed November 29 and where a field was built on a grassy plain. The Aola Bay affair was an expensive waste of men and equipment—at a time when both were at a premium—and Marine HQ heaved a sigh of relief when "Turner's Folly" was finally abandoned.

Vandegrift had not waited a month to move all the troops from Aola, however. Carlson's Raiders had barely landed before they were ordered to march overland toward Koli to intercept any Japanese forces attempting to retire from the area. They were in time to make contact with the enemy retreating south and west toward the Mount Austen area and in an epic 30-day jungle march covering 150 miles (aided by both native porters and native scouts, who themselves killed many of the enemy) sorely harassed the already distressed Japanese forces. The Raiders entered the American perimeter on December 4, having fought twelve separate actions and accounted for over 450 of the enemy at a cost to themselves of sixteen killed and eighteen wounded.

On October 24, President Roosevelt sent a mem-

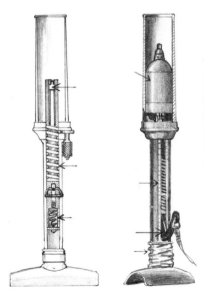

Weight of shell: 1 lb. 12 oz. Range of shell: 130–700 yards Range with Model 91 hand grenade (with propellant and primer added): 40–200 yards Weight: 10¼ lbs. Length of barrel: 10" Length, total: 24" Barrel was held in hand. Spade rested on log or ground (not on knee—as was discovered through painful experience by some Marines on Guadalcanal). Range governed by regulating amount of firing pin projecting into barrel (thus varying volume of gas in chamber). Trigger cocks and fires piece in one operation.

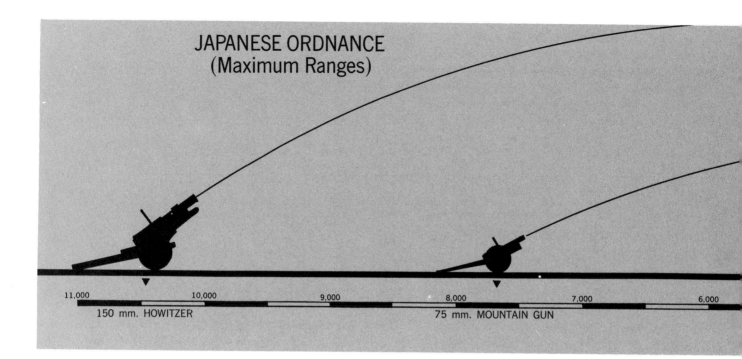

JAPANESE ORDNANCE
(Maximum Ranges)

| 11,000 | 10,000 | 9,000 | 8,000 | 7,000 | 6,000 |

150 mm. HOWITZER   75 mm. MOUNTAIN GUN

orandum to the Joint Chiefs of Staff expressing a desire that every effort be made to send reinforcements to Guadalcanal. This despite heavy losses in the Atlantic (U-boats sank eighty-eight ships in October, totaling over 585,000 tons); Operation Torch, then at sea en route to North Africa; and the buildup for the projected Operation Bolero cross-channel drive hopefully scheduled for 1943. In accordance with this decision (heartily approved by Admiral King) the new battleship *Indiana* and her supporting group of cruisers and destroyers were earmarked for the South Pacific, as well as a number of transports. The U. S. Army's 25th Infantry Division (then in Hawaii) was alerted for a move south and, besides other Army and Marine units, 8th Marines were to be brought from Samoa. The reinforcements also included more submarines for the Solomons area, more

Single-seater Long-range Fighter
Span: 52'
Length: 37'10"   Height: 9'10"
Weight empty: 12,264 lbs.
Max. speed: 395 mph at 25,000 ft.; 347 mph at 5000 feet.
Range: 400 miles at 33 mph at 25,000 ft., 900 miles at 219 mph at 10,000 feet. (Drop tanks increased this to 1750 miles at 213 mph at 10,000 ft.)
Power: two 1225-hp Allison 12-cylinder Vee engines
Armament: one 20-mm. cannon and four 0.5 MGs., all nose-mounted. Plus two 1000-lb. bombs or two 21-inch torpedoes

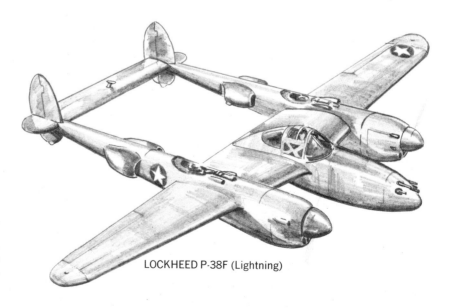

LOCKHEED P-38F (Lightning)

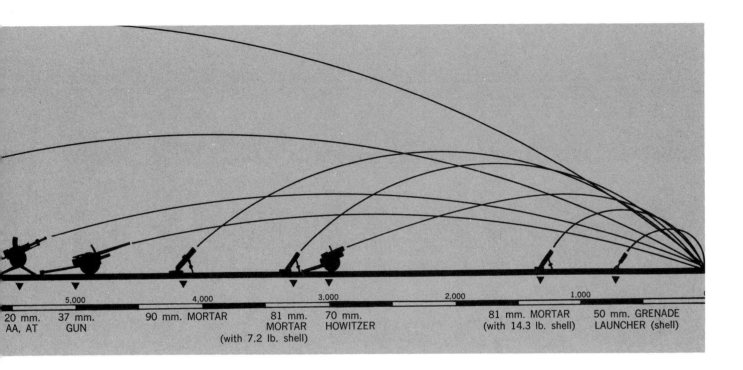

	5,000	4,000		3,000	2,000	1,000	

| 20 mm.
AA, AT | 37 mm.
GUN | 90 mm. MORTAR | 81 mm.
MORTAR
(with 7.2 lb. shell) | 70 mm.
HOWITZER | | 81 mm. MORTAR
(with 14.3 lb. shell) | 50 mm. GRENADE
LAUNCHER (shell) |

torpedo boats and last, but not least, more planes. These were to include eight P-38s, promised by MacArthur.

Combat losses, accidents, bombardments, and just plain wear and tear kept Cactus Air Force constantly short of planes. (On October 26, there were only 29 planes fit to fly.) But a steady trickle of men and machines kept arriving, along with plane loads of spare parts. A few more heavy bombard-

ment planes were becoming available, and three squadrons of this type were temporarily diverted from Australia to New Caledonia. By mid-November, aviation units on Guadalcanal totaled over 1700 officers and men.

As a result of this welcome augmentation of Operation Shoestring, men, guns, and supplies began to arrive on the island in fair quantities. On November 2, *Alchiba* and *Fuller* landed supplies,

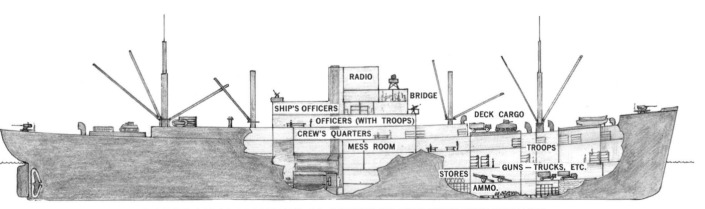

C-3 TYPE CARGO-PASSENGER CONVERTED TO ATTACK TRANSPORT (APA)

Displacement: c. 10,000 tons   LOA: 492   Beam: 69½   Draft: 26½ feet.
Single screw.   8500 hp=18.4 knots
Armament (varied): four 3 in., Small AAs

ammunition, and two batteries of 155-mm guns —one Army, one Marine, thus assuring effective counterbattery fire for the first time. And on November 4, the reinforced 8th Marines of Colonel R. Hall Heschke arrived in Sealark Channel.

Vandegrift was anxious to resume his interrupted offensive on the Kokumbona area and when it was obvious that the Japanese at Koli Point were contained, 3rd Battalion of the 7th and 164th Infantry and some supporting units were brought back from Koli by boat and truck on November 9. The following day, 8th Marines, 1st and 2nd Battalions of the 2nd Marines, and the 1st Battalion of the 164th Infantry moved west from Point Cruz. Attacking on a three-battalion front on November 11, the troops reached the point of farthest advance

made on November 4. Opposition was mounting and had the advance continued, some stiff fighting would have ensued. Hyakutake had given the task of keeping the Americans away from the vital Kokumbona area to a new commander, Major General Takeo Ito, Infantry Group Commander of the 38th Division, who had landed November 5 at Tassafaronga. Ito had deployed 5000 men in the jungle-covered hills parallel to the American line of advance and some 2½ miles south of the beach with the intention of taking his enemies in flank and rear. But once again threats of a major Japanese offensive induced Vandegrift to recall his legions within the boundaries of his little empire. By November 12, all units had withdrawn east of the Matanikau and the bridges were destroyed.

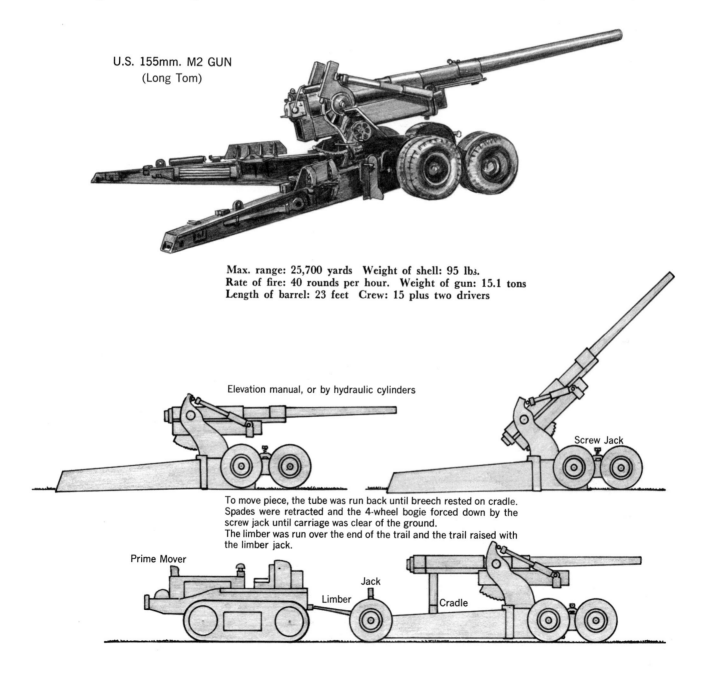

U.S. 155mm. M2 GUN
(Long Tom)

Max. range: 25,700 yards Weight of shell: 95 lbs.
Rate of fire: 40 rounds per hour. Weight of gun: 15.1 tons
Length of barrel: 23 feet Crew: 15 plus two drivers

Elevation manual, or by hydraulic cylinders

Screw Jack

To move piece, the tube was run back until breech rested on cradle. Spades were retracted and the 4-wheel bogie forced down by the screw jack until carriage was clear of the ground.
The limber was run over the end of the trail and the trail raised with the limber jack.

Prime Mover

Jack

Limber

Cradle

XII
"Get the Big Ones First"

THE FIRST BATTLE OF GUADALCANAL

While Vandegrift's men had been fighting on both sides of their defense perimeter, there had been a slow but steady buildup of Japanese forces. In almost nightly runs, the Tokyo Express had succeeded in putting a considerable number of men ashore, although these excursions were not always without incident. The arrival at Tulagi on October 25 of a second group of four PT boats meant that, even with courier and escort duties, there would be some boats available for anti-Express patrol. While no striking successes were scored, their very presence in the area added to the worries of the Japanese commanders.

On the night of November 5–6, four boats were on patrol. PT 39 had a brush with two destroyers but escaped without damage. On the following night, PT 48 fired four torpedoes at close range

at a destroyer off Koli Point. A tremendous explosion was seen and an oil slick sighted next day, but there are no records of any Japanese destroyer being sunk that night. (On November 8, however, some sources say destroyer *Mochizuki* was damaged slightly by a torpedo. The PT boats made no claim to any hits at that time so there may have been a confusion in dates.) The premature explosion of a torpedo, viewed from the ship which launched it, could very easily be confused with an actual hit.

On November 7, eleven destroyers, carrying an advance unit of 1300 men of the 38th Division were heavily attacked by fighter-escorted bombers from Henderson Field. The escort of six Zeros was shot down but Tanaka says no ships were hit, the troops were landed and all destroyers arrived

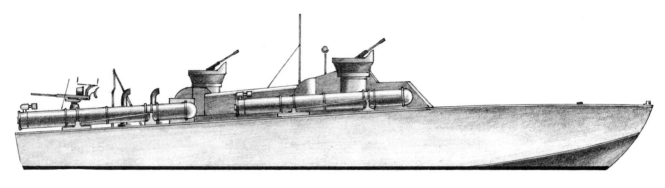

U.S. PT 103 CLASS (358 Boats)

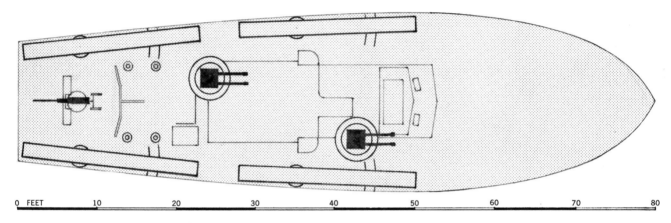

Launched 1942–1945 Displacement: 38 tons LOA: 80 Beam: 20¾ Draft: 5 feet
Triple screw. 3 Packard gasoline engines 4050 hp=40 knots Armament: four 21 in.
torpedo tubes or drop racks, one 20 mm., four .50 cal. MG. Complement: 14
(Note: Armament varied. Some boats later carried one 37 mm. and one 20 mm. forward,
four .50 cal. MGs., and one 40-mm aft plus radar and depth charges.)

safely in Shortlands next day. Morison and the Naval Analysis Division of U. S. Strategic Bombing Survey state that DDs *Naganami* and *Takanami* received major damage in this attack. If they were hit at all, however, damage must have been light as *Naganami* and *Takanami* (as well as torpedoed *Mochizuki*) sortied with Tanaka from Shortlands on November 12.

There was further action on the night of November 8–9. A force of five destroyers had been sighted heading for Guadalcanal and the PTs were ordered to intercept. Because of inadequate base facilities and wear and tear on both boats and men, only three boats were available. They made contact and five torpedoes in all were launched, all of which missed. One boat had its bow blown off by a shell while another was damaged by splinters. Both injured boats returned to Tulagi safely. Two nights later, five destroyers, bringing in Lieutenant General Tadayoshi Sano and six hundred men of the 38th Division, beat off an attempt by three PTs to interfere with the landing operation.

American supplies continued to arrive with comparatively little loss. Destroyer *Lansdowne* brought in 90 tons of ammunition on November 7. While she was unloading, the 2200-ton Navy cargo ship *Majaba*, anchored nearby, was struck by a torpedo launched by submarine *I-20*. *Lansdowne* joined in the ensuing hunt but the submarine escaped. However, on November 10, minesweeper *Southard* sank *I-172* off Cape Recherche, San Cristobal. In the meantime, a considerable reinforcement was on the way under command of Rear Admiral Turner.

This armada of Turner's, designated TF 67, was in three groups. TG 67.1—the transport group—*McCawley, Crescent City, President Adams* and *President Jackson* carried the 182nd Infantry, less 3rd Battalion, 4th Marine Replacement Battalion, and Naval Defense Force personnel. It was escorted by part of the Support Group, TG 67.4, consisting of five cruisers and ten destroyers under Rear Admiral Daniel J. Callaghan. Of this Support Group, two destroyers, *Gwin* and *Preston,* and heavy cruiser *Pensacola* were detached (to join Kinkaid). Heavy cruiser *Portland* and three destroyers accompanied Turner and his transports, leaving Nouméa on November 8. They rendezvoused with Callaghan and his remaining three cruisers and five destroyers off San Cristobal on November 11. The third group, TG 62.4, consisted

JAPANESE I 15 CLASS SUBMARINE (20 Ships)

Displacement: 2584 (submerged 3654).   LOA: 356½   Beam: 30½   Draft: 16¾ feet.
Twin screw.   Diesel 12,400 hp=23½ knots (surface)
Electric 2000 hp=8 knots (submerged) Armament: one 5.5 in., two 25-mm. AA (1✕2),
six 21 in. torpedo tubes (bow) Aircraft: 1 Complement: 100
   (Aircraft was unarmed, single-seat spotting plane, carried disassembled, in watertight hangar.
90-knot speed, 3-hr. range. It took about one hour to recover and stow plane and prepare to
dive.)

of light cruiser *Atlanta* and four destroyers, escorting three attack cargo ships (AKAs) carrying 1st Marine Aviation Engineer Battalion, Marine Air Wing 1 ground personnel, Marine replacements, ammunition, provisions, and matériel. This group was commanded by Rear Admiral Norman Scott and left Espiritu Santo on November 9.

The duty of protecting Turner's Task Force against a large scale attack had been assigned by Halsey to Rear Admiral Kinkaid—Task Force 16—with *Enterprise* (repair crews still working on her battle damage), with cruisers *Northampton* and *San Diego* (*Pensacola* joined later) and six destroyers. For a heavy ship-to-ship punch there was Task Force 64—Rear Admiral Willis A. Lee, Jr.—with new battleships *Washington* and *South Dakota* (also not fully repaired) and two destroyers (two of Callaghan's joined later). *Enterprise* had been kept at Nouméa as long as possible while frantic efforts were made to repair the bomb damage received at Santa Cruz. The battleships remained with her and the combined force did not leave Nouméa until November 11. Thus when word was received of strong Japanese forces gathering for an assault on Guadalcanal, the heaviest American ships in the area were too far away to assist.

Scott had hoped to avoid being sighted by long range Japanese planes but a seaplane from one of the I-class submarines (fitted with hangars) spotted his convoy on November 10. The plane thoroughly investigated TG 62.4 from just outside the range of Scott's AA fire and the American admiral knew that as soon as he reached the island (the time of his arrival would be broadcast by Japanese radio on Guadalcanal) planes with the familiar meat-ball markings would be on their way.

Lunga Point was reached at first light on November 11, and the Marines began to go ashore as soon as the hooks splashed down. The expected attack was not long in coming—dive bombers from *Hiyo*, then cruising northwest of Guadalcanal. The

Vals met a hot fire from the ships' AA and from fighters of Cactus Air Force.

They made no direct hits, but a near miss on AKA *Zeilin* damaged her hull and some flooding resulted. Damage to the other two AKAs, *Betelgeuse* and *Libra,* was slight. A later raid of some twenty-seven Bettys from Rabaul concentrated mostly on the airfield. AA fire forced them to fly high and damage was slight. Both raids had interrupted unloading, however, and all three AKAs had cargo still aboard when they withdrew to In-

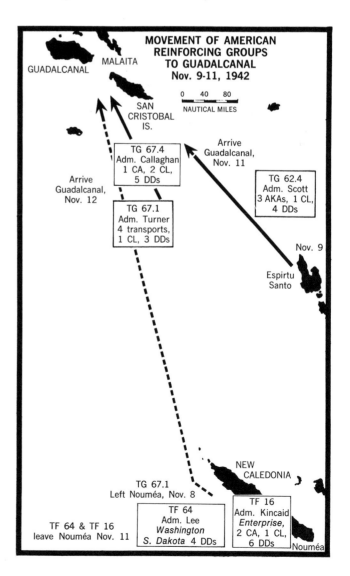

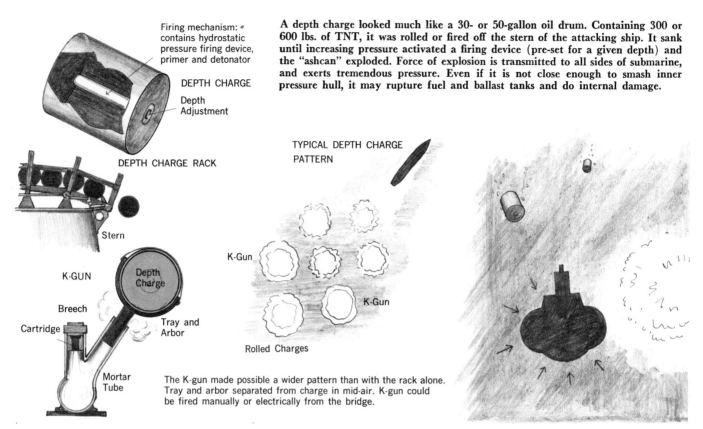

Firing mechanism: contains hydrostatic pressure firing device, primer and detonator

DEPTH CHARGE

Depth Adjustment

A depth charge looked much like a 30- or 50-gallon oil drum. Containing 300 or 600 lbs. of TNT, it was rolled or fired off the stern of the attacking ship. It sank until increasing pressure activated a firing device (pre-set for a given depth) and the "ashcan" exploded. Force of explosion is transmitted to all sides of submarine, and exerts tremendous pressure. Even if it is not close enough to smash inner pressure hull, it may rupture fuel and ballast tanks and do internal damage.

DEPTH CHARGE RACK

Stern

TYPICAL DEPTH CHARGE PATTERN

K-GUN

Depth Charge

Breech

Cartridge

Mortar Tube

Tray and Arbor

K-Gun

K-Gun

Rolled Charges

The K-gun made possible a wider pattern than with the rack alone. Tray and arbor separated from charge in mid-air. K-gun could be fired manually or electrically from the bridge.

dispensable Strait at 1800. It was decided that *Zeilin's* buckled hull made it necessary for her to return to base, so she departed for Espiritu Santo with destroyer *Lardner* as escort.

At 2200, Callaghan, who had come on ahead of Turner with his three cruisers and five destroyers, joined Scott's group. Together the warships made a sweep around Savo Island. No enemy were sighted and the ships spent the night patrolling in Sealark Channel. The two AKAs joined Turner's group when it came up later that night and all six ships began to unload at daybreak on November 12.

Turner had also been "snooped" on his way up from Nouméa and he was anxious to get his vessels emptied and out of the area as soon as possible. Troops were sent ashore at once, with but one unit of fire and two days' rations. Debarkation was well under way when, about two hours after Turner's arrival, Japanese 150-mm guns opened up on *Betelgeuse* and *Libra* from near Kokumbona. Neither ship was hit and fire from warships and American heavy artillery soon silenced the enemy battery. During unloading, *San Francisco, Helena,* and *Portland* steamed in a semicircle around the anchored ships while *Juneau, Atlanta,* and eleven destroyers formed an outer screen. An underwater contact at 0600 set off a flurry of antisubmarine activity, but the booming depth charges brought up nothing but white water.

All troops were ashore and the unloading of supplies was progressing rapidly when, at 1317, a message was received from Coastwatcher Mason at Buin that a raid was on the way. Unloading was stopped, the ships were got under way and Turner's command took up a defensive formation. The four transports and two cargo ships in two parallel columns, formed the center of the formation. The five cruisers, *San Francisco* ahead and the others on each bow and quarter of the columns, and eleven DDs, plus two fast minesweepers, formed a protective circle bristling with AA guns of all calibers.

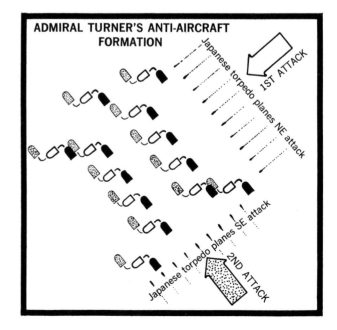

ADMIRAL TURNER'S ANTI-AIRCRAFT FORMATION

Japanese torpedo planes NE attack

1ST ATTACK

Japanese torpedo planes SE attack

2ND ATTACK

About 1410 the Japs arrived. While some twenty-five Bettys escorted by Zeros attacked the airfield, twenty-one twin-engine torpedo bombers roared low over the southeastern end of Florida Island. Forming a line they came in at wave-top height. They were not yet within effective range of the screen's antiaircraft guns, but *San Francisco* and *Portland* fired several salvos with their main battery guns, shooting short so that the shells threw up great waterspouts through which the attackers had to pass. No planes were hit but the attack now split into two groups, one circling to attack from the northeast, the other from the southeast.

As soon as the move for the two pronged port and starboard bow attack became evident, Turner swung his formation so as to provide a tempting target for the northeastern group. Without waiting for the other group to circle into position, the first group bored in. It was met with a murderous hail of AA. The waters of the sound were lashed into foam by a storm of bursting projectiles and hurtling shell fragments. Here and there a plane disintegrated in a flash of fire, or plunged into the sea streaming smoke. But through the wall of dirty-brown shell bursts broke the surviving Japanese planes. Torpedoes splashed into the water, but Turner had signaled for a turn away, and the ominous streaks paralleled his formation.

Overhead, had anyone on board any of the ships had time to glance upward, a furious dog fight was going on between fighters from Henderson and the attacking Bettys and their attendant Zeros. Some American fighters detached themselves from the battle to attack the southerly group of torpedo bombers. Hit by Wildcats, who followed them in through the American AA fire, the attackers were again shown the retreating sterns of Turner's vessels and again no torpdoes hit. Then suddenly it was all over and one surviving Japanese torpedo plane began its flight back to Rabaul. Four American planes were lost.

Several vessels received minor damage but *Buchanan* was so badly battered topside she had to return to base. Most serious damage was to *San Francisco*. A burning Japanese plane crashed into her after superstructure, wrecking the after control station, the after main battery director and FC radar and wiping out three 20-mm guns and their crews—heroes who kept their weapons pumping out shells until the moment of impact. The ensuing gasoline fire burned out Battle II (the secondary conning station) and did considerable other damage before it was brought under control. The crash and fire cost the lives of twenty-four men and as many more were injured.

Reports had reached Turner of a powerful Japanese squadron, including two battleships, on the way toward Guadalcanal. A fleet of transports had been sighted further north. Empty or not, the American transports and cargo vessels would have to leave. *McCawley* and *President Jackson* had been completely unloaded. The others had managed to put ashore an average of almost half their cargoes. All personnel had been landed, including a Marine battery of 155-mm howitzers. At 1815, *McCawley* led the force out of the anchorage, preceded by the warships. In Indispensable Strait Turner parted company with Callaghan and Scott, and set course for Espiritu Santo. With him as escort went damaged *Buchanan*, *Shaw* and *McCalla* (short on fuel) and DMS *Southard* and *Hovey*.

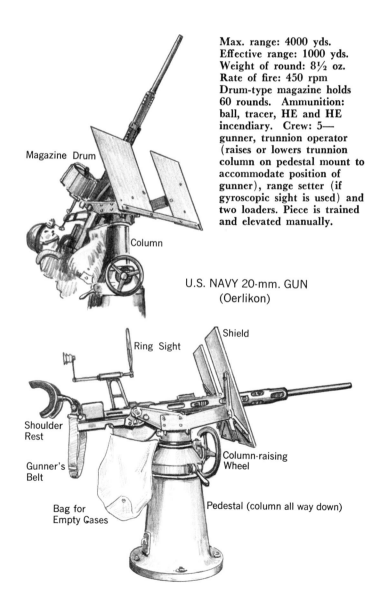

Max. range: 4000 yds. Effective range: 1000 yds. Weight of round: 8½ oz. Rate of fire: 450 rpm Drum-type magazine holds 60 rounds. Ammunition: ball, tracer, HE and HE incendiary. Crew: 5—gunner, trunnion operator (raises or lowers trunnion column on pedestal mount to accommodate position of gunner), range setter (if gyroscopic sight is used) and two loaders. Piece is trained and elevated manually.

Magazine Drum

Column

U.S. NAVY 20-mm. GUN (Oerlikon)

Ring Sight

Shield

Shoulder Rest

Gunner's Belt

Column-raising Wheel

Bag for Empty Cases

Pedestal (column all way down)

AMERICAN AND JAPANESE NAVAL FORCES AT THE FIRST BATTLE OF GUADALCANAL, NOVEMBER 12–13

		Class	Tonnage	Speed	Armament	Launched	
San Francisco	(CA)	Astoria	9,950	32.7	9 8-in., 8 5-in.	1933	
Portland	(CA)	Indianapolis	9,800	32.7	9 8-in., 8 5-in.	1932	
Helena	(CL)	Brooklyn	10,000	34	15 6-in., 8 5-in.	1938	
Atlanta	(CL)	Atlanta	6,000	32	16 5-in., 8 21-in. TT	1941	°
Juneau	(CL)	"	"	"	" "	"	°°
Fletcher	(DD)	Fletcher	2,050	37	5 5-in., 10 21-in. TT	1942	
O'Bannon	(DD)	"	"	"	" "	"	
Laffey	(DD)	Benson	1,630	37	4 5-in., 5 21-in. TT	1941	°
Aaron Ward	(DD)	"	"	"	" "	"	
Barton	(DD)	"	"	"	" "	"	°
Monssen	(DD)	"	1,620	"	5 5-in., 10 21-in. TT	1940	°
Sterett	(DD)	Craven	1,500	36.5	4 5-in., 16 21-in. TT	1938	
Cushing	(DD)	Mahan	1,465	36.5	4 5-in., 12 21-in. TT	1935	°
Hiei	(BB)	Kongo	31,720	30.5	8 14-in., 16 6-in., 8 5-in. AA	1912	°
Kirishima	(BB)	Kongo	31,980	30.5	" " "	1912	
Nagara	(CL)	Nagara	5,170	36	7 5.5-in., 2 3-in. AA, 8 24-TT	1921	
Terutsuki	(DD)	Akitsuki	2,700	33	8 3.9-in., 4 24-in. TT	1941	
Akatsuki	(DD)	Akatsuki	2,090	38	6 5-in., 9 24-in. TT	1932	°
Ikazuchi	(DD)	"	"	"	" "	"	
Inazume	(DD)	"	"	"	" "	"	
Amatsukaze	(DD)	Kagero	2,030	35.5	6 5-in., 8 24-in. TT	1939	
Yukikaze	(DD)	"	"	"	" "	"	
Asagumo	(DD)	Asashio	1,960	35	6 5-in., 8 24-in. TT	1937	
Harusame	(DD)	Shiratsuyu	1,580	34	5 5-in., 8 24-in. TT	1935	
Samidare	(DD)	"	"	"	" "	"	
Yudachi	(DD)	"	"	"	" "	1936	°
Murasame	(DD)	"	"	"	" "	1935	

° Sunk in action
°° Torpedoed and sunk next day

Callaghan and Scott returned to Savo Sound via Lengo Channel about 2200. Crews were already at battle stations and Callaghan had ordered his dispositions for the battle lineup. This, a long column, with four DDs ahead of the cruisers and four behind, has been criticized as being unwieldy and used mainly because Scott had successfully used such a formation at the Battle of Cape Esperance. Actually it was not such a bad formation as some Monday morning quarterbacks have made out. The waters around Savo and between Guadalcanal and Florida Island are restricted, and a column formation is well suited to the twists and turns of such an area, especially at night. Separation of forces led to the danger of confusion of friend with foe or, if the groups were too far apart, defeat in detail as happened at Savo. Furthermore, if the whole destroyer force had been stationed ahead (as some have suggested) and a sudden reversal of course became necessary, the destroyers would automatically find themselves in the rear instead of the van.

Where Callaghan did make a mistake, now generally acknowledged, was in flying his flag in a ship not equipped with the most effective radar apparatus in his squadron. Instead he had to rely on information relayed to him via TBS—a serious handicap at a time when every second was vital, and the equivalent of a man driving a car with windshield and windows painted over, coached by a friend with his head through the sun roof. Worse, in a way, as in moments of stress the TBS became choked with orders, inquiries, reports, etc. But in his defense it must be remembered that radar was still in its infancy and many officers, remembering its teething troubles, were not inclined to put too much trust in it. It is also possible that greater latitude as to the exact time and method of attack might have been given to Commander Thomas Stokes and Captain R. G. Tobin, commanders of the van and rear destroyer groups respectively.

So it was that the precious time won for the American force by *Helena's* first contact at 0124 was thrown away—time in which the column might have steered across the path of the oncoming Japanese—time in which some of the eighty-nine torpedo tubes available might have been fired to advantage.

The battle line as it steamed along the coast that night was; *Cushing, Laffey, Sterett, O'Bannon; Atlanta, San Francisco, Portland, Helena, Juneau; Aaron Ward, Barton, Monssen,* and *Fletcher.* Distance between types—800 yards; between destroyers—500 yards, with 700 yards between cruisers.

The Japanese squadron then steaming south was a powerful one. Vice-Admiral Hiroaki Abe flew his flag in battleship *Hiei.* With him was her sister ship *Kirishima,* light cruiser *Nagara* and eleven destroyers. Three other destroyers were sent to patrol in the area between the Russell Islands and Cape Esperance. Abe's was a bombardment mission—to render Henderson Field inoperable and to destroy or damage the planes based on it. That mission accomplished, a major military reinforcement would be landed in the Tassafaronga area and another drive be begun against the American perimeter. These troops, the 229th and 230th Regiments of the 38th Division, with artillery and engineer units, plus a naval landing force and many tons of supplies were already embarked in eleven fast transports. These vessels were escorted by twelve destroyers. The whole force, under command of Rear Admiral Tanaka, left Shortlands at 1800 on November 12. As usual, the Combined Fleet was in support, ready to beat down any major American naval counterthrust. It was also prepared to move into the waters around Guadalcanal when the all-important field had been neutralized, to prevent either attempts at reinforcement or evacuation.

At 1030 the Japanese Bombardment Group had been sighted by a B-17 and its composition fairly accurately reported (three battleships or heavy cruisers, one cruiser, and six destroyers 335 miles north of Guadalcanal). An afternoon report of a sighting of Japanese aircraft carriers 265 miles to the west proved to be false. There were two Japanese carriers in the area, *Hiyo* and *Junyo,* but they were some distance north of the reported position and they were not sighted.

At about 1530, Abe ordered his squadron to take up a double half-ring formation—five DDs fanned out 8000 meters in front of *Nagara* and an inner semicircle closer in to the cruiser. *Hiei* followed 2000 meters behind, with *Kirishima* the same

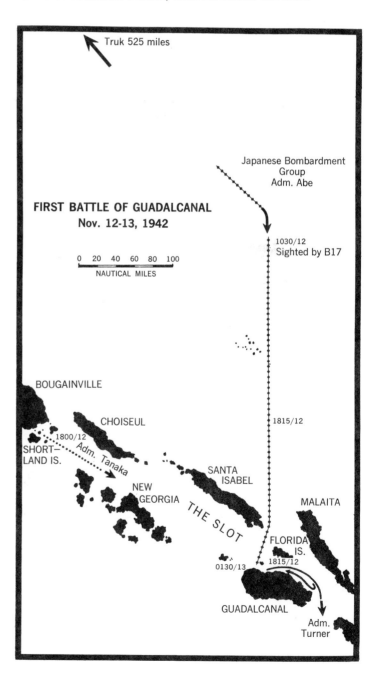

Truk 525 miles

Japanese Bombardment Group
Adm. Abe

FIRST BATTLE OF GUADALCANAL
Nov. 12-13, 1942

0 20 40 60 80 100
NAUTICAL MILES

1030/12
Sighted by B17

BOUGAINVILLE

CHOISEUL

1815/12

1800/12

Adm. Tanaka

SHORT-
LAND IS.

SANTA
ISABEL

NEW
GEORGIA

THE SLOT

MALAITA

FLORIDA
IS.

0130/13   1815/12

GUADALCANAL

Adm.
Turner

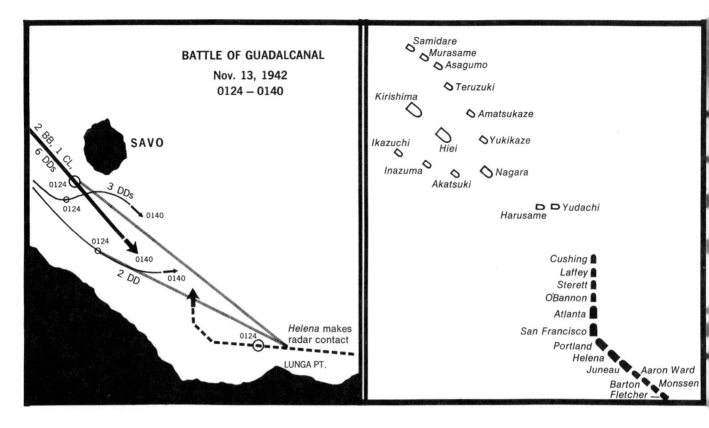

BATTLE OF GUADALCANAL
Nov. 13, 1942
0124 – 0140

SAVO

2 BB, 1 CL.
6 DDs

0124
0124
3 DDs
0140
0124
0140
2 DD
0140

Helena makes
radar contact
0124

LUNGA PT.

Samidare
Murasame
Asagumo
Teruzuki
Kirishima
Amatsukaze
Ikazuchi
Hiei
Yukikaze
Inazuma
Akatsuki
Nagara

Harusame
Yudachi

Cushing
Laffey
Sterett
O'Bannon
Atlanta
San Francisco
Portland
Helena
Juneau
Aaron Ward
Barton
Monssen
Fletcher

distance behind *Hiei*. An hour after the defensive formation was complete, a float plane was launched to reconnoiter the Savo Sound area. At 1800 the force ran into a heavy squall. Sheets of rain and gathering darkness cut visibility to a few yards. Despite danger of collision Abe maintained speed, keeping pace with the tropical storm moving south overhead.

For hour after hour the Japanese warships steamed south at a steady 18 knots, while the drenching rain provided a protective curtain, forming perfect cover from plane observation or attack. After hours of silence, at 2300 the float plane radioed a sighting of more than a dozen enemy warships off Lunga Point. And still the warm tropical rain poured down.

At midnight, still proceeding toward his target area under the increasing downpour, Abe received a radio message from observers on Guadalcanal reporting that they too were enveloped in sheets of rain. This was no weather for a bombardment and the Japanese admiral ordered a 180° turn. Despite the complex formation all ships executed the turn, although during the long advance in almost zero visibility the screening destroyers had lost alignment.

Forty minutes later the rain ended and Abe once more ordered an about-face. In about 20 minutes Guadalcanal reported clear weather but

no ships in sight. Another half-hour brought the Japanese to within 12 miles of the island and the admiral ordered the main batteries to load with bombardment ammunition.

Through the darkness, *Helena*'s radar had picked up targets and at 0124 she reported two groups of ships, the nearest at 27,000 yards with more behind at 35,000 yards. Three minutes later Callaghan ordered a slight change in course to starboard and at 0130 *Helena* reported targets 14,500 yards on her port bow. At this moment the opposing squadrons were heading almost directly toward each other, and the range was closing fast. Callaghan held his fire. The initial advantage given the Americans by their radar was being thrown away and still no command came to fire either guns or torpedoes.

At 0137 the American admiral, handicapped in his solution of the rapidly changing problem by his flagship's lack of effective radar and by the overburdened TBS channel (choked with requests for information as well as orders as to speed and course, and squalling like an angry Donald Duck), ordered course changed to due north, hoping perhaps to cross the approaching enemy's T. (i.e., with the Japanese formation at right angles to the center of his own battle line).

If this was his intention he was a little too late. The leading Japanese destroyers, *Yudachi* and

Harusame, were about to cross the bows of his own lead destroyer and at 0141, *Yudachi* reported "enemy sighted." *Cushing* saw enemy destroyers ahead, passing from port to starboard, and swung hard left to avoid collision. The unsignaled move threw the American line into confusion as the van destroyers turned in *Cushing's* wake. *Atlanta* also went hard left and the flagship at once wanted to know what she was doing. "Avoiding our own destroyers" was the reply over TBS. After a moment's hesitation *San Francisco* also swung left, followed by the rest of the squadron.

The move headed Callaghan's squadron smack into the Japanese formation and the following melee has never been accurately plotted. It was both brief and bloody, perhaps the most vicious night action in history, with armored ships engaging at point-blank range, destroyers raking battleships with automatic weapons and torpedoes streaking toward targets so close that the warheads had no time to arm. But before the shooting began there was a curious pause, as precious minutes passed without any order from the American admiral to open fire. *Cushing's* captain finally asked permission to fire torpedoes, but by the time the request was made and granted, the enemy destroyers had vanished in the darkness. At 0145 came, "Stand by to open fire," but it was not until 0150 when Japanese searchlights illuminated *Atlanta* and as both sides opened up with shell and star shell, that Callaghan ordered, "Odd ships commence fire to starboard, even ships to port."

The Americans, although forewarned, had, by bad management, thrown away an opportunity and themselves into confusion. The Japanese, through poor judgment on their admiral's part, were thoroughly surprised. Abe had made the mistake of assuming that the warships reported earlier in the sound would have left at sunset, relinquishing control over the waters off Guadalcanal to the ships of the Imperial Japanese Navy. The contact found him with his ships in cruising formation and with his battleships main batteries loaded with incendiaries. (Hara, who was present as commander of *Amatsukaze*, says that during the few minutes between the sighting and the first shots the special bombardment ammunition was sent below and armor-piercing shell brought up from the magazines. But some, at least, still remained in the turrets. The bases of a couple of these shells were found in *San Francisco* after the battle, as well as many of the incendiary cases with which they were filled—short pieces of pipe, some 3 inches

long and about 1 inch in diameter, filled with a powdered aluminum and magnesium mixture and fused at both ends. The nose fuses of these incendiary shells must have been very sensitive, as the thin-walled projectiles, while passing through ordinary half-inch plating before bursting, broke up against armor. Had they been of armor-piercing type, or even ordinary high explosive bombardment shells the damage to *San Francisco* might have proved fatal.) However, the disciplined Japanese crews soon recovered from their surprise and the American column was the target of a hail of shells and dozens of torpedoes.

Everything was happening at once and the major part of the action was over in 15 minutes. In that time, three destroyers had gone down with most of their crews, three more and a cruiser were on fire and sinking, seven other vessels (three of them cruisers and one a battleship) were limping off, battered and blazing, while almost all the other ships engaged had suffered some damage. Close to 50,000 tons of fighting ships were on the bottom or on the way there—and some 1300 seamen, including two admirals, were dead. It was a shattering encounter, one of the swiftest and deadliest on record. To many of those who survived, it was a nightmare of ear-splitting crashes, blinding flashes, torrents of tracers, billowing flames, tangled wreckage, sprawled bodies, and oil-slicked debris. No one, not even the officers who fought their ships there, could tell afterward exactly what happened, nor even if all the ships they fired into, or received fire from, were those of the enemy.

It was *Cushing* who, at 0141, sighted two enemy

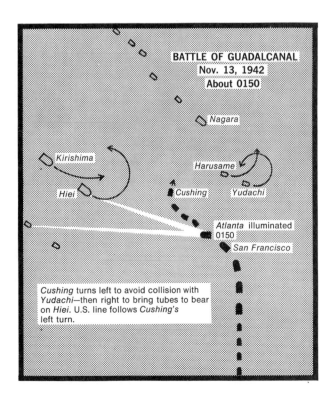

BATTLE OF GUADALCANAL
Nov. 13, 1942
About 0150

Nagara

Kirishima

Harusame

Hiei

Cushing *Yudachi*

Atlanta illuminated
0150

San Francisco

Cushing turns left to avoid collision with *Yudachi*—then right to bring tubes to bear on *Hiei*. U.S. line follows *Cushing's* left turn.

destroyers ahead. Her captain, Lieutenant Commander Edward Parker, swung her hard left and, when no command to open fire came from the flagship, requested permission to fire torpedoes. The Japanese, *Yudachi* and *Harusame,* were well past by the time he received it, and the opportunity was lost. A few minutes later the Sound exploded in a glare of searchlights, muzzle flashes, and shell bursts. *Cushing*'s gunners, like those on all the other twenty-six darkened hulls racing through the inky waters that night, were ready. A Japanese destroyer was sighted to starboard and several five-gun salvos flashed out at her. But *Cushing* headed the American line, and star shell, searchlights, and the glare of gunfire were turning night into day. In little more than a minute Japanese gunners found their mark and *Cushing* was struck amidships. Power lines were cut and she began to lose way. At that moment battleship *Hiei* came into view to port, her guns flaming and her topsides and huge pagoda control tower already sparkling with hits. Parker went hard right to bring his tubes to bear and at a scant 1000 yards let fly six fish as the giant came on. If any hit, they were duds or exploded prematurely, but *Hiei* had seen the tracks and turned left and away. *Cushing,* her power lost, slid to a halt and as she did so, a probing searchlight lit full on her. In an instant she was the target for a dozen guns. Bursting shells tore her bridge and upperworks to scrap and wrecked her battery. Flames shot up and drew more fire. At 0220 the order to abandon ship was given. Parker and a few diehards remained aboard but at 0315 they too gave up. *Cushing* burned throughout the day until about 1700 when the intense heat set off her magazines and she went down. Down with her went some sixty officers and men.

Destroyer *Laffey* followed *Cushing*'s sudden left turn. She was even closer to *Hiei* and her skipper, Lieutenant Commander W. E. Hank, had to make a violent change of course to avoid a collision. Two torpedoes were fired at such close range that they failed to arm and skidded up the underwater bulge of the battleship's hull like salmon trying to jump a fall. As *Laffey* tore across the oncoming bow, her gunners let loose with everything that would bear. Pouring torrents of 20-mm and 1.1-inch automatic fire into the towering bridge structure they set it on fire, killing Captain Suzuki and wounding Abe and others. But the battleship's turret guns roared and 14-inch shells smashed into the destroyer's engine rooms. At the same moment a torpedo exploded in her stern and she started to settle fast. Ruptured fuel lines and incendiaries turned her midships into a roaring inferno and "abandon ship" was ordered. As the stern slid under, the racked depth charges went up in a huge blast, killing many of those in the water and sending the stricken ship down with a rush. With her went nearly all her crew and her captain—posthumously awarded the Navy Cross for his attack on *Hiei.*

Third in line was *Sterett.* As one of the odd ships, her captain, Commander J. D. Coward, directed her 5-inchers at a vessel to starboard. For some three minutes *Sterett* pumped out round after round. Then, somewhere off to port, a Japanese gunnery officer caught her in his cross hairs and a salvo smashed into her stern, wrecking her steering gear, while a stray shell brought her radar down in a mess of wreckage. At that moment she, too, caught sight of *Hiei* and, steering with the screws, Coward brought *Sterett* round and fired four torpedoes. Like all the others loosed at *Hiei* that night they missed or failed to function.

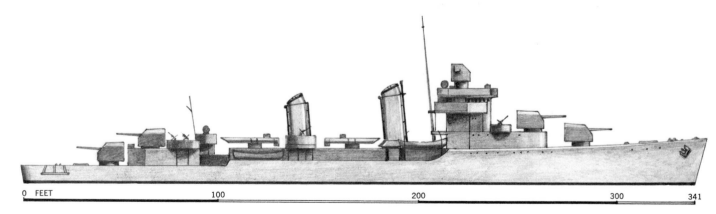

BENSON-LIVERMORE CLASS DESTROYER (96 Ships)

Launched October 1939–February 1943 Displacement: 1620–1630 tons LOA: 347¾
Beam: 36¼ Draft: 10¼ feet Twin screw. 50,000 hp=37 knots Armament: four 5 in.,
8–20 MM., ten 21 in. torpedo tubes (2✕5) Complement: 250
(Note: Changes made later in some ships: No. 3 5 in. and/or after TT mount replaced by
40-mm. and 20-mm. AA.)

ATLANTA CLASS LIGHT (Anti-aircraft) CRUISER (11 Ships)

Launched July 1941–March 1946 Displacement: 6000 tons LOA: 541½ Beam: 53¼ Draft 16½ feet Twin screw. 75,000 hp=32 knots Armor: belt 3½ in., deck 2 in. Armament: sixteen 5 in. D.P. (8×2), eight 40-mm.+20-mm. AA; eight 21 in torpedo tubes (2×4) Complement: 800

(Note: sixteen 5-in. in 1941 ships only. In later ships twin 40-mm. replaced port and starboard 5-in. mounts.)

The battleship's destroyer screen concentrated on the American ship, knocking out all but her forward 5-inchers, smashing her superstructure and setting ready-service charges alight. But her engine spaces were unhit and, though burning and with many casualties, her skipper brought her safely out of action.

The Japanese flagship, considerably battered by now, also caught a blast of fire from *O'Bannon*, last in line of the van destroyers. Lieutenant Commander E. R. Wilkinson, sheering out to avoid *Sterett*, found himself so close to *Hiei* that her main battery guns could not be depressed enough to bear. *O'Bannon's* 5-inch, 20-mm, and 1.1-inch automatics plastered the huge target and two torpedoes ran straight and true. The American destroyermen would have given much for a torpedo as deadly and reliable as those in the Japanese tubes that Friday the 13th—for *O'Bannon's* pair also failed to score. She then made a sharp turn to avoid the sinking *Laffey*. As *O'Bannon* swept past, crewmen threw life jackets to the men in the water. Suddenly their ship received a terrific jolt which jarred her engines as *Laffey* blew up. The whole area was by now a maelstrom of churning screws, blazing and exploding ships, smoke, shell splashes, and red arcs of tracers. Not knowing friend from foe, Wilkinson wisely decided to clear the area and get his bearings. There was a good chance that Jap transports might be trying to slip by so *O'Bannon* steamed down the coast of Guadalcanal and out of the battle.

Heading the cruiser column, and possibly the first American vessel to fire a shot that night was *Atlanta*, flagship of Rear Admiral Scott. It was she who was first to be caught in the glare of a Japanese searchlight, to which she promptly replied with a storm of 5-inch from her main turrets.

But with the light came an answering hail of projectiles from Japanese gunners. One salvo (Hara says it was from *Hiei*) smashed *Atlanta's* bridge, killing Scott and nearly everyone else stationed there. Shells from all sides crashed into her and deadly "long lances" were streaking in her direction. "Lucky A's" luck had run out. One torpedo (perhaps two), struck hard in her engine spaces. The 6000-ton hull heaved to the explosions, then smashed down again. Mortally wounded, she staggered into *San Francisco's* line of fire and the latter's 8-inch armor-piercing projectiles (most of which passed through the thin metal of her superstructure without exploding) added to the carnage aboard. The glare of an immense explosion somewhere behind her revealed her identity, and it was this incident which prompted Callaghan to order, "Cease firing own ships." In the confusion the order, intended only for *San Francisco's* gunners, went out on TBS. Most ships had clear targets anyway but the order, which seems to have puz-

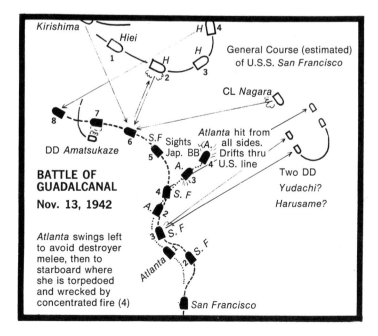

General Course (estimated) of U.S.S. *San Francisco*

BATTLE OF GUADALCANAL
Nov. 13, 1942

Atlanta swings left to avoid destroyer melee, then to starboard where she is torpedoed and wrecked by concentrated fire (4)

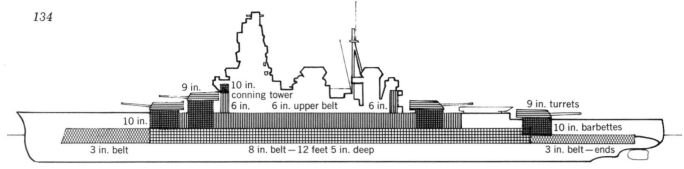

VERTICAL ARMOR OF KONGO CLASS BATTLESHIP

Main belt closed forward by armored bulkhead 6 in.–5 in., after bulkhead 8 in.–6 in. Decks total 7 in. Anti-torpedo bulges (see diagram on page 139) fitted 1930, 1936. Port and starboard engine rooms divided by unpierced fore and aft bulkhead.

zled a few captains, may have stopped some indiscriminate shooting.

Atlanta was a doomed ship. Ten minutes after fire was opened she was a blazing wreck, her engines dead, her hull ripped by torpedoes, her upperworks holed by upward of fifty medium to large caliber hits and seven of her eight turrets out of action. Heroic efforts were made to save her. By morning she had drifted toward Lunga Point and all wounded and non-essential personnel were taken off by landing craft. Tug *Bobolink* took her in tow about 0930 and she still had enough fight left in her to drive off a Betty which seemed about to attack. At 1400 she anchored off Kukum but it was obvious that she could not be saved and as the Japs were expected back in force that night she was scuttled and went down just after dark.

The flagship *San Francisco* played a valiant part that night. When the shooting began, her 5-inchers illuminated an enemy destroyer to starboard and she got off seven main battery salvos at a range of less than 2 miles, setting the target afire. Fire was then switched to a vessel ahead (this may have been *Atlanta* mistaken for an enemy destroyer) but then Japanese battleships were sighted. Admiral Callaghan gave his last order: "We want the big ones! Get the big ones first!" *Hiei* was crossing *San Francisco*'s bow and Captain Young swung left to bring his after turret to bear. The Japanese battleship also turned left and the two flagships steamed by each other on opposite courses about 2500 yards apart. It was a naval duel reminiscent more of the eighteenth century than the twentieth, fought at (for modern naval guns of those calibers) point-blank range.

San Francisco fired first—a salvo ranged at 2200 yards, all of which, except one shell, fell short. *Hiei* (whose fire control and ranging apparatus

must have been already badly shot up) fired short —two 4-gun salvos which burst on impact and sent up showers of green-white incendiaries. *San Francisco*'s guns then went to rapid fire and scored many of the hits which ultimately doomed the 31,000 ton giant. (*Hiei* and her sisters of the Kongo class had been built originally during World War I as battlecruisers, sacrificing armor for speed. In a slugging match at close range even 5-inch shells would penetrate their lightly [3-inch] armored ends while an 8-incher could go through their 8-inch main armor belt.) At the same time *San Francisco* was taking hits from *Hiei*'s secondary battery of 6-inchers and her 5-inch AA guns, as well as from light cruiser *Nagara* (ahead of *Hiei* and on *San Francisco*'s starboard quarter) and from *Kirishima*, on the American cruiser's port side. Then *Hiei*'s third salvo hit abreast *San Francisco*'s bridges with shattering effect. Admiral Callaghan and three of the lieutenant commanders of his staff were killed, Captain Young was mortally wounded, and the ship's navigator blown off the bridge onto a gun mount two decks below. Another shell tore through the roof of hastily repaired Battle II, killing everyone inside including the executive officer. Steering control was temporarily lost but was switched to the conning tower, the Officer of the Deck, Lieutenant Commander Bruce McCandless, one of the few survivors of the bridge area, handled the ship during the rest of the action. About this time a Japanese destroyer (Hara's *Amatsukaze*) crossed ahead and raced down *San Francisco*'s port side, her guns blazing. Fortunately she was so close that the 4 fish which she fired as she sped by failed to arm, although the Japanese believed they heard them strike. As it was, her 5-inch guns completed the wrecking of *San Francisco*'s portside secondary battery.

The Japanese battleships were pulling away now

Diagram showing hits of various calibers on U.S.S. San Francisco in night action of November 12, 1942. Large circles show hits estimated as 8 in. or over. Small holes are 6 in., 5.5 in. and 5 in. Black—port side. White—starboard. Most of major caliber hits were estimated by Navy inspectors as 8 in. However, as no Japanese heavy (8-in. gun) cruiser was present, it is likely that these "8 in." were from 14″ bombardment projectiles with reduced bursting charges. Not shown are many hits by automatic weapons and shell fragments.

and fire was slackening. *Kirishima* fired a few parting salvos which splashed close aboard, but *San Francisco's* fighting was over for a while. Some twenty-five fires were raging aboard and water was pouring in through holes near the waterline. Forty-five hits were later counted, many of them from 14-inch projectiles. Casualties amounted to eighty-three killed and 106 seriously wounded—low, considering the beating she had taken. Early in the morning there was a brief alarm when a cruiser, afterward identified as *Helena*, challenged. The signal board showing the correct answer was now twisted scrap and only a hasty reply by blinker saved the flagship from a further pounding. Despite the heavy damage topside, her engine spaces were unhit and she was able to rendezvous with the survivors of the squadron later in the morning.

Portland, "Sweet Pea" to her crew, opened fire on targets to starboard. She was following in the flagship's wake, her guns still slamming at a dimly seen vessel 3 miles away when one of the many Japanese torpedoes, then darting toward the American squadron, tore a great gash in her stern. Twisted plates from the ruptured hull pulled *Portland* round in a complete circle. She completed the first involuntary turn in time to catch *Hiei* in her sights and her forward turrets added to the wreckage aboard that battered battleship. This was the extent of *Portland's* fighting for the night. Condemned by her shattered stern to steam in circles, she played no further part in the battle until early morning. Daylight then revealed a burning Japanese destroyer, *Yudachi*, some 12,500 yards away. Still circling out of control, *Portland* fired six salvos from her forward turrets. One of the thirty-six shells must have found a magazine, as

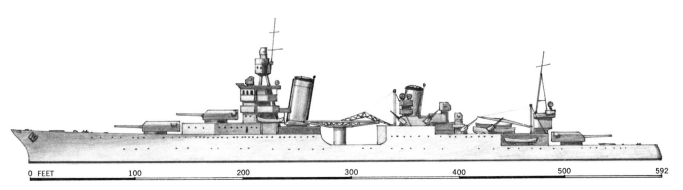

INDIANAPOLIS CLASS HEAVY CRUISER (2 Ships)

Launched November 1931, May 1932
Displacement: 9950 (Portland 9800)   LOA: 610¼   Beam: 66¼   Draft: 17¼ feet
4 screws.   107,000 hp=32.7 knots
Armor: belt 4 in., deck 4 in., turret 3 in.
Armament: nine 8 in. (3×3), eight 5 in. (8×1), 40-mm. and 20-mm. added.
Aircraft: three   Complement: 1150

FLETCHER CLASS DESTROYER (175 Ships)

Launched May 1942–June 1944
Displacement: 2050 tons LOA: 376½ Beam: 39½ Draft: 17¾ feet
Twin screw. 60,000 hp=37 knots
Armament: five 5 in. D.P., six to ten 40-mm., numerous 20-mm., ten 21 in. torpedo tubes
Complement: 300 (Ships of this class differed somewhat in minor details, especially make-up
and arrangement of AA weapons) SC Radar

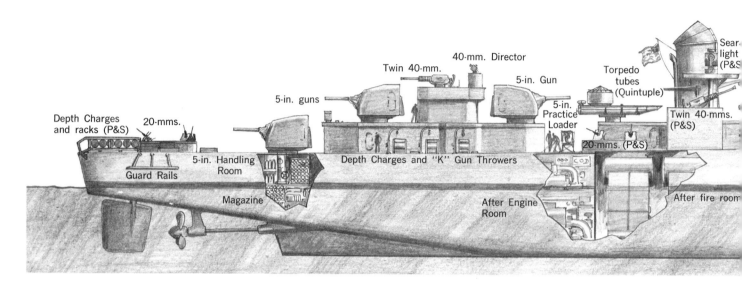

Yudachi, already abandoned, blew up with a roar. With busy *Bobolink* pushing against "Sweet Pea's" starboard bow she finally crawled into Tulagi Harbor after dark.

Helena was lucky that night. Although her gunners poured out shells at target after target, she received only minor topside damage. Her skipper, Captain Gilbert C. Hoover conned her successfully through the huddle of damaged or sinking ships ahead and miraculously avoided any of the "tin fish" which laced the waters. At 0126 she fired her last salvo at the retreating enemy.

Last in the cruiser column, *Juneau* was less fortunate. Firing hard she swept along behind *Helena* until a "long lance" drove into her forward fire room. The blast put the light cruiser out of action. Down by the bows, with a list, one of her two propeller shafts damaged and with several shell hits, she limped out of the battle to meet a sad fate a few hours later.

Aaron Ward, flagship of Squadron Commander Captain R. G. Tobin, after firing at targets some 7000 yards away and finding the range repeatedly fouled by friendly ships, finally headed into the melee, shooting at such targets as presented themselves. A hit which wrecked her director necessitated a shift to local control; then one of a series of hits holed her badly, flooding her engine room,

while others brought down her mast and radar, smashed her searchlights and left fifteen of her crew dead and fifty-seven wounded. She was finally towed toward Tulagi.

Barton's story is short and tragic. She opened fire, then loosed four torpedoes at a swiftly moving target, probably one of the three destroyers of Abe's starboard screen. She made a sudden stop to avoid collision with a vessel looming up ahead and as she came to a halt, screws frantically beating the water under her fantail, two torpedoes tore her in half. One moment she was there, 347 feet of steel, crammed with intricate machinery and weapons, manned by 250 highly trained fighting men. An instant later she was gone—vanished in a churning, boiling cauldron of blazing oil, wreckage, and bodies, some 225 of them. She had been in commission less than 5½ months. She had been in action seven minutes.

Racing in *Barton's* wake came *Monssen.* Caught in the general uproar as the first guns went off she soon found targets to port and starboard. As her guns flashed out, a battleship was sighted to starboard and the destroyer launched a salvo of five torpedoes—followed by five more, also to starboard, at a second target. With a flash and roar her next ahead suddenly broke in two and vanished —so close that *Monssen's* bow plowed through the

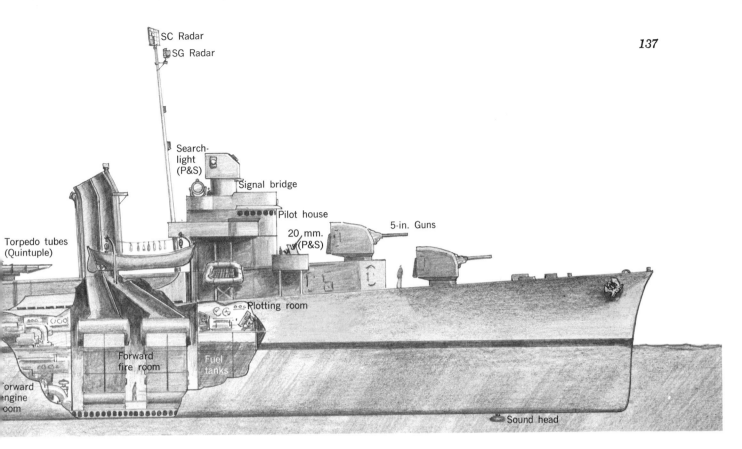

SC Radar

SG Radar

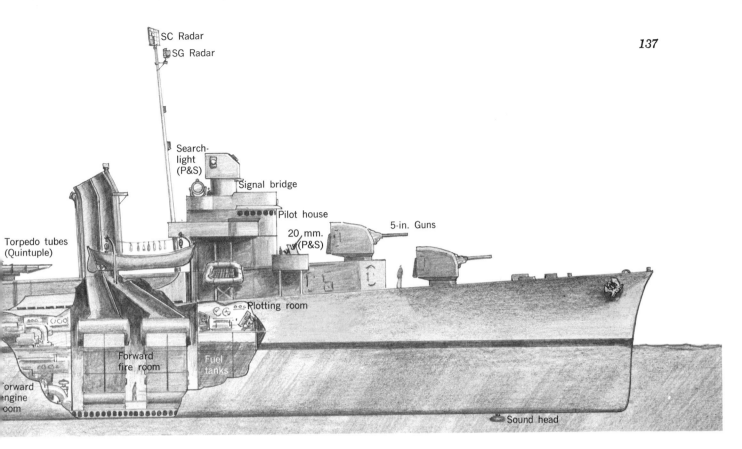 Search-
light
(P&S)

Signal bridge

Pilot house

20 mm.
(P&S)

5-in. Guns

Torpedo tubes
(Quintuple)

Plotting room

Forward
fire room

Fuel
tanks

Forward
engine
room

Sound head

spread of oil, wreckage, and struggling humans which marked *Barton's* grave.

Then tragedy overtook *Monssen.* Star shells burst overhead, bathing the ship in ghostly greenish-white brilliance. Her captain, Lieutenant Commander C. E. McCombs, was certain the shells came from an American ship and he ordered recognition signals turned on. Immediately two searchlights fastened on her, followed by a deluge of shells which reduced her to a flaming wreck. Some thirty-seven shells struck, blowing 5-inch guns overboard, crashing into her fire rooms and engine rooms, smashing her bridge and killing some 130 of her crew. The survivors went overside at 0220. *Monssen* burned until noon, then blew up and sank.

Fletcher, last ship in Callaghan's battle line, bore a charmed life. She carried the new SG radar and used it efficiently—switching her 5-inchers from target to target. Of the two ships next ahead, one was sunk and the other in flames but *Fletcher's* captain, Commander W. M. Cole, finally managed to get his ship clear of the melee. Dodging torpedoes and deluged by near misses, he steered north, avoiding the cruiser action. Then, using his radar to pick his way, he turned south and headed for the enemy. His screen showed him a large target some 7000 yards away and he loosed a spread of 10

torpedoes. A great glow was seen to go up at the proper time in the direction of the target, but Savo Sound was full of sudden flares and flashes that night and it is doubtful if any of *Fletcher's* torpedoes hit. Her tubes empty, Cole headed back to Sealark Channel. *Fletcher* was the only ship in the American squadron to escape without a scratch.

The maneuvers of the ships of Abe's squadron are even harder to follow than those of Callaghan's. The Japanese admiral's formation, hardly suited to an engagement, was somewhat disjointed after a long run in zero visibility and two 180° turns. Her two lead destroyers, *Yudachi* and *Harusame,* were far ahead of the battleships, while light cruiser *Nagara* was also somewhat ahead of her assigned position. The three other destroyers of the outer semicircle were out of station and instead of being on *Hiei's* port bow were now on *Kirishima's* port quarter. In the mixed-up brawl which followed it possibly did not make a great deal of difference, although had they been in their assigned stations they would have been in a better position to use their torpedoes before the opposing forces became hopelessly tangled. According to Hara, the five destroyers steaming in an arc 8000 meters ahead of *Nagara* had already had to reverse course (before receiving *Hiei's* initial order to turn 180°) because they were approaching too close to Guadalcanal.

SHIRATSUYU CLASS DETROYER (10 Ships)

Launched April 1935–March 1937 Displacement: 1580 tons LOA: 860 Beam: 32½ Draft 11½ feet Twin screw. 42,000 hp=34 knots Armament: five 5 in. D.P. (2×2, 1×1 [No. 2 Mount]); four 25-mm. (2×2), eight 24 in. torpedo tubes (2×4) Complement: 180

Yudachi's captain admitted that when *Cushing* loomed up, heading as if to hit *Yudachi* amidships, he was completely taken by surprise and not ready to fire. She and *Harusame* ran on until they saw gunfire, then *Yudachi* turned back toward the melee, while *Harusame* tailed after *Nagara*. *Yudachi*, firing rapidly, ran through the American formation, cutting across in front of *Aaron Ward*, then swinging right. This maneuver, which brought her parallel to the American line, also brought her under the guns of *Juneau*. That cruiser opened a heavy fire on *Yudachi*, who replied with gunfire and a salvo of eight torpedoes. These torpedoes missed but a couple from off the starboard, fired by *Amatsukaze*, did not. *Yudachi's* skipper, who did not relish a gun duel with the American cruiser's fourteen 5-inchers, was relieved to see a column of flame and water rise from his adversary, marking the end of her fighting for the night. *Yudachi* then attacked a cruiser (believed to be *Portland*) with torpedoes and claimed a hit. She was then involved in a gun duel (possibly with *Aaron Ward*) and set on fire. She burned all night and was finally abandoned, her crew taken off by *Samidare*. As related above, she was sunk later by long-range gunfire from *Portland*.

At the commencement of the action Hara's *Amatsukaze* found herself behind *Hiei* when that ship was receiving fire from *Cushing*. Overs were splashing down around Hara's ship and he put on speed and made a run parallel to the American formation. Star shells from *Nagara*, then heading east ahead of the battleships, lit up a column of four American destroyers (the rear formation). Hara fired eight torpedoes, one or more of which sank *Barton*, then swung around and headed back. Up ahead in the distance Hara could see *Hiei* outlined by the fires in her superstructure. A few minutes later a cruiser was made out to port silhouetted by the glare of her guns. This was *Juneau* firing on her port side at *Yudachi*. Hara loosed four

torpedoes at this target and a red flash showed that at least some of his fish had hit.

Still proceeding toward his flagship, the only vessel he could recognize, Hara saw a rising glow to the west (probably the beginning of the end of *Yudachi*) and noted the time—0213. A moment later he nearly collided with a vessel (*San Francisco*) heading toward him on his port side. Flashing on his searchlight, Hara recognized her for an enemy cruiser and *Amatsukaze* tore down the vessel's port side, firing everything she had, at the same time loosing her last four torpedoes. As noted before they were too close to arm, a fact which undoubtedly saved the American flaghip from sudden disaster.

As in so many other cases, the use of searchlights often proved a two edged weapon. Hara left his on too long and a cruiser he believed to be *Helena* landed a salvo aboard. Darkened now, and making smoke, Hara tried to get away; but *Amatsukaze's* steering gear was out of order, among other damage, and she made two circles in her own smoke, taking a few more hits meanwhile, before she could switch to manual steering and withdraw.

Terutsuki, astern of *Amatsukaze* as Abe's squadron came into action, is credited by Hara with sinking *Cushing* after that ship's attack on *Hiei*. *Akatsuki* was the lead ship of the three destroyers on the Japanese flagship's starboard side. She became involved in the general melee and must have passed close by the badly battered destroyers of the American van formation. Through the smoke and glare came *Atlanta*, and *Akatsuki's* torpedo officer had her in his sights. One or more of the spread he fired hit the American cruiser and gave her her death blow. Then, so Hara says, she came under a heavy cross fire between *San Francisco* and another American destroyer and went down blazing in a hail of shells, taking most of her crew with her.

Light cruiser *Nagara* led the Japanese battle line

in and led it out again when Abe decided to withdraw. She was followed by *Yukikaze*, who did not receive a scratch in the action. She later returned to stand by *Hiei*.

Asagumo, Murasame, and *Samidare,* the three van destroyers which had fallen astern in the mixup resulting from the poor visibility and Abe's two countermarches, arrived late to the fray. Of the three only *Murasame* received any serious damage. She was hit in her forward boiler room but could still steam, if but slowly. *Samidare* later stood by *Yudachi* and removed her crew. *Inazume,* following *Akatsuki,* was not damaged but *Ikazuchi,* who was astern of her, received damage to her forward gun mount.

Flagship *Hiei* took a terrible pounding. Set on by several destroyers, who shot up her pagoda and set fire to her superstructure, she also received many 8-inch hits from *San Francisco* and *Portland.* Her engines were damaged, her rudder jammed, and her topsides were a shambles. Japanese accounts say she was hit eighty-five times, although her main battery guns were still in working order and she had received little underwater damage. The intensity of the fire which lashed at his flagship, as well as the surprise and ignorance as to the strength of the opposing squadron induced Abe (who had a reputation in the Japanese Navy for extreme caution) to break off the action a scant 15 minutes after it began by ordering his two battleships north.

Hiei did not get very far. Her damaged machinery could only move her at a crawl and daylight found her just north of Savo Island. Combined

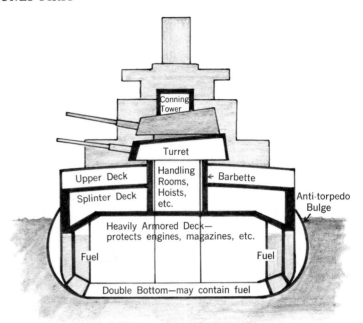

ARMOR PROTECTION OF A BATTLESHIP

Fleet ordered *Kirishima* to take her still-smoking sister ship in tow, but Abe's chief concern was to get his squadron as far away from Henderson Field as possible. *Yukikaze* stood by the crippled flagship as the expected air attacks began. *Hiei* was hit by fliers from Henderson, as well as by torpedo planes from *Enterprise* en route to Guadalcanal as a reinforcement (*Enterprise*'s elevator was still jammed in the up position—it was said that even Halsey himself would not have dared push the "down" button—and this slowed her flying operation, hence the transfer of planes to the field).

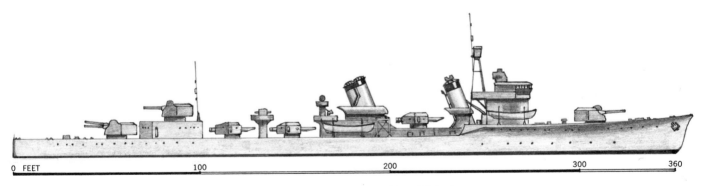

AKATSUKI CLASS DESTROYER (4 Ships)

Launched October 1931–June 1932
Displacement: 2090 tons LOA: 371½ Beam: 34 Draft: 10¾ feet
Twin screw. 50,000 hp=38 knots
Armament: six 5-in. D.P. (3×2), two 13-mm. AA, nine 24-in. torpedo tubes (3×3)
Complement: 200

Torpedoes in *Hiei's* stern set her steaming in a circle, others holed her along her sides. Bombs ripped through her decks while fighters strafed her AA positions. Flying Fortresses from Espiritu Santo dropped fifty-six bombs around her (only one is believed to have hit) and by 1430 *Hiei* was blazing from stem to stern and dead in the water about 5 miles NNW of Savo. She was still afloat, though, and to the frustrated American pilots she appeared unsinkable. But she was beyond salvage and her crew was removed by *Yukikaze* and other destroyers which had returned to the scene. Abe finally gave the order to scuttle (which infuriated Yamamoto and helped lose Abe his job). The great ship, red hot from the fires raging within her, went hissing to the bottom, the first Japanese battleship sunk since the war began.

Kirishima received only minor damage and was back again two nights later—a sortie from which she would not return.

And so ended the First Battle of Guadalcanal. Without any doubt the Japanese had won a tactical victory. At the cost of an old battleship and two destroyers sunk, Abe's squadron had sunk one cruiser and four destroyers, and seriously damaged three cruisers and two destroyers. American casualties far outnumbered those of the Japanese and included two admirals. Strategically the victory was an American one. Abe had come south to wreck Henderson Field and he had turned north without putting a single shell into it. To rub salt into that wound the planes which later in the day reduced his flagship to a drifting inferno operated from the very field he had been sent to destroy.

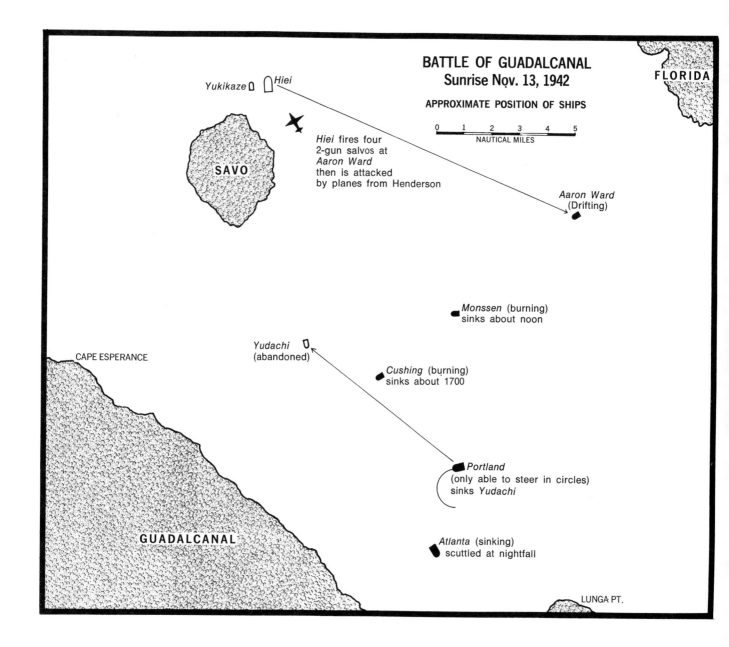

BATTLE OF GUADALCANAL
Sunrise Nov. 13, 1942

APPROXIMATE POSITION OF SHIPS

0   1   2   3   4   5
NAUTICAL MILES

FLORIDA

Yukikaze   *Hiei*

Hiei fires four 2-gun salvos at *Aaron Ward* then is attacked by planes from Henderson

SAVO

Aaron Ward (Drifting)

Monssen (burning) sinks about noon

CAPE ESPERANCE

Yudachi (abandoned)

Cushing (burning) sinks about 1700

Portland (only able to steer in circles) sinks *Yudachi*

Atlanta (sinking) scuttled at nightfall

GUADALCANAL

LUNGA PT.

XIII
Tanaka the Tenacious

THE SECOND BATTLE OF GUADALCANAL—
AND A CONVOY GOES DOWN

The naval events of November 12–13 should rightly be considered as only the first act of a three-act drama, which did not ring down its final curtain until late on November 15 and it is only as a matter of convenience that it is here broken down into two chapters. It was a continuous performance and dramatic episodes followed one another in rapid succession.

Even while the battered Japanese flagship *Hiei* was undergoing her first aerial attacks of the day, disaster struck the retiring American squadron. At daybreak *Helena's* Captain Hoover, as senior surviving officer, headed the remnants of Callaghan's force through Indispensable Strait and southeast toward Espiritu Santo. There submarine *I-26* sighted the three American cruisers in a shaky

column formation (*Juneau* alternately sheering to port and starboard due to her underwater damage) guarded by badly damaged *Sterett, Fletcher,* and *O'Bannon* (whose sonar gear had been put out of commission by the exploding *Laffey*).

A little after 1100 the submarine loosed a salvo of torpedoes at *San Francisco.* They passed ahead of that vessel but one or more raced on to strike *Juneau* some 1500 yards away. To quote McCandless, on watch on *San Francisco* at the time of the attack: "*Juneau* didn't sink—she blew up with all the fury of an erupting volcano. There was a terrific thunderclap and a plume of white water that was blotted out by a huge brown hemisphere a thousand yards across, from within which came the sounds of more explosions . . ." A twin 5-inch

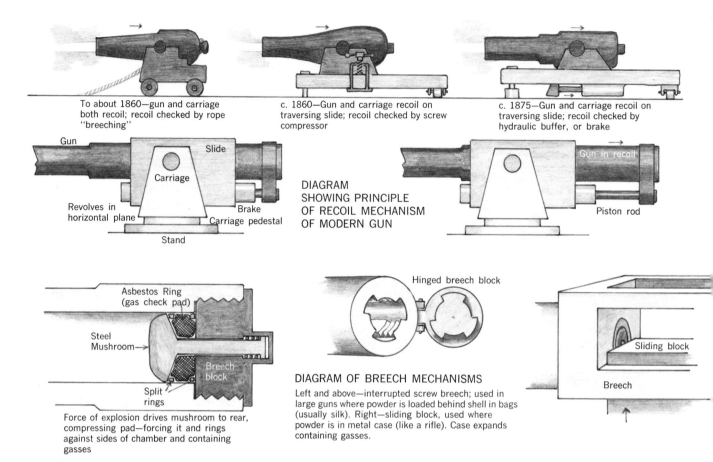

To about 1860—gun and carriage both recoil; recoil checked by rope "breeching"

c. 1860—Gun and carriage recoil on traversing slide; recoil checked by screw compressor

c. 1875—Gun and carriage recoil on traversing slide; recoil checked by hydraulic buffer, or brake

Gun
Slide
Carriage
Revolves in horizontal plane
Brake
Carriage pedestal
Stand

DIAGRAM SHOWING PRINCIPLE OF RECOIL MECHANISM OF MODERN GUN

Gun in recoil
Piston rod

Asbestos Ring (gas check pad)
Steel Mushroom
Breech block
Split rings

Force of explosion drives mushroom to rear, compressing pad—forcing it and rings against sides of chamber and containing gasses

Hinged breech block

DIAGRAM OF BREECH MECHANISMS

Left and above—interrupted screw breech; used in large guns where powder is loaded behind shell in bags (usually silk). Right—sliding block, used where powder is in metal case (like a rifle). Case expands containing gasses.

Sliding block
Breech

gun turret was seen to rise slowly above the cloud, then drop back out of sight. A long piece of plating smashed into *San Francisco*'s bridge while a smaller piece of debris broke a seaman's legs. When the pall of smoke drifted away, the 6000-ton vessel had vanished.

Over a hundred of her crew lived through the blast but it was considered that stopping to search for possible survivors was too hazardous in those submarine-infested waters and the squadron steamed on. A B-17 overhead was requested to relay a report of the sinking to Halsey's headquarters. The message was never received. Days later a PBY rescued six men from a raft. Three more paddled to an island where they were tended by a white trader. The sole survivor of one raftload was picked up by a destroyer on November 20. It was a bad foulup—one that, fairly or not, cost Captain Hoover his command.

The scene now changes to the north. Here great things were afoot and fresh squadrons flying the flag of the Rising Sun were getting under way,

their destination Guadalcanal. The core of the Japanese advance, although the slowest and most vulnerable, was the all-important troop convoy led by Tanaka. These ships had left the Shortlands at 1800 on November 12. On receiving orders from Combined Fleet that the debarkation had been delayed until the 14th, Tanaka turned back to Shortlands about 0200 and arrived there later on November 13. An hour later he sailed again, this time preceded by Mikawa in *Chokai*. Mikawa was leading his Support Group consisting of *Chokai*, *Kinugasa*, *Isuzu*, and two DDs—and a Bombardment Group, *Suzuya* (flagship of Rear Admiral Shoji Nishimura) and *Maya*, *Tenryu*, and four DDs. The main cover for Tanaka's Reinforcement Group, however, was Kondo's Attack Group consisting of two heavy cruisers, *Atago* and *Takao*, with light cruiser *Sendai* and five destroyers, to which were added *Kirishima*, *Nagara*, and four destroyers—veterans of Abe's battle of November 12–13. Distant cover was supplied by Kurita's Carrier Support Group; carriers *Junyo* and *Hiyo*, battleships *Kongo* and *Haruna*, heavy cruiser *Tone* and attendant destroyers.

It was a formidable force, and to meet it Kinkaid was steaming north as fast as possible with Task Force 16 (*Enterprise* and attendant cruisers and destroyers) and Task Force 64 (Lee and his two battleships and escorting destroyers). As noted in the preceding chapter, there had been a report on the afternoon of November 12 of Japanese carriers within striking distance of Guadalcanal and at dawn on November 13 a ten-plane search flew off *Enterprise* to locate them. Task Force 16 was still 340 miles SSE of Guadalcanal and the planes made no sightings. Later nine Avengers and six Wildcats were sent to Henderson (the planes which made the initial attack on *Hiei*).

B-17s and Catalinas made several contacts far to the north on November 13—including a sighting of Tanaka and his transports. And *Enterprise* was also spied on, by a Kawanishi flying boat which was promptly shot down by the carrier's CAP. Meanwhile, reports of Japanese naval units heading for Guadalcanal prompted Halsey to order Lee to be ready for a fast run to Guadalcanal. At about 1830 the order came to proceed to the island. But Kinkaid's progress north had been slow—there had been time-consuming end runs around areas of suspected submarine activity, and the slight southerly wind meant that to fly off and recover planes *Enterprise* had to steam at full speed directly away from her objective. Thus Halsey's order found Lee some 350 miles from Guadalcanal—too far for him to be able to head off a bombardment of Henderson Field that night. So when just after midnight Mikawa arrived off Savo Island the defense of the field rested on the frail hulls of the Tulagi PT boats.

The valiant assaults made by two of the PT boats scored no hits but the suddenness of the attack and the probability that the speedy little warships with their deadly loads were out in force quite possibly helped hasten the Japanese retirement. But the bombardment came off as scheduled. *Suzuya* and *Maya* escorted by *Tenryu* and four destroyers steamed along the coastline off Lunga and deluged Henderson Field with some one thousand rounds of high explosive from their 8-inch guns. Once again the field's defenders burrowed into foxholes and dugouts as shells screamed into their positions—positions brightly lit by flares from Washing Machine Charley droning around overhead. The field area was soon lit by other flares as precious planes went up in flames. Unwilling guests at the performance were hundreds of survivors from *Atlanta* and the sunken destroyers.

For over half an hour the big projectiles roared in. When Nishimura steamed off to rejoin Mikawa some eighteen planes had been destroyed.

It was not enough. At first light on November 14, scout planes from Henderson and long range search aircraft from Espiritu Santo were combing the waters north and west of Guadalcanal. A couple of hours later, Tanaka's Reinforcement Group had been spotted 150 miles up The Slot heading for the island, and Mikawa's retiring Support Group, about 140 miles away south of New Georgia.

A small strike (six TBFs, seven SBDs, and seven F4Fs) hit Mikawa about 0800. A torpedo hit was claimed on *Kinugasa*, and *Isuzu* was struck by dive bombers and set afire. *Enterprise* was now about 200 miles SSW of Guadalcanal. Search planes went up shortly after 0600 and a seventeen-plane strike of dive bombers was readied on her flight deck. On receiving a report of enemy planes some 140 miles away this strike took off. No more was heard of the enemy planes but shortly after 0900 a couple

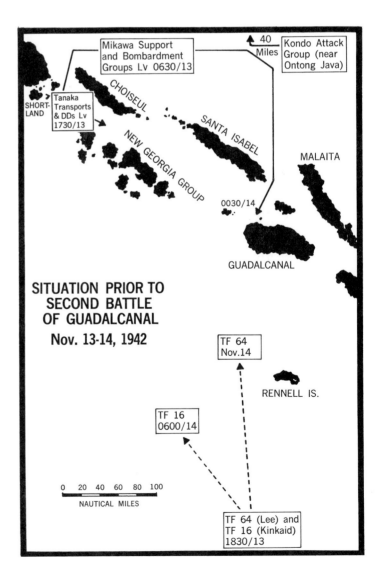

SITUATION PRIOR TO
SECOND BATTLE
OF GUADALCANAL
Nov. 13-14, 1942

↑ Kurita (Carrier Support Group) 0630
20 miles

↑ Kondo
20 miles

BOUGAINVILLE

Buin

Faisi

CHOISEUL

Adm. Mikawa—4 CA, 2 CL, 6 DD

Depart 0630/13

SHORTLAND

Depart 1730/13

Arrive 1600/14

Reinforcement Group
Adm. Tanaka—11 transports,
11 DD

THE SLOT

NEW GEORGIA GROUP

SANTA ISABEL

0830

6 Transports sunk—
1 badly damaged, returns
to base

1015 Several
Attacks

0915

RENDOVA

0800

1150

1245

1345—1530 Repeated
Attacks

MALAITA

FLORIDA IS.

B-17s From Espirito
Santo

RUSSELL IS.

CA *Kinugasa* sunk
CA *Isuzu* heavily damaged
CA *Chokai* lightly damaged
CA *Maya* lightly damaged
DD *Michishio* lightly damaged

GUADALCANAL

BATTLE OF GUADALCANAL

Air Attacks on Tanaka and Mikawa
NOVEMBER 14, 1942

0   30   60   90   120
NAUTICAL MILES

0630: Kinkaid
195 Miles

↓ 0630:
Lee 58 Miles

---

of scout planes sighted Mikawa's squadron about 25 miles due west of the southern tip of Rendova. The *Enterprise* strike at once headed for this target while the two sighting planes, their scouting mission accomplished, attacked already-damaged *Kinugasa* and scored a couple of near misses which started some plates and left her listing. The *Enterprise*'s SBDs arrived over the target at 0950. *Kinugasa* was hit once more and went down. In the series of attacks which lasted some two hours, *Isuzu* was hit again and heavily damaged. *Maya*, *Chokai*, and destroyer *Michishio* received light damage.

Tanaka's group had been sighted north of New Georgia about 0700. He writes that he was attacked at dawn by two B-17s and four SBDs. No damage was suffered and two SBDs shot down. There

seems to be no confirmation of this from American sources, although two of *Enterprise*'s scout planes found him and attacked about 0830. A near miss was scored on a transport and one SBD shot down by the escorting Zeros. Tanaka reports another attack by two SBDs, both of which were destroyed and it is possible that this is the attack made by the scout planes mentioned above. There is considerable discrepancy between American and Japanese accounts as to times and numbers and types of planes, although very little as to actual results.

Enterprise's planes were occupied with Mikawa (fortunately for Tanaka) but Henderson Field had been heavily reinforced in the last few days and the main attacks on the Reinforcement Group came from there. The total air strength on the island had been raised to forty-one F4Fs, thirty SBDs, nineteen TBFs, and two P-400s. To this must be added eight of the long awaited P-38s which flew in on the 12th from Espiritu Santo, while eight more from MacArthur's command made the long hop from Milne Bay on November 13. Despite damage to planes and runways by Mikawa's cruisers on the night of the 13th, planes from Henderson attacked Tanaka's group the next morning, concentrating on the transports.

The first strike, seven TBFs, eighteen SBDs, and twelve F4Fs hit just before noon. The transports had been advancing steadily in four-column formation, surrounded by the destroyers. The ships commenced evasive action while the destroyers poured out rolling clouds of smoke and studded the sky with shell bursts. Neither frantic maneuvering nor heavy AA fire stopped the Cactus fliers. Torpedoes ripped open *Nagara Maru* and *Canberra Maru*, and *Sado Maru* was crippled by bomb hits. By the time the planes withdrew the two Marus had sunk and destroyers were busy picking up survivors. *Sado Maru,* too badly damaged to proceed, was ordered back to Shortland with *Amagiri* and *Mochizuki* as escort.

At 1245 another attack roared in—seventeen SBDs escorted by fighters. *Brisbane Maru* went down this time; pilots saw her break in two, and *Kawakaze* dashed in to pull survivors out of the water. An hour later twenty more SBDs, closely followed by ten more, screamed down through the protective curtain of fire to sink *Arizona Maru* and *Shinanogawa Maru*. It was a wild scene as Tanaka remembered it: ". . . carrier bombers roaring toward targets as though to plunge into the water, releasing bombs and pulling out barely in time; each miss sending up towering columns of mist and spray; every hit raising clouds of smoke and fire as transports burst into flame and take the sickening list that spells their doom. Attackers depart, smoke screens lift and reveal the tragic scene of men jumping overboard from burning, sinking ships."

B-17s from Espiritu Santo added to the carnage. At 1430, fifteen Fortresses dropped tons of bombs from three miles up, scoring at least one hit and several near misses and shooting down several of the air escort.

At 1530 an *Enterprise* strike of eight SBDs plus fighters found Tanaka some 60 miles from Savo Island, doggedly leading the battered survivors of his armada toward the debarkation point. This attack left *Nako Maru* afire and sinking. A seven plane group from Henderson, unescorted, gave Tanaka's Zeros a chance for revenge. They shot down three SBDs, badly damaged two more and drove off the remaining two before they could do any damage.

At a cost of five planes, six of Tanaka's transports and a heavy cruiser had been sunk and other warships and a transport damaged. Estimates as to how many aboard the transports perished vary. Many were picked up by the destroyer escort but it is believed that some 3000 went down with the ships and many of those rescued must have been burned or wounded.

Still Tanaka kept on. Nightfall had put an end to the air attacks but over half of his Marus were gone, his destroyers were crammed with survivors and it was now evident that, even by pushing his remaining Marus to their maximum speed, they could not reach the beaches much before sunrise on the 15th. But his orders were to land the troops and land them he would. By now he had some powerful assistance for ahead of him in the darkness Kondo's Attack Group was approaching Savo Island.

During the night of November 13, Lee and Task Force 64 were steaming northward at high speed. It was too late by then to ward off Mikawa's cruisers and the men at Henderson Field had to weather the bombardment as best they could. The 14th saw Lee marking time some one hundred miles S by W of the island, waiting for dark before moving into Savo Sound.

Kondo's advance had not gone unreported. His squadron had left its position near Ontong Java about 1000, November 14, and proceeded south on a course designed to bring it toward Savo past the eastern end of Santa Isabel. Kondo's track brought his ships in range of submarine *Trout*, who fired a salvo which nearly hit flagship *Atago. Trout* then surfaced and sent a report in clear—which alerted Kondo that the American command had been warned. At 1600 an aerial scout reported him about 150 miles north of Guadalcanal.

By evening, Lee was closing the island, sweeping around the western end and ultimately passing Savo Island some 15 miles to the west of it. The American squadron was in extended column with destroyers *Walke, Benham, Preston,* and *Gwin* about 4000–5000 yards ahead of *Washington* and *South Dakota.* Although some distance apart both fleets were rapidly approaching each other but at 2110 Lee made a sharp turn to starboard heading due east. At 2148 he turned to starboard again, on a SSE course passing east of Savo, until 2252 when he turned to starboard once more, heading due

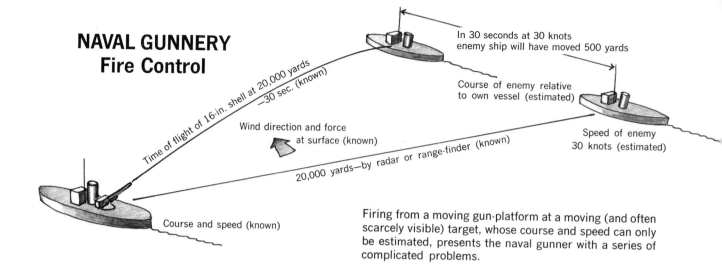

NAVAL GUNNERY
Fire Control

Time of flight of 16-in. shell at 20,000 yards—30 sec. (known)

In 30 seconds at 30 knots enemy ship will have moved 500 yards

Course of enemy relative to own vessel (estimated)

Wind direction and force at surface (known)

Speed of enemy 30 knots (estimated)

20,000 yards—by radar or range-finder (known)

Course and speed (known)

Firing from a moving gun-platform at a moving (and often scarcely visible) target, whose course and speed can only be estimated, presents the naval gunner with a series of complicated problems.

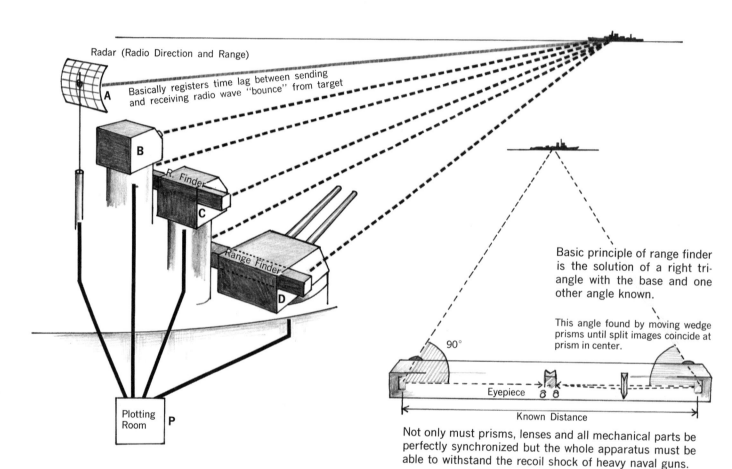

Radar (Radio Direction and Range)

Basically registers time lag between sending and receiving radio wave "bounce" from target

A

B

R. Finder **C**

Range Finder **D**

Plotting Room **P**

Basic principle of range finder is the solution of a right triangle with the base and one other angle known.

This angle found by moving wedge prisms until split images coincide at prism in center.

90°

Eyepiece

Known Distance

Not only must prisms, lenses and all mechanical parts be perfectly synchronized but the whole apparatus must be able to withstand the recoil shock of heavy naval guns.

Into the intricate calculating instruments in the plotting room (far below decks) comes data from the numerous range-taking and observation stations in various parts of the ship. Ranges are taken by radar and/or range finders like that in the diagram to the right. Among the factors which have to be computed for are: range; course and speed of both vessels; direction and strength of wind; temperature of powder (this affects the velocity of the shell, as does gun erosion and wear which has to be allowed for); drift of shell, due to the twist of the rifling, the added or subtracted velocity due to the vessels approaching or leaving the target; barometric pressure and air temperature and humidity.

Not only must prisms, lenses and all mechanical parts be perfectly synchronized but the whole apparatus must be able to withstand the recoil shock of heavy naval guns.

From control (B) fall of shot is spotted and course of enemy estimated and sent to P. From director (C) range is taken, sent to P, as also from range finders in turret (D). This data is processed and the correct elevation and deflection (from the center line of the ship) is transmitted to guns. In "director control" firing Chief Fire Control Officer in (C) fired all or selected guns electrically when target is lined in crosshairs of his scope. In control firing, gun pointer (elevation) does not follow target in his cross wire continuously, but all guns are set to fire when roll of ship brings CFCO's crosshairs on target.

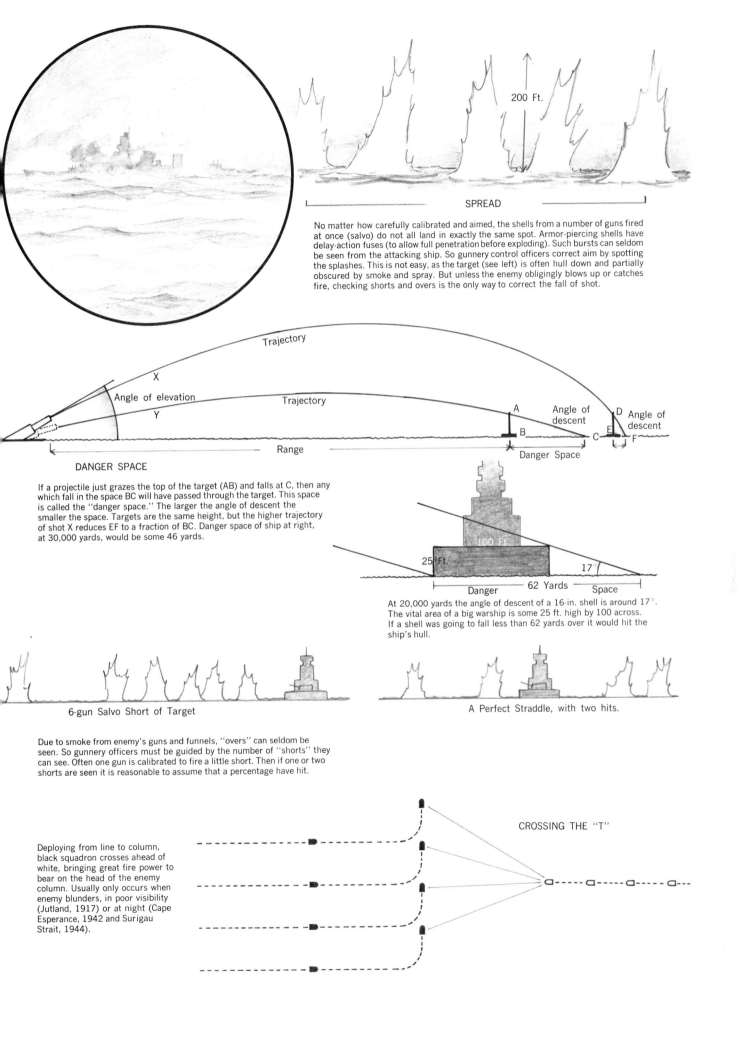

SPREAD

No matter how carefully calibrated and aimed, the shells from a number of guns fired at once (salvo) do not all land in exactly the same spot. Armor-piercing shells have delay-action fuses (to allow full penetration before exploding). Such bursts can seldom be seen from the attacking ship. So gunnery control officers correct aim by spotting the splashes. This is not easy, as the target (see left) is often hull down and partially obscured by smoke and spray. But unless the enemy obligingly blows up or catches fire, checking shorts and overs is the only way to correct the fall of shot.

DANGER SPACE

If a projectile just grazes the top of the target (AB) and falls at C, then any which fall in the space BC will have passed through the target. This space is called the "danger space." The larger the angle of descent the smaller the space. Targets are the same height, but the higher trajectory of shot X reduces EF to a fraction of BC. Danger space of ship at right, at 30,000 yards, would be some 46 yards.

At 20,000 yards the angle of descent of a 16-in. shell is around 17°. The vital area of a big warship is some 25 ft. high by 100 across. If a shell was going to fall less than 62 yards over it would hit the ship's hull.

6-gun Salvo Short of Target

A Perfect Straddle, with two hits.

Due to smoke from enemy's guns and funnels, "overs" can seldom be seen. So gunnery officers must be guided by the number of "shorts" they can see. Often one gun is calibrated to fire a little short. Then if one or two shorts are seen it is reasonable to assume that a percentage have hit.

CROSSING THE "T"

Deploying from line to column, black squadron crosses ahead of white, bringing great fire power to bear on the head of the enemy column. Usually only occurs when enemy blunders, in poor visibility (Jutland, 1917) or at night (Cape Esperance, 1942 and Surigau Strait, 1944).

west. Eight minutes later *Washington's* radar picked up a target almost due north. (A few minutes before Lee's last turn he had requested information from Guadalcanal, using his name as no call sign had been assigned. Guadalcanal had replied, "We do not recognize you." Lee, an old friend of Vandegrift's, signaled, "Tell your big boss Ching Lee is here and wants the latest information . . ." using his Naval Academy nickname. At the same time TBS conversation between three patrolling PT boats was overhead—one boat noting the passage ". . . of two big ones, but I don't know whose they are." Again the admiral used his nickname and requested Cactus to "Call off your boys." The "boys" were duly called off and Lee's squadron passed unmolested.)

Kondo's approach had been made in three sections: an outer screen of light cruiser *Sendai* and three destroyers; an inner screen of *Nagara* (Rear Admiral Kimura) and six destroyers; and *Atago*, *Takao*, and *Kirishima*. At 2210 *Sendai* (Rear Admiral Hashimoto) reported, "Two enemy cruisers and four destroyers," north of Savo (Lee's force was on its SSE course). Hashimoto sent two of his destroyers, *Ayanami* and *Uranami*, to scout round Savo while he and *Shikinami* headed after the enemy. Kondo now split Kimura's group: *Nagara* with four destroyers to steam at full speed west of Savo; two destroyers to remain with the heavy ships. It was an involved plan, further complicated by the fact that the Japanese ships did not have radar.

At 2300, when *Washington* made her radar contact (with *Sendai*) the Japanese were advancing south in four groups. *Sendai* was tracked for 12 minutes, by which time she was visible through the

AMERICAN AND JAPANESE NAVAL FORCES AT SECOND BATTLE OF GUADALCANAL, NOVEMBER 14–15

		Class	Tonnage	Speed	Armament	Launched
Washington	(BB)	North Carolina	35,000	28	9 16-in., 20 5-in.	1940
South Dakota	(BB)	South Dakota	35,000	28	9 16-in., 15 5-in.	1941
Gwin	(DD)	Benson	1,630	37	5 5-in., 10 21-in. TT	1940
Walke	(DD)	Sims	1,570	38	5 5-in., 12 21-in. TT	1939 *
Preston	(DD)	Mahan	1,480	36.5	5 5-in., 12 21-in. TT	1936 *
Benham	(DD)	Craven	1,500	36.5	4 5-in., 16 21-in. TT	1938 *
Kirishima	(BB)	Kongo	31,980	30.5	8 14-in., 16 6-in.	1913 *
					8 5-in. AA	
Takao	(CA)	Takao	13,160	34.25	10 8-in., 8 5-in. AA	1930
					16 24-in. TT	
Atago	(CA)	"	"	"	(Same as Takao)	"
Sendai	(CL)	Sendai	5,195	35.25	7 5.5-in., 8 24-in. TT	1923
Nagara	(CL)	Nagara	5,170	36	7 5.5-in., 8 24-in. TT	1921
Terutsuki	(DD)	Akitsuki	2,700	33	8 3.9-in., 4 24-in. TT	1941
Ikazuchi	(DD)	Akatsuki	2,090	38	6 5-in., 9 24-in. TT	1932
Hatsuyuki	(DD)	Fubuki	2,090	34	6 5-in., 9 24-in. TT	1927
Shirayuki	(DD)	"	"	"	" "	1928
Uranami	(DD)	"	"	"	" "	"
Ayanami	(DD)	"	"	"	" "	1929 *
Shikinami			"	"	" "	"
Asagumo	(DD)	Asashio	1,960	35	6 5-in., 8 24-in. TT	1937
Samidare	(DD)	Shiratsuyu	1,580	34	5 5-in., 8 24-in. TT	1935

* Sunk in action

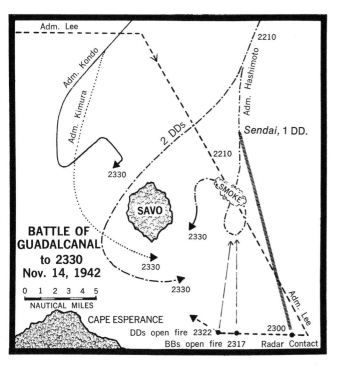

Adm. Lee

Adm. Kondo

Adm. Kimura

Adm. Hashimoto

2210

2 DDs

Sendai, 1 DD.

2210

SMOKE

2330

SAVO

BATTLE OF GUADALCANAL to 2330 Nov. 14, 1942

2330

2330

2330

2330

0 1 2 3 4 5
NAUTICAL MILES

CAPE ESPERANCE

DDs open fire 2322
BBs open fire 2317

Adm. Lee

2300

Radar Contact

ing *Sendai.* Almost immediately the American destroyers came under a heavy and accurate fire from Kimura's squadron. With Savo looming up behind them the Japanese showed no silhouettes, while the land mass obscured the radar picture. The American destroyermen had only gun flashes to fire at, and so complete is the confusion of a night action that afterward many American gunners thought they had been engaging shore batteries on Savo Island.

The destroyer action was soon over. There were six Japanese destroyers and a light cruiser and they shot fast and straight. Before the action was five minutes old, *Preston's* superstructure was ablaze and a concentrated fire being poured into her hull. Both fire rooms were wrecked, her stack came crashing down and she began to list and settle by the stern. At 2336 the order to abandon was given and as the men took to the water she capsized and sank. Some 115 officers and men went with her, including her captain, Commander C. M. Stormes.

Walke was also badly hit. Her captain, Commander T. E. Fraser, tried to bring his tubes to bear but she fell off to port, her guns still in action. Then a terrific blast tore off her forecastle. Salvos of 24-in. torpedoes had been sent streaking toward the American formation and one had slammed into *Walke's* bow, probably touching off a magazine. With everything forward of the bridge gone, the destroyer settled fast. Men were still sliding overboard into the oil and debris when the stern went under. Then the depth charges, which had been reported on "safe," began to go off, killing many of the survivors.

main battery director telescopes. At 2316, the order to open fire when ready was given and at 2317 both battleships opened fire. *Sendai* promptly retired, making smoke, followed by *Shikinami.*

While *Sendai* was racing north behind her smoke screen, *Ayanami* and *Uranami,* followed by *Nagara* and her four destroyers, were rounding Savo from the west and were entering the sound on a course opposite but roughly parallel to the advancing American column. A few minutes after Lee's battleships began shooting at *Sendai, Walke,* leading the American squadron, opened fire at enemy ships seen to starboard. *Benham* and *Preston* also opened up on these targets (*Ayanami* and *Uranami*) while *Gwin* fired star shells over retreat-

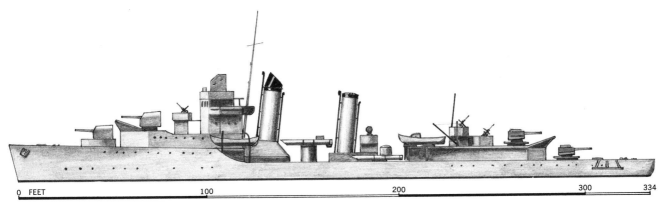

MAHAN CLASS DESTROYER (18 Ships)

Launched September 1935–September 1936
Displacement: 1450–1500 tons LOA: 341½ Beam: 35½ Draft: 10 feet
Twin screw. 49,000 hp=36.5 knots
 Armament: four 5-in. D.P. (Smaller AA varied, 20-mm. and 40-mm. added), twelve 21 in.
torpedo tubes (3×4)
Complement: 172

FUBUKI CLASS DESTROYER (20 Ships)

Launched September 1927–June 1931
Displacement: 2090 tons   LOA: 388½   Beam: 34   Draft: 10½
Twin screw.   50,000 hp=34 knots   Armament: six 5 in. (in 9 of the class, 5 in. were D.P.)
(3×2), two 13-mm MGs.; nine 24-in. torpedo tubes (3×3)   Complement: 197

Astern of *Walke*, *Benham* was also victim of a torpedo. Her guns were pounding away at dimly seen Japanese vessels to starboard when at 2338 a violent explosion threw the vessel over on her port side. When the spray and smoke vanished, a sizable piece of *Benham's* bow had gone, too. Though mortally hurt, she could still steam and at 5 knots she staggered out of the battle.

Gwin, last in line, soon found herself the only destroyer in action. She traded salvos with the Japanese forces to the north and took a shell in her engine room and others topside. One of them jarred the safety devices on her tubes and the missiles slid out—so *Gwin* loosed no torpedoes that night, either. She fired while there were targets in sight—then *South Dakota* went rushing by and *Gwin's* part in the action was over.

The Japanese had not escaped without injury. *Ayanami* headed north in sinking condition, with *Uranami* standing by. As the American battleships' secondary armament came into action, *Nagara* and her destroyers turned away westward. Radar echoes from Savo confused *Washington's* gunners, while

South Dakota had suffered a temporary power failure which brought practically everything to a standstill. It is doubtful if Kimura's force suffered any but minor damage from this encounter.

Lee was now passing through the wreckage of his vanguard destroyer division and he swerved *Washington* left to avoid them. *South Dakota* made a sharp right to avoid *Benham* and in so doing not only closed the range toward Kimura but, lacking radar, lost sight of the flagship. Her power was back on again at 2336, with radars, guns, directors, etc. functioning once more. She let fly a few salvos from her main battery at *Sendai,* now returned from her brief flight north and quietly working up behind the American column. Lee had not ordered his battleships' planes flown off before the action, and a blast from *South Dakota's* after turret set the planes on her fantail catapults alight. The bonfire could have been serious, but a second salvo blew the blazing planes overboard, with no harm done.

South Dakota's right turn brought her close to Kondo's advancing column and his two lead de-

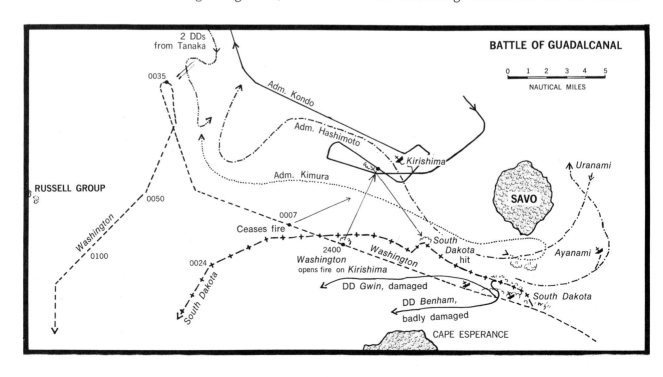

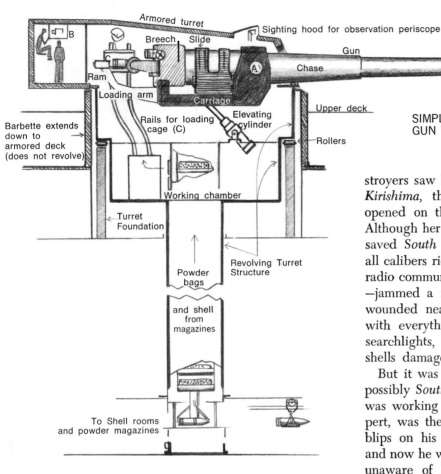

Armored turret

Sighting hood for observation periscope

Breech Slide

Gun

B

Ram

Chase

Muzzle

A

Loading arm

Carriage

Upper deck

Barbette extends
down to
armored deck
(does not revolve)

Rails for loading
cage (C)

Elevating
cylinder

Rollers

Working chamber

Turret
Foundation

Powder
bags

Revolving Turret
Structure

and shell
from
magazines

To Shell rooms
and powder magazines

SIMPLIFIED DRAWING ON LARGE-CALIBER
GUN TURRET

**The turret is the upper, heavily armored, part of the re-
volving turret structure. At the rear is the control chamber
with turret range-finder apparatus (B). The gun moves in
the slide (which includes the recoil cylinders) and rotates
(for elevation) around the trunnions (A). The carriage supports the slide and is itself supported by the revolving turret structure. This is rotated horizontally by electro-hydrau-
lic power, and extends down to the magazine handling
rooms below decks. Armor on turret face is usually heavier
ports the slide and is itself supported by the revolving tur-
Carolina (below) is 18 in. thick.**

stroyers saw her and flipped on their searchlights.
Kirishima, the two heavies and the destroyers,
opened on the American battleship like a flash.
Although her 18-inch armor belt and turret facings
saved *South Dakota* from vital damage, shells of
all calibers riddled her superstructure, knocked out
radio communications and all but one of her radars
—jammed a 16-inch turret in train, and killed or
wounded nearly a hundred men. She shot back
with everything that would bear, aiming at the
searchlights, and it is probable that some of her
shells damaged *Atago* and *Takao*.

But it was *Washington* who saved the day—and
possibly *South Dakota* as well. *Washington's* radar
was working perfectly, and Lee, an old radar expert, was the man to get the most out of it. The
blips on his screen had kept him well informed
and now he was able to open on a Japanese column
unaware of his presence. Kondo's heavies were
busily concentrating on *South Dakota*, illuminated
both by searchlights and by fires in her superstructure. At 8400 yards *Washington* sent salvo
after salvo crashing into *Kirishima*. At least nine
main battery shells, each weighing over a ton,
smashed into her, while *Washington's* starboard
secondary battery of ten 5-inchers scored some
forty hits. In seven minutes the veteran Japanese

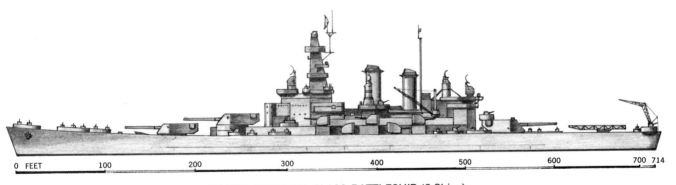

NORTH CAROLINA CLASS BATTLESHIP (2 Ships)

Launched June 1940
Displacement: 35,000 tons LOA: 729 Beam: 108¼ Draft: 26¾
4 screws. 121,000 hp=28 knots
Armor: belt 16 in., decks total 10 in., turret 18 in.
Armament: nine 16 in. (3×3), twenty 5 in. D.P. (10×2), forty 40-mm., forty 20-mm.
(added 1942–45) Aircraft: three Complement: 2500

battleship was finished. With flames pouring from her topsides, her steering gear wrecked and her engines damaged, she staggered out of line.

Both his heavy cruisers had been hit, although not badly, and Kondo decided he had had enough. He turned away (NE) and then to a west northwesterly course. Lee paralleled the Japanese cruisers some seven miles to the south. Then having, as it were, seen them off the premises he turned toward the south. As he turned (about 0035) there was a brief flurry of action as two of Tanaka's destroyers (which he had sent to support Kondo) launched torpedoes at *Washington*, some of which exploded in the turbulent water of her wake. That was the end of the battle, and Kondo led his forces on a northeasterly course to clear Santa Isabel.

Northwest of Savo *Sendai* and four destroyers were standing by *Kirishima*. The great ship was beyond salvage, blazing while internal explosions racked her hull. Having in mind what happened to *Hiei* the day after the previous action, *Kirishima's* captain ordered her scuttled and she went down about 0300.

Benham got as far as the south coast of Guadalcanal on her voyage to Espiritu Santo when she began to break up. *Gwin* took off her crew (she had only had seven men wounded) and sank her by gunfire.

At 0900 *South Dakota* joined *Washington* and both set course for Nouméa. The flagship, which was uninjured, had done a great job for the Navy and Lee must have been proud of her. Lee, too, had done a great job. The last major Japanese effort to smash Henderson Field and to transport a sizable force with all its equipment to the island had failed. It was not done without cost—three destroyers sunk and a battleship and a destroyer damaged. But the Japanese had lost more than a battle—they had lost a campaign.

The end of the drama was played out in the early hours of the morning. Tanaka had been forced to withdraw while the battle was raging. Now, while destroyers were still searching for survivors and the glare from a burning ship (probably *South Dakota*) could be seen to the southward, the tenacious little admiral steered once more for Tassafaronga with his four remaining transports. It was obvious that they could never be unloaded and away before daylight so Tanaka ordered them run on the beach. By break of day they were hard aground, and Tanaka led his overcrowded destroyers back up The Slot at top speed.

Troops began to go ashore from the beached ships almost as soon as they struck but it is doubtful if much of the material aboard ever reached the shore. As soon as it was light enough to see, Cactus fighters found and strafed the stranded transports, followed by attacks by SBDs which lasted all day. Long-range Marine artillery bombarded the helpless vessels, and destroyer *Meade*, just arrived at Tulagi, worked them over with her 5-inchers and newly installed 40-mms. Soon all four transports were on fire, and some material which had been landed was destroyed on the beaches. In all about two thousand troops were put ashore. Thousands of men, thousands of tons of supplies, eleven transports totaling over 77,000 tons, and all the heavy equipment and artillery of a division had gone to the bottom. Of the Japanese naval covering and bombardment forces, two battleships, a heavy cruiser, and three destroyers had been sunk with other cruisers and destroyers damaged, plus an indeterminate number of planes and pilots lost. It was a major strategic victory for the U. S. Navy; costly in ships and men, but one which was to bring decisive results. The Tokyo Express would run again, and more American ships would go down. But never again would major Japanese units steam proudly into Ironbottom Sound to pour shells into Henderson Field or do battle for the control of the dark and bloody waters around the ill-omened island of Savo.

XIV

Mayhem at Midnight

THE BATTLE OF TASSAFARONGA

While the Navy had been fighting the battles which finally established American supremacy in the waters off Guadalcanal, General Vandegrift had once more been planning an advance west of the Matanikau. The exhausted and disease-ridden veteran 1st Marine Division had been alerted to leave the island, but the newly arrived 182nd Infantry Regiment and the comparatively fresh 164th Infantry gave the general enough troops for a limited advance.

General Edmund Sebree of the Americal Division was to be in tactical command and as a first objective the plan was to clear Point Cruz and capture a ridge formed of several low hills, with Hill 66 on its southern end about 2500 yards inland from the beach west of the Point. The

ground to the west of the Matanikau is different from the jungle areas to the east and south. Rocky ridges, several hundred feet high and covered with tall grass and brush, run from north to south, while the beach area is flat and sandy. Deep jungled ravines (like the one in which the Japanese 4th Infantry took such a beating from Puller's battalion on October 9) divided the ridges. The original plan called for an advance with 1st Marines on the southern wing—ready to move north and take in flank any opposition encountered by the frontal attack.

Unfortunately, the withdrawal of 1st Marines forced a cancellation of this part of the program. Even more unfortunate was the fact that the Japanese 38th Division, although weakened by losses

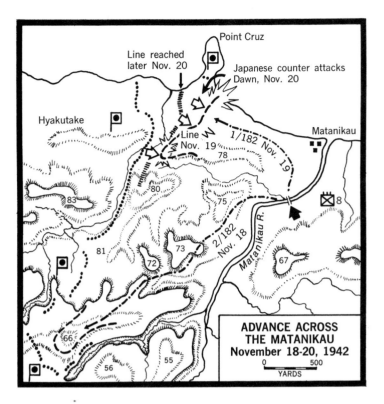

Point Cruz

Line reached later Nov. 20

Japanese counter attacks Dawn, Nov. 20

Hyakutake

Line Nov. 19

Matanikau

1/182 Nov. 19

78

83

80

75

8

2/182 Nov. 18

81

73

72

67

66

55

56

ADVANCE ACROSS THE MATANIKAU
November 18-20, 1942

0   500
YARDS

in transit and without its heavy equipment, was also planning an advance east of the river. At the same time, other Japanese units, under General Ito, were to occupy Mount Austen.

So when the advance began (November 18), the Japanese were in considerable strength, dug in positions on the reverse slopes and defiladed from mortar and artillery fire.

The attack began when 2nd Battalion of the 182nd Infantry crossed the Matanikau on two footbridges (thrown across by the engineers about 700 yards from the river mouth), and advanced toward Hill 66. The troops had been ashore less than a week and the unaccustomed damp heat slowed their advance; so that the hill, just over a mile from the bridge, was not reached until noon. The men dug in on Hill 66 and next day 1st Battalion of the 182nd Infantry crossed the river and moved along the flat coastal area toward Point Cruz. Eighth Marines were in position on the east side of the river, but Company B crossed to cover the 1st Battalion's left flank. The 1st met only slight resistance but Company B of the 8th Marines ran into heavier fire and could not make headway. About noon, 1st Battalion of the 182nd was halted just east of Point Cruz and dug in for the night, while the Marine company recrossed the river and rejoined its regiment.

Japanese troops from Kokumbona had been moving east, and under cover of darkness took up posi-

tions facing 182nd Regiment's 1st Battalion. Artillery and mortar fire hit the 1st Battalion lines during the night and at dawn on November 20 the Japanese attacked. The first assault came on the battalion's left flank. This held, but succeeding attacks on the battalion's front forced the companies on the low ground to fall back. They were rallied by General Sebree and other staff officers, and with support from artillery and planes regained their positions by 0900.

The battalion then advanced again and reached the beach west of Point Cruz. There the infantry was stalled by mortar and artillery fire—the point of land itself remaining in Japanese hands.

General Sebree now ordered up 164th Infantry Regiment of the Americal Division from reserve to move into the gap between 1st and 2nd battalions of 182nd. This was done during the night of November 20–21 and the regiment advanced at dawn. But the Japanese to the west were well dug in, with many well camouflaged positions roofed with logs and earth; mutually supporting, with interlocking fields of fire for automatic weapons and the whole well covered by mortars and artillery. The soldiers of the 164th Infantry were halted after making average gains of only 40 yards, nor did 1st Battalion of the 182nd have any better success. They cleared out the Japanese on Point Cruz, but got no further. Both regiments attacked again on November 22 but again failed to make any headway.

On November 23, after a 30-minute bombardment by more than three battalions of artillery, the 8th

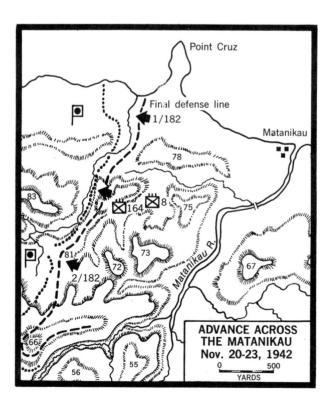

Point Cruz

Final defense line
1/182

Matanikau

78

83

164   8   75

81   73

72

67

2/182

66

56   55

ADVANCE ACROSS THE MATANIKAU
Nov. 20-23, 1942

0   500
YARDS

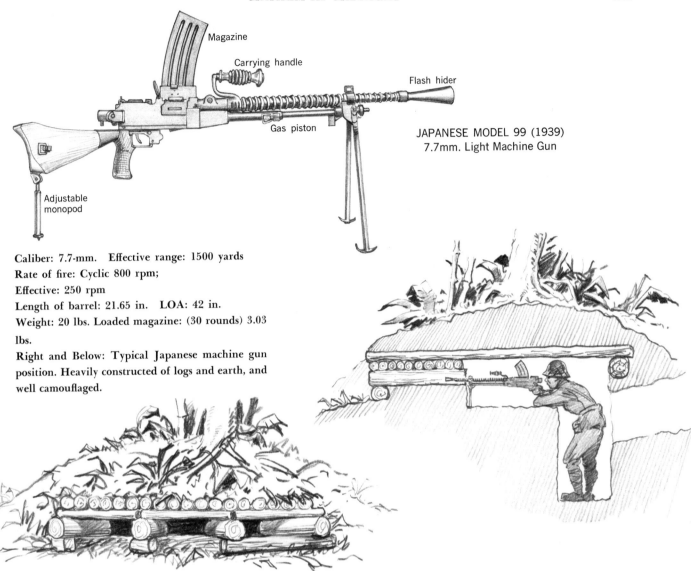

Magazine

Carrying handle

Flash hider

Gas piston

Adjustable
monopod

JAPANESE MODEL 99 (1939)
7.7mm. Light Machine Gun

Caliber: 7.7-mm. Effective range: 1500 yards
Rate of fire: Cyclic 800 rpm;
Effective: 250 rpm
Length of barrel: 21.65 in. LOA: 42 in.
Weight: 20 lbs. Loaded magazine: (30 rounds) 3.03
lbs.
Right and Below: Typical Japanese machine gun
position. Heavily constructed of logs and earth, and
well camouflaged.

Marines (brought up the evening before) passed through the 164th Infantry and delivered a series of attacks, supported by artillery. The artillery succeeded in putting a shell close enough to Hyakutake's command post to slightly wound him and his chief of staff. It did not succeed in demolishing the Japanese strong points or in silencing the enemy artillery (which caused many casualties during the day) and the 8th Marines gained no ground either.

The American commanders now decided that any gains in ground by frontal assault would be too costly and the order was given to dig in and fortify on the line Hills 66–80–81–Point Cruz. And here the lines stayed until January. The frontal assault had gained little ground and casualties had

been fairly high. Between November 19 and 25, the 164th Infantry had 117 killed and 208 wounded and other units had suffered in proportion. The days of the great Japanese banzai attacks, with swarms of enemy troops assailing American positions in costly frontal attacks, were over. Now it was the American fighting man who would discover how difficult and costly it was to rout a determined enemy from prepared positions well furnished with machine guns and artillery.

While the abortive attempt to drive to the west was in progress, a seaborn patrol scouted the southwestern and western coast of Guadalcanal. On November 21, a small coasting schooner left Lunga Point carrying thirteen men of 164th Infantry, two Marine radiomen, two Marine Navajo

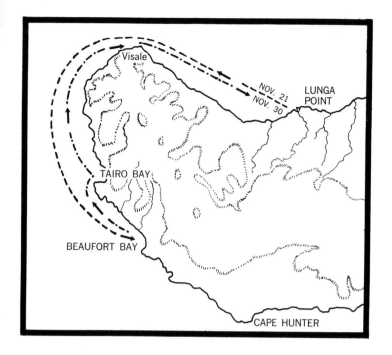

talkers, and a native police boy. The patrol was under command of 1st Lieutenant F. T. Flo, 164th Infantry. The vessel proceeded around Cape Esperance and touched first at Beaufort Bay. Flo was met by Father de Klerk, a Belgian missionary who had refused to be evacuated from his station and had since served as a coastwatcher and recruiter of native labor. The priest informed Flo that there were no enemy troops at that time between Beaufort Bay and Tiaro Bay to the north. The patrol then sailed to Tiaro Bay. For the next eight days, the patrol scouted the coastal areas as far as Visale and on their return to Lunga on November 30 reported that, while there were a few small parties of Japanese in the area, the enemy forces were concentrated well east of Cape Esperance.

The plight of the enemy troops on the island was becoming serious. There are no accurate records as to the exact number of Japanese troops on Guadalcanal at any one time—or rather there are several records but they do not agree. By the end of November there were probably between 25,000 and 30,000 men of all branches. The supply problem had become acute. The destroyer runs of the Express had been mainly devoted to bringing in reinforcements and of the thousands of tons of supplies loaded aboard regular transports, most had been sunk or destroyed. The island itself afforded little in the way of food, and many units had long since been on half rations. This was later cut to one-third the regular allowance, supplemented by coconuts, bamboo sprouts, roots, a few

wild potatoes and even grass and ferns. The medical arrangements were pitifully inadequate and malaria—which was becoming a serious problem to the Americans—was far more prevalent in the Japanese forces.

To quote Tanaka once more: "Almost daily came radio messages reporting the critical situation on the island and requesting immediate supplies. It was indicated that by the end of November the entire food supply would be gone, and by the latter part of the month we learned that all staple supplies had been consumed. The men were now down to eating wild plants and animals. Everyone was on the verge of starvation, sick lists increased, and even the healthy were exhausted."

There would be no more expensive attempts to send escorted transports and freighters down The Slot. But destroyers were not suitable for carrying and landing deck cargoes of supplies in the limited time in which the Express could remain off the beaches. Experiments were therefore made in loading supplies in metal drums—with enough air space to give them buoyancy. These drums were to be loaded aboard destroyers, some 200 to 240 drums apiece, and each 40 or 50 drums linked together with rope. When off the beach, the crew of each vessel would roll the drums overboard. Ship's boats would then tow the ends of the lines ashore after which the destroyer picked up speed for its return dash up The Slot.

After a trial run, it was decided to land the first loads of drums on the night of November 30. Tanaka was, of course, elected and eight destroyers placed at his disposal. Six were loaded with drums—after their spare torpedoes were removed—but no drums were put aboard Tanaka's flagship, destroyer *Naganami*, nor *Takanami*, carrying the commander of Desdiv 31. The admiral led his force from Shortland the night of November 29.

The naval forces under Halsey's command had meanwhile been reorganized. *Saratoga* was on her way back to the war zone and would have a group built around her under Rear Admiral DeWitt Ramsey. Another carrier group was formed around *Enterprise* under Rear Admiral Frederick C. Sherman. *Washington* had been joined by her sister ship *North Carolina*, whose torpedo damage had been repaired, and a third member of this battleship task force, *Indiana*, joined later. Battleships *Maryland* and *Colorado* were in the Fijis, and two of the new escort carriers, *Nassau* and *Altamaha*,

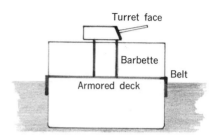

A CRUISER'S ARMOR

was necessarily skimpy. Much of her displacement was devoted to machinery and weapons leaving little for protection. A narrow belt (in some vessels just a patch amidships) ran along the sides from the forward to the after barbettes and was often only at its thickest (maybe 4 inches) amidships, tapering off to 1½ or 2 inches. The ends usually had no vertical armor. An armored (sometimes 2) deck usually starting at the forward end of the belt, ran to the stern and gave some protection to the machinery spaces, magazines and firerooms. The conning tower was armored, as were the communication tubes from the main control stations, and sometimes the control stations themselves. Barbettes and turret faces were armored, and sometimes their roofs and sides.

were ferrying planes up to New Caledonia and Espiritu Santo.

A cruiser task force was formed of heavy cruisers *New Orleans*, *Northampton*, and *Pensacola* and light cruisers *Helena* and *Honolulu*. These, with attached destroyers, were based on Espiritu Santo and were under command of Rear Admiral Kinkaid. This force was to be ready to intercept any major attempts by the Japanese to reinforce their troops on Guadalcanal.

On November 24, Admiral Kinkaid arrived at Espiritu Santo to take command of the cruiser force and by November 27 had completed a plan of operations to be followed in the event of a night action. This plan, embodying some hard-won lessons from previous battles, called for the force to be divided in three groups. The destroyers, in the van on the cruisers' engaged bow, were to use their radars to enable them to deliver a surprise torpedo attack, after which they were to clear the area to avoid any chance of a mixup with their own cruisers. The cruisers, in two groups, were to withhold fire until the destroyers' torpedoes had reached their targets. They were to attempt to stay at least 12,000 yards from the enemy, thus taking advantage of their radar-controlled gunnery and to present distant and difficult targets for the inevitable shoals of Japanese torpedoes. Each group was to contain at least one vessel equipped with efficient SG radar. No searchlights were to be used, and recognition lights were only to be switched on when being actually fired on by friendly ships. Signals had been clarified, and lastly the float planes were to be catapulted off to scout any enemy approach and to be ready to drop flares when requested by the commanding officer.

Unfortunately, on November 28, Kinkaid was detached by Halsey's orders (he was to command the Northern Pacific Force) and replaced by Rear Admiral Carleton Wright. Wright brought with him a reinforcement in the shape of heavy cruiser *Minneapolis*, but the admiral, unlike Kinkaid, had had little experience in the waters around Guadalcanal and it was doubly unfortunate that he was to be faced with a night action only two days after taking command.

While the cruiser group at Espiritu was changing hands, another weapon in the Japanese arsenal made its first appearance in the waters off Guadalcanal. A midget (two-man) submarine, carried by fleet submarine *I-16* and released near the northern entrance to Indispensable Strait, torpedoed the AKA *Alchiba* off Lunga Point. The naval freighter, in company with transport *Barnett* and five destroyers, had arrived at the island and on November 28 was unloading a cargo of gasoline, ammunition, and bombs when a torpedo struck her. She burst into flames forward and took a heavy list. There was a good chance she would either explode or sink but her captain ran her hard aground. At the same time, every effort was made to save her and her cargo. Despite roaring fires and exploding

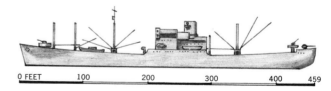

CARGO SHIP (AK) ALCHIBA (Ex-Mormacdove)

Launched June 1939 Deadweight tonnage (cargo capacity) 8656 LOA: 459 Beam: 63 Draft: 25¾ feet Single screw. 6000 hp=15.5 knots. Armament: one 5 in. (stern) four 3 in. (4×1) plus smaller AA.

158

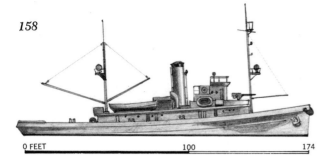

BIRD CLASS MINESWEEPER (22 Ships)

0 FEET   100   174

Launched March 1918–May 1919 Displacement: 840
tons LOA: 188 Beam: 35½ Draft: 9 feet
Single screw. 1400 hp=14 knots
Armament: two 3 in. AA Complement: 72

ammunition, her damage-control parties fought the blaze, aided by hoses from *Bobolink*. Japanese planes dropped bombs close aboard the inviting target about 0330. Fire fighting and unloading went on all day November 29. She burned for four days, but while the Navy wrote her off as a total loss, she managed to survive the war.

On November 29, Admiral Wright held a conference with his commanding officers and it was agreed that Kinkaid's operational plan should stand. On the evening of the same day he received word from Halsey that an enemy force of eight destroyers and six transports might be expected at Guadalcanal on the night of November 30. Wright was ordered to intercept it and at 2300, his ships cleared Espiritu and headed north at 28 knots. The float planes were shot off and flew up to Tulagi to wait until needed.

As Admiral Wright's force was approaching Lengo Channel on the evening of November 30, it met an eastbound convoy of three transports and five destroyers. Halsey ordered two of the escort, *Lamson* and *Lardner*, to join Wright. As there was no time for detailed explanations they were ordered to fall in behind the cruiser column.

The lineup of the American forces was as follows: destroyers *Fletcher*, *Perkins*, *Maury*, and *Drayton*; cruisers *Minneapolis*, *New Orleans*, *Pensacola*, *Honolulu*, and *Northampton*, followed by *Lamson* and *Lardner*. *Drayton*, last of the van destroyers, steamed 2 miles ahead of *Minneapolis*, and the cruisers followed the flagship at 1000-yard intervals.

AMERICAN AND JAPANESE NAVAL FORCES AT THE BATTLE OF TASSAFARONGA

		Class	Tonnage	Speed	Armament		Launched
Minneapolis	(CA)	Astoria	9,950	32.7	9 8-in.,	8 5-in.	1933
New Orleans	(CA)	"	"	"	"	"	"
Pensacola	(CA)	Pensacola	9,100	32.7	10 8-in.,	8 5-in.	1929
Northampton	(CA)	Northampton	9,050	32.7	9 8-in.,	8 5-in.	1929 °
Honolulu	(CL)	Brooklyn	9,650	34	15 6-in.,	8 5-in.	1937
Fletcher	(DD)	Fletcher	2,050	37	5 5-in.,	10 21-in. TT	1942
Lardner	(DD)	Benson	1,630	37	5 5-in.,	10 21-in. TT	1942
Maury	(DD)	Craven	1,500	36.5	4 5-in.,	16 21-in. TT	1938
Lamson	(DD)	Mahan	1,480	36.5	4 5-in.,	12 21-in. TT	1936
Drayton	(DD)	"	"	"	"	"	"
Perkins	(DD)	"	1,465	"	"	"	1935
Naganami	(DD)	Yugumo	2,077	35.5	6 5-in.,	8 24-in. TT	1942
Takanami	(DD)	"	"	"	"	"	" °
Makanami	(DD)	"	"	"	"	"	"
Oyashio	(DD)	Kagero	2,033	35.5	"	"	1938
Kurashio	(DD)	"	"	"	"	"	"
Kagero	(DD)	"	"	"	"	"	"
Kawakaze	(DD)	Shiratsuyu	1,580	34	5 5-in.,	8 24-in. TT	1936
Suzukaze	(DD)	"	"	"	"	"	1937

° Sunk in the action

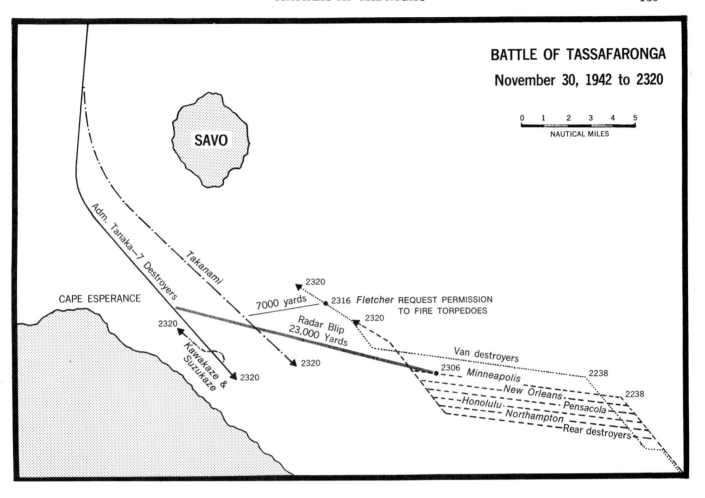

The American force entered the sound through Lengo Channel at 2225, heading northwest. A few minutes later a simultaneous turn to 280° brought the ships in line of bearing. The waters of the sound were smooth and glassy and the night black as ink. While lookouts vainly strained their eyes, radar operators intently scanned their screens for the moving pips which would indicate a contact with enemy vessels. At 2306, *Minneapolis* picked up a blip at 23,000 yards range, almost due west. The force was informed and a 40° course change ordered, bringing the ships into column once more. The blips now indicated an enemy formation of several ships, heading southeast. At 2314, Admiral Wright turned his column 20° to the left and the American battle line steadied on course 300°.

When the American flagship first made contact, Tanaka was some 4 miles due east of Cape Esperance, heading southeast. Earlier in the day, a Japanese reconnaissance plane had reported twelve destroyers and nine transports in the Guadalcanal area so that the Japanese admiral was alerted for possible trouble. His mission was to drop supplies, not indulge himself in midnight mayhem, but although his laden squadron would be at considerable disadvantage the aggressive Tanaka signaled all ships that "utmost efforts will be made to destroy the enemy without regard to the unloading of supplies."

Takanami steamed some distance off *Naganami*'s port bow and the flagship was followed by *Makinami, Oyashio, Kuroshio, Kagero, Kawakaze,* and *Suzukaze*. Having no radar, Tanaka was unaware of the approaching American squadron. But his lookouts were awake. As he approached the designated off-loading area off Tassafaronga, he reduced speed to 12 knots and his destroyers broke formation and prepared to roll off their cargo drums. Before this could be accomplished, *Takanami* sighted enemy ships, bearing 100°. Tanaka immediately ordered unloading to stop and ships to take battle stations and increase speed. There was no time to resume formation, however, and in the ensuing engagement each Japanese destroyer captain had to take independent action.

The two squadrons were now approaching each

KAGERO CLASS DESTROYER (18 Ships)

Launched June 1938–March 1941
Diplacement: 2033 tons LOA: 388¾ Beam: 35½ Draft: 12⅓
Twin screw. 52,000 hp=35½ knots
Armament: six 5 in. D.P. (3×2), four 25-mm. AA (2×2), two 13-mm. MGs., eight 24 in.
torpedo tubes (2×4) Complement: 240

other on opposite courses—distant some 5 miles. *Fletcher*, Commander Cole, had an enemy (*Takanami*) on her port bow at 2316, range 7000 yards, and asked permission to fire. Once more an opportunity for a torpedo attack was lost by an American admiral delaying too long in giving an order which might better have been left to the discretion of the destroyer commodore. Four minutes elapsed before the order came and by that time it was too late. Tanaka's destroyers, pouring on speed, were racing by abeam before the American warheads were on their way. An overtaking shot at long range gave little chance of success. Only twenty torpedoes were launched by the four van destroyers and none found a mark.

As the last of the American torpedoes splashed into the water, Wright ordered his cruisers to open fire. All ships opened up and a storm of shells sought the speeding Japanese vessels at ranges of

less that 10,000 yards. Five-inch star shells illuminated the scene, but the super-brilliant airplane flares which might have made all the difference to the American gunners were lacking. The float planes were vainly taxiing over the glass-smooth waters off Tulagi, unable to get enough lift to become airborne.

Sharp eyes on Tanaka's flagship had spotted the American vessels a few seconds before the first star shells burst. If any of the Japanese destroyermen were taken by surprise they failed to show it, and their reactions were swift and deadly. *Takanami*, nearest the enemy, fired torpedoes and turned away. American gunnery radars picked her up and a heavy fire was concentrated on her. Her own gunners made good practice and fires blazed up in the American line. But the big destroyer was soon on fire and in a badly crippled state. *Naganami* opened fire on a cruiser, reversed course, and let loose eight torpedoes at 5000 yards. She came under a terrific fire but, though showered with splinters from near misses, she received no direct hits.

Despite the embarrassment of deck loads of cargo drums, the six supply destroyers also got off their missiles and, five minutes after the American cruisers opened fire, salvos of the huge Japanese torpedoes were nearing the American line. At 2327, just as the American flagship, *Minneapolis*, was loosing her ninth main battery salvo, two torpedoes struck her. One hit forward—doing such damage that 60 feet of her bow hung down like a giant ramp—while the other smashed into her number 2 fire room. *New Orleans*, next astern, swung right to avoid the battered flagship and was herself struck between the two forward magazines. A great blast tore off the forward part of the ship up to number 2 turret, and men on deck aft saw the bow of their ship grinding down their port side, to be lost in the darkness astern.

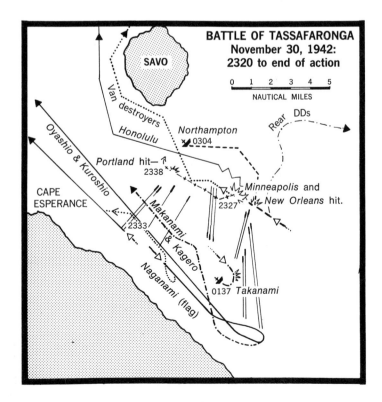

BATTLE OF TASSAFARONGA
November 30, 1942:
2320 to end of action

0 1 2 3 4 5
NAUTICAL MILES

SAVO

Van destroyers

Honolulu

Northampton
0304

Portland hit—
2338

Minneapolis and
New Orleans hit.
2327

CAPE
ESPERANCE

Oyashio & Kuroshio

Makanami
& Kagero

2333

Naganami (flag)

Rear DDs

0137 Takanami

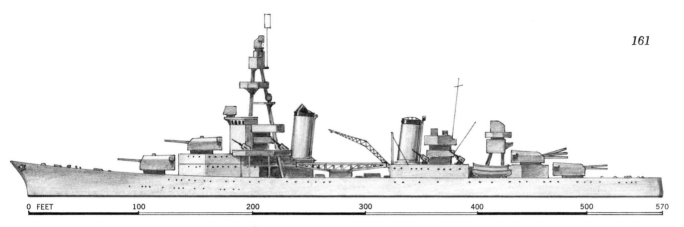

PENSACOLA CLASS HEAVY CRUISER (2 Ships)

Launched January–April 1929 Displacement: 9100 tons LOA: 585¾ Beam: 65¼ Draft: 16¼ feet 4 screws. 107,000 hp=32.7 knots Armor: belt 3 in., deck 3 in., turret 1.5 in. Armament: ten 8 in. (2×2, 2×3), eight 5 in. (8×1), 20-mms. and 40-mms. added during war. Aircraft: two Complement: 1200

Pensacola swung out of line to avoid the blazing wrecks ahead—then, as she returned to course, was herself hit abreast the mainmast. A huge fire flared up, three turrets were knocked out, and the after engine room flooded so fast that only one man got out.

Honolulu, her six-inchers blazing, zigzagged down the disengaged side of the flaming wrecks ahead, thus avoiding torpedoes and the danger of being silhouetted against the glare of the fires. She was not hit but *Northampton* was not so lucky. Two torpedoes struck her aft, ripping open her engine room and igniting her fuel tanks. The doomed ship, listing badly to port, finally came to a stop, roaring like a furnace.

Wright's van destroyers, after making their belated and abortive torpedo attack, bore off to the northwest to clear their cruisers, finally rounding Savo Island before heading back toward the scene of the engagement. *Lamson* and *Lardner,* following *Northampton,* were too far away to take any part in the action. The gun crews of such of the crippled cruisers' weapons as were still operable were understandably edgy, and after both rear destroyers had drawn fire from friendly vessels they wisely withdrew, turning first north and then east.

Takanami, burning and exploding, had drawn much of the fire from the American line. She now lay dead in the water some 9 miles southeast of Cape Esperance. By midnight Tanaka had collected his scattered destroyers and was heading homeward. Only *Takanami* did not answer the roll call, and *Kuroshio* and *Oyashio* were sent back to the debris-strewn battle area to look for her. They found her slowly sinking and began rescue

operations. Before these could be completed the near approach of some American vessels forced them to withdraw. Many of *Takanami*'s crew, in boats and rafts, managed to land near Japanese held positions on the nearby shore. She sank some two and one-half hours after first sighting the enemy.

With the withdrawal of Tanaka's destroyers, the action came to an end. In the space of twenty minutes, three American heavy cruisers had been badly damaged—enough to keep them out of the war for months—and a fourth was sinking. The cost to the Japanese was one destroyer. True, not many drums of supplies were off-loaded—if any, at least not that night. But, taken any way you

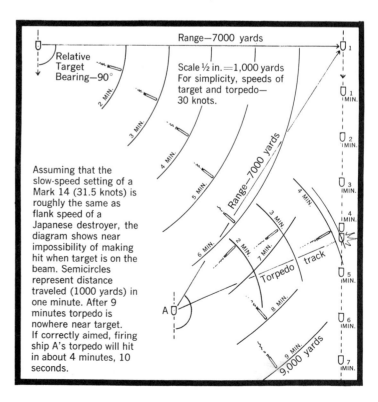

Range—7000 yards

Relative Target Bearing—90°

Scale ½ in.=1,000 yards For simplicity, speeds of target and torpedo— 30 knots.

Range—7000 yards

Assuming that the slow-speed setting of a Mark 14 (31.5 knots) is roughly the same as flank speed of a Japanese destroyer, the diagram shows near impossibility of making hit when target is on the beam. Semicircles represent distance traveled (1000 yards) in one minute. After 9 minutes torpedo is nowhere near target. If correctly aimed, firing ship A's torpedo will hit in about 4 minutes, 10 seconds.

Torpedo track

9,000 yards

like, tough, tenacious little Tanaka had won a smashing victory.

The ships of the Japanese squadron retired unmolested to their base. Of the Americans'—*Northampton* went down at 0304, December 1, despite valiant efforts to save her. By jettisoning heavy movables and pumping oil overside, *Minneapolis* managed to crawl into Tulagi at 3 knots, with freeboard reduced to a few feet. *New Orleans* had lost 120 feet of her bow and was drawing 40 feet at number 2 turret. But her engineering spaces were undamaged and she managed to make 5 knots toward Tulagi. *Pensacola* also made Tulagi, with fires still raging and ammunition "cooking off" in her red-hot gun positions. It was twelve hours later when the last fire was extinguished. The subsequent patching and jury-rigging of the damaged vessels for the long voyage home was a miracle of American engineering and ingenuity.

The sharp defeat brought some sharp comments —by Halsey and others. Cole was blamed for loosing his squadron's torpedoes at too long range and for leaving the scene afterward. But the failure of the torpedo attack was scarcely his fault, and the Kinkaid-Wright plan called for him to clear the cruisers. Where the plan fell down was in tying him too closely to the cruiser admiral's orders. Had the moment for firing torpedoes been left to the destroyer commander's discretion there would almost certainly have been no disastrous delay. There was even a long string tied to the float planes. When these machines finally got into the air and appeared over the enemy formation they did not drop their flares because they were to do so only when ordered by the flagship. But their flagship was by then battered and burning, struggling to keep afloat. No orders, so no flares. Overwhelming strength and fancy electronic devices were no substitute for initiative.

The American torpedoes were launched too late at targets already receding. The fact that none of them hit was disappointing but not, perhaps, surprising. But, despite destruction of *Takanami*, American gunnery that night was more than disappointing. Except for a few splinter scratches no other enemy ships were damaged, although for several minutes they were subjected to a hail of shells of all calibers. It was obvious that American captains and crews needed the rigorous training in night battle tactics and firing which made the Japanese seamen such dangerous opponents.

On the credit side of the naval war was the fact that while American planning at the higher levels showed considerable daring, ingenuity, and flexibility, that of the Japanese was characterized by a peculiarly rigid and unimaginative approach, coupled with a reluctance to risk much to gain much. As Yamamoto had a reputation as a poker player, the caution with which he played his game of naval strategy subsequent to the Pearl Harbor attack is still puzzling. It followed that, as American seamen gained the experience which (with their superior equipment and almost limitless resources) made them the equal of their Japanese opponents, the balance of power at sea inevitably shifted.

The battle of Tassafaronga was the last surface action off Guadalcanal in which any major U.S. vessels were engaged. Hereafter the task of combating the runs of the Tokyo Express would fall to the PT squadrons and to Cactus Air Force. It was considered that between reports of the coastwatchers, air reconnaissance, and submarines, there would be sufficient warning of any threat by major Japanese units. The covering forces in the area and at Espiritu, while not close enough to be unduly exposed to any concerted Japanese submarine or air attack, were still close enough to be available to cover the island in case of need.

It was a wise decision and had the effect of reversing the positions of the Japanese and American forces. Instead of the U. S. Navy risking major warships in confused night actions with Japanese destroyers, these latter valuable vessels were now exposed to attacks by numbers of speedy (and comparatively expendable) motor torpedo boats. The shoe would now be on the other foot. And while actual damage done by the PTs (one destroyer and one submarine sunk, and one destroyer damaged) was less than was believed at the time, their presence alone was a deterrent to the enemy and had a marked effect on Japanese operations.

XV

"Take the High Ground"

THE ASSAULT ON MOUNT AUSTEN

The beginning of December 1942 found the Americans on Guadalcanal in some strength, with almost complete control over the sky and sea approaches to the island. On November 29, Vandegrift reported that there were 188 planes on the island's airstrips. These included U. S. Army, Navy, Marine Corps, and Royal New Zealand Air Force.

Henderson Field itself was improving. More surface had been steel matted, making it possible to use part of the strip in all weather. Fighter strip number 1 was being regraded and needed a large amount of matting but by the end of December a second fighter strip, coral surfaced, was nearly finished and was used by U. S. Army fighter pilots and those of the RNZAF. The Aola Bay fiasco was over and work progressing on a bomber strip at Koli Point (Carney Field).

Rear Admiral McCain had recommended that, if Henderson Field was to be used as a staging point and base for heavy and medium bombers, storage tanks of 1,000,000 gallons capacity be built and work on these had begun.

No amount of air cover or antiaircraft weaponry could guarantee that a surprise attack by single planes or small groups might not occasionally break through to raid the field. But the days of concerted attacks were over, as were the almost nightly bombardments from the sea. Pistol Pete no longer peppered the field with long-range artillery fire and the only annoyance was the arrival at dark of Washing Machine Charley. The scattering of light bombs from these planes did little actual damage; but even when the missiles were no more destructive than empty beer bottles (whose acoustical properties were such as to give a lively imitation of

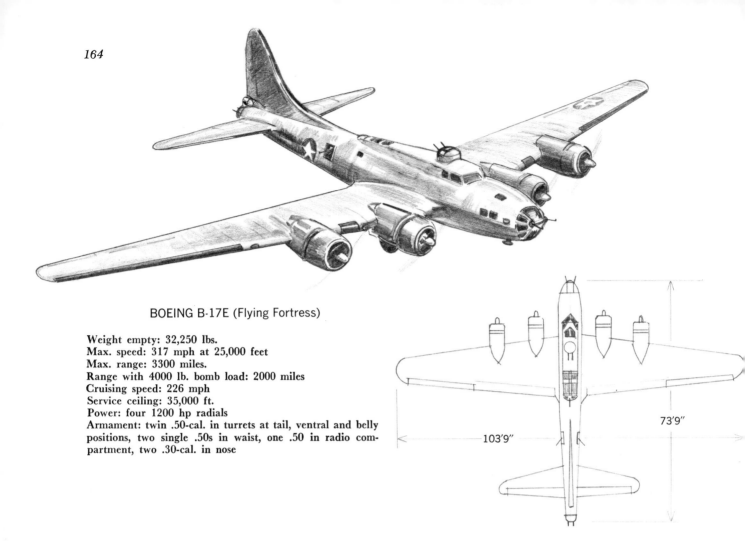

BOEING B-17E (Flying Fortress)

Weight empty: 32,250 lbs.
Max. speed: 317 mph at 25,000 feet
Max. range: 3300 miles.
Range with 4000 lb. bomb load: 2000 miles
Cruising speed: 226 mph
Service ceiling: 35,000 ft.
Power: four 1200 hp radials
Armament: twin .50-cal. in turrets at tail, ventral and belly positions, two single .50s in waist, one .50 in radio compartment, two .30-cal. in nose

103'9"   73'9"

the whistle of a falling bomb) they, like Macbeth, did murder sleep.

As an indication of the growing strength and importance of the Army Air Force in SoPac, it was decided early in December that all such forces were to constitute a new command, designated Thirteenth Air Force.

Besides planes actually operating from Guadalcanal there had been a considerable buildup in the heavy bomber strength of the USAAF in the area. 11th Heavy Bombardment Group, operating from Espiritu since July, had been joined by 5th Heavy Bombardment Group—eight squadrons in all, plus two squadrons of medium bombers (B-26s). On occasion some of these planes staged through Henderson Field, but the chronic shortage of gasoline and the poor condition of the field in bad weather seriously hampered such operations. However, conditions at Espiritu Santo improved and many sorties were flown in support of the ground forces on Guadalcanal, against enemy shipping en route to the island and against Japanese bases and staging areas in the lower Solomons. Distances were

too great (it was some 1300 miles from Espiritu to Rabaul) for raids far to the north. It was not until increased fuel supplies and improvement of Henderson Field by the use of steel matting that attacks with sizable bomb loads could be mounted against Rabaul.

In the meantime, much of the tonnage dropped on Rabaul and the northern bases were delivered by MacArthur's planes from Port Moresby. Between the middle of September and the end of November about forty sorties were flown by Catalinas against Buka, thirty-eight by Catalinas and forty-seven by B-17s against Buin and eleven by Catalinas and 180 by B-17s against Rabaul. A small effort by European Theater standards, but it all helped.

To the disappointment of many USAAF men, a large percentage of the sorties flown by B-17s had been for reconnaissance. At the time it may have seemed a waste to use a heavily armed machine, designed to carry a bomb load for a great distance, for work which might as well be performed by planes such as the Catalina. Actually, the Catalina, although a fine plane, was highly vulnerable to air attack. With a speed almost 100 mph less than the Fortress it was far less heavily armed, with three .30-caliber and two .50-caliber machine guns, as opposed to the eight .50s and one .30-caliber weapons of the B-17E. The Catalina pilots' old joke, "Have sighted enemy carrier. Please notify next of kin" was not always funny. On the other hand, one Flying Fortress maintained contact with a Japanese carrier force for two hours and claimed to have shot down six Zeros of the enemy's CAP. The advantages of a comparatively fast reconnaissance plane with enough armor and armament to fight its way through to its objective and back again was obvious. And while Catalina and RAAF Hudsons continued to fly search missions it was not until the long-ranged twin-engined Lightning fighters became available in quantity and proved their worth at photo and recon work that the B-17 resumed its true duties as a bomb carrier.

Actually, except for cratering enemy airstrips and plastering areas known to conceal enemy installations, heavy bombers found few worthwhile targets. The most important were enemy vessels, but unfortunately these made poor targets and less than one percent of hits were scored against moving ships. Successful attacks on vessels under way called for pattern bombing by formations of a minimum of nine planes (a mathematical formula had shown that the probability of 7 percent hits on a moving enemy carrier, attacked under ideal conditions from 14,000 feet, could only be attained by a formation of eighteen to twenty Fortresses). Even when nine planes were available at Espiritu it took so long to get them into the air (and longer to land) from the inadequate runway facilities then existing that such formations were impractical. The

CO of the 11th Bomber Group, Colonel LaVerne Saunders, was lucky if he could fly a vee of three. So the B-17, as operated in SoPac, never lived up to its vaunted reputation as a "drop-'em-in-a-pickle-barrel-from-15,000-feet" high level bomber. But it was a work horse, never the less, and much credit is due to the men who flew them—sometimes seventeen days of consecutive sorties, each perhaps of eleven to thirteen hours. And to the men (very often aided by the weary crews) who helped service them under impossible conditions and who often gassed them up by means of a bucket brigade, owing to the lack of the proper tankers and pumpers.

The buildup of naval and air strength made any major Japanese drive to retake the island unlikely. But the reduction of the Japanese positions to the west called for more troops than were immediately available. For the veteran 1st Marine Division had been ordered out. While actual combat losses had not been excessive—774 killed, died of wounds or missing, presumed dead, and 1962 wounded—the division was riddled with disease (the incidence of malaria was estimated at 75 percent) and worn out—as much from fighting the climate, the insects, and the tropical jungle as the Japanese.

In preparation for the 1st Marine Division withdrawal, staff officers of the Americal Division moved into Marine staff sections. On December 1, Americal supply sections took over responsibility for supplies and a week later Americal staff officers had taken over completely. Evacuation began on December 9, with the 5th Marines the first to go, and by the end of the month the remainder had

LOCKHEED A-29 (Hudson)

Span: 65'6" **Length** 44'3" **Weight empty:** 12,810 lbs. **Max. speed:** 260 mph at 12,500 feet **Max. range:** 1800 miles **Range with 1400 lb. bomb load:** 1500 miles **Power:** two P&W 1050 radials **Armament:** two .50-cal. in dorsal turret, two .50-cal. in nose, one .50 belly gun **Bomb load:** 1400 lbs. (A sturdy workhouse often known as "Old Boomerang" —always came back)

gone, too. On the same day Vandegrift was relieved by Major General Alexander M. Patch, commanding general of the American Division and now to direct tactical operations on Guadalcanal, though still under Halsey's over-all command. At the same time, the island now being under Army control, Admiral Turner was relieved of his duty of defending the island, although he was still responsible for the transport of troops and supplies.

The American Division—unusual in that it was the only division in the U. S. Army that had a name and not a number—had been activated in New Caledonia (hence the name) on May 27, 1942, formed of troops sent to defend that island after its inhabitants overthrew the pro-Vichy Government and declared for De Gaulle and his Free French. Its main units were the 132nd, 164th (on Guadalcanal since mid-October), and 182nd Infantry regiments (two battalions of which had landed in mid-November); the 221st, 245th, 246th, 247th Field Artillery battalions; the 57th Engineer Combat Battalion; 101st Quartermaster Regiment; 101st Medical Regiment; 26th Signal Company and a Mobile Combat Reconnaissance Squadron (a special motorized unit using jeeps, with 37-mm anti-tank guns, mortars, and automatic weapons. Guadalcanal was too hilly and its jungles too thick for motorized operations, so the unit fought on foot).

Most of the division was on the island by mid-December though most of its units were understrength. On December 11, the division's total strength was 13,169—3125 below its authorized strength.

Besides the American Division, Patch had the 147th Infantry, 2nd and 8th Marines of 2nd Marine Division, and the Marine Defense Battalions. The 147th and the 2nd Marine Regiments were also understrength and feeling the wear and tear of jungle warfare. To bring the American forces on the island to the strength needed for a resumption of the offensive, the Army's 25th Infantry Division, commanded by Major General J. Lawton Collins, then in Hawaii, was ordered to the South Pacific.

Due to lack of shipping space at Pearl Harbor the ships carrying the 25th were not combat-loaded. Normally this would have been done at Nouméa before heading for the combat zone. But for various reasons (mainly improper scheduling—which sometimes saw the arrival of forty-eight or more ships a month when only twenty-four could be handled) there was great confusion and congestion at that little port. There were often thirty cargo ships at anchor there—sometimes three times as many—and some cargoes sat in various holds as long as three months. To save time, Lieutenant General Millard F. Harmon, commanding general of U. S. Army troops in the South Pacific area, took a chance on unloading the ships in the combat zone and ordered the 25th Division's transports to bypass Nouméa and proceed direct to Guadalcanal. The gamble paid off and the transports, under sea and air escorts, landed their troops and supplies without incident. On December 17, the 35th Regimental Combat Team landed; on January 1, the 27th disembarked, followed on January 4 by the 161st. Also on the 4th, there arrived the 6th Marines and the 2nd Marine Division's headquarters.

The situation of the American forces was steadily improving. But the very factors which brought about that improvement—surer command of the sea, fresh troops and equipment, and increasing mastery of the skies—meant a steady worsening of the enemy's position. Malnutrition, malaria, shortage of ammunition and supplies of all kinds including medicine, lack of artillery, and vehicles all added up to an impending defeat. Worst of all was the fact that now few—very few—fresh troops could be sent in to bolster the defenders. Some of the Japanese on the island were survivors of the initial landing force—others veterans of the Tenryu fight and Bloody Ridge. Many were unfit for duty. It was reported that a Japanese commander classified his men as those who could fight and still move, those who could only fight from fixed positions, and those who were unable even to lift a rifle. From a peak of 30,000 men, Japanese strength had dropped to about 25,000 in the beginning of December. All were riddled with disease and half-starved. And all but the most optimistic and fanatical must have realized that things were not going well. More and more enemy planes roared into the field they had tried so hard to retake—more and more American transports and supply ships anchored in Lunga Roads. If all was as rosy as Radio Tokyo said then where were the emperor's ships—and the emperor's planes?

A new command had been set up in Rabaul. The 8th Area Army, headed by General Hitoshi Imamura, had come down from Java. But 50,000 fresh troops and a new general in the north meant little to the weary men on the island and General Hyakutake and his Seventeenth Army staff had to meet the coming American drive with the dwindling forces at their disposal.

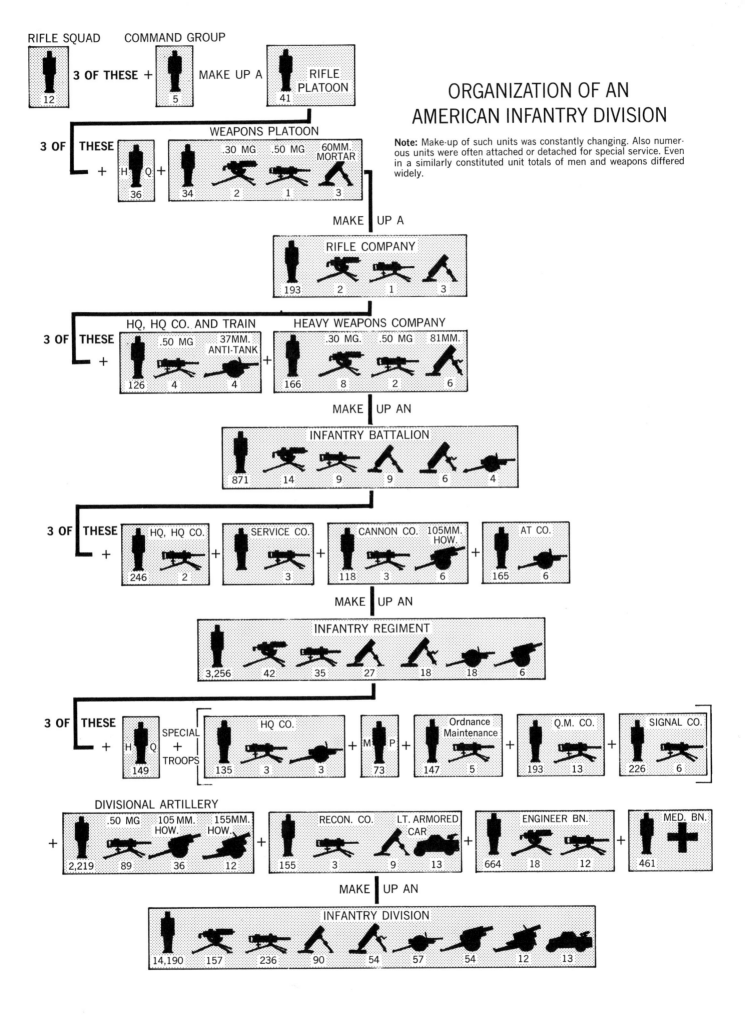

RIFLE SQUAD   COMMAND GROUP

12   **3 OF THESE** +   5   MAKE UP A   41   RIFLE PLATOON

ORGANIZATION OF AN AMERICAN INFANTRY DIVISION

Note: Make-up of such units was constantly changing. Also numerous units were often attached or detached for special service. Even in a similarly constituted unit totals of men and weapons differed widely.

3 OF THESE +   HQ 36   +   WEAPONS PLATOON   .30 MG   .50 MG   60MM. MORTAR   34   2   1   3

MAKE UP A

RIFLE COMPANY   193   2   1   3

3 OF THESE +   HQ, HQ CO. AND TRAIN   .50 MG   37MM. ANTI-TANK   126   4   4   +   HEAVY WEAPONS COMPANY   .30 MG.   .50 MG   81MM.   166   8   2   6

MAKE UP AN

INFANTRY BATTALION   871   14   9   9   6   4

3 OF THESE +   HQ, HQ CO.   246   2   +   SERVICE CO.   3   +   CANNON CO.   105MM. HOW.   118   3   6   +   AT CO.   165   6

MAKE UP AN

INFANTRY REGIMENT   3,256   42   35   27   18   18   6

3 OF THESE +   HQ 149   SPECIAL + TROOPS   HQ CO.   135   3   3   +   MP 73   +   Ordnance Maintenance   147   5   +   Q.M. CO.   193   13   +   SIGNAL CO.   226   6

+   DIVISIONAL ARTILLERY   .50 MG   105 MM. HOW.   155MM. HOW.   2,219   89   36   12   +   RECON. CO.   LT. ARMORED CAR   155   3   9   13   +   ENGINEER BN.   664   18   12   +   MED. BN.   461

MAKE UP AN

INFANTRY DIVISION   14,190   157   236   90   54   57   54   12   13

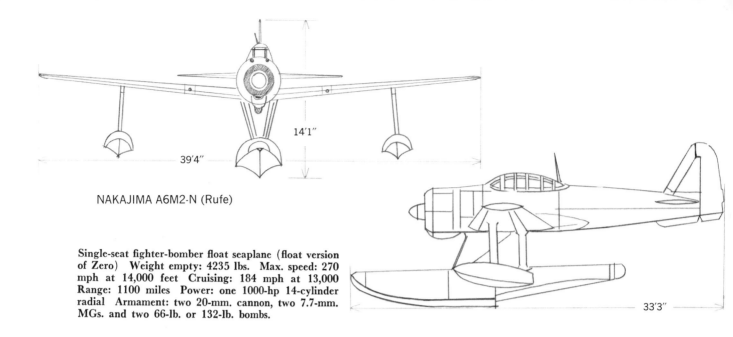

NAKAJIMA A6M2-N (Rufe)

Single-seat fighter-bomber float seaplane (float version of Zero) Weight empty: 4235 lbs. Max. speed: 270 mph at 14,000 feet Cruising: 184 mph at 13,000 Range: 1100 miles Power: one 1000-hp 14-cylinder radial Armament: two 20-mm. cannon, two 7.7-mm. MGs. and two 66-lb. or 132-lb. bombs.

Tanaka and his veteran destroyermen were meanwhile persisting in their efforts to run in supplies to their hungry countrymen. On December 3, coastwatchers and air reconnaissance reported ten enemy destroyers on their way down to Guadalcanal. By the late afternoon these were attacked by dive bombers, torpedo planes, and fighters. Tanaka's force—destroyers *Naganami* (flagship), *Makinami*, and *Yugure* acting as escorts for seven others loaded with drums—were covered by twelve Zero float planes (Rufes) from the Shortlands. These tangled with the attackers, shooting down two and losing three of their own in the action. A near miss damaged *Makanami* but did not halt the squadron. About midnight the force passed southwest of Savo and neared the coast off Tassafaronga. Drums were rolled overboard, linking ropes hauled ashore, boats hoisted, and the force got under way. The PTs were not in action and Tanaka's squadron reached Shortland safely.

Of the 1500 drums dropped, Tanaka reports that only 310 were picked up by dawn. Lack of personnel to haul in the drums, the shore parties feebleness and the fact that when drums caught on underwater projections, the hauling ropes broke was blamed for the failure. Any drums found floating by daylight were sunk by machine-gun fire from strafing planes or PTs. On his return to base, the disgusted admiral strongly recommended that the island be evacuated.

A ten-destroyer run on December 7 under Captain Torajiro Sato was attacked by bombers, torpedo planes, and fighters. Again a near-miss. This one blew a hole in *Nowake* and flooded her engine spaces and fire rooms. She had to be towed home

by *Naganami*, escorted by two other destroyers. The remaining 6 were attacked by PT boats. Torpedoes and automatic weapons fire prompted Sato to retire, his mission unaccomplished.

On December 11, Tanaka led an eleven-vessel Express in his new flagship, the recently commissioned 2500-ton destroyer *Teruzuki*. His escorting planes had turned for home when, off New Georgia, he was subjected to the expected air raid. SBDs attacked but no hits were scored and the operation was proceeding according to plan when PT boats were sighted. A brisk and confused action began, with tracer arcing in all directions, shell bursts from the Japanese destroyers' guns, and the black waters streaked with foaming wakes and the tell-tale bubbles of American torpedo tracks. One or more of the racing "fish" intercepted Tanaka's brand-new flagship. A stunning blast hurled the Japanese admiral to the deck and he regained consciousness to find *Teruzuki* on fire and sinking. Destroyers took off Tanaka and most of *Teruzuki*'s crew before the flames reached her after magazines and she blew up. PT 44 was sunk by gunfire.

The PTs had done well for themselves. Two nights before, PT 59 had caught the 2000-ton *I-3* on the surface near Cape Esperance. One of 59's torpedoes hit and a huge explosion marked the end of another attempt to supply Guadalcanal.

The December 11 foray was Tanaka's last trip to Ironbottom Sound. On the 12th, an order came from the fleet halting all reinforcement attempts temporarily "because of moonlit nights." At the end of the month, the chief engineer of so many runs of the Tokyo Express was transferred to the

Naval General Staff. By that time it had been finally decided that the only possible course was to evacuate the island, a decision which had the tough little admiral's hearty approval.

In the meantime the necessity of increasing their facilities—particularly airfields—in the northern and central Solomons (a move long advocated by Tanaka) had finally become apparent to the Japanese High Command. Increasingly heavy air attacks on Rabaul and the anchorage at Shortland Island (two tankers were hit by B-17s on December 10) showed that more fighter protection was necessary, while a forward airfield within easy striking distance of Henderson Field would not only make possible a far greater bombing effort against American positions, but would also ensure full fighter protection for extended periods. The strip at Buin, at the southern end of Bougainville, was small and the float planes which were based at a couple of other sheltered locations in the area were not capable of meeting the American fighter planes on equal terms.

It was decided therefore to build a forward field in the New Georgia group. A coconut plantation at Munda Point on the southwestern end of New Georgia, about 10 miles south of Kula Gulf and only some 180 miles from Henderson Field, was chosen as a likely spot, and on November 24, a convoy arrived off the Point and work was begun on the field. The work was carefully camouflaged. As trees were cut, the fronds were suspended from wires, other palms were left standing to be removed at the very last minute.

But the convoy and its escorts had not escaped notice. Any suspicious activity brought increased

American aerial reconnaissance and, by December 5, photographs definitely established that a Japanese airfield was in the making. Next day, P-39s from Guadalcanal strafed Munda at treetop height and brought back reports of earth rollers, trucks and carts and the beginning of two airstrips. A strike of B-17s on December 9 followed, and in the ensuing weeks Munda received constant attention by planes of all types, including night nuisance raids by PBYs. During the month of December alone, B-17s of the 5th and 11th Groups would raid Munda twenty-one times.

Although the combatants of neither side knew it, the outcome of the campaign was now a foregone conclusion. Despite costly Allied defeats such as Savo and Tassafaronga, it was the Imperial Japanese Navy which was feeling the need to conserve its ships.

To date, the Guadalcanal campaign had cost the Japanese a small carrier, two elderly battleships, two heavy cruisers, a light cruiser, and eleven destroyers. Allied losses had been heavier—two fleet carriers, five heavy cruisers, two light cruisers, and thirteen fleet destroyers. But American shipyards were shifting into high gear. Surface warships of destroyer size and up launched in 1942 included: six fleet carriers, fifteen escort carriers, three battleships, nine cruisers, and 105 destroyers. In comparison, Japanese output of these types in 1942 was minuscule—three light cruisers and eleven destroyers. Japanese plane losses had also been very heavy and even more damaging was the loss of trained pilots. In December 1941, Japanese Navy pilots were as good or better than any in the world. But no provision for training the great numbers of

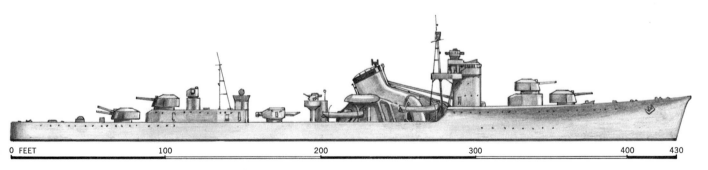

0 FEET   100   200   300   400   430

AKITSUKI CLASS DESTROYER (12 Ships)

Launched July 1941–December 1944
Displacement: 2701 tons   LOA: 440⅓   Beam: 38   Draft: 13½ feet
Twin screw.   52,000 hp=35 knots
Armament: eight 3.9 AA (4×2), four 25-mm. (2×2), four 24 in. torpedo tubes (1×4),
seventy-two depth charges
Complement: 290

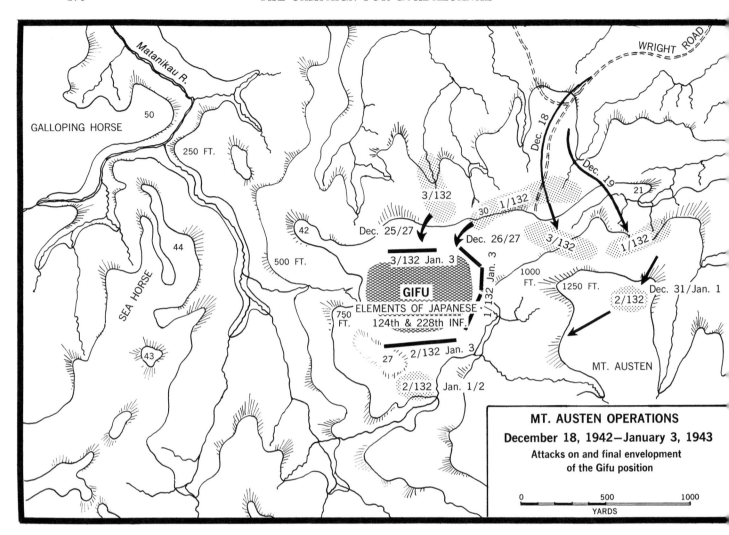

MT. AUSTEN OPERATIONS
December 18, 1942—January 3, 1943
Attacks on and final envelopment
of the Gifu position

0   500   1000
YARDS

men needed for a long war had been made. In 1940, a proposal was made by a far-seeing naval airman for training 15,000 pilots. It was dismissed as a wild dream. When an extended training program finally got under way, it was too late. American pilots were quick to note the sharp decline in the quality of Japanese airmen as the war progressed and as the superbly trained first-line pilots were killed off.

The imminent arrival of reinforcements allowed the American commander on Guadalcanal, General Patch, to implement plans for a renewed drive to the west. But before the thrust along the coast could be set in motion, the Japanese-held area on and around Mount Austen had to be cleared of the enemy. Once that was done, the plan was for two divisions to drive to the west

while a third held the airfields. But the "Mountain" proved a hard nut to crack.

Mount Austen is a low spur of the island's spinal mountain ridge. It is situated about 6 miles southwest of Henderson Field and its jungle-covered 1514-foot summit afforded a good view of the American airstrips, the anchorage off Lunga Point, and of American activities in general. It had been used as such an observation point since the beginning of the campaign, and reports broadcast to Japanese headquarters on the island and then to Rabaul.

Mount Austen does not rise in a single peak but is only the highest point in a series of precipitous, heavily wooded ridges, falling away to grass covered foothills. The area was a most difficult one in which to fight and one of the first things done in preparation was to hack out a trail, suitable for jeep traffic, from the coastal road as far up the foothills as the terrain and the enemy would permit. This was begun early in December and reached some 5 miles in southwest from Lunga Point. Here 60 percent grades halted motor traffic and from here supplies were carried by available soldiers and by the "Cannibal Battalion" of native porters.

The assault on the mountain was to be made by the 132nd Infantry, Colonel LeRoy E. Nelson. The regiment had only landed on December 8 and was new to combat. The 3rd Battalion was to lead the attack; 1st Battalion in reserve and 2nd Battalion to remain in the Lunga defense perimeter. Army 105-mm howitzers and Marine 75-mm pack howitzers were to furnish fire support, as would planes of Cactus Air Force.

Little was known about Japanese strength in the area. A reconnaissance in force on December 17 reported sighting no enemy, but concealment in thick jungle is easy and when the battalion moved to the attack on December 18, fire from rifles and machine guns pinned it to the ground. Artillery was called in on the suspected whereabouts of the enemy but the battalion failed to advance. A more thorough reconnaissance of the ground might have dispelled the optimism which led the commanding general and his staff to assume that a battalion of green troops, only a few days out of overcrowded transports and with no chance to become acclimated, could walk over even lightly held enemy positions in country such as that. Checked as much by the country as Japanese fire, 3rd Battalion of the 132nd Regiment dug in for the night. Casualties were one man wounded.

Actually, the Mount Austen area was held by understrength battalions of 38th Division regiments under Colonel Oka. These units, though desperately short of ammunition and supplies, were well dug in. Strong points for machine guns and riflemen had been constructed, some with three layers of logs covered with earth on top and walls, two logs in thickness, dug in so only firing slits were above ground. Impervious to any but direct hit by bomb or shell, hidden in dense jungle and mutually supporting, they proved a formidable obstacle.

On December 19, 1st Battalion of the 132nd was brought up in support, but little progress was made. The colonel of 3rd Battalion of the same regiment was killed and Japanese infiltrators disorganized the Americans by firing into the combined battalion command post, as well as harassing supply parties and the working parties on the jeep trail. December 20 and 21 saw more casualties but no advance. Japanese infiltrators still shot up working parties and fired on litter bearers so often that some took off their Red Cross brassards and took to carrying rifles. Their work was difficult enough without being the target of enemy marksmen. The steep ravines and jungle-filled hollows made removal of the litter cases a back-breaking task. Later skids were fastened to Navy basket-style litters and these were lowered down the slopes with ropes. Some of the deeper clefts were negotiated by use of steel cables and pulleys. Once at the jeep trail, the wounded were loaded aboard jeeps and jolted down the winding track to the perimeter.

A request for release of 2nd Battalion of the 132nd Regiment was turned down by General Sebree. (To lighten the command structure and provide General Patch with more staff, a Corps Headquarters was set up and the Guadalcanal-Tulagi area incorporated as XIV Corps. Patch was moved up to Corps Commander and Sebree replaced him as commander of the Americal Division.) On December 23, the two battalions prepared to advance again but little progress was made. The main enemy resistance was a strong point, or interlocking series of strong points, garrisoned by some five hundred of Oka's men and named by them the Gifu, after a prefecture in Honshu. Jungle hid most of the positions from air observation while others were in defilade and thus protected from artillery fire.

JAPANESE STRONG POINT
CENTRAL BUNKER AND FLANKING MG PITS

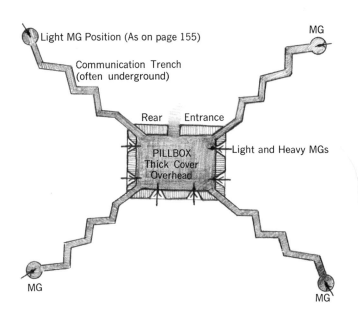

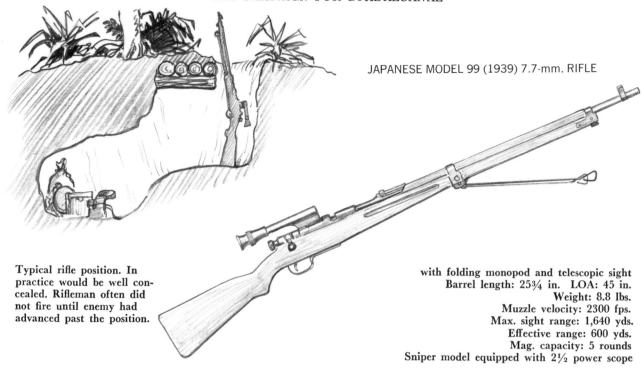

JAPANESE MODEL 99 (1939) 7.7-mm. RIFLE

Typical rifle position. In practice would be well concealed. Rifleman often did not fire until enemy had advanced past the position.

with folding monopod and telescopic sight
Barrel length: 25¾ in.   LOA: 45 in.
Weight: 8.8 lbs.
Muzzle velocity: 2300 fps.
Max. sight range: 1,640 yds.
Effective range: 600 yds.
Mag. capacity: 5 rounds
Sniper model equipped with 2½ power scope

Probing attacks continued for several days, directed mainly against the complex of hills of which the Gifu was a part. The fighting dragged on—the two battalions had lost over three hundred men and were in poor shape physically and mentally. The fresh 2nd Battalion was now ordered up (December 30), and on January 1, began the advance and took the slopes of one of the outlying hills—Hill 27—close to the Gifu. The commander of the 132nd, worn out and ill from malaria, asked to be relieved and Colonel Alexander George took over. To prove his contention that the Japanese riflemen were not as effective as his troops believed, the colonel inspected his front positions walking erect, clad in shorts and a fatigue cap and carrying a rifle. Japanese "snipers" obligingly fired at him and missed. (By now the word sniper was usually misused. The proper use of the term is to describe a highly trained marksman, often equipped with a weapon with a telescopic sight, who could conceal himself carefully and patiently wait to pick off an enemy, often at long range. To the citizen-soldier, any solitary rifleman was a "sniper.")

Perhaps the colonel's little demonstration was needed. Certainly the 132nd's advances thus far had been less than spectacular. At any rate, 2nd Battalion of the 132nd took Hill 27—only to be vigorously counterattacked before it could dig in. Six assaults, each preceded by mortar fire, were

beaten back. That night the Japanese almost surrounded the battalion but their advances were stopped by heavy concentrations of artillery fire.

By January 3, the three battalions were in contact with one another and they now dug in on a stoutly fortified position ringing the Gifu on the north, east, and south. The remaining Japanese on the Gifu were thus contained, if not driven out. But the 132nd was worn out. Nearly four hundred were dead or wounded and many others sick. No further advances were undertaken until the position was taken over by 2nd Battalion, 35th Infantry of the 25th Division. Americans were finding out the hard way that rooting Japanese troops (even if they were cut off, half starved, low on ammunition, and without artillery support) out of carefully prepared positions was a slow and costly job. A man who is fanatically determined to die where he stands rather than give up his position is a tough opponent.

While the 132nd Infantry was battling around the Gifu, the naval front had shifted temporarily to New Georgia. Despite U.S. air attacks, work on the airstrip and installations was progressing. Admiral Tanaka, although still suffering from his injuries, made several trips to Munda with troops and supplies. These were not without incident. American planes and submarines were active. On December 16, a pair of SBDs bombed and damaged destroyer *Kagero* and on Christmas Day, the transport *Nankai Maru* was hit by a torpedo and subsequently sank. During the excitement of the counterattack, destroyer *Uzuki* collided with the transport and had to be towed back to base. On December 26, a near-miss set destroyer *Ariake* on fire and killed and wounded nearly seventy of her crew. Planes from Guadalcanal also sank a small transport and a freighter en route to Wickham, an anchorage on Vangunu Island, south of New Georgia, where a small base was being established.

A major concentration of shipping at Rabaul drew added attention, both from bombers based on Henderson Field and from MacArthur's command. A transport was sunk, others damaged, and destroyer *Tachikaze* had her bow blown off.

At the same time, the submarine war against Japanese shipping was continuing.

Convoys to and from Truk and Rabaul were attacked and several freighters sunk. Naval losses included light cruiser *Tenryu* (sunk on December 18 off New Guinea by *Albacore*) and several submarines. By a line of reasoning peculiar to the Japanese, their fine fleet submarines were not used against American supply lines but, when not operating with the fleet against naval targets, were used to supply outlying garrisons such as Guadalcanal. As we have seen, one of these, *I-3*, had been sunk by a PT. *I-4* went down southeast of Rabaul December 20—victim of *Seadragon*, and later *Grayback* sent *I-18* to the bottom. Reported sinkings by U.S. forces do not always coincide with

Japanese records, but in November and December, five submarines disappeared in the Guadalcanal-New Guinea area.

These actions were only incidental to the Guadalcanal campaign, however, and the base at Munda (which was being used by Zeros by mid-December) was still the chief concern of the American commanders. On December 24, dive bombers, escorted by fighters, made an early morning raid on the strip and caught the Japanese off guard. Some dozen fighters were destroyed on the ground, ten more just as they were taking off, and four more in mid-air. A second raid later in the day beat up ten landing barges laden with troops and supplies. But although the almost daily raids were doing damage, it was decided that what the field needed was a good pasting by naval gunfire.

Accordingly, Task Force 57 was reorganized, under Rear Admiral Walden "Pug" L. Ainsworth. The force was split up—the bombardment group (light cruisers *Nashville*, *Helena*, and *St. Louis*, with destroyers *O'Bannon* and *Fletcher*) to hit the field, while a distant support group (heavy cruiser *Louisville*, light cruisers *Honolulu*, *Columbia*, and H.M.N.Z.S. *Achilles*, and destroyers *Lamson*, *Drayton*, and *Nicholas*, under Rear Admiral Tisdale) was to cruise southeast of New Georgia. The bombardment was scheduled to coincide with the movement to Guadalcanal of the 6th Marine Regiment, Divisional Headquarters of the 2nd Marine Division, and the 161st Combat Team of the Army's 25th Division. The warships would escort the transports to the island on the morning of January 4, then steam north toward Rendova.

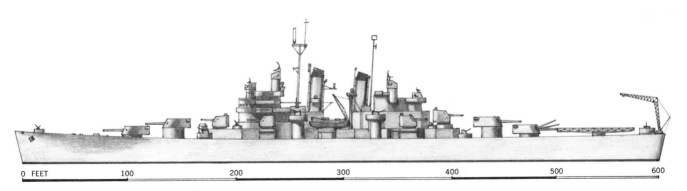

CLEVELAND CLASS LIGHT CRUISER (27 Ships)

Launched January 1941–April 1945
Displacement: 10,000 tons LOA: 608⅓ Beam: 63 Draft: 20 feet
4 screws. 100,000 hp＝35 knots Armament: twelve 6 in. (4✕3), twelve 5 in. (6✕2),
twenty-four–twenty-eight 40-mm./20-mm. AAs Aircraft: four Complement: 1200

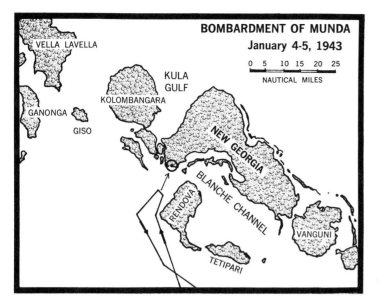

Submarine *Grayback* was to take station off the west coast of that island and act as a navigational point. Night fighting Catalinas were to fly spotters for the cruisers over the target area during the shoot.

The bombardment went off without a hitch. About midnight, *Nashville,* the flagship, rounded the southwestern tip of Rendova and turned northeast parallel to the coast. Around 0100, January 5, the column swung left to a northwesterly course to bring all guns to bear and a few minutes later opened fire. Projectiles arced up and away toward Munda and observers noted the pulsating glare of burning gasoline or ammunition stores mingled with the flashes of exploding shells. When the ships turned away, about 0150, some 3000 rounds of 6-inch and 1400 of 5-inch had smashed into the field and its surrounding positions and the glow of fires was visible for many miles.

The two squadrons rendezvoused south of Guadalcanal on the morning of January 6. The day was fine and a CAP from Henderson was covering the Task Force while more planes flew an antisubmarine patrol farther out. Yet four Japanese dive bombers managed to arrive unannounced and near-missed *Honolulu,* while another planted a bomb square on *Achilles* number 3 turret. The turret roof was pierced and the turret wrecked but the ship maintained her place in formation. Two of the four planes were shot down.

At Imperial GHQ in Tokyo, meanwhile, there had been heard (from some of the more outspoken and realistic) the first discreet hints that the troops on Guadalcanal could no longer be supported. This was, at first, regarded as defeatism by the powers-that-were, particularly those wearing the Army uniform. Troops had died by the thousands—there were more troops. And Imamura with his Eighth Area Army was now assembled at Rabaul, awaiting the word to proceed to the relief of the island. But the burden of transporting them there rested on the Navy, and while there might be no shortage of troops willing and ready to die for the emperor, there was already a decided shortage of shipping. U.S. submarine doctrine differed sharply from that of the Imperial Navy and by January 2, 1943, some 614,000 tons of cargo and transport ships had been sunk by submarine attack alone. Many precious destroyers now littered the floor of Ironbottom Sound and the waters of The Slot, while more had limped back to base in various states of disrepair. There were other theaters of war to consider (the campaign in the Aleutians was not going well, either) and there was, above

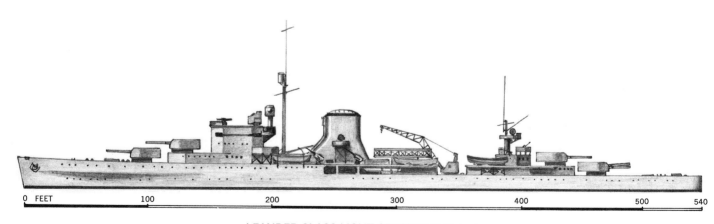

0 FEET   100   200   300   400   500   540

LEANDER CLASS LIGHT CRUISER (5 Ships)

Launched September 1931–March 1934
Displacement: 6840–7140 tons LOA: 554½ Beam: 55 Draft: 15½ feet
4 screws. 72,000 hp=32.5 knots Armor: belt 4 in., deck 2 in., turrets 1 in. Armament:
eight 6 in. (4×2), eight 4 in. AA (4×2), (in Achilles above) four 4 in. (4×1), four 3
pdr., eight 21 in. torpedo tubes (2×4) Aircraft: 1 (Ajax 2) Complement: 550

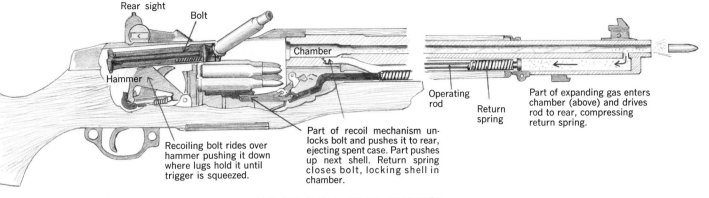

Rear sight

Bolt

Hammer

Chamber

Recoiling bolt rides over hammer pushing it down where lugs hold it until trigger is squeezed.

Part of recoil mechanism unlocks bolt and pushes it to rear, ejecting spent case. Part pushes up next shell. Return spring closes bolt, locking shell in chamber.

Operating rod

Return spring

Part of expanding gas enters chamber (above) and drives rod to rear, compressing return spring.

U.S. RIFLE, CAL. .30 M1 (GARAND)

Diagram showing basic principle of operation gas operated, auto-loading (not automatic) rifle. Clip feed. 8 cartridges. Clip ejects after last round is fired. Over-all length: 43 inches Weight: 9 pounds Effective range: 5–600 yards

all, the expected confrontation with the U. S. Pacific Fleet. There was also a suspicion that the Army was not pulling its weight. So far the air offensive against Guadalcanal had been borne almost exclusively by Navy planes and Navy pilots. And the successive waves of confident troops and overconfident generals, which the Navy had transported to the island at such cost, had not only repeatedly failed to annihilate the enemy, but now were on the verge of starvation and defeat. Yamamoto, as we have mentioned, was noted for his poker. And one of the requisites of a good player is ability to realize when it is time to throw in his hand.

By the end of November the unpalatable truth that Guadalcanal must be abandoned had become increasingly apparent and a withdrawal was finally decided upon. Such a momentous decision—Japan's first retreat (and a tacit admission that dozens of ships, hundreds of planes, and thousands of men had been sacrificed for nothing)—had to have approval from the Throne. This was granted on December 31, 1942, and a few days later a shocked Imamura received the news. Equally reluctant to admit defeat was the naval commander at Rabaul, Vice-Admiral Jinichi Kusaka. But the orders had the Imperial sanction, and plans for the evacuation in early February were begun at once. These top secret plans were not even made known to the commanding officers in the field, and it was not until mid-January that General Hyakutake was informed by a special messenger.

On Guadalcanal the Army's 25th Infantry Division prepared to resume the advance, while the 2nd Marine Division worked along the coast. The

beginning of the main American drive (the clearing of Mount Austen had been considered a preliminary to this) was set for January 10, 1943. The offensive was to push west along and at right angles to the coast—from the lines (Point Cruz to Hill 66) established at the end of the fighting of late November. At the same time, a push southwest from Hill 55 and from positions on the western slopes of Mount Austen (south of the Gifu) was to advance the American line to a position running at right angles to the coast and ending

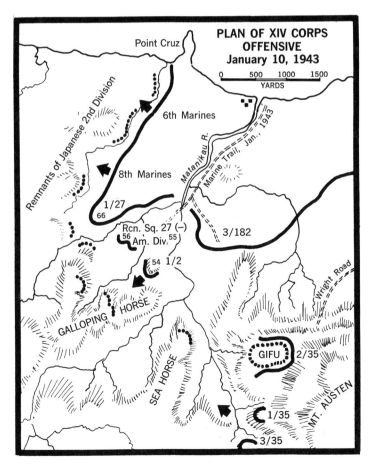

PLAN OF XIV CORPS OFFENSIVE
January 10, 1943

0   500   1000   1500
YARDS

Point Cruz

Remnants of Japanese 2nd Division

6th Marines

8th Marines

1/27
66

Matanikau R.

Marine Trail, Jan., 1943

Rcn. Sq. 27 (–)
56 Am. Div. 55

3/182

54 1/2

GALLOPING HORSE

SEA HORSE

GIFU 2/35

Wright Road

1/35

MT. AUSTEN

3/35

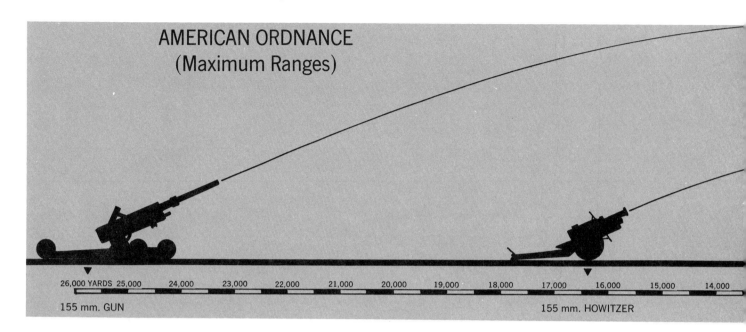

AMERICAN ORDNANCE
(Maximum Ranges)

26,000 YARDS 25,000   24,000   23,000   22,000   21,000   20,000   19,000   18,000   17,000   16,000   15,000   14,000

155 mm. GUN   155 mm. HOWITZER

some three miles inland. Of the Americal Division, the 182nd Infantry, the Reconnaissance Squadron, and the 2nd Battalion of the 132nd Regiment were included in the attacking forces, the rest of the Division were to hold the perimeter. Considerable artillery forces were available to assist in the attack, including a 155-mm howitzer battery and a 155-mm gun battery. Air support was, of course, on call, as was naval gunfire; while some B-17s were to be used to drop supplies to isolated units. Supply was a considerable problem, as the main jeep trail (from the coast track at the mouth of the Matanikau to Hill 55) was inadequate and beyond that point supplies had to be manhandled. There was often a severe water shortage, a terrible hardship in a place where men quickly became dehydrated, and both food and ammunition were sometimes in short supply. Use of assault boats and light draft barges, heaved bodily up the shallow upper reaches of the Matanikau, and known as the Pusha Maru Line, helped somewhat. The Pusha Maru was also used to evacuate wounded.

The attack southwest from Hill 55 was to be made by the 27th Infantry. The hill complex it was to assault—held by elements of the Japanese 228th and 230th Infantry regiments—was, from its shape, known as the Galloping Horse. At 0550

on January 10, six artillery battalions opened a concentrated fire. Time-on-target fire was used, possibly the first divisional TOT shoot of the war. (In TOT fire the time of flight of the shells from each battery is subtracted from the time the shells are to arrive at the selected target. The time on target is given to all batteries engaged and each gun fires on the calculated split second. Firing is from grids—laid over the map—or from range data previously recorded. No ranging shots are fired, so that the enemy has no warning before the simultaneous arrival of the initial salvo—in this case, seventy-two shells—in the target area.) In thirty minutes, 5700 rounds were poured into the Japanese positions. When the barrage stopped, at 0620, twelve P-39s (each carrying one 500-lb. bomb) and twelve SBDs, each with three 325-lb. depth charges, bombed positions protected from the artillery fire by steep slopes.

Thanks to the TOT concentration, the leading companies of 1st Battalion of the 27th Regiment met only fire from three machine guns and reached its first objective, Hill 57, by 1140. The 3rd Battalion had a tough fight for another strong point on the Galloping Horse, Hill 52. It had not been included in the preliminary bombardment and several enveloping attacks failed. At 1430, a com-

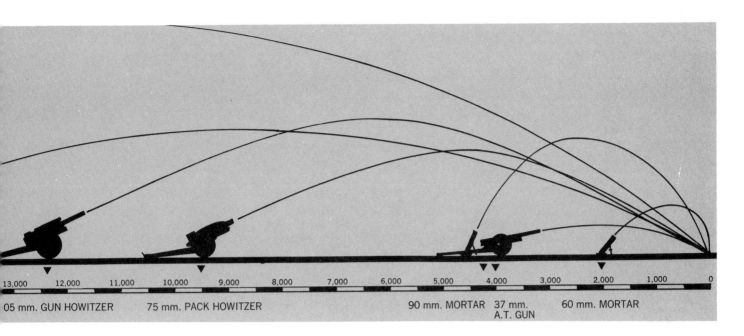

13,000   12,000   11,000   10,000   9,000   8,000   7,000   6,000   5,000   4,000   3,000   2,000   1,000   0

05 mm. GUN HOWITZER   75 mm. PACK HOWITZER   90 mm. MORTAR   37 mm.
A.T. GUN   60 mm. MORTAR

bined artillery and air bombardment was put down on the position and, under cover of the battalion's 37-mm guns and mortars, the hill was rushed with fixed bayonets. Thirty Japanese were killed and six machine guns which had survived the bombardment were taken. By nightfall of the first day, 1st Battalion of the 27th and 3rd Battalion of the same regiment had taken more than half of the Galloping Horse with light casualties. Second Battalion of the 27th, in regimental reserve, moved up in contact. The 161st Infantry, in Division reserve, had not been called in.

There was a serious water shortage in the forward positions on the Galloping Horse. Water had been sent up the trail to the front but little reached the forward units. When 3rd Battalion of the 27th resumed the attack on January 11, many men had only what was left in their canteens after the blazing hot fighting of the previous day. Efforts to take Hill 53, the southwestern tip of the Galloping Horse, failed and the exhausted battalion was brought back into reserve. Next day, 2nd Battalion of the 27th tried again but, despite seventeen artillery concentrations called for by the battalion commander and intensive mortaring by the battalion's weapons, fire from the well-hidden, protected Japanese bunkers held up all advances.

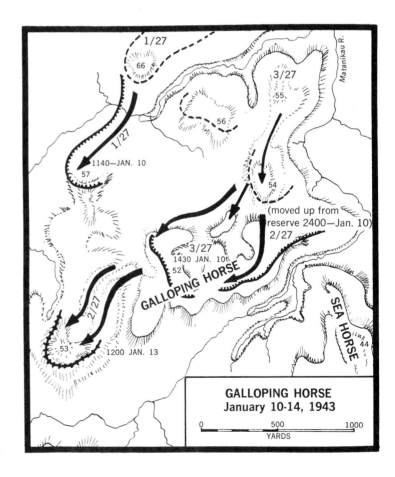

GALLOPING HORSE
January 10-14, 1943

0   500   1000
YARDS

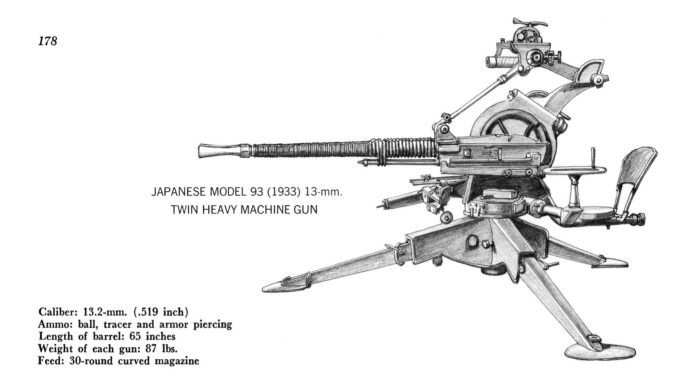

JAPANESE MODEL 93 (1933) 13-mm.
TWIN HEAVY MACHINE GUN

Caliber: 13.2-mm. (.519 inch)
Ammo: ball, tracer and armor piercing
Length of barrel: 65 inches
Weight of each gun: 87 lbs.
Feed: 30-round curved magazine

On January 13, 2nd Battalion of the 27th tried again. The enemy covering positions were such that they could not be reached by artillery or mortar fire—even when the 61-mm tubes were elevated almost to the vertical. The position was at last taken when Captain Charles Davis (the 2nd Battalion Executive Officer) and four men crawled to within ten yards of the strong point and lobbed in grenades. Some of the enemy ran; the captain and his men then rushed in among the survivors with rifles and pistols and killed

them all. Seeing this gallant action (which earned Captain Davis the Medal of Honor), the company leading the attack sprang up the hill and carried it. The crest of Hill 53 was now subjected to an intensive fire by three artillery battalions. Attacking the moment the last shells exploded, the troops overran what little organized resistance was left and by noon the last positions of the Galloping Horse were in American hands.

At the same time as the 27th Infantry began its attack on the Galloping Horse, the 35th Infantry moved to clear the Japanese out of the Gifu and from the areas south and west of it. The Japanese held the open crests of two hills, 43 and 44, east of the Gifu. This open area showed up on aerial maps in the shape of a sea horse, and its capture would isolate enemy units still holding out in the Gifu and surrounding jungle. On January 10, 3rd Battalion of the 35th Regiment managed to reach the slopes of the southernmost hill of the Sea Horse, Hill 43, against stubborn resistance. A surprise counterattack by some of Oka's men on an isolated position scattered some American riflemen and knocked out one or two light machine guns. Two soldiers, Sergeant William Fournier and T/5 Lewis Hall, recovered the abandoned machine gun and opened fire on the Japanese. To bring the weapon to bear on the enemy, then in a low stream bed, Sergeant Fournier lifted the weapon on its tripod while Hall fired. The Japanese attack was broken up but not before

GALLOPING
HORSE

2/27

CAPTURE OF THE
SEA HORSE
January 8-11, 1943

0   500

YARDS

44

SEA HORSE

3/182

JAN. 11

2/35 (−)

GIFU

43

JAN. 11

2/35 (−)

27

JAN. 10/11

3/35

JAN. 9

JAN. 10

Fournier and Hall were mortally wounded. Both were posthumously awarded the Medal of Honor. By the time the slopes of Hill 43 were reached, it was too dark to continue the action and the battalion dug in.

Attacking on January 11, 3rd Battalion of the 35th pressed on despite enemy machine-gun fire and by night had cleared both Hill 43 and Hill 44. The Sea Horse was in American hands and the Gifu encircled. During the next few days (January 12–16) 1st Battalion of the 35th Regiment and the 3rd Battalion, same regiment, cleared out all pockets of resistance between the Sea Horse and the north-south line which was the Corps' objective. Enemy dead were estimated at over five hundred. Seventeen prisoners were taken, some too weak to walk. Two 70-mm cannon were captured along with forty-eight machine guns. The attackers had outrun their supply lines and drops were made by B–17s. Few cargo parachutes were available and some supplies were wrapped in burlap and tossed out of low-flying planes. Of food supplies some 85 percent was usable, but little ammunition and few water cans survived the drops.

While its two sister battalions were taking the Sea Horse area, 2nd Battalion of the 35th had begun the task of clearing the Gifu. The battalion met with strong resistance on the 10th and attacks on the following days met with little success. The position of the defenders was hopeless. Their last rations were gone and so was their commander. Colonel Oka and his regimental staff of the 124th Infantry had made their way out through the American positions. He later ordered Major Inagaki and the remaining troops to work their way out through the jungle. So many men were sick or wounded that the major decided to fight to the last rather than abandon them. They continued to defend their pillboxes stubbornly and by January 16 their positions were still almost intact, despite heavy pressure and concentrated mortar attacks.

The commanding officer of the 2nd Battalion was relieved and preparations by the new CO were made for an all-out assault. While a heavy artillery preparation was being organized, appeals to surrender were made by loud speaker. This effort only netted five half-starved prisoners and, on January 17, two battalions of 105-mms and two of 155-mms registered on the position and at 1430 began a bombardment which dropped more than 1700 rounds into an area some 750 yards long by 500 deep. At the same time, all available mortars also fired into the Gifu. To clear the line of fire the attacking units of the 35th had to pull back. By the time they regained their positions, it was too near dark to risk an advance and the chance of overrunning the dazed and shaken defenders was lost. The fighting went on, pillbox by pillbox, for the next few days and it was not until January 22 when a Marine Corps light tank (brought up with a great deal of effort) succeeded in knocking out several strong points, that any real headway was made. That night about one hundred of the strongest of the defenders, led by Major Inagaki, made a desperate counterattack. The attackers were cut to pieces by automatic weapons' fire. Eighty-five Japanese, including Inagaki, another major, eight captains, and fifteen lieutenants fell in this assault.

When next day the battalion advanced in skirmish order there was little resistance and the position was finally cleared. The garrison was all but wiped out—over five hundred bodies and forty machine guns were found. But the Gifu defenders had held out for more than a month and it had required the efforts of five battalions to reduce the stronghold. The enemy defense is all the more remarkable when it is considered that they had no air support, no artillery, almost no food or medical supplies, and no hope of relief. It was a foretaste of what American troops could expect in later days and on other islands.

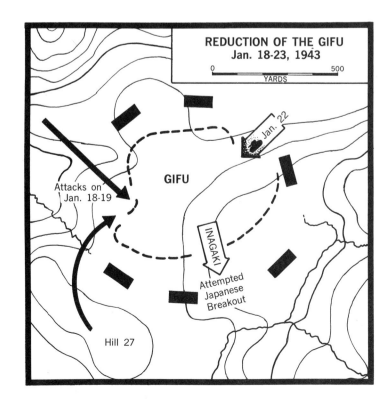

REDUCTION OF THE GIFU
Jan. 18-23, 1943

0   500
YARDS

Jan. 22

GIFU

Attacks on
Jan. 18-19

INAGAKI

Attempted
Japanese
Breakout

Hill 27

The offensive along the coast, which did not suffer from the logistic problems of the units operating further inland, began on January 13. The 2nd Marine Division attack was to be delivered in echelons from left to right. This plan was dictated by the strongly held Japanese positions outflanking each of the numerous wooded ravines running at right angles to the coast. The idea was for the units on the Americans' left flank to move forward and clean out the machine-gun nests at the head of each ravine—thus permitting the main advance to cross the ravines unexposed to flanking fire.

The 2nd Marines, supported by the 6th, were assigned the southern end of the advance and the 8th the right, nearest the coast. The 2nd advanced some 800 yards but the 8th was held up by heavy Japanese machine-gun, mortar, and rifle fire. The 6th Marines now relieved the 2nd, who moved back into the perimeter defenses in preparation for their evacuation from the island. The 2nd Marine Regiment had been in the area since August 7 and were in urgent need of rest and change of climate.

The 8th attempted to gain ground across the ravine in their front again on January 14, but little was accomplished. Tanks were ordered into action on January 15 but it was not until a flame-thrower was brought into play later in the day that any impression could be made on the Japanese bunkers. It took until the evening of January 17 before the 8th had cleared the ravine and brought its front in line with 6th Marines on their left. As a measure of the intensity of the fighting, 2nd Marine Division reported that, from January 13 to 17, it had advanced 650 yards and killed 643 Japanese and taken three 75-mm field howitzers and seventy-one machine guns.

On January 18 the 8th Marines were withdrawn and sent into bivouac and 147th Infantry (less one battalion) was attached to the 2nd Marine Division, as was the 182nd (less one battalion). This composite Army-Marine Division (CAM), was to continue the coastal advance, while the 25th Division continued their advance westward farther inland (2nd Battalion of the 35th Regiment was still busy with the Gifu). The ground facing the two divisions was generally similar to that just won—north-south ravines in the coastal area and higher hill complexes farther inland.

The offensive began on January 22. The 27th was to make a holding attack on the right while the 161st moved to envelop and attack a three-hill formation dominating the area. It was thought that these hills, 87, 88, 89, would be strongly held, but after a heavy artillery bombardment the 27th found so little opposition that, while the assault battalion of the 161st was still deep in the jungle, the regiment was able to push on and take all three hills. Both corps and division commanders were quick to take advantage of the situation. New orders sent the 25th Division ahead toward Kokumbona and by 1700, 1st Battalion of the 27th Regiment had reached the high ground a half mile southeast of that place. The rapid advance called for some major moves by the supporting artillery battalions (25th Division artillery had fired nearly 70 tons of shells since morning). On January 23, 1st Battalion of the 27th entered Kokumbona, 2nd Battalion of the 27th moved south and west of the village, and the regiment's 3rd Battalion faced east, boxing in the enemy still opposing CAM Division near the coast.

The Japanese were unaware that the Americans had cut behind them and reached the beach. That night (January 23–24) a party of the enemy marched westward along the coastal road, pulling a 37-mm gun. They were talking and using lights

as if there were no Americans within miles. They carelessly marched into a 27th Regiment unit blocking the road. The unit held its fire until the Japanese were close, then cut loose with everything they had. Some fifty bodies were counted in the morning.

Running from Kokumbona to Beaufort Bay on the southwestern coast is the Beaufort Trail, a 20-mile-long native track winding through the mountains. This and the coast road to Cape Esperance were the only escape routes open to the Japanese. To block this trail (most of which had been explored by U.S. patrols in December) a small force of the 147th Infantry under Captain Charles Beach had been sent in two tank landing craft from Kukum. Rounding Cape Esperance at night they had landed at Father Klerk's mission on Beaufort Bay on January 9. Beach defenses were set up, while part of the force went up the trail and established a block some 6 miles from the coast near the headwaters of the Poha. No Japanese were encountered, and after the capture of Kokumbona and the crossing of the Poha River the force finally proceeded north to the coast.

CAM's 6th Marines, 147th Infantry, and 182nd Infantry moved forward on January 22, the three

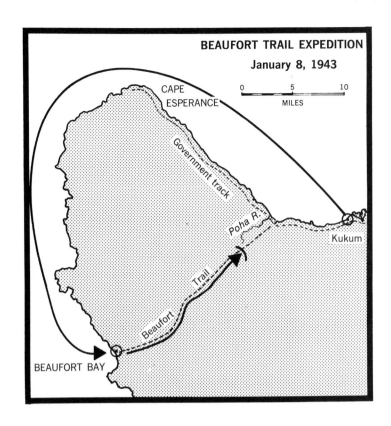

regiments abreast. The attack was supported by air and by naval gunfire from destroyers offshore, as well as Americal Division and 2nd Marine Division artillery. Resistance on the left was light

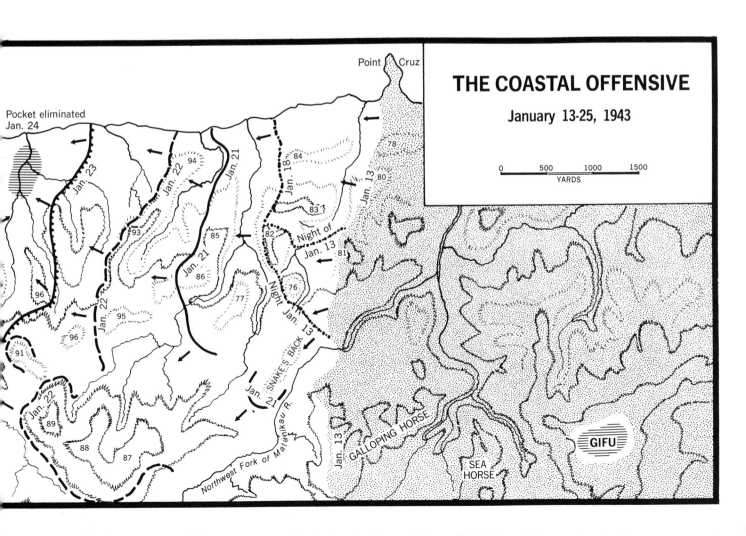

but the Marines met heavy antitank and machine-gun fire and the advance halted for the night with gains all along the line of from 500 to 1000 yards. The advance continued next day and by nightfall the Marines had crossed a ravine and taken the high ground in front of them. Besides machine guns, they destroyed three 150-mm guns, two 37-mm guns, and a light tank. On the next day, CAM Division made contact with the 27th Regiment units—wiping out the remaining Japanese caught between the two forces.

About a mile and a half west of Kokumbona—where landing craft were now unloading supplies—is the mouth of the Poha River. The 27th Infantry Regiment attempted to reach this ob-jective on January 24, but was held up by a sharp defense. Next day the advance was pushed by the 3rd Battalion of the regiment and the swampy river delta was reached in late afternoon. There was some confusion as to which of the streams was the main river. The battalion commander, after crossing six streams, requested the artillery to drop one shell offshore opposite the true river mouth. The shell exploded behind him. The Poha had been crossed! The second battalion was mopping up inland and the two linked up on the morning of January 26. Besides killing some four hundred Japanese, the troops captured a radar station, trucks, landing craft, and fifteen pieces of artillery.

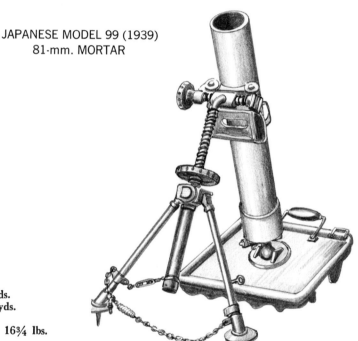

JAPANESE MODEL 99 (1939)
81-mm. MORTAR

Max. range: 7.2 lb. shell 3280 yds., Min.: 545 yds.
Max. range: 14.3 lb. shell 1312 yds., Min.: 207 yds.
Rate of fire: 15 rounds per minute
Weight: barrel 17¾ lbs., baseplate 18 lbs., bipod 16¾ lbs.
Length: 25¼ inches

XVI

"One More River to Cross"

THE ADVANCE TO CAPE ESPERANCE
AND THE EVACUATION

Although the Japanese High Command had decided upon the evacuation of Guadalcanal, it was still necessary to supply the thousands of troops now being steadily driven westward toward Cape Esperance. By January 20, submarines were engaged in bringing supplies to the island, and occasional runs were made by the Tokyo Express. These last now rarely entered Ironbottom Sound without an encounter with the PTs, which often disrupted or forced cancellation of the supply drops.

On January 10, for instance, coastwatchers reported eight destroyers heading down The Slot. The news came too late for a plane strike before dusk, but eight PTs went out on patrol. In the following action, PT 112 was sunk; PT 43 was hit, abandoned, towed ashore by the Japanese

and finally destroyed by gunfire from a Royal New Zealand Navy trawler; and *Hatsukaze* was holed by a torpedo. The damaged destroyer managed to limp off to base, but the PTs conducted a shoot next morning, using unrecovered drums as targets.

The night of January 14–15, nine Japanese destroyers brought supplies and six hundred fresh troops (as far as is known, the last to reach the island) to help in the rear-guard actions then in progress. Thirteen PTs were on patrol and several attacks were made, but no hits. Despite the pitch black, squally night Japanese planes, guided by the dazzling phosphorescent wakes, bombed and strafed some of the PTs—unsuccessfully, as it turned out. Next day, fifteen dive bombers from Guadalcanal attacked the retiring squadron. Apart from damage

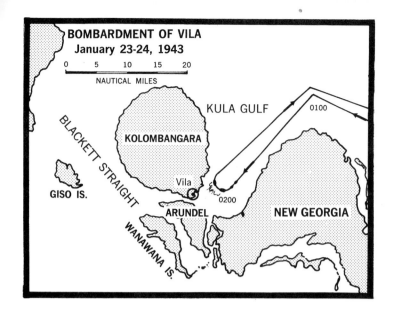

BOMBARDMENT OF VILA
January 23-24, 1943
0   5   10   15   20
NAUTICAL MILES

BLACKETT STRAIGHT

GISO IS.

KOLOMBANGARA

KULA GULF

0100

Vila

0200

ARUNDEL

NEW GEORGIA

WANAWANA IS.

to the rudder of one vessel and a few .50-caliber bullet holes in another, the enemy returned to base unscathed, but a furious air battle cost the Japanese a number of their fighter cover.

Experience at Henderson Field had shown that even heavy bombardment could not knock out an airstrip for long. However, it was decided to attack a nearly completed Japanese strip then building at Vila, a plantation on the flat coastal area of volcanic Kolombangara Island, west of Kula Gulf. On the evening of January 23, Rear Admiral Ainsworth left the New Hebrides with Task Force 67. Light cruisers *Nashville* and *Helena,* with destroyers *De Haven, Radford, O'Bannon,* and *Nicholas* made up the bombardment force, while *Honolulu, St. Louis* and destroyers *Drayton, Lamson,* and *Hughes* were to cruise south of Guadalcanal in support. A couple of Japanese planes flew over the bombardment group about midnight, but they were not fired upon and they finally flew off, evidently thinking the ships were friendly.

On entering Kula Gulf, *O'Bannon* took station as picket near Kolombangara while *Nicholas* scouted nearby. At 0200, the cruisers began their shoot, correcting their aim in accordance with information from spotters in Black Cats over the target. When they ceased fire, the two destroyers added their 5-inchers to the show. In all nearly two thousand 6-inch shells and some fifteen hundred 5-inch plowed into the target area. Counterbattery fire was scattered and inaccurate. Large fires could be seen as the squadron withdrew. Half an hour later Japanese planes arrived overhead, but by dodging into rain squalls Ainsworth avoided damage. Antiaircraft fire was directed by radar and *Radford* scored a hit by this means on an unseen

target—a fiery ball plunging out of a cloud proving the claim.

For the first time the enemy dropped float flares to mark the position of the American ships, as well as colored identification flares and illuminants. (The reason for this Fourth of July spectacle would become apparent on another occasion.) Despite the fireworks no ship was hit and the two squadrons rendezvoused on the 26th and returned to base.

On the 23rd *Saratoga,* sortieing from Nouméa, had flown her air group to Guadalcanal, and on January 24, twenty-four SBDs and seventeen TBFs, escorted by eighteen F4Fs, dropped twenty-three tons of bombs on battered Vila. In retaliation, on January 25 thirteen bombers escorted by over seventy Zeros approached Guadalcanal. The ploy was to entice the American fighters into positions from which the nimble Zeros could launch their attacks. The American fighter pilots refused to fall into the trap and the Japanese finally made off— leaving four of their number behind. A second attack on the 27th cost them a dozen planes, while the Cactus Air Force lost four.

American submarines continued their hunt for Japanese vessels in the Bismarck-Solomons area. Although still plagued with defective torpedoes, from January 9 to the end of the month they sank seven merchantmen, a destroyer, and a patrol boat. Japanese submarines, meanwhile, were continuing their supply runs. Some 40 to 50 tons of cargo could be carried inside, and a further 20 to 30 tons on deck. Kamimbo Bay, just west of Cape Esperance, was a favorite spot for off-loading and it was near here that *I-1* met her end. She was attacked by gunfire from the Royal New Zealand Navy trawler, *Kiwi*—one of four operating off Guadalcanal; then rammed, shot up some more, rammed again and finally beached in sinking condition. The surviving crew members attempted to destroy her and her ship's papers, but they did not do a very thorough job as important documents were found in the wreck after the evacuation.

The Japanese evacuation plans were a well-kept secret, disclosed only to top-ranking Japanese officers. A buildup of transport shipping at Rabaul and Buin and much naval activity near Ontong Java, was therefore (reasonably enough) thought by the American command to presage another large-scale reinforcement of the island. Halsey now had considerable naval forces at his disposal— two fleet carriers, two escort carriers, three new battleships, twelve cruisers, and twenty-five destroyers. These put to sea in six groups, to be on hand in case the Japanese fleet came down on the island in force. One of these, Task Force 18, under Rear Admiral Robert C. Giffen, was to rendezvous with the four destroyers (based at Purvis Bay near Tulagi and known as the "Cactus Striking Force") off Cape Hunter on the south-western coast of Guadalcanal. He was then to make a sweep up The Slot. Task Force 18 consisted of three heavy cruisers, three light cruisers, two escort carriers, and eight destroyers; but the escort carriers were slow, only capable of 18 knots, and their CAP and antisubmarine patrols entailed constant maneuvering into the wind to fly off or take on planes. Giffen was impatient (he was getting late for his rendezvous) so he left the two CVEs with two destroyers for escort and pushed on. But Task Force 18's passage had been reported by Japanese submarines and an air attack was already being mounted. Giffen's destroyers were in a semicircle ahead, with the six cruisers in two columns astern. Despite warning blips on his radars, Giffen maintained his formation; one which, well suited for swift deployment into battle order, was not the ideal one for warding off an attack from the air.

At dusk of January 29, several ships dismissed from General Quarters and no special attention was paid by the flagship to the reports of bogies over the horizon. As the daylight faded, a force of torpedo-carrying Bettys attacked from the cruisers' starboard quarters. No hits were made and some planes were shot down. But the formation was not altered and soon float flares and other pyrotechnics heralded another attack. This time heavy cruiser *Chicago* took two torpedoes in her engine spaces and slid to a stop.

The force now changed course and reduced speed (to cut down the tell-tale wakes) while *Louisville* took *Chicago* in tow for Espiritu Santo.

Halsey now ordered the remaining cruisers to Efate. A tug took over the tow and six destroyers circled *Chicago* as a shield. Carrier *Enterprise* headed for the crippled cruiser as did the two CVEs. But despite all precautions, a dozen torpedo planes launched another attack late in the afternoon of January 30. Wildcats from *Enterprise* shot down three. Of the remaining nine, seven were downed, but not before four more torpedoes had slammed into the wounded *Chicago*, which sank in twenty minutes. Another torpedo flooded destroyer *La Vallette*'s forward engine room but she managed to make port.

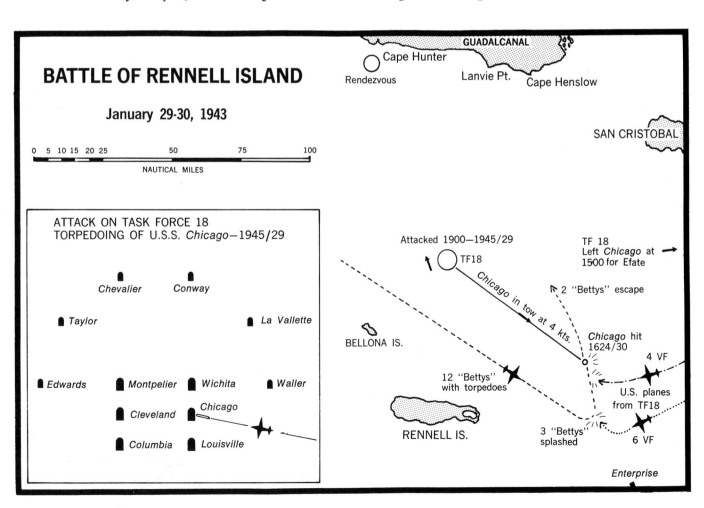

BATTLE OF RENNELL ISLAND

January 29-30, 1943

0 5 10 15 20 25   50   75   100

NAUTICAL MILES

GUADALCANAL

Cape Hunter

Rendezvous   Lanvie Pt.   Cape Henslow

SAN CRISTOBAL

ATTACK ON TASK FORCE 18
TORPEDOING OF U.S.S. *Chicago*—1945/29

Chevalier   Conway

Taylor   La Vallette

Edwards   Montpelier   Wichita   Waller

Cleveland   Chicago

Columbia   Louisville

Attacked 1900–1945/29

TF18

TF 18
Left *Chicago* at 1500 for Efate

2 "Bettys" escape

BELLONA IS.

Chicago in tow at 4 kts.

Chicago hit 1624/30

4 VF

12 "Bettys" with torpedoes

U.S. planes from TF18

RENNELL IS.

3 "Bettys" splashed

6 VF

Enterprise

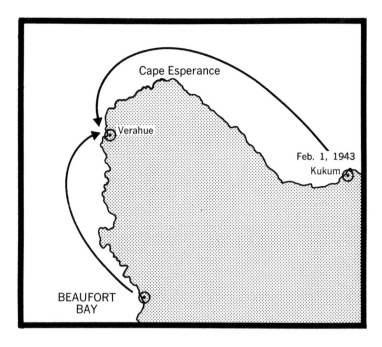

Cape Esperance

Verahue

Feb. 1, 1943

Kukum

BEAUFORT
BAY

For the operations which followed the crossing of the Poha the Japanese, both Army and Navy, deserve great credit. On the Army side—a few troops (mainly the six hundred who had landed on the night of January 14–15) fought a stubborn rear-guard action against greatly superior forces, which had powerful support from artillery, naval gunfire, and aerial bombing and strafing. The Japanese Navy's destroyermen performed with their usual brilliance. They risked not only attack by aircraft during their Tokyo Express runs down and up The Slot and at night while off the beaches, but action with destroyers and numerous PT boats based at Tulagi, and minefields. Yet in three night operations they successfully evacuated all their remaining troops, amounting to 11,706 men. And this was accomplished without the American high command being any the wiser. It was a notable feat of arms and one which somewhat dimmed the luster of the American victory.

Critics of the campaign have wondered why, since from mid-November the seas around the island could be safely said to be American property—at least in the daytime—that an amphibious landing was not resorted to with the object of outflanking the enemy and forcing him to fight on two fronts. The answer lay in the scarcity of proper landing craft. It was not until January, when six LCTs (Landing Craft, Tanks) arrived at Tulagi, that an end run could be contemplated. On January 21 naval forces were available to make a landing on the western tip of the island. A reconnaissance party from the troops of the 147th Infantry Regiment holding the beachhead at Beaufort Bay sailed up the coast in a small island schooner. In the meantime, the reinforced 2nd Battalion of the 132nd Infantry embarked, complete with trucks and artillery, at Kukum in five LCTs and seaplane tender *Stringham*. At 0400, February 1, 1943, the expedition and its escort of the "Cactus Striking Force" left Kukum and proceeded around Cape Esperance. The reconnaissance patrol found Verahue, some 10 miles southwest of Cape Esperance, was not defended and there the expedition landed.

The 40-odd mile trip had been uneventful but on the return trip destroyers *De Haven* and *Nicholas*, escorting three empty LCTs, were attacked by enemy dive bombers south of Savo Island. By some foul-up all the fighter escort were flying cover for *Radford* and *Fletcher*, who were escorting the other landing craft, then some miles astern. *De Haven* was hit by three bombs while another exploded close alongside. She went down in two minutes, taking 167 of her crew with her. One plane was shot down by the landing craft, who picked up 146 survivors. *Nicholas* was near missed and escaped with two dead and minor damage.

Early the same afternoon, word came that twenty

LANDING CRAFT, TANK (LCT)
MARK V

Length: 112 Beam: 32 Draft: (loaded) 3 ft. 1 in. forward, 3 ft. 9 in. aft. Displacement (loaded) 286 tons Triple screw. Three 225-hp diesels=9 knots Cruising radius: 500 miles at 8½ knots. Capacity: 8 light, 6 medium or 3 heavy tanks or approx. 162 tons. Armament: two 20-mm. Crew: ten

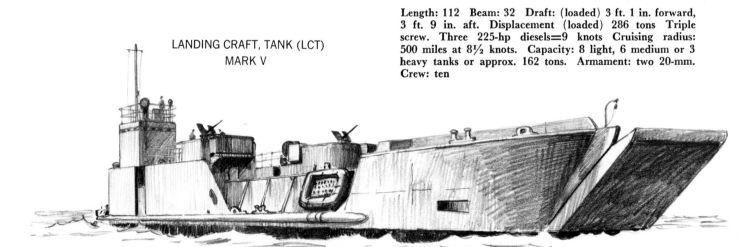

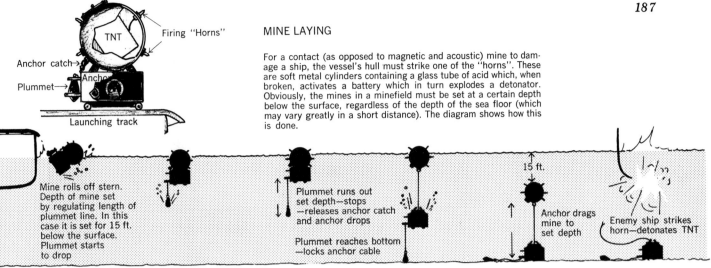

MINE LAYING

For a contact (as opposed to magnetic and acoustic) mine to damage a ship, the vessel's hull must strike one of the "horns". These are soft metal cylinders containing a glass tube of acid which, when broken, activates a battery which in turn explodes a detonator. Obviously, the mines in a minefield must be set at a certain depth below the surface, regardless of the depth of the sea floor (which may vary greatly in a short distance). The diagram shows how this is done.

enemy destroyers were on their way down The Slot and preparations were made to turn back what appeared to be a major attempt at reinforcement. At dusk a force of seventeen SBDs and seven TBFs, with an escort of seventeen F4Fs, struck at the oncoming squadron. The American fighters fought a furious air battle with thirty escorting Zeros, losing four planes. *Makinami* took a bomb hit which stopped her, but the rest of the force kept on. As night fell, three destroyer-minelayers, *Preble, Tracy,* and *Montgomery,* laid a minefield between Doma Cove and Cape Esperance. *Radford, Nicholas,* and *Fletcher* moved out to be ready to intercept and the PTs, eleven of them, took station to harass the enemy. The actions which followed were as confused as are most night actions. Cactus Striking Force had no luck. The Japanese force had been escorted by night-flying aircraft and these prevented the three de-

stroyers from getting in to position for an attack. These same planes also attacked the PTs and one managed to plant a bomb square on the stern of PT 123, which went up in a great burst of flame.

Other PTs tangled with the enemy but without doing damage. Two boats, PTs 111 and 37, were sunk by gunfire and PT 48 was beached on Savo Island but towed off next day. A night attack by six SBDs scored no hits. The only Japanese casualty was *Makigumo*, who steamed into the new minefield and went down.

Although the Americans did not know it, the Tokyo Express that night was taking off the first batch of troops to be evacuated. Despite the minefields, PTs, and aircraft, eighteen destroyers made their pickup and by daylight were well on their way up The Slot. An attack by SBDs and TBFs did little damage, if any. Even *Makinami* made it back under tow.

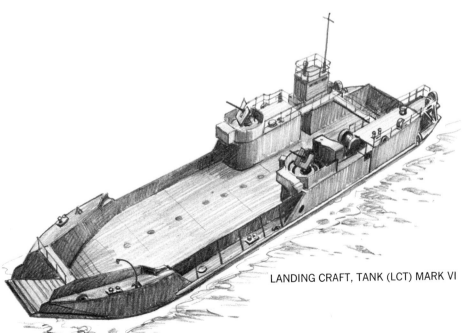

LANDING CRAFT, TANK (LCT) MARK VI

**Length: 120
Beam: 32
Displacement (loaded): 320 tons
Triple screw.
Three 225-hp diesels=9 knots
Armament: two 20-mm.**

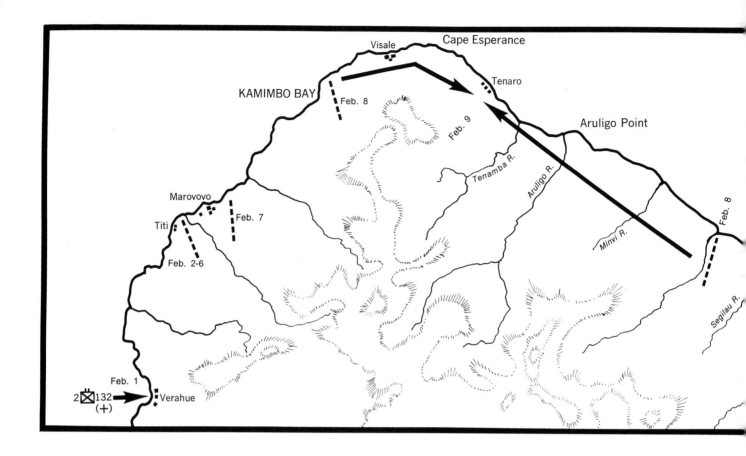

While the Japanese were making preparations for the final evacuation, General Patch's men were slowly battling their way westward. The general's orders called upon his troops to "effect the kill through aggressive and untiring offensive action." Had it been realized that the enemy was on the point of escaping perhaps the Army's efforts might have been a little more "aggressive and untiring." As it was, the infantry's advance was slow and methodical in the extreme. Gains of only a thousand yards against light opposition were sometimes followed by a day to regroup. Artillery preparations were thorough and often supported by shelling from the sea. Gains were registered in yards and from January 25 to February 7, when it finally dawned on the Americans that the enemy was going or gone, the average day's gain for the thirteen days was only some 870 yards. Small wonder that the Japanese commanders felt grateful for thus being allowed to escape. General Hyakutake stated afterward that resolute attacks would have destroyed his army.

The advance was largely without incident. The CAM Division attacked from the Poha on January 26 and advanced a thousand yards against light opposition. Next day, the Division reached the Nueha River some two thousand yards farther

on. There followed a two-day delay, during which there was some shuffling of units, then on January 30, the 147th Infantry, with 6th Marines in support, advanced to the Bonegi River. Here there was a check. The Japanese appeared to be holding the river in some strength. Attempts to cross failed on the 30th, 31st, and February 1 despite heavy artillery support and a bombardment by destroyers *Anderson* and *Wilson*. These last, steaming close to shore, poured 1100 rounds of 5-inch into the Japanese positions.

The river was finally crossed on February 2. The 147th's casualties in the crossing operation amounted altogether to two killed and 67 wounded and the few hundred Japanese opposing them had gained valuable time. A little ground was gained on the 3rd, and on the 4th the Americans were some one thousand yards east of the Umasami River. The 5th was spent in patrol activity. On February 6 the 161st Infantry passed through the 147th and reached the river. They crossed it the next day and reached Burina. Resistance was very slight and on February 8 they reached Doma Cove.

On the southwest, the force landed at Verahue had established itself at Titi. There it stayed until February 7, when it advanced a few hundred yards to Marovovo. When the advance was re-

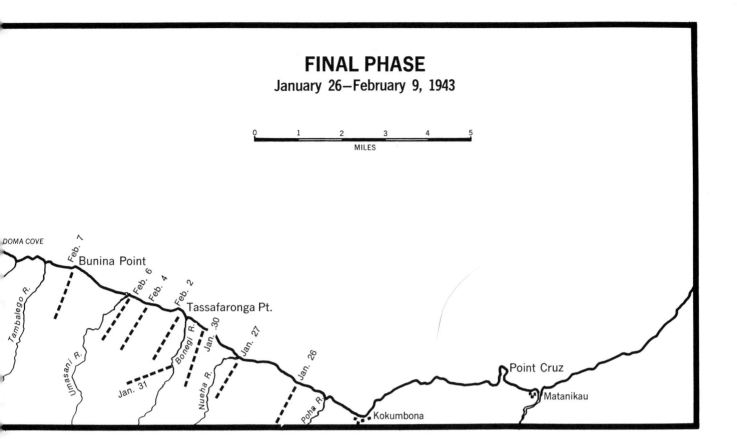

FINAL PHASE
January 26–February 9, 1943

sumed next day, abandoned landing craft and supplies were found on the beach. Finally realizing that the Japanese were evacuating the island, the force pushed on to Kamimbo Bay.

It was too late. The enemy had already gone. On the nights of February 4–5 and 7–8, massive Express runs had taken off all but a few stragglers. The run on February 4, twenty-two destroyers and a cruiser, had been attacked in the evening by dive bombers and one, *Maikaze*, was disabled while another was damaged. Ten U.S. planes and seventeen Zeros went down in the ensuing dog fights. The PTs failed to make contact that night and the destroyers of Cactus Striking Force had gone back to base for rest and refit. A few SBDs attacked with bombs while Black Cats illuminated with flares, but no hits were scored. The final lift was on February 7–8. Eighteen destroyers were reported coming down The Slot and attacked by fifteen SBDs. Two vessels were hit but kept on coming. There was no further action and the enemy peacefully picked up the remainder of the troops; their top-ranking officers clambered aboard—and the campaign for Guadalcanal was over. Troops from the southern expedition passed Cape Esperance on February 9 and met the men of the 161st in the village of Tenaro. Scattered material on

the beaches and landing craft cut adrift and abandoned were the only signs of the enemy. Close to 12,000 veterans had been snatched from under the very noses of Patch's victorious troops, many to recover, regroup, and fight again.

Though the campaign itself ended for the Americans in some feelings of anticlimax and disappointment, the results were far-reaching. For the Japanese it represented the first ebbing of the tide of fortune which had followed their arms since Pearl Harbor. Midway might be brushed off as a solitary incident—a combination of bad luck and poor judgment. But the six months' campaign for the island was another matter. Despite every effort of thousands of their best troops, and after losing hundreds of planes and over two dozen warships, they had been forced to retreat. The skillful handling of the withdrawal could afford the Japanese soldier and sailor some satisfaction. But it was a retreat, nevertheless, and wars are not won nor empires secured by "advances to the rear."

There were many reasons given by ranking Japanese Army and Navy officers for their defeat. Tanaka named several: (1.) Confused command, resulting in conflicting orders from Combined Fleet, Eighth Fleet, and Eleventh Air Fleet. (2.)

Lack of long-range plans, resulting in hastily assembled units being committed to battle piecemeal. (3.) Almost total lack of coordination between Army and Navy. (4.) Consistent underestimation of enemy strength, both from faulty intelligence and from unwillingness to admit a defeat. "Enemy successes were deprecated and alibied in every instance. It was standard practice in inflate our own capabilities to the consequent underestimation of the enemy's. This was fine for the ego but poor for winning victories."

On the technical and material side, there was the lack of ship-borne radar; the refusal of the Army to furnish sufficient planes and pilots (thereby throwing most of the burden on the Navy —with subsequent impairment of carrier operations), and a chronic lack of landing barges and transports.

The defeat had cost the Japanese heavily in men. More than 24,000 of some 36,000 landed on the island were killed or died of sickness and starvation, while thousands more perished en route. Air losses, mostly Navy, had also been heavy. Japanese sources list Navy losses, both combat and operational, for the period August 1942 through February 1943 as: fighter planes—909, torpedo planes and dive bombers—330, medium bombers—291, float planes—268 and, flying boats—29. Naval losses included two battleships, a light carrier, three heavy cruisers, one light cruiser, twelve destroyers, and six submarines—totaling almost 138,000 tons. Besides warships, a good number of transports had been sunk or beached.

Allied naval losses were almost as great: two fleet carriers, six heavy and two light cruisers and fourteen destroyers—126,400 tons. Of some 60,000 Army personnel and Marines, 1600 were killed, 4250 wounded, and several thousand incapacitated from disease. Plane losses were high, particularly those lost on the ground through enemy action and operational hazards. Pilot losses were not as severe due to efficient rescue work.

There is no doubt that the victory was worth the price. Tanaka wrote: "There is no question that Japan's doom was sealed with the closing of the struggle for Guadalcanal." Admiral Mitsumasa Yonai, Navy Minister in various cabinets, stated that: "When we had to retreat [from Guadalcanal] taking the whole situation, I felt that there was no further chance of success." And, when after the Japanese surrender, an interrogator asked Admiral Kurita: "At what stage in the war did you feel that the balance had swung against you?" Kurita answered simply, "Guadalcanal."

JAPANESE UNIFORMS

At the outbreak of war, tropical wear did not differ greatly in design from the heavier regulation uniforms. Leather belts, holsters, cartridge pouches, etc. had mostly given way to those of canvas or rubberized fabric. Later uniforms were often very thin—too thin to ward off the ever-present mosquito. The officer at left wears a tropical helmet. Others wore variations of the field cap. The steel helmet, right, was held in place by tapes tied under the chin or at the back of the head. Officers wore riding boots, leather leggings or puttees. Light packs were also carried and usually a map case. Officers and warrant officers, and some noncoms carried a sword.

The Japanese soldier was a prodigious marcher. Footwear varied—besides stout leather boots, many troops wore the split-toed sneaker called the TABI. The soldier at lower left wears a lightweight tropical uniform. The men at lower right are in full marching order, with gas mask under left arm. Uniforms were of khaki or olive green. Navy detachments known as "Special Landing Forces" (there were no "Imperial Marines") wore navy uniforms or khaki.

U.S. UNIFORMS IN THE SOUTH PACIFIC

were anything but uniform. Clothing, at least on land, was often in short supply and it was a case of "anything goes." Light green fatigues, with or without leggings or undershirts, were the normal wear. Spit and polish applied only to "shootin' irons" and on these, Marine and soldier lavished loving care. Bayonets were honed to a fine edge as were an assortment of non-reg. knives. The Marine below holds a .45-cal. Thompson submachine gun. Also used was the .45-cal H & R Reising submachine gun—both useful weapons in short-range jungle fighting. The infantryman at right wears his plastic helmet-liner. An extra canteen and a machete often added weight to the sweating GI's burden. At battle stations, topside, the sailor below would wear his "tin hat" while the "talker," above, wore an outsize helmet designed to cover his bulky earphones.

APPENDIX

CHRONOLOGY: PEARL HARBOR TO GUADALCANAL
December 7, 1941 to August 7, 1942

December, 1941

7 Japanese carrier planes attack Pearl Harbor, Hickam, and Wheeler airfields. Battleships *Oklahoma, Arizona, California* and *West Virginia,* minelayer *Oglala* and target ship *Utah* sunk. Damaged—battleships *Nevada, Pennsylvania, Tennessee, Maryland,* light cruisers *Raleigh, Honolulu, Helena,* destroyers *Cassin, Shaw,* and *Downes,* seaplane tender *Curtiss* and repair ship *Vestal* . . . 188 Naval and Army aircraft destroyed. Killed or missing—Navy 2004, Marines, 108, Army 222. Wounded—Navy, 912, Marine, 75, Army, 360. Japanese losses—five midget submarines, twenty-eight aircraft, and less than one hundred men. Two Japanese destroyers bombarded Midway.

8 Japanese bombard Wake and Guam. Air attacks on Philippines, Hong Kong, and Singapore. Many U.S. planes destroyed on Clark and Iba Fields (P.I.). Japanese from Indochina cross Thai border. Drive on Bangkok. Land on Malay Peninsula near Kotabharu. Seize International Settlement at Shanghai. Move troops toward Kowloon, opposite Hong Kong. River gunboat *Wake* (only U.S. ship to surrender in war) surrenders at Shanghai after attempt to scuttle fails. Minesweeper *Penguin* sunk by bombers at Guam. U. S. Marines and nationals interned at Shanghai and Tientsin.

9 Japanese occupy Bangkok. Land on Tarawa and Makin, Gilbert Islands.

10 Guam surrenders to Japanese landing force. Japanese land on Gonzaga and Aparri on Luzon, P.I. Cavite navy yard heavily damaged by enemy air attacks. Destroyer *Peary,* submarines *Seadragon* and *Sea Lion,* minesweeper *Bittern* damaged (Cavite). Submarine *I-170* sunk by carrier planes off Hawaii. British battleship *Prince of Wales* and battlecruiser *Repulse* sunk by Japanese planes near Kuantan, Malaya.

11 Marines repulse Japanese attack on Wake Island. Destroyers *Hayate* and *Kisaragi* sunk (*Hayate* by gunfire, *Kisaragi* by aircraft). Japanese bomb airfield Tavoy in lower Burma.

12 Japanese go ashore at Legaspi, Luzon. Heavy air attacks on U.S. airfields in Philippines. Heavy fighting continues in Malaya. Japanese invade Burma.

14 Wake Island relief expedition (Rear Admiral Frank Jack Fletcher) leaves Pearl Harbor.

15 Kahului and Maui (Hawaiian Islands) shelled by Japanese submarine.

16 British evacuate Penang, Malaya. Japanese invade British Borneo. Johnston Island (Hawaii) shelled by Japanese submarine. Admiral Chester W. Nimitz relieves Admiral Husband E. Kimmel as Commander in Chief, Pacific Fleet.

18 Japanese invade Hong Kong Island. Destroyer *Shinonome* sunk by mine, Miri, Borneo.

20 Admiral Ernest J. King named Commander in Chief, U. S. Fleet. Japanese troops land at Davao, Mindanao, P.I.

22 American troops (Brigadier General Julian F. Barnes) arrive at Brisbane, Australia. Japanese landings in Lingayen Gulf area (P.I.). Heavy air attacks on Wake. Relief force delayed for refueling.

23 Japanese naval force put ashore on Wake, garrison overwhelmed. Relief force some 400 miles away, turns back to Midway. Palmyra Island shelled by Japanese submarine. Japanese landings at Kuching, Sarawak (Borneo).

25 Hong Kong surrenders. Admiral Thomas C. Hart turns over remaining naval force (P.I.) to Rear Admiral Francis W. Rockwell. Hart sails in sub for Java to establish HQ of Asiatic Fleet.

26 Manila declared open city.

29 First Japanese air attacks on Corregidor Island.

January, 1942

2 Manila and Cavite fall to Japanese.

4 Japanese begin air offensive against Rabaul.

6 Japanese occupy Brunei Bay, Borneo.

7   U.S. and Philippine forces complete withdrawal to Bataan Peninsula. Japanese break through Slim River positions in Malaya, drive toward Kualalumpur.

9   Japanese assault on Bataan begins.

10 Japanese take Kualalumpur. Japanese begin daylight raids on Singapore airfields.

11 Japanese invade Netherlands East Indies at Tarakan, Borneo, Menado, and Kema (Celebes). Japan declares war on the Netherlands. Japanese submarine shells naval station at Pago Pago, Samoa. *Saratoga* damaged by submarine 500 miles SW of Oahu.

14 British on Malaya withdraw into Johore.

15 ABDACOM established. Headquarters at Batavia, Java.

16 Japanese invade Burma from Thailand.

17 Japanese force lands at Sandakan, British North Borneo.

19 British North Borneo surrenders to Japanese. Japanese take Tavoy in Burma.

20 Heavy Japanese air raids on Rabaul, Kavieng, New Ireland.

21 Japanese begin air offensive against New Guinea.

22 Japanese land on Mussau Island, north of New Ireland.

23 Japanese land at Rabaul and Kavieng. Small Australian garrison at Rabaul overrun. Japanese land on Kieta, Bougainville (Solomon Islands).

25 Japanese submarine shells Midway.

28 Japanese land on Rossel Island, off New Guinea.

29 Japanese land at Badoeing Island and Mampawan Island (Celebes).

30 Japanese invade Amboina Island (N.E.I.). Japanese attack Moulmein (Burma).

31 British complete withdrawal to Singapore Island.

February, 1942

1   Units of U. S. Pacific Fleet (2 carriers, 5 cruisers, and 10 destroyers) attack Kwajalein, Wotje, Waloelap, Jaluit, and Mili in Marshall Islands and Makin in Gilbert Islands. *Enterprise* and *Chester* damaged. U.S. naval base established at Sydney, Australia.

3   Japanese bomb Surabaya, Java. Air attacks on Port Moresby.

4   Japanese bomb Allied fleet in Madoera Strait. Two U.S. cruisers (*Houston* and *Marblehead*) and one Netherlands cruiser damaged. Garrison (AUS) of Amboina Island surrenders.

7   Anzac Force activated under the command of Vice-Admiral Herbert F. Leary, USN. Naval Forces, Southwest Pacific area (Vice-Admiral William A. Glassford, USN) establish headquarters at Tjilatjap, Java.

8   Japanese submarine shells Midway. Japanese troops land at Gasmata, New Britain. Submarine S-37 sinks destroyer *Natsushio* in Makassar Strait.

9   Japanese aircraft bomb Batavia, Surabaya, and Malang, Java. Japanese land on Singapore Island.

10 Japanese submarine shells Midway.

13 All remaining British shipping leaves Singapore. Japanese take Bandjermasin in SE Borneo.

14 Vice-Admiral C. E. L. Helfrich, RNN, relieves Admiral Thomas C. Hart, USN, as Commander in Chief, Allied Naval Forces, Southwest Pacific. Japanese invade Sumatra.

15 Singapore surrenders.

18 Japanese invade Bali.

19 Night action—Badoeing Strait—One RNN destroyer sunk, two RNN cruisers, and one U.S. destroyer damaged. One Japanese destroyer damaged. Destructive air raid on Darwin, Australia. Much shipping and many aircraft destroyed. Destroyer *Peary* sunk.

20 Japanese invade Timor. Submarine *Swordfish* evacuates President Manuel Quezon and other officials from Luzon.

22 President Roosevelt orders MacArthur to leave Philippines.

23 Japanese submarine shells oil refinery at Elwood, California. First U.S. air attack against Rabaul. Conquest of Amboina Island completed. In Burma, Japanese drive to Sittang River.

24 *Enterprise* task force under Vice-Admiral William F. Halsey bombards Wake Island.

25 ABDACOM dissolved.

26 USS *Langley* sunk en route to Java by Japanese planes.

27 Japanese land on Mindoro Island (P.I.). Battle of Java Sea. Naval force under Rear Admiral K. W. F. Doorman, RNN (five cruisers and eleven destroyers) attack enemy covering Java invasion convoy. Two RNN cruisers, one RNN destroyer, two RN destroyers sunk. One U.S. and one RN cruiser damaged.

28 Japanese invade Java.

March, 1942

1   Battle of Sunda Strait. Allied vessels surviving Battle of Java Sea attacked by Japanese forces. USS *Houston* and destroyer USS *Pope*, one RAN cruiser, and one RNN destroyer sunk. Four Japanese transports sunk. U.S. destroyers *Edsell* and *Pillsbury* sunk by naval forces south of Christmas Island.

2   Japanese land at Zamboanga, Mindanao, P.I.

3   Heavy Japanese air raid on Broome, Australia.

4   Planes from *Enterprise* raid Marcus Island.

5 Batavia evacuated. Japanese take Pegu in Burma.

7 Japanese invade Lae and Salamaua in New Guinea. Japanese take Rangoon.

9 Java surrenders.

10 Japanese invade Finschhafen, New Guinea. Aircraft from *Lexington* and *Yorktown* bomb Japanese shipping at Salamaua and Lae.

11 General MacArthur, family, and staff leave Corregidor.

12 U.S. force, 17,500 men, under Major General Alexander M. Patch, reach Nouméa. British evacuate Andaman Islands.

13 Japanese land at Buka in Solomon Islands.

18 U. S. Engineers and Infantry arrive at Efate, New Hebrides, to build airfield.

23 Japanese take Andaman Islands.

30 Pacific area divided into two commands: Pacific Ocean Area—Admiral Chester W. Nimitz; Southwest Pacific Area—General Douglas MacArthur. Japanese occupy Christmas Island.

April, 1942

1 Japanese occupy Buka and land on Dutch New Guinea.

4 Japanese sink British cruisers *Dorsetshire* and *Cornwall* near Colombo, Ceylon.

5 Japanese occupy Manu Island in Admiralty Islands.

9 U.S. forces on Bataan surrender. Trincomalee, Ceylon, heavily attacked by Japanese carrier planes. Aircraft carrier HMS *Hermes* sunk off coast.

10 Japanese invade Cebu, P.I.

13 Vice-Admiral Robert L. Ghormley designated commander of South Pacific Area.

14 Burma oil fields ordered destroyed.

18 General MacArthur assumes supreme command, Southwest Pacific Area. Sixteen B-25s, Lieutenant Colonel James H. Doolittle, launched from *Hornet;* raid Tokyo and other cities.

20 Japanese hold Cebu and Panay.

29 Admiral King establishes South Pacific Amphibious Force. Japanese begin final offensive for Mindanao. Japanese take Lashio, terminus of Burma Road.

30 Japanese complete conquest of central Burma. British withdraw across Irrawaddy.

May, 1942

3 Japanese invade Tulagi. Japanese land on Northern Mindanao.

4 Japanese air and artillery attack on Corregidor reaches peak. Battle of Coral Sea begins. Carrier planes from *Yorktown* attack Tulagi, sink destroyer *Kikutsuki.* Japanese transports leave Rabaul for Port Moresby. British evacuate Akyab, Burma.

5 Allied Fleet under Rear Admiral Frank Jack Fletcher, USN, move to intercept Japanese Port Moresby invasion group. Japanese land on Corregidor.

6 Corregidor and Manila Bay forts surrender.

7 Battle of Coral Sea. Japanese carrier planes sink destroyer *Sims* and oiler *Neosho.* Aircraft from *Lexington* and *Yorktown* sink carrier *Shoho.* From Manila, General Jonathan M. Wainwright broadcasts terms of surrender to forces in Philippines.

8 Coral Sea. *Lexington* sunk. Carriers *Yorktown* and *Shokaku* damaged. Japanese invasion group turns back. Japanese occupy Myitkyina in Burma.

9 U.S. troops arrive at Tongatabu (Tonga Island).

10 Brigadier General William F. Sharp directs Visayan-Mindanao force to surrender in Philippine Island.

12 Japanese cross Salween in Burma.

17 *I-28* sunk by submarine *Tautog* near Caroline Islands. *I-164* sunk by submarine *Triton* SE of Ryushu.

20 Conquest of Burma completed.

26 Task force under Rear Admiral Raymond A. Spruance (carriers *Enterprise* and *Hornet*) arrives at Pearl Harbor from South Pacific. Midway reinforced.

27 *Yorktown* force, Admiral Fletcher, arrives in Pearl Harbor from South Pacific. Japanese carrier striking force, Vice-Admiral Chuichi Nagumo, leaves Japan for Midway. Transports sail from Saipan, cruisers and destroyers from Guam. New Caledonia—American Division activated in New Caledonia (General Patch). Marines and Seabees occupy Wallace Island, South Pacific.

28 Main Japanese fleet, Admiral Isoroku Yamamoto, leaves Japan for Midway. Admiral Spruance's force leaves Pearl Harbor for Midway. U.S. troops arrive at Espiritu Santo, New Hebrides.

30 *Yorktown* force sails for Midway from Pearl Harbor. Japanese task force leaves Japan for Aleutians.

31 Japanese midget submarines raid Sydney harbor.

June, 1942

2 Fletcher and Spruance task forces rendezvous about 350 miles NE Midway.

3 Midway-based planes attack transports about 600 miles west of Midway. Japanese carrier planes bomb Dutch Harbor, Alaska.

4 Battle of Midway. Planes from four Japanese carriers hit Midway installations. U.S. carrier planes sink or fatally damage four Japanese carriers—*Kaga, Soryu, Akagi,* and *Hiryu. Yorktown* damaged.

6 Planes from *Enterprise* and *Hornet* attack retreating Japanese force. Heavy cruiser *Mikuma* sunk. U.S. destroyer *Hammann* sunk.

7 *Yorktown* sunk by Japanese submarine. Japanese invade western Aleutians, land on Attu and Kiska.

9 Japanese conquest of Philippines completed.

14 5th Marines of 1st Marine Division arrive in New Zealand.

19 Admiral Ghormley assumes command of South Pacific Area with headquarters at Auckland.

20 Japanese submarine shells Vancouver Island, B.C.

21 Japanese submarine shells Fort Stevens, Oregon.

25 Japanese destroyer *Yamakaze* sunk by *Nautilus* off Honshu.

July, 1942

2 Joint Chiefs of Staff issue directive for offensive—New Britain-New Ireland-New Guinea area. First phase—lower Solomons—date set for August 1, postponed to August 7. Boundary between Southwest Pacific Area and South Pacific Area altered to put lower Solomons with South Pacific zone.

4 Japanese destroyer *Nenohi* sunk by *Triton* off Aleutians.

7 *Saratoga* and *Enterprise* sail from Pearl Harbor for South Pacific.

8 MacArthur and Ghormley recommend offensive be postponed until forces are strengthened. Nimitz issues attack plan. South Pacific force to take Santa Cruz Island and Tulagi-Guadalcanal area in Solomons.

10 Joint Chiefs of Staff rule offensive be conducted as planned.

14 Major General Millard F. Harmon named commander, U. S. Army Forces in South Pacific Area (USAFISPA). 7th Marines, 1st Marine Division on Samoa alerted for Solomons on four days' notice.

18 Amphibious Force, South Pacific Area established (Rear Admiral Richmond Kelly Turner).

21 Japanese occupy Buna, New Guinea.

22 98th Squadron, 11th Heavy Bombardment Group, lands in New Caledonia. Solomons Amphibious Force sails from Wellington, New Zealand, with 1st Marine Division.

23 42nd Squadron, 11th Heavy Bombardment Group arrives New Caledonia. Japanese advance over Kokoda Trail toward Port Moresby.

24 431st Squadron, 11th Heavy Bombardment Group arrives in Fiji Islands.

25 26th Squadron, 11th Heavy Bombardment Group arrives at Efate.

26 Solomons expeditionary force rendezvous southeast of Fiji Islands. Japanese take Kokoda.

28 Solomons expeditionary force (Task Force 61) begins rehearsal for invasion of Solomons at Koro, Fiji. Tokyo orders all-out drive for eastern New Guinea.

31 Task Force 61 sails from Fiji for Solomons. B-17s from New Hebrides start attacks on Tulagi and Guadalcanal.

August, 1942

7 Marines land on Guadalcanal and Tulagi and islets of Tanambogo and Gavutu.

CHRONOLOGY: THE GUADALCANAL CAMPAIGN
August 7, 1942 to February 9, 1943

August, 1942

7 Marines land on Guadalcanal and Tulagi and islets of Tanambogo and Gavutu. Japanese planes attack. Destroyer *Mugford* damaged. Vice-Admiral Mikawa and cruiser force leave Rabaul for Guadalcanal.

8 Landing field taken. Tulagi, Tanambogo, and Gavutu secured. Japanese planes set AP *George F. Elliot* on fire, damage destroyer *Jarvis.*

8–9 Battle of Savo Island. CAs H.M.A.S. *Canberra* and *Astoria, Quincy, Vincennes* sunk. CA *Chicago,* DDs *Ralph Talbot,* and *Patterson* damaged.

9 Amphibious and air support forces retire. Japanese carrier planes sink DD *Jarvis*. Engineers start to work on uncompleted airfield (named Henderson Field, in honor of Major Lofton Henderson, Marine flier killed at Midway leading VMSB 241).

10 CA *Kako* sunk by submarine *S-44* near Kieveng.

12 First plane (amphibious Catalina) makes trial landing on Henderson Field. U.S. reconnaissance patrol west of Matanikau River ambushed and wiped out.

13 Imperial General Headquarters orders Japanese Seventeenth Army at Rabaul to take charge of ground operations on Guadalcanal.

15 Destroyer transports (APDs) land gas and ammo at Guadalcanal. Marine rations cut.

16 Rear Admiral Raizo Tanaka leaves Rabaul with transport group for Guadalcanal.

17 Henderson Field ready for planes.

17/18 Six Japanese destroyers land nine hundred men at Taivu Point. Short bombardment of U.S. positions.

19 Marines take Matanikau and Kokumbona villages, then retire to Lunga Point. Japanese transports and destroyers leave Rabaul for Guadalcanal.

20 Three APDs land 120 tons of rations on Guadalcanal. First flight of USMC planes land on Henderson from escort carrier *Long Island*.

21 Battle of Tenaru River.

22 Part of USAAF 67th Fighter Squadron (P-400s) lands on Henderson. AKs *Alhena* and *Fomalhaut* land supplies at Tulagi. DD *Blue* torpedoed by Japanese destroyer in Ironbottom Sound.

24 Battle of Eastern Solomons. CV *Ryujo* sunk. Seaplane carrier *Chitose* damaged. *Enterprise* damaged. Navy dive bombers land on Henderson.

24/25 Seven Japanese destroyers bombard U.S. positions on Guadalcanal.

25 Marine Corps dive bombers from Henderson hit CL *Jintsu*. Sink transport *Kinryu Maru*. DD *Mutsuki* sunk by B-17s. DD *Uzuki* damaged. Tanaka returns to Faisi Harbor, Shortlands. Raids on Guadalcanal by Japanese planes.

27 Reconnaissance in force west of Matanikau. Meets stiff opposition. Force withdrawn to perimeter next day. Nine P-400s of 67th Fighter Squadron arrive at Henderson Field.

28 First echelon of 3500 Japanese in four destroyers attempt to land on Guadalcanal. Attacked by Marine dive bombers. *Asagiri* blows up. *Shirakumo* and *Yugiri* damaged. No troops landed.

29 Five destroyers from Shortlands land some 1000 men near Taivu Point.

30 Nineteen Wildcats of VMF 224 and twelve SBDs of VMSB 231 land at Henderson. Air strike sinks APD *Colhoun*.

30/31 Destroyer *Yudachi* and two patrol boats land troops.

31 *Saratoga* torpedoed while on defensive patrol. Out for nearly three months.

31/1 Japanese run eight destroyers with General Kiyotake Kawaguchi and 1200 men to Guadalcanal.

September, 1942

1 Transport *Betelgeuse* lands two 5-inch guns at Tulagi.

2 Kawaguchi starts cutting trail from Taivu to position south of Henderson Field.

3 *Fomalhaut* and three APDs land supplies.

4/5 Three Japanese destroyers escorting landing force sink APDs *Little* and *Gregory*.

5 Marine planes from Henderson attack barges carrying Japanese reinforcements.

8 Edson's Raiders make landing east of Tasimboko. Village taken, large quantities of supplies, guns, and ammunition destroyed. Transports *Fuller* and *Bellatrix* unload supplies at Lunga.

8/9 *Sendai* and eight Japanese destroyers bombard Tulagi.

11 Twenty-four Wildcats arrive Guadalcanal from Espiritu Santo.

12 Kawaguchi begins battle of Bloody Ridge. Four "Zekes" and ten bombers shot down in raid. Cruiser and three destroyers bombard Guadalcanal. 7th Marines and elements of 5th Defense Battalion arrive at Espiritu Santo.

13 Eighteen F4Fs from *Hornet* and *Wasp* and twelve SBDs and six TBFs from *Saratoga* arrive at Henderson Field.

13/14 Seven Japanese destroyers begin a bombardment and Japanese furiously assault Bloody Ridge. Beaten back by automatic weapons and artillery fire.

14 Attack on Marine positions on west side of perimeter by Colonel Akinosuka Oka's men beaten off. Six transports with 7th Marine Regiment sail from Espiritu Santo with destroyers and cruisers under Admiral Turner. Covering task force with *Hornet*, and *Wasp* and *North Carolina*, seven cruisers, and thirteen destroyers about one hundred miles from transports.

15 *Wasp*, *North Carolina*, DD *O'Brien* torpedoed by Japanese submarines. *Wasp* is later sunk by U.S. destroyer. *O'Brien* partially repaired. Sinks on way to U.S.

18 Turner lands 7th Marines, guns, vehicles, etc. in twelve hours. Destroyers *Monssen* and *MacDonough* shell enemy positions. MacArthur's fliers bomb Rabaul airfields. AK *Bellatrix* and two APDs land gasoline.

23 Second U.S. attempt to clear area west of Matanikau begins. Meets stiff opposition.

26 Fighting along Matanikau River continues.

27 Matanikau River action ends. Many casualties and no advantage to U.S. Heavy Japanese air raids on Guadalcanal.

28 Heavy air raids. Japanese lose twenty-three bombers, one fighter out of sixty-two planes. U.S. none.

October, 1942

5 Japanese destroyers *Minegumo* and *Murasame* damaged by SBDs from Henderson.

7 Third action to clear Matanikau area begins.

8 Fighting along Matanikau continues. Great increase in Japanese shipping noted in Shortlands.

9 Cruiser *Tatsuta* and five destroyers land General Hyakutake and troops on Guadalcanal. Transport group carrying 164th Infantry Regiment of American Division leaves Nouméa with 3 covering forces (Rear Admiral L. W. Murray with *Hornet*, Rear Admiral Willis A. Lee with *Washington*, Rear Admiral Norman Scott with cruiser group). Fighting on Mantanikau concludes with heavy Japanese losses. Marines withdraw across the river.

10 Marines attack two villages 25 miles east of perimeter. Kill thirty Japanese, destroy much equipment.

11 Japanese from Rabaul raid Henderson Field with about thirty-five bombers and thirty fighters. Lose eight bombers and four fighters. Do little damage but keep Henderson fliers busy.

11/12 Japanese bombardment group (three cruisers and two destroyers) plus reinforcing group (two seaplane carriers and six destroyers carrying troops, guns, and supplies) approaching Guadalcanal.

Bombardment group spotted by B-17s at 1810 less than a hundred miles from Savo. Scott arrives Guadalcanal, off Savo. Battle of Cape Esperance. CA *Furutaka*, DD *Fubuki* sunk. *Aoba* and *Kinugasa* damaged. DD *Duncan* sunk. *Boise*, *Farenholt*, and *Salt Lake City* damaged. Japanese reinforcement group lands soldiers, supplies, and 150-mm howitzers.

12 Two destroyers of reinforcement group sunk by Marine dive bombers from Henderson while picking up survivors of cruiser and destroyer. Four PT boats arrive at Tulagi.

13 Turner lands 164th Infantry Regiment. Heavy Japanese air raids. Japanese 150-mm howitzers (Pistol Pete) fire on Henderson Field.

13/14 Japanese battleships *Kongo* and *Haruna*, with light screening forces, bombard Henderson Field. Many planes destroyed.

14 Japanese transports and destroyers leave for Guadalcanal. Four dive bombers and seven F4Fs with bombs attack. Slight damage to one destroyer.

14/15 CAs *Chokai* and *Kinugasa* shell Henderson Field.

15 Japanese transports unload in daylight off Tassafaronga. Little gas at Henderson. Few planes still flying bomb transports—as do B-17s from Espiritu Santo. Three Japanese transports beached, other three damaged and withdraw. Some 4500 troops put ashore. Nimitz says situation critical. Destroyer *Meredith* sunk towing barge of gas and bombs.

15/16 CAs *Myoko* and *Maya* put 1500 8-inch shells into U.S. positions. Submarine *Amberjack* ferries 9000 gals. of gas and bombs to Tulagi. Some gas flown in from Espiritu Santo.

16 *Hornet's* planes raid Rekata Bay, Santa Isabel, destroy twelve seaplanes. Also raid Japanese positions on Guadalcanal. Admiral Halsey replaces Admiral Ghormley. Seaplane tender *McFarland* damaged by bombing off Lunga.

17 DDs *Aaron Ward* and *Lardner* bombard Japanese positions west of Kokumbona with two thousand rounds of 5-inch. Task force with *Indiana* ordered to South Pacific, also U. S. Army's 25th Infantry Division. Fifty fighters, more submarines, and more B-17s to Espiritu Santo. *Enterprise* repaired, back to South Pacific.

20 Japanese fighter strip at Buin, Bougainville, ready. Thirty Zekes fly in. Heavy artillery fire against U.S. on Matanikau line.

21 Japanese tank attacks are repulsed near Matanikau River mouth.

22 Destroyer *Nicholas* puts a thousand 5-inch into Japanese lines.

23 Heavy Japanese artillery fire. Tanks and infantry attack. Twelve tanks destroyed, many Japanese killed. Western assault on Henderson beaten.

24 *Enterprise* with *South Dakota* rejoins fleet.

24/25 Japanese night attack on ridge beaten off. Heavy Japanese losses.

25 Eight Japanese destroyers and CL *Yura* sink tug, tender off Tulagi—are bombed. *Yura* damaged (sunk by own forces) and one destroyer damaged. *President Coolidge*, carrying 172nd Infantry, 43rd Division, sunk in U.S. minefield off Espiritu Santo. All equipment lost. Twenty-seven Japanese planes downed during day.

25/26 Second Japanese night attack on perimeter beaten off with severe loss. Air contacts with Japanese fleet. Catalinas attack *Zuikaku*, no hits. U.S. forces round Santa Cruz Islands. Second group of PTs arrive at Tulagi.

26 Battle of Santa Cruz. *Zuiho*, *Shokaku*, CA *Chikuma* damaged. DD *Porter* torpedoed by submarine. *Hornet* set on fire by Japanese planes and later abandoned. Torpedoed and sunk by Japa-

nese destroyers. *South Dakota,* slight damage. CL *San Juan* damaged. DD *Smith* damaged.

29/30 CL *Atlanta* and four destroyers escort transports with Marines and heavy (155-mm) artillery.

30 Escort bombards Japanese positions.

31 American engineers throw footbridge over Matanikau in preparation for new U.S. drive.

November, 1942

1 Advance across Matanikau begins. CA *San Francisco,* CL *Helena,* and a destroyer shell Santa Cruz area. 2nd Battalion of 7th Marines moves east past Tenaru.

2 Advance across Matanikau continues. Two destroyers shell Japanese positions between Point Cruz and mouth of Umasami River. AK *Alchiba* and *Fuller* land two batteries of 155-mm guns. 2nd Battalion of the 7th cross Metapona River, dig in near Koli Point.

2/3 Tokyo Express lands 1500 men near Koli Point.

3 *San Francisco, Helena,* and two DDs shell new Japanese positions near Koli. Ground fighting continues. Action in Kokumbona area curtailed.

4 Transports land men, guns, Seabees at Aola Bay. 8th Marines arrive at Guadalcanal. Carlson's Raiders begin a pursuit of Japanese retreating from Koli toward Mount Austen.

6 Koli Point cleared of Japanese.

7 Japanese DDs land 1300 men of 38th Division. Cargo ship *Majaba* torpedoed while unloading. DD *Lansdowne* brings in ammunition to Guadalcanal.

8/9 PTs in action with Japanese destroyers. Two PTs damaged.

9 Rear Admiral Scott in *Atlanta* with four destroyers, escorting three AKAs leaves Espiritu Santo.

10 Operations toward Kokumbona resumed. Scott's force sighted north of San Cristobal by plane from Japanese submarine. *I-127* sunk by DMS *Southard* off San Cristobal.

10/11 Five DDs bring in Lieutenant General Sano and six hundred men of 38th Division. Beat off PT attack.

11 Scott's group arrives off Lunga Point. AKA *Zeilin* damaged in air raid. *Enterprise* and two battleships under Admiral Thomas C. Kinkaid leave Nouméa. Advance to west of perimeter halted.

12 Rear Admiral Turner with four transports, and four cruisers and eight DDs under Rear Admiral Daniel J. Callaghan arrive Lunga Point. Eight P-38s arrive from Espiritu Santo. Heavy air raid on shipping. *San Francisco* and DD *Buchanan*

damaged. Many Japanese planes downed. Heavy Japanese units reported heading toward Guadalcanal. Turner leaves with cargo and transport vessels with three DDs as escort. Tanaka with eleven transports and twelve DDs leaves Shortlands. Japanese Bombardment Group (two battleships plus light forces) nears Guadalcanal. Area to east of perimeter cleared. All troops withdraw to perimeter.

12/13 First Battle of Guadalcanal. U.S. losses, one CL, four DDs sunk. Japanese, two DDs sunk, BB *Hiei* badly damaged.

13 *Juneau* sunk by torpedo. *Hiei* sunk by planes from Guadalcanal and *Enterprise.* Rear Admiral Lee with two battleships ordered to Guadalcanal. Eight P-38s arrive from Milne Bay.

13/14 Japanese cruisers shell Henderson Field.

14 Planes from Henderson Field and *Enterprise* attack retiring Japanese bombardment force. CA *Kinugasa* sunk, two CAs, one CL, one DD damaged. Kondo starts south with strong force. Lee steaming north. Planes begin attacks on Tanaka's transports. By evening, six are sunk, one damaged.

14/15 Second Battle of Guadalcanal. U.S. loses three DDs, *South Dakota* damaged. Japanese lose *Kirishima* and one DD. Tanaka beaches four remaining transports. Some 2000 troops get ashore. Air attacks and shore artillery set vessels afire, most of supplies lost.

18 New advance west of Matanikau begins. Japanese in strength and well dug in.

20 Japanese counterattacks gain, then lose ground. Beach west of Point Cruz reached.

21 Point Cruz cleared. Seaborne patrols round Cape Esperance to Beaufort Bay. Scouts area for eight days. Reports very few Japanese west of Cape Esperance.

23 Frontal attacks too costly. U.S. forces dig in from Hill 66 to Point Cruz.

24 Rear Admiral Kinkaid takes command of cruiser force at Espiritu Santo. Japanese convoy arrives Munda Point, New Georgia. Work begun on airfield.

28 Rear Admiral Carleton H. Wright relieves Kinkaid at Espiritu Santo. *Alchiba* torpedoed by midget sub from *I-16* off Lunga Point.

29 3rd Battalion, 142nd Infantry Regiment, artillery, and Seabees land at Koli Point to construct airfield. Halsey informs Wright that force of Japanese DDs and fast transports are on way to Guadalcanal.

30/31 Wright's force enters Ironbottom Sound. Japanese force (Tanaka with eight DDs, six of them loaded with drums) off Tassafaronga.

Battle of Tassafaronga. Three U. S. CAs torpedoed and damaged plus one sunk. One Japanese destroyer sunk.

December, 1942

3   Aola force moved to Koli Point. Express run of ten Japanese destroyers reported on way down Slot. Attacked by planes. One damaged.

3/4   Japanese DDs unload supply drums off Tassafaronga.

4   Carlson's Raiders reach Lunga perimeter after month-long march.

5   Photo reconnaissance shows Japanese building field at Munda.

6   P-39s from Guadalcanal strafe Munda airfield. First of many raids.

7   By this date, Army staff officers of Americal Division have taken over from 1st Marine Division. Express run. Ten Japanese DDs attacked by planes in Slot. One damaged.

7/8   Six Japanese DDs attacked by PTs. Retire without dropping supplies.

8   132nd Regimental Combat Team lands on Guadalcanal.

9   5th Marines leave Guadalcanal. First of 1st Division to go. General Alexander Patch relieves General Alexander Vandegrift.

9/10   *I-3* sunk by PT 59 off Cape Esperance.

11   Express run, eleven destroyers under Tanaka. Plane attacks do no damage.

11/12   Night action with PTs. *Teruzuki* torpedoed. Tanaka injured. PT 44 sunk by gunfire.

12   18th Naval Construction Battalion (Seabees) and 2nd Division Signal Company arrives at Guadalcanal.

13   3rd Battalion, 182nd Infantry and Marine Engineers arrive Guadalcanal.

17   35th Regimental Combat Team lands on Guadalcanal. Reconnaissance in force of northeast side of Mount Austen.

18   Drive on Mount Austen begins.

20   Engineers complete jeep road as far as Hill 35.

24   Early morning air raid on Munda catches many Japanese planes on ground. Others destroyed in air. In Mount Austen fighting, Americans held up by strong defenses of Gifu.

26   Advance elements of 2nd Marine Air Wing arrive on Guadalcanal.

31   Emperor Hirohito grants approval to plan to evacuate Guadalcanal.

January, 1943

1   27th Regimental Combat Team, 25th Division, arrives on Guadalcanal.

2   XIV Corps activated. General Patch in command.

3   Japanese forces in Gifu strong point contained.

4   161st Regimental Combat Team, 25th Division, 6th Marines, and HQ, 2nd Marine Division arrive on Guadalcanal.

4/5   Cruiser force under Rear Admiral Walden Ainsworth bombards Munda Field, much damage.

9   Small U.S. force sent in 2 LCTs round Cape Esperance, land at Beaufort Bay. Push up Beaufort Trail.

10   Assault begins on Japanese in Galloping Horse and Sea Horse.

10/11   Action between PTs and eight Japanese destroyers. PT 112 and PT 43 destroyed. *Hatsukaze* damaged.

11   Sea Horse positions taken. Gifu surrounded.

13   Galloping Horse positions in American hands. Attack along coast begins. Progress is slow.

14/15   Nine Japanese destroyers bring six hundred reinforcements. Action with PTs. No damage.

23   *Saratoga* flies air group to Guadalcanal. Kokumbona taken, Gifu position finally cleared.

23/24   Nearly completed airstrip at Vila, Kolombangara Island, bombarded by force under Ainsworth.

24   Heavy air raid on Vila.

25   U.S. forces cross Poha.

27   U.S. forces reach Nueha River.

29   *I-1* destroyed by RNZN corvettes in Kamimbo Bay.

30   CA *Chicago* torpedoed and sunk by air attack.

February, 1943

1   U.S. amphibious force rounds Cape Esperance, lands at Verahue. Destroyer *De Haven*, returning from escorting Amphibious Force, sunk by dive bombers. Twenty Japanese destroyers (on first evacuation run) attacked by planes from Guadalcanal. One damaged. U.S. minefield laid off Japanese-held beaches.

1/2   Action with PTs. PT 123 sunk by dive bomber; PTs 111 and 37 by gunfire; destroyer *Makigumo* by mine.

2   U.S. forces cross Bonegi River.

4   Twenty-two Japanese destroyers and a CL on evacuation run. Attacked by dive bombers. Two damaged, remainder pick up many troops, despite night bombing attacks.

7   U.S. forces cross Umasami River, reach Burina.

7/8   Final evacuation. Eighteen destroyers pick up remaining troops.

8   U.S. forces reach Doma Cove.

9   Troops from amphibious force pass Cape Esperance, meet main force in Tenaro Village, ending the campaign.

BIBLIOGRAPHY

Adams, Captain Henry A., U.S.N.R., *1942: The Year That Doomed the Axis*, New York, David McKay.

Bradford, George and Morgan, Len, *Fifty Famous Tanks*, New York, Arco Publishing Company, 1967.

Casey, Robert J., *Torpedo Junction*, Indianapolis. The Bobbs-Merrill Company, 1942.

Charles, Roland W., *Troopships of World War II*, Washington, D.C., The Army Transportation Association, 1947.

Cooper, Bryon, *PT Boats*, New York, Ballantine Books, 1970.

Fahey, James C., *The Ships and Aircraft of the U. S. Fleet*, New York, Ships and Aircraft, 1965.

Feldt, Commander Eric A., R.A.N., *The Coast Watchers*, New York, Oxford University Press, 1946.

Francillon, Dr. René J., *Japanese Bombers*, Windsor, England, Hylton Lacy Publishers, Ltd., 1969.

Fuchida, Midsuo and Okumiya, Masatake, *Midway: The Battle That Doomed Japan*, Annapolis, Naval Institute, 1955.

Green, William, *Famous Bombers of the Second World War*, New York, Doubleday & Company, Inc., 1967.

————, *Famous Bombers of the Second World War*, Second Series, New York, Doubleday & Company, Inc., 1967.

————, *Famous Fighters of the Second World War*, Hanover House, 1960.

————, *Famous Fighters of the Second World War*, Second Series, New York, Doubleday & Company, Inc., 1967.

Griffith, Brigadier General Samuel B., II, *The Battle for Guadalcanal*, Philadelphia, J. B. Lippincott Company, 1963.

Hara, Tameichi, Saito, Fred and Pineau, Roger, *Japanese Destroyer Captain*, New York, Ballantine Books, 1961.

Hashimoto, Mochitsura, *Sunk*, New York, Henry Holt & Company, 1954.

Holmes, W. J., *Undersea Victory*, New York, Doubleday & Company, Inc., 1966.

Hough, Lieutenant Colonel Frank O., Ludwig, Major Verle E. and Shaw, Henry I., Jr., *History of the United States Marine Corps in World War II*, U.S.M.C., Historical Branch G-3, Division Headquarters, 1960.

Jane's Fighting Ships, Annual Volumes, New York, Macmillan Company, 1936–1941.

Japanese Aircraft Carriers and Destroyers, translated from the Japanese, London, Macdonald and Company, 1964.

Japanese Battleships and Cruisers, translated from the Japanese, London, Macdonald and Company, 1963.

Jablonski, Edward, *Flying Fortress*, New York, Doubleday & Company, Inc., 1965.

Johnston, Stanley, *Queen of the Flat-Tops*, New York, E. P. Dutton & Co., 1942.

Kafka, Roger and Pepperburg, Roy L., *Warships of World War II*, New York, Cornell Maritime Press, 1946.

Kirk, John and Young, Robert Jr., *Great Weapons of World War II*, New York, Bonanza Books, 1961.

Leckie, Robert, *Challenge for the Pacific*, New York, Doubleday & Company, Inc., 1965.

————, *Helmet for My Pillow*, New York, Random House, 1957.

Lenton, H. T., *American Fleet and Escort Destroyers*, Volumes 1 and 2, New York, Doubleday & Company, Inc., 1971.

Lord, Walter, *Incredible Victory*, New York, Harper & Row, 1967.

MacIntyre, Captain Donald and Bathe, B. W., *Man of War*, New York, McGraw-Hill, 1969.

Military Intelligence Service, U. S. Army Intelligence bulletins and publications.

Miller, John, Jr., *United States Army in World War II*, Boston, Little, Brown & Company, 1949.

Munson, Kenneth, *Aircraft of World War II*, New York, Doubleday & Company, Inc., 1968.

Naval Analysis Division, *The Campaigns of the Pacific War*, U. S. Strategic Bombing Survey Pacific, 1946.

Naval Weapons and Their Uses, Annapolis, U. S. Naval Institute, 1943.

Newcomb, Richard F., *Savo*, New York, Holt, Rinehart & Winston, 1961.

Newman, James R., *The Tools of War*, New York, Doubleday & Company, Inc., 1942.

Office of the Chief of Military History, Dept. of the Army, *Command Decisions*, London, Methuen and Company, Ltd., 1960.

Okumiya, Masatake and Horikoshi, Jiro (with Martin Caidin), *Zero*, New York, Ballantine Books, 1956.

Personal files, U. S. Navy, U.S.A.A.F. and U. S. Army.

Potter, E. B. and Nimitz, Admiral Chester W., editors, *The Great Sea War*, New York, Bramhall House, 1960.

Potter, John Deane, *Yamamoto*, New York, Viking Press, 1965.

Pratt, Fletcher, *The Marines' War*, New York, William Sloane Associates, 1948.

Roscoe, Theodore, *U. S. Destroyer Operations in World War II*, Annapolis, U. S. Naval Institute, 1953.

————, *U. S. Submarine Operations in World War II*, Annapolis, U. S. Naval Institute, 1949.

Roskill, Captain S. W., *The War at Sea*, Volumes I and II, Her Majesty's Stationery Office, 1956.

Silverstone, Paul H., *United States Warships in World War II*, New York, Doubleday & Company, Inc., 1965.

Smith, S. E., editor, *The United States Navy in World War II*, New York, William Morrow & Company, 1966.

Smith, W. H. B., *Small Arms of the World*, Harrisburg, Military Service Publishing Company, 1943.

Tregaskis, Richard, *Guadalcanal Diary*, New York, Random House, 1943.

V-4 Airforce Historical Division, *The Army Air Force in World War II*, Chicago, University of Chicago Press, 1950.

Wagner, Ray, *American Combat Planes*, New York, Doubleday & Company, Inc., 1968.

Watts, Anthony J., *Japanese Warships of World War II*, New York, Doubleday & Company, Inc., 1971.

————, and Gordon, Brian G., *The Imperial Japanese Navy*, New York, Doubleday & Company, Inc., 1971.

Wise, William H. and Company, Inc., *Pictorial History of Second World War*, 10 Volumes, 1949.

Wolfert, Ira, *Battle for the Solomons*, Boston, Houghton Mifflin Company, 1943.

Zimmerman, Major John L., *The Guadalcanal Campaign*, Historical Division, Headquarters, U.S.M.C.

INDEX